BEFORE & AFTER

US Foreign Policy and the War on Terrorism

by Phyllis Bennis • foreword by Noam Chomsky

ARRIS
BOOKS

An imprint of Arris Publishing Ltd
Gloucestershire

First published in Great Britain in 2003 by

ARRIS BOOKS
An imprint of Arris Publishing, Ltd
Unit 1a Fosseway Business Centre
Stratford Road
Moreton-in-Marsh
Gloucestershire GL56 9NQ
www.arrisbooks.com

Printed and bound in Canada by Webcom Ltd.

BEFORE & AFTER

CONTENTS

FOREWORD

I n the culture of the streets, the criminal underworld, and the arena of international affairs, it is often considered more important to be feared than to be liked. For those with the will and capacity to dominate, to be "disrespected" is unacceptable. There is a term for this stance in the rhetoric of statecraft and international relations: "establishing credibility." That is commonly a significant factor in affairs of state, rather strikingly so for the present US administration. Mostly holdovers from the Reagan years, when much the same was true, Bush #2 planners make no secret of their intent to use the means of violence at their command, which are overwhelming and rapidly expanding, to organize the world in what is called "the national interest"—typically the special interest of narrow sectors that have inordinate influence over the political system.

In this book, Phyllis Bennis reviews many illustrations of this stance: the systematic demolition of treaties and barring of new ones, arrogation of extraordinary executive authority, and more generally, the purposeful brazen contempt for basic principles of law and world order.

The stance is a virtual reflex, even when it serves little purpose other than the pleasures of intimidation and avoidance of diplomacy. Thus, when Saudi Prince Abdullah visited the US in April 2002 to urge Washington to pay some attention to the difficulties caused for its allies in the Arab world by its support for Israeli terror and repression, he was bluntly informed that his concerns did not matter. One official explained to the press the message conveyed to the errant Prince: "The idea was, if he thought we were strong in Desert Storm, we're 10 times as strong today... This was to give him some idea what Afghanistan demonstrated about our capabilities." A prominent military analyst outlined the thinking of senior Defense Department officials: if the United States "was firm, tough, acted with resolve, especially in that area of the world, the rest of the world will come along and respect us for our toughness and won't mess with us."

In short, "You're either with us or with the terrorists," as the

President had declared, and if you don't follow us, you'll be pulverized. Abdullah can go home and chew on that.

To establish credibility is a good reason for bombing countries like Afghanistan, blasting creatures huddling in caves with every weapon we have short of nuclear bombs, reveling in the praise for the brilliance of our military hardware—and who could possibly care if miserable Afghan peasants are torn to shreds or tortured and massacred afterward? We have to show what we're capable of doing if someone disrespects us. The consequences for Afghans generally are immaterial. They were scarcely considered in the first place, and will never be known, even investigated. Also insignificant is the fact that little evidence was available when the President informed Afghans that they would be bombed until they turned over terrorist suspects (the demand that they overthrow the regime was an afterthought, announced as a war aim weeks later). Eight months after the bombing began, FBI director Mueller testified to Congress that intelligence now "believes" that the "idea of the September 11 attacks" was hatched in Afghanistan, though implementation and financing trace elsewhere. The consequences for terrorism rank higher in the scale of values, but not much. In June US intelligence concluded that the bombing probably increased the threat by scattering the al-Qaeda network and spawning others like it. Nonetheless, the operation was a spectacular success: it "demonstrated our capabilities," and that is of prime importance.

As Bennis explains, the US rejected Security Council authorization for the assault, knowing that there would be no veto. Britain's support is routine. France would not have objected. Russia and China eagerly joined the "coalition against terror" in the expectation that they would receive authorization for their own terrorist atrocities. Russia was also surely pleased that it at last received the support of the "international community" as the US joined the Russia-Iran-India coalition backing the Northern Alliance. For similar reasons, Washington dismissed tentative offers of extradition of suspects, whether serious or not, only ideologues know.

There is nothing new in the resort to violence to establish credibility. Not long ago, Serbia was bombed primarily for that reason, as Clinton, Blair, and others explained in their more candid moments. Humanitarian aims were routinely professed, but that carries zero information in the technical sense; it is a predictable concomitant of the reliance on force. In this case, there was ample reason to be skeptical about the protestations at the time, and it requires real dedication to take them seriously in the light of voluminous evidence later released by Western sources. Parliamentary records reveal that in late January 1999, the British, the most hawkish element in the alliance, still attributed most atrocities in Kosovo to the KLA guerrillas, and the rich documentation provided by the State Department, NATO, KVM monitors, the UN, and other high-level Western sources indicate that nothing changed substantially until the US withdrew the OECD monitors in preparation for the bombing that immediately followed. NATO Commander Wesley Clark, who had informed the press at once that escalation of Serbian atrocities after the bombing was "entirely predictable" and that "the military authorities fully anticipated the vicious approach that Milosevic would adopt, as well as the terrible efficiency with which he would carry it out," has since revealed that several weeks earlier, in the planning stage, he had informed Secretary of State Madeleine Albright that as soon as air strikes commenced, "Almost certainly [the Serbs] will attack the civilian population" and NATO will be able to do nothing to prevent it. But the officially-announced aim of "bolstering the credibility of NATO" was a sufficient reason, whatever the human consequences; and the reference, of course, is not to the credibility of Belgium or Italy.

There are many earlier examples. Similar reasons motivated President Kennedy, forty years earlier, when he ordered his staff to subject Cubans to the "terrors of the earth" until Castro was eliminated. "The very existence of his regime... represents a successful defiance of the US," Kennedy planners advised, "a negation of our whole hemispheric policy of almost half a century," based on the principle of subordination to the will of the Colossus of the North. The "defiance" was the resistance to the Bay of Pigs invasion. US reaction to that show of disrespect "is not a legal issue," senior statesman Dean Acheson informed the American Association of International Law, nor do legal issues ever arise in the case of response to a "challenge... [to the]... power, position, and prestige of the United States."

Castro's "successful defiance" added further urgency to the earlier reasons for overthrowing his regime: that Cuba was providing an "example and general stimulus" that might "encourage agitation and radical change" in other parts of Latin America, where "social and economic conditions... invite opposition to ruling authority" and susceptibility to "the Castro idea of taking matters into one's own hands" and grave dangers when the "poor and underprivileged, stimulated by the example of the Cuban revolution" demand "opportunities for a decent living." That was bad enough, but successful resistance to invasion alone is an intolerable threat to credibility, warranting the "terrors of the earth" and destructive economic warfare.

The example captures a good deal of the essence of policy—before, after, and during the Cold War, to adapt Bennis's title. "Taking matters into one's own hands" is an unacceptable challenge to credibility, only enhanced when accompanied by "successful defiance," and passing beyond the bounds of the tolerable when the miscreant threatens to become a "virus that will infect others," a "rotten apple that will spoil the barrel," in the terminology of the guardians of state and private power. The Russian threat was perceived in much the same light from the origins of the Cold War in 1917, as recognized even by leading advocates of the "traditional" framework of Soviet guilt and Western reaction.

The resort to violence to intimidate—"terrorism," in the technical sense of US official documents—has long been a standard tool of domination. The British commander in Palestine during the Arab revolt of 1936–39 ordered "rigorous repressive measures [to] intimidate the Arab population sufficiently to bring lawless acts to an end." The end result, a senior colonial administrator observed, "could have been expressed in a simple provision empowering the High Commissioner to take any action he wished." The commanding officer responsible for the Amritsar massacre in India twenty years earlier defended his actions on the grounds that "the mob... were there to defy the arm of the law," so it would have been "a criminal act of folly" to keep to a "small amount of firing" to disperse them: "It was no longer a question of merely dispersing the crowd, but one of producing a sufficient moral effect, from a military point of view, not only on those who were present but more specially throughout the Punjab." Churchill's impassioned advocacy of "using poisoned gas against uncivilised tribes" shortly after was based on similar reasoning. Dismissing with contempt the "squeamishness" of those who worried about popular reaction to what was then regarded as the most criminal weapon of war, Churchill pointed out that it "would spread a lively terror" among those chafing under British rule—"recalcitrant Arabs" (mostly Afghans), as the military called them. Murderous bombing of civilian targets was justified on the same grounds. And like its successor in global dominance, Britain undermined international conventions that might retard such practices because we must "reserve the right to bomb niggers," as the distinguished statesman Lloyd George recorded in his diary after Britain's success in excluding aerial bombardment of civilians from a 1932 disarmament treaty. There is no need to review the practice in earlier years, or among those who do not fall within the category of "enlightened states."

For a very powerful state, threats of irrational behavior can also serve to intimidate and enhance credibility, frightening potential adversaries or allies who are dragging their feet. That is second-nature for the Reaganites in the current Administration, now freed from the limited deterrence of their first heady experience with awesome power. They doubtless recall their success at the Tokyo Summit of industrial democracies in May 1986, when Europe was unwilling to sign on to the demonization-of-Libya crusade the Reagan adminsitration launched on assuming office, under the pretext of a "war on terror." To counter such defiance, the Reaganites themselves circulated a position paper warning Europe to get on board to make sure "that the crazy Americans won't take matters into their own hands again," as they had just done in the terror bombing of Tripoli and Benghazi. It worked. Europe approved Washington's condemnation of Libya, while commentators at home exulted that European "wimps" had learned proper behavior.

Clinton planners also recognized the effectiveness of this device. In a major study entitled "Essentials of Post-Cold War Deterrence," Clinton's Strategic Command (STRATCOM) stressed that nuclear weapons must be at the heart of US military strategy because "Unlike chemical or biological weapons, the extreme destruction from a nuclear explosion is immediate, with few if any palliatives to reduce its effect," and whether actually used or not, "nuclear weapons always cast a shadow over any crisis or conflict." Furthermore, planners must "maintain ambiguity." "It hurts to portray ourselves as too fully rational and cool-headed," they advised. "That the US may become irrational and vindictive if its vital interests are attacked should be a part of the national persona we project." It is "beneficial" for our strategic posture if "some elements may appear to be potentially "'out of control'"— "crazy Americans," in Reaganite rhetoric.

The concept may have been pioneered by Israel in the mid-1950s, when Defense Minister Pinhas Lavon "constantly preached in favor of acts of madness and taught the army leadership the diabolical lesson of how to set the Middle East on fire," if necessary performing "acts of despair and suicide," Foreign Minister Moshe Sharett recorded in his diary. Lavon's doctrine, according to Sharett, was "We will go crazy" ("Nishtagea") if crossed—the origins of the "Samson doctrine," recalling Samson's bringing down the Temple walls and killing more Philistines than during the rest of his lifetime. At that time the threat was limited, though not after the acquisition of a substantial nuclear arsenal.

Policy intellectuals explain that it is right and proper for the US leaders to resort to coercion and violence unilaterally. Missile defense will provide the US with "absolute freedom in using or threatening to use force in international relations," Lawrence Kaplan writes in the liberal *New Republic*, that will "cement US hegemony and make Americans 'masters of the world'". In the neoconservative *National Interest*, Andrew Bacevich cites him approvingly, providing historical and philosophical depth. History, he explains, "has a discernible direction and destination. Uniquely among all the nations of the world, the United States comprehends and manifests history's purpose," so that US "hegemony" should be welcomed, as the realization of history's purpose. The merest truism, the doctrine "defines the parameters within which the policy debate occurs," a spectrum that excludes only "tattered remnants" on the right and left. The principle that America is a "historical vanguard," and therefore must be free to act as its leaders choose, is "so authoritative as to be virtually immune to challenge." And by the same token, requires no argument and is immune to evidence.

The sentiments are not original, either in American history or among earlier aspirants to hegemony. History provides some lessons as to what to expect, as does simple common sense.

It is hardly surprising that the conceptions of executive power that inspire the reactionary statists who defame the term "conservative" should extend to the domestic arena as well. One illustration of the return to some of the worst days of domestic repression is the declared right to imprison without even a bow to minimal legal safeguards, a standard practice in client states as well: Israel and Turkey, for example, both now virtual offshore US military bases and closely aligned, with over ten percent of Israel's naval and air forces (the latter larger and more advanced than any European NATO power) now permanently stationed in Eastern Turkey along with massive US deployments, nuclear-armed, poised as visibly as possible toward Iran and Iraq. Turkish legal standards need not be discussed; Israel is reported to have detained some 600,000 Palestinians over the years in the occupied territories (and more within Israel) on flimsy pretexts or none at all, many for long periods and with credible charges of torture.

In this connection, it might also be wise to recall some words of Churchill's: "The power of the executive to cast a man into prison without formulating any charge known to the law, and particularly to deny him the judgment of his peers, is in the highest degree odious, and the foundation of all totalitarian government whether Nazi or Communist." Churchill's warning against such abuse of executive power for alleged intelligence and preventive purposes was in 1943, when Britain was facing threats that were not exactly trivial.

There is ample reason to share Bennis's deep concern about the developments she expertly reviews, and no less, to attend closely to her final words. To reverse the current course will not be easy, but it is surely possible.

—Noam Chomsky, August 2002

PREFACE

On the morning of September 11, 2001, "all changed, changed utterly." What was born, however, was not Yeats' "terrible beauty" but an incomprehensible horror. Following the attacks on the World Trade Center and the Pentagon, over the course of minutes, then hours and days, everything seemed to change utterly. Images of the carnage were inescapable.

I had arrived back home in Washington from Amsterdam less than eighteen hours before. On the morning of the 11th I was still jet-lagged, and the attacks seemed slightly surreal—as well as unreal—throughout the day. All that was clear was the sense that what we did and how we lived, in Washington and elsewhere around the country, was profoundly and permanently altered.

Last September, it was still perhaps too soon to draw out all the lessons that had to be learned, but it was not too soon, even in the epicenter of that anguish, to begin to ask questions, to ask why. Why human beings could even contemplate, let alone carry out, such an act. Why we here in the US had never imagined or believed that we would come face-to-face with what *The Independent*'s Robert Fisk described as "the wickedness and awesome cruelty of those who claim to speak for a crushed and humiliated people."

For weeks after the attacks, the city of Washington remained under siege: the airports were largely closed, F-16 fighter jets patrolled the skies, and military helicopters flew constant patterns over our neighborhoods. The Institute for Policy Studies (around the corner from the White House and within the new security perimeter) was evacuated, and we had the strange experience of sitting outside on our doorstep, drafting an analysis of Congress's then-pending, support-the-war resolution at the request of some members of the beleaguered Progressive and Black Caucuses of Congress. As we went line-by-line with a red pen, black vans filled with secret service agents and busloads of camouflage-clad soldiers roared down the closed-off street in front of our office, heading into the driveway between the White House and the Treasury building.

From the first moments after the attack, it became clear things were likely to get even worse, probably very soon. Thousands were dead, we would not know for days how many thousands. The victims would include people from more than 60 countries—restaurant workers, stock traders, janitors, and tourists—as well as the police, firefighters, and ordinary people-turned-rescue workers. The drumbeats of war were already ratcheting up the calls for retaliation and vengeance rather than for mourning and justice, and voices of sanity were quickly drowned out. Serious discussion about how to respond to this crime against humanity, how to seek justice for the perpetrators without creating more innocent victims, and how to prevent horrific events like this from ever happening again—discussion that focused on root causes, as anachronistic as that notion suddenly seemed—was rare.

The memorial service at the National Cathedral started out with what was most appropriate in a singular moment such as this. A number of clergy spoke of honoring the victims and the rescuers, of mourning and remembrance, of coming together and keeping faith in people. But then President Bush took over the pulpit with his call for armed vengeance against an undifferentiated "them," followed by a military chorus singing the "Battle Hymn of the Republic," including the usually-discarded verses about dying in the service of God, further increasing the volume of the call for revenge and war.

The attacks on the World Trade Center and the Pentagon changed utterly the terrain of public policy work. Everything we now said and did had to recognize the new fears and new anger and new grief that had suddenly reshaped people's thinking and emotions and reactions—including some of our own. Our work challenging the Bush administration's preexisting penchant for empire's privilege became much more difficult. Our campaign for Palestinian rights and an end to Israeli occupation had to be completely recalibrated. Our work on democratizing the UN now had to take into account Washington's latest success in winning unanimous support, not simply for an appropriate condemnation of these appalling acts, but for language that would, however misleadingly, be claimed as a Security Council endorsement of US military strikes. All our work now had to take into account a new and dangerous escalation of racist attacks on Arabs, Arab-Americans, and Muslims and the serious erosion of all of our civil rights—including the right to oppose this clearly imminent war.

The attack on the World Trade Center was a crime—a crime against humanity of unspeakable magnitude, but a crime nonetheless. If the US claim to be a country ruled by law was accurate, the US goal—even for those outside the law such as the September 11 terrorists—would have been to bring the perpetrators to face international justice, not to turn them into dead-or-alive targets for F-16-flying bounty-hunters.

More than any single policy, the biggest cause of international anger against the United States is the arrogance with which US power is exercised—international law dismissed, UN resolutions ignored, binding treaties abandoned. Washington demands that other countries strictly abide by UN resolutions and international law, imposing sanctions or threatening military assault in response to violations, but holds itself accountable only to a separate law of empire that applies to the US alone.

In an article I wrote just days into the crisis, I asked, "What might a war against bin Laden look like?… Many things remain uncertain. But if the US refuses to pull back from its self-declared intended abyss of war against an unseen but omnipresent enemy, the coming war will present far more serious challenges than Junior's father ever dreamed of." Unfortunately, the grim forecasts of war and an increase in Washington of the arrogance of power proved accurate.

We know now that a weak, ultimately illegitimate president saw the September 11 crisis as a great gift, enabling him to consolidate his faltering credibility (domestic and international), and to implement long-standing goals of the right-wing Republican agenda. Aside from domestic policies that destroyed once-cherished civil liberties protections and undermined hard-won environmental defenses, September 11 brought the Bush presidency a shift of vastly enhanced power to the executive branch, military force asserted in place of diplomacy, rejection of treaties, and foreign policy imposed on the rest of the world through an unchallenged law of empire. The September 11 crisis opened what the satirist Tom Lehrer once called, "a good year for the war buffs."

Among the many changes the events of that day brought about were in US foreign policy, but for the most part not in the ways that either Osama bin Laden or George W. Bush anticipated. What changed in US foreign policy—and what stayed the same—is the central question this book tries to answer.

Since those frightening and dark days after September 11, some small possibilities of a different sort of tomorrow have reemerged.

International responses to the attacks, from people even more than from governments, began not with calls for vengeance but with human solidarity, sympathy for the victims on a global level rarely experienced in this country. And then, as Bush's calls for war went out around the world, throughout Europe, the Middle East, and elsewhere people refused to accept their governments' frightened acquiescence to Washington's hegemonic demands. Hundreds of thousands took to the streets to protest. In the United States, campuses, places of worship, and community centers erupted with teach-ins and demonstrations, with hundreds, then thousands, then tens of thousands of people determined to learn, to question, and to criticize their governments' actions. Family members of victims killed in the September 11 bombings urged a response of justice, not war—and "not in our name" became a rallying cry for peace. In the spring 100,000 people came to Washington to demand an end to Washington's borderless and limitless war on terror. A few brave members of Congress broke out of the bipartisan toe-the-line mode to begin challenging the stripping of civil rights protections that formed Bush's anti-terror war at home.

One night in September, during those first crazed weeks of mobilization and response, I woke at three a.m. with an overwhelming sense of déjà-vu. Thinking back, I remembered a conversation I had with the late Eqbal Ahmad, the brilliant Pakistani scholar/activist, during the last few weeks before the Gulf War began in January 1991, a moment that felt very much like what we were living through now. We were in Chicago, and like so many others around the country, we had both been running like crazy people, writing too many leaflets, speaking at too many teach-ins, sleeping too little, and drinking too much coffee, as we all tried so hard to organize a movement strong enough to prevent a war that by those last weeks we knew was already unstoppable. It was in a moment of exhaustion and despair that Eqbal said that if we stopped now, we would lose the fight even to contain the war that we knew was coming, or to learn lessons from it after.

And I realized that this time, more than a decade later, we had to move forward to mobilize in that same way once again. Eqbal was right. Even if we failed to stop this futile but murderous war, we had at least to continue trying. We had to fight for a different response to the crimes of September 11, one based on international justice instead of savage vengeance, even after the war began.

ACKNOWLEDGMENTS

W riting is by its nature a solitary activity; responding to the crises of September 11—the crisis of war and foreign policy but also the crisis shaking our collective understanding, national character, and human identity—was by its nature a social undertaking. This book relied on both. And while the faults and omissions are mine alone, this book could not have been written without the wide range of friends, colleagues, and comrades on whose work and support I relied. Collaborations and discussions with my colleagues at the Institute for Policy Studies helped shape the approach and analysis of this book. I must especially thank John Cavanagh, Marc Raskin, Sarah Anderson, and Sanho Tree for their generous support. Similarly, I gained new insights from discussions (across oceans or otherwise) with fellows and staff of the Transnational Institute in Amsterdam. My activist colleagues in the peace and justice movements, on Iraq and Israel-Palestine especially, have given me ideas, criticism, help, and understanding when I disappeared to write. In the US they include Denis Halliday, Laura Flanders, Peter Lems, Nadia Hijab, Naseer Aruri, Kathy Bergen, David Wildman, and Mona Younis. Many others continue their difficult work under the dangerous conditions of Israeli occupation—continuing despite suffocating curfews, armed attacks and the deaths of far too many innocents—and I remain grateful for their example. Friends across the country provided desperately needed support throughout a very tough year, and my gang in Washington replenished me with sufficient movies, hiking, and weekends in West Virginia. Michel Moushabeck at Interlink first urged me to write this book and, with his staff, in particular Pam Thompson, Elizabeth Porto, and Juliana Spear, labored diligently and quickly to get the project finished.

I am deeply grateful to Noam Chomsky for making room in his overwhelmed schedule to write his remarkable foreword to *Before & After*. To Edward W. Said for providing an exemplar for us all in refusing to give in. And most of all to my father, who taught me to love ideas, and who died just before the book went to press.

ONE

BEFORE: THE BUSH ADMINISTRATION STEPS INTO THE WORLD

I n November 2000, the Bush–Gore election appeared to be in a dead heat. After weeks of partisan wrangling, culminating in his narrow selection by a partisan Supreme Court, George W. Bush was named president. On January 20, 2001, the Bush team positively strutted into office, brimming with self-righteousness and hubris, acting as would befit a new president with a commanding electoral victory behind him. Bush had campaigned with a call for a more humble foreign policy, but somehow the humility appropriate to an unelected president never seemed to touch the new "Leader of the Free World."

From their first moments in office, Bush officials brought to the White House an aggressive brand of unilateralism, characterized by disdain for global opinion and contempt for international law and institutions. This was not an administration uneasy with or embarrassed by their chief's utter lack of foreign policy experience. No one in the administration or in the proudly isolationist contingent in Congress expressed any concern over Junior's lack of frequent-flier miles. It was only three years, after all, since the National Security Caucus Foundation reported that a full one-third of the members of the House and Senate did not even have passports.[1]

The Clinton administration, when they came into office eight years earlier, claimed "assertive multilateralism" as their basis for foreign policy. That commitment was always more rhetorical than real, as Clinton was far more committed to the appearance of leading a global coalition than to any real consultation, let alone power-sharing, in global decision-making. In fact, during eight years of Clintonian multilateralism, treaties on everything from the rights of children to the International Criminal Court to the prohibition of anti-personnel land mines were rejected. The United Nations Charter was repeatedly violated and Security Council decision-making circumvented. US dues to the UN remained billions of dollars in arrears.

After the "Black Hawk Down"[2] Somalia debacle of 1993, the slogan "assertive multilateralism" dropped off the White House and State Department agendas. But versions of the catchphrase continued to surface on occasion, because it somehow continued to resonate with the American people. The idea, if not the reality, of the US moving in concert with the international community, participating with, rather than isolated from other countries, shaped a popular paradigm for post-Cold War foreign policy. And many people believed the rhetoric. Many were prepared to accept the Clintonites' claims that most of Washington was on the right track, that it was only because of the right wing in Congress, or a few recalcitrant senators, that the US failed to pay its UN dues or to ratify treaties on the rights of children or to support the International Criminal Court.

There was thus hardly any public recognition of the roots of Bush's supposedly new approach, nor of how much it followed (albeit with more potency) the broad trajectory of US foreign policy in recent years. When the Senate voted against ratification of the Comprehensive Test Ban Treaty (CTBT) in October 1999, many claimed then that the new isolationism of the Republican Party's right-wing had triumphed. That so-called isolationism, though, was actually a more virulent strand of unilateralism in which Washington's solitary decision-making, including decisions to send troops to other countries and to ignore or violate international laws on a whim, was asserted as a point of pride rather than implemented in the shadows.

Bush Junior followed, and certainly expanded, a powerful unilateralist inclination in foreign policy. But it was a pre-existing trend—he didn't invent it. In the first months of his presidency, Bush's unilateralism differed less in substance, and more in rhetoric and emphasis, from Clinton's approach. Clinton, for example, sat silently on the Comprehensive Test Ban Treaty, refusing to send it to the Senate for ratification. Bush, on the other hand, announced his official intention to actually abandon the Anti-Ballistic Missile (ABM) treaty, long deemed the cornerstone of international strategic arms control.

The multilateral gloss of the Clinton years had captured a certain part of the public imagination, however, so the shift under Bush seemed more significant than it really was. When George Bush Junior came into office in January 2001 following his bitterly contested and ultimately false claim of victory, it was against the image and rhetoric of the "multilateral" Clinton years that Bush foreign policy would be measured.

BUSH BEGINS

Even before the disputed vote tallies in Florida were settled by Supreme Court fiat, many more thoughtful US policymakers and pundits expressed fear of an inexperienced, untrained president in whom US allies would have little confidence. Around the world, writers, politicians, and cartoonists were already having a field day mocking the intellectual lightweight and Texas good ol' boy whose family bought him admission to Yale and raised him to be president. As Washington's newest first family and its minions settled into the city, early foreign policy decisions indicated the growing global fears were right.

From the start Bush asserted a boldly unilateralist voice, one that catered to both the far-right social conservatives and the most belligerent military hawks of the Republican Party. After the election, one of the first decisions of the new administration was to reimpose an international gag order—withholding US aid to any family planning service provider anywhere in the world if its staff (with separate, non-US funds) provided, lobbied for, or even mentioned abortion or abortion rights to its patients. Many in the US, women in particular, and many in the UN and other international health agencies, were outraged.

Bush had inveighed against "nation-building" during his campaign, condemning US participation in Balkan peacekeeping and hinting at a unilateral withdrawal from Bosnia and/or Kosovo. Europe was not amused. Some of the new administration's earliest foreign policy prescriptions further antagonized allies—especially its withdrawal from the Kyoto Protocol and its announced intention to abandon the Anti-Ballistic Missile treaty (ABM), long viewed as the linchpin of the global, especially US-Russian, arms control regime. The Comprehensive Test Ban Treaty (CTBT), for which the Clinton administration had failed to win Senate ratification, fell completely off the agenda, and in March the US suspended missile talks with North Korea. Furthermore, from the first moments of his presidency, George Bush took on the role of cheerleader number one for the so-called missile defense shield against mythical future missiles that might be fired some day from states such as North Korea, Iran, or Iraq. The plan was rooted in the long-discredited

Star Wars of Ronald Reagan and soon became emblematic of the Bush administration's extremism and militarism.

There was broad trepidation right from the beginning. Fears of this "retreat from international engagement" shaped headlines across the country and around the world. In April, at the height of tensions with China over the downed spy plane, an Australian television journalist interviewing an American analyst said, "I saw President Bush on television last night, and he didn't look very confident." His guest, Charles Kupchan of Georgetown University, agreed, saying:

> I think it would be fair to say that George Bush is right now a fish out of water. He has very little international experience—he's traveled abroad three times in his adult life, other than trips to Mexico—and so here he is sitting in the Oval Office dealing with a major international situation and he really hasn't had time to get up to speed.[3]

Newspaper editorials and pundits, already concerned about Bush's proudly proclaimed ignorance of foreign affairs, expressed discomfort about the consequences of these high-profile withdrawals from global commitments. Among the public, there was also some unease about the increasingly go-it-alone tendencies of US policy pronouncements.

All of Bush's major foreign policy advisers, most of them older than the baby boomer president, had earned their political stripes fighting or analyzing the Cold War. That group, including Vice President Dick Cheney, Defense Secretary Donald Rumsfeld, his deputy Paul Wolfowitz, Secretary of State Colin Powell, and National Security Adviser Condoleezza Rice, as well as their respective deputies and assistants, were a seasoned, experienced team, and they agreed on one fundamental point: that post-Cold War US hegemony on a global scale unprecedented by any previous empire was not only possible, but fitting. They agreed that for the US, might really does make right, that American values, interests and directions were inherently good, simply because they were American.

Within that broad political agreement, however, there was a serious strategic divide over just how that US domination could best be maintained. The debate began right at the beginning of the new presidency, during the early 2001 Senate confirmation hearings for Bush's cabinet nominees. The debate was drawn most sharply between Secretary of State Colin Powell on the one hand and the Pentagon chiefs, Secretary of Defense Donald Rumsfeld and his deputy, Paul

Wolfowitz, on the other. Powell envisioned a US-dominated international consensus, however artificial or coerced it might be, in whose name US policies could be imposed on the world. On the other side was what the US media quickly dubbed the "Wolfowitz cabal," grouped around the deputy secretary and the semi-official Defense Policy Board made up of hard-line Pentagon hawks. This group saw a unilateral assertion of US power, especially military power, as the first-choice option. And their belief in the perks due an unchallenged superpower led to the conviction that the US need pay little attention to the views of its allies.

The rift between the two wings of the administration first emerged during the February round of confirmation hearings for the various cabinet posts. Policy toward Iraq (along with that toward North Korea) had emerged as the sharpest reflection of that highly contentious debate. Testifying before the Senate, Powell argued for the continuation of sanctions. He outlined a spin-driven "smart sanctions" proposal designed to deflect growing domestic and international concern over the deadly impact of economic sanctions on Iraqi civilians, and that prioritized maintaining some semblance of an allied, especially allied Arab, coalition to support the US position. Protection of the Gulf War coalition, already in tatters after the decade-long humanitarian crisis raging in Iraq, was Powell's chief strategic goal.

Wolfowitz, during the same period, emerged strongly as the voice of the administration's hard-core rightists. Backed by Rumsfeld, Wolfowitz brought to the debate the voices of the military unilateralists. (It should be noted, however, that the Bush hawks toned down their rhetoric somewhat from the overheated language they used during the Clinton years.) Their policy was overtly aimed at overthrowing Saddam Hussein, if not the Iraqi regime, in what was primly known as "regime change"; they cared little for the niceties of coalition politics. They had spent the Clinton years in the private sector, using their out-of-office positions of influence to urge ever-more reckless military escalation, particularly against Iraq, on what they perceived as a hopelessly soft administration.

It appeared for a while that Vice President Dick Cheney was a staunch backer of the Wolfowitz side—but questions remained because of his stance during the 1990s as CEO of Halliburton Oil Industries. In that role, while his company signed multi-million dollar contracts with Iraq for oil equipment repair, Cheney had backed an anti-sanctions and almost pro-normalization approach to Iran, and many observers at first anticipated expansion of that approach to Iraq. Cheney, despite his role in the arm-the-Iraqi-opposition contingent during his 1990s years in the private oil sector, told CNN on March 4, 2001 that "I don't believe [Saddam Hussein] is a significant military threat today...we want to make sure he does not become one in the future." (Actually, Cheney's oil-driven loyalties were clear long before: as a member of the House of Representatives, Cheney supported the 1981 sale of AWAC planes to Saudi Arabia, despite Israeli opposition, and in 1979 he voted against the windfall profits tax on oil revenues. And, just to fill out the record, Cheney also voted against the Panama Canal Treaty [1979], against the Department of Education [1979], against South African sanctions [1985], and against safe drinking water standards [1986].)

Even Wolfowitz, long identified as the most committed to arming the Iraqi opposition, said at his Senate confirmation hearing that, while he supports US military backing for an opposition force inside Iraq, "I haven't yet seen a plausible plan" for doing so. National Security Adviser Condoleezza Rice, whose previous White House experience was during the Reagan years as a young Soviet specialist, was an unknown factor in the internal debate. And, perhaps significantly, George Bush's own position vis-à-vis the warring factions of his team remained uncertain.

PLANES OVER CHINA

When the spy plane incident erupted over China in the spring of 2001, first indications were that the Wolfowitz approach of militarizing diplomacy had won the day. The White House rhetoric was tough and uncompromising, and fear of further confrontation settled over Washington and the media. The slow-flying, US EP-3 plane, bristling with the most advanced listening equipment in Washington's arsenal, was cruising off the Chinese coast in an area China has long claimed as within its territorial waters, but which the US claimed was international jurisdiction. China dispatched two F8 fighter jets to intercept the spy-plane. Sources differ about what happened next, but, according to *The Guardian* in London,

> It seems that the Chinese jets 'hemmed in' the much bigger American plane, in an apparent manoeuvre to make it change course. According to

the Chinese foreign ministry, the US plane suddenly veered to the left, hitting one of the single-seater jets on its tail. The Chinese machine crashed into the sea and the pilot is missing, presumed dead.[4]

The damaged US plane limped to the closest airstrip, on China's Hainan Island, where Beijing took the crew and the plane into custody. Tensions mounted. Bush demanded immediate return of the crew and the plane, saying the incident threatened severe damage to US-Chinese relations. China demanded an apology for the pilot's death and for the unauthorized landing on Chinese territory; the US refused. Stalemate ensued, and rhetoric remained tough.

One week into the crisis, however, Colin Powell expressed "sorrow" for the incident. Three days after that, as negotiations continued, China's official media reported his earlier statement. Eleven days after the crash, the crisis ended. The Bush administration claimed that the US did not apologize, but the US letter of understanding, relying on an artful use of the past tense as a diplomatic dodge, provided a different story. According to China's Xinhua News Agency, the letter read "Both President Bush and Secretary of State Powell have expressed their sincere regret over your missing pilot and aircraft.... Please convey to the Chinese people and to the family of pilot Wang Wei that we are very sorry for their loss." In what Chinese Foreign Minister Tang Jiaxuan called a "humanitarian gesture," the crew was then released.[5]

The China spy-plane crisis of the spring faded quickly, yet it provided a hint that, despite the hawkish rhetoric and the still unresolved power struggle between Powell's rule-by-coalition pragmatists and the unrepentant military unilateralists grouped around Rumsfeld and Wolfowitz, the new Bush administration would, in the main, lean toward pragmatism. At the rhetorical level, the unilateralist trajectory of the Bush White House remained dominant. But, for the moment, that rhetoric did not reflect the nuances of actual policies. Brookings analyst James M. Lindsay described how, "When ideology meets reality, reality usually wins.... At the end of the day, this administration will look a lot like its predecessors."[6]

While unilateralism was not a new phenomenon in Washington, several factors began to emerge that marked distinctions between the new White House and its predecessor. These differences may have reflected more style than substance, more rhetoric than reality, but they soon became major indicators of a new US view of its role in the world.

One had to do with the Bush administration's public pride in its assertion of unilateral US power—a far cry from Clinton's determination to appear as a global actor. One example was Colin Powell's approach to the US-British military attacks in the "no-fly zones" in northern and southern Iraq. Whereas Bill Clinton had mendaciously claimed that "enforcement" of the zones was a US obligation under UN resolutions, no UN resolution on Iraq ever authorized, or indeed even mentioned, creation of such zones, let alone enforcing them with warplanes and bombing raids. But Clinton, the ostensible multilateralist, remained determined to justify the unilateral military policy by claiming a UN imprimatur. Powell, on the other hand, had no such compunction. Instead, in testimony before the Senate, Powell identified the "no-fly zone" enforcement as being "essentially between us and the United Kingdom," thus acknowledging unabashedly that the no-fly zones and the bombing of the zones were not authorized by UN resolutions.

It was perhaps that contrast of style between Clinton and Bush that soon gave rise to a worldwide chorus of anger toward Bush Junior's supercilious dismissal of the concerns of non-US humanity. Newspaper editorials, journalists, and pundits around the world demeaned Bush's ignorance of international issues, his perceived paucity of intellectual capacity, and his penchant for mispronunciation. Clinton's justly famed ability to convince even international audiences that he "felt their pain" camouflaged at least some of his presidential power drive. His administration's claimed commitment to operating in the name of global cooperation had masked much of the essentially unilateral nature of the decision-making that undergirded such military operations as those in Haiti, Somalia, and East Timor, among other places. Bush could not convince anyone that he felt their pain—but on the other hand, he did not try.

It should not have been surprising then that another significant difference became visible very early in the Bush administration. By the spring of 2001, as international anger toward US arrogance was on the rise, there appeared some reason to hope that a global challenge—of whatever sort—might take shape to defy the policies that were emerging as exemplars of untrammeled US domination and control. Back in 1999, when French intellectuals began identifying the US as a "hyper-power," Prime Minister Lionel Jospin had identified US unilateral behavior as "a new problem on the international scene." Foreign Minister Hubert Vedrine called for "a system both multilateral and multipolar associating all or part of the 185 countries of the world" to challenge Washington's "dominant power with its means of influence."[7] At the time the critique seemed idealist, the usual French challenge to US power, but a challenge from which the rest of the world, out of fear and intimidation, seemed distant.

By 2001 that was beginning to change. *New York Times* columnist Thomas Friedman described how "America is referred to as a 'rogue state' in Europe now as often as Iraq."[8] A Boston University scholar described in the spring how

> the United States at the end of 2000 was an unrivaled superpower presiding over a Pax Americana. But the new White House team seems determined to alienate and possibly lose America's friends abroad, while antagonizing other nations (notably China and Russia) so they turn into foes rather than partners. During last year's campaign, candidate George W. Bush admonished the United States to practice humility. Now, as president, he insists others bow to whatever new rules are devised by his administration. He ignores understandings and consensus built up among many parties over many years.[9]

The clearest indication of a new international mood popped up on May 3, 2001, at the United Nations, when nations from around the world, led by Western Europe, voted to boot the US off the Human Rights Commission. The move surprised those who had not followed developments carefully, and it astounded some US officials, who had come to take for granted their right to what had seemed an unofficially permanent seat. Some in Washington, however, were less than surprised; Secretary of State Colin Powell said that the vote against the United States was "a vote looking for a venue to happen." [10] That same day, Washington also lost its seat on the International Narcotics Control Board that it had held for two terms. And for the first time it began to look as though a collaborative multilateral challenge to post-Cold War US power might just be taking shape as something more than a pipedream.

The US response was angry and combative. Noting that Sudan had just been voted in to one of Africa's rotating seats on the Human Rights Commission, US officials and pundits alike excoriated the 56 member states of the Commission for allegedly replacing the US with the human rights pariah Sudan. In fact, the US was replaced by Sweden—

a country against whom Washington would fair poorly on almost any human rights standard. The Sudan reference was simply convenient for spin-control. As is the practice in most UN agencies, regional groups determine nominees for Commission membership. Certainly Africa could have nominated a country less egregiously symbolic of human rights violations than Sudan. But the Africa Group is far more democratic than the Western Group; it rotates virtually all its countries onto the Commission in turn rather than choosing to exclude those who might actually learn something or even be pressured to improve its practices while functioning as a Commission member. South Africa, Senegal, and Cameroon were among the African members when Sudan was voted in. The Western Group, which includes the US and Europe, was allotted three open seats for this election cycle, but fielded four candidates—France, Austria, Sweden, and the U.S. Withdrawal by any one of those European allies would have guaranteed the US another term. Instead, Sweden won the third highest votes among the group's candidates, beating out the US, which polled the lowest.

The US setback was not the result of some back-room campaign orchestrated by human rights violators or enemies of the US. Rather it was an expression of growing frustration by Washington's friends and allies, especially in Western Europe, at what they saw as increasing US rejection of the United Nations and other international commitments. As Harold Hongju Koh, human rights chief in the Clinton administration, described it, "the world was trying to teach us a lesson."11

Human rights were only part of the problem, but that issue sharpened international anger about a host of other examples of US unilateralism and hypocrisy. European diplomats explaining the Human Rights Commission vote pointed to the US's use of the death penalty; its refusal to sign or ratify numerous treaties and conventions including the CTBT, those guaranteeing the rights of women and children, prohibiting land mines, and supporting the International Criminal Court; its abandonment of the Kyoto protocol on global warming; its threats (at that time still unrealized) to the ABM treaty; and Washington's rejection of international protection for the Palestinians.

Bush's National Security Adviser Condoleezza Rice called the loss of the Commission seat an "outrage," claiming it was because other countries resent US support for human rights. In the House of

Representatives, the response was a decision to withhold the partial payment of back dues to the UN they had approved several months earlier. As former US Ambassador Dennis Jett put it, the congressional tantrum "has cemented the claim that the US is now the world's only super-pouter."12

The willingness of countries to stand up to the US on UN commission seats gave some additional hope to the idea that the United Nations could serve as a venue of challenge. Even if full-scale global insurrection against US unilateral domination was not on the agenda, maybe the UN could at least become a center for collective efforts to hold Washington accountable to the basics of international norms. The US, however, continued to hold itself above the international law it demanded others adhere to. In late March the *New York Times* editorialized a warning.

> Europe may seem like familiar territory to Bush administration officials, many of whom dealt with the continent during the cold war years when European leaders were more deferential to Washington's wishes than they are now. Administration policy makers must adjust their thinking to Europe's new mood or risk conflicts over the environment, arms control, NATO and trade.13

"Cheer up, ugly Americans," wrote one national columnist, assuring them that Europe really didn't hate the US quite as much as it seemed to. He agreed that "powerful American influence at the outset of the 21st century will rile some nations, be perceived as threatening to some, and spur envy among others. But Europe has not become a fortress of anti-American hatred."14

Yet when the president traveled to Europe in June 2001 for his first outing as leader of the Atlantic alliance, Europe was largely unimpressed. The Swedish Prime Minister Goran Persson, then president of the European Union, praised the EU as "one of the few institutions we can develop as a balance to US world domination."15 European leaders may have been relieved that the malaprop-prone president pronounced all their names right, but Secretary of State Powell, still serving as fire marshal of the Bush administration, stomping out brushfires of international outrage as they cropped up, was still busy. Just before Bush's trip, Powell had to assure NATO allies that the administration's *pro forma* discussions to promote its no-compromise commitment to missile defense did not constitute "phony consultations."[16] Few seemed convinced. In fact, when the NATO foreign ministers gathered in Budapest at the end of May, Powell could not even win agreement that there was a "common threat" of missile attack. His team had tried to ratchet up language that would be stronger than the same body's 2000 reference to a "potential threat." But they failed, and the only compromise they could achieve was an agreement to continue assessing the threat level.

Given the European resistance to the US threat assessment, it was no surprise that the NATO ministers had no interest in the Star Wars-style missile shield defense plan the US was trying to impose. The NATO meeting was less than four weeks after the UN Human Rights Commission debacle, and clearly Bush and his team still didn't get it. The *New York Times* editors lectured again:

> Wisely, the Bush administration has stepped back from early rhetoric that suggested its missile defense plans were set and the world would simply have to adapt to them. But consultation must involve more than showcasing American proposals.... During the cold war, Washington could simply impose its will on NATO when it came to missiles and nuclear weapons policies. Those days are over.[17]

The Bush administration, however, did not see things that way. November 2001 was the target for adopting a new protocol aimed to strengthen enforcment of the 1972 Biological Weapons Convention— the germ warfare treaty. As originally drafted, the treaty prohibits possession, development, and production of biological weapons. More than 140 countries ratified it, including the US. But the terms of the treaty never dealt with verification and compliance. Negotiations had been under way throughout the 1990s to change that situation, and put some teeth into the treaty. It was understood that international inspections would have to be at the heart of any verification mechanism; the debate was over the nature, scope, and authority of those inspections. For the US officials negotiating in Geneva, unannounced inspections were viewed as an infringement on the commercial, industrial, and patent rights of the US laboratories, pharmaceutical manufacturers, and other potential targets of international observers concerned about possible "dual use" dangers by some US biological production facilities.

The 2001 draft, at US insistence, had already seriously compromised the power of international inspectors. Arms control experts disagreed on whether it would be better to endorse a weakened protocol or to continue working to strengthen the proposal. But in the run-up to the planned November conference, Bush administration negotiators in Geneva made clear that they did not want either one. They had no intention of acquiescing to international inspections of US commercial or governmental production facilities, and they made no effort to help craft a new protocol. In May Bush's inter-agency review team dismissed the terms of the compromise proposal and made clear the administration's intention to reject the protocol decision in November. One member of the Federation of American Scientists' working group on biological weapons verification, while recognizing that the proposed protocol was less than perfect, said that Bush's rejection of it would nevertheless "reinforce the perception that his administration is controlled by those who never saw an arms control treaty that they liked, and that his administration is only willing to give lip service rather than leadership to multilateral security efforts."[18]

By July the Bush team made it official: the US would not accept the new protocol. Europeans, in particular, were outraged. Sarcastic writers at London's *Independent* noted

> For six years everybody talks of the importance of verification. And then, America discovers that its facilities, too, would have to be verified. The brazen nerve! America might be treated as though it were just another country! Mr. Bush's America seems in danger of convincing itself that it can force everybody to make concessions, while itself remaining impervious to change.[19]

The US remained the leading producer of germ weapons seed stock in the world. Officially, the only weapons-related germ research had to do with creating a defense against others' biological weapons, which required a stock of offensive material against which to craft such a defense. (No one in the US took note of the irony that Washington's continuing sanctions and bombing of Iraq were because of Baghdad's very similar resistance to international inspections of biological facilities.)

When the international disarmament conference opened in Geneva in mid-November, the US put forward its own set of proposals; it ignored the fundamental issue of inspections and left out creation of an international implementation agency, focusing instead on the responsibility of signatories to monitor their countries' own biological production. Further, the Bush administration, led by US

Undersecretary of State for Arms Control and longtime UN-basher John Bolton, insisted that its own weak package of substitute proposals be accepted as part of the conference's final document but not as a legally binding component of the treaty. On December 7, as the *Washington Post* noted, the meeting "disbanded in chaos and anger."[20] The conference decided to suspend its work for at least a year rather than accept the US-orchestrated collapse and a permanent end to the negotiations. European diplomats, in particular, were furious. But this was post-September 11, after all, and Europe's anger remained muted.

Earlier in the year, European and broader international animosity had been growing. In August, polls commissioned by the Council on Foreign Relations and the *International Herald Tribune* proved what pundits and international travelers were already reporting: Europe, in particular, was very angry. The poll examined public opinion in Europe's four largest countries, and the view of the Bush administration in Britain, Italy, Germany, and France was not pretty. On missile defense and US withdrawal from the ABM treaty, opposition was at 66% in Britain, 65% in Italy, 75% in France, and a whopping 83% in Germany. When it came to US abandonment of the Kyoto Protocol on global warming, opposition soared to 80% in Italy, 83% in Britain, 85% in France, and 87% in Germany. Asked for an overall assessment of Bush's handling of international policy, the "disapprove" levels were somewhat smaller—from 46% in Italy up to 65% Germany. But it was perhaps even more telling that Bush's confidence ranking among Europeans was barely on a par with that of Russian President Vladimir Putin. In France, 77% had little or no confidence in Putin, but 75% had little or none in Bush. Among both Italians and Britons asked who was likely to do the right thing in world affairs, Bush ranked even lower than Putin.[21]

Growing international anger was not lost on US opinion and policymakers. After all, unilateralism, even isolationism, might be fine for us, but being isolated by others was certainly not acceptable. US punditry took up the challenge, and headlines like "There's a Point to Going It Alone: Unilateralism Has Often Served Us Well"[22] and "Empire or Not? A Quiet Debate Over US Role"[23] began to pop up with greater frequency. The latter sympathetically reported that "a handful of conservative defense intellectuals have begun to argue that the United States is indeed acting in an 'imperialist' fashion—and that it should embrace the role." The former went on the offensive, claiming that "Unilateralism has always been a centerpiece of American foreign policymaking, and the world is the better for it." Yet there were voices of criticism in the US as well; some mainstream Democrats, including Senate Majority leaderTom Daschle and House Minority leader Richard Gebhardt, took the White House to task for a go-it-alone attitude.

THE WORLD AGAINST RACISM— THE US AGAINST THE WORLD

Much of the debate among Washington insiders faded, however, as the US prepared for its next US versus the World scenario. That would take place in Durban, South Africa, at the World Conference Against Racism, Racial Discrimination, Xenophobia, and Related Intolerances, the UN's third effort in a quarter of a century to confront national problems of racism with international solutions. The 2001 conference, in planning for over five years, followed earlier anti-racism conferences in 1978 and 1983. The US had boycotted both of those earlier efforts, but this time around, throughout the early preparatory process during the Clinton era, there were indications that things would be different. High-level official participation from the US seemed a much more realistic goal, although it was clear early on that Washington's agenda was already clashing with the organizers' goals.

Like other global conferences the UN sponsored (the 1992 Rio Earth Summit, the 1993 Human Rights Conference in Vienna, the 1994 Population Conference in Cairo, the 1995 Social Development Summit in Copenhagen, the 1995 Fourth World Conference on Women in Beijing, and others), the World Conference Against Racism (WCAR) combined an official diplomatic meeting with a parallel conference of non-governmental organizations (NGOs) and national and global social movements focusing on anti-racist and other kinds of anti-discrimination campaigns.

Inevitably, the conflict between the interests of the official and the NGO sectors was sharp. Institutionally, the UN was committed to a serious and ambitious anti-racist agenda. But a number of governments devoted enormous efforts to excluding or marginalizing activists committed to highlighting their own governments' responsibility for long-standing and continuing attacks. These activists included the lower-caste Dalits in India, the Roma in a number of European countries, Australia's aboriginals, Palestinians living under Israeli occupation, Tibetans challenging China, advocates for asylum seekers and refugees across the wealthy world, African-Americans, and other people of color in the US. Participation of all those groups, both as advocates and lobbyists within or against official national delegations, and as independent participants in the NGO Forum, ensured a kaleidoscopic picture of the diversity and energy of the world's peoples.

Among US policymakers and the media, the run-up to Durban quickly put aside the broad range of demands and participants to hone in on the two issues that would continue to shape—and limit—how Americans saw the WCAR. Those were the criticism of Israel's treatment of Palestinians and the demand for reparations for victims of the transatlantic slave trade and their descendants. Objecting to the criticism of Israel, the US deemed irrelevant Israel's long-standing and well-documented history of violations of international law, the Geneva Conventions, and numerous UN resolutions. The reparations debate reflected many years of effort in the US to force official acknowledgement of responsibility for the horrors of slavery and serious engagement on the question of what kind of reparations to former slaves, their descendants, and their countries of origin should be paid.

Negotiations over the language of the final communiqué, under way long before the meeting began, were bitter. By the time conference participants arrived in Durban in the last week of August, battle lines had long been drawn. Colin Powell, the first African-American secretary of state, had decided, "regretfully" he said on one occasion, not to attend and to send only a low-level delegation to the conference. The official reason was the US claim that Israel was being "singled out" for criticism of its treatment of Palestinians. Many US activists, however, believe that resistance to the reparations effort was actually an equally, or even more significant, ground for official US opposition to WCAR than concern about Israel.

The language regarding Israeli treatment of Palestinians, nevertheless, continued to shape US public understanding of the conference. The US media was filled with commentary about WCAR resurrecting the "Zionism equals racism" language of a 1970s-era UN resolution, overturned in 1991. At the time of the May 2001 preparatory committee meeting in Geneva, a few countries, largely reacting to the rapidly escalating violence by Israel in the occupied territories, had indeed proposed similar language. The US delegates hinted that they would stay away from WCAR altogether, much as the US had done during similar UN anti-racism conferences in 1978 and 1983, if such language was even on the agenda for discussion in Durban. Reaction to Washington's heavy-handed approach was swift, and the May talks stalled.

New talks among 21 of the countries involved were set for June. When they failed as well, a final preparatory session was convened on July 31, only a month before the conference was to convene, in a last chance to agree on the language. When that session opened, the European Parliament described the WCAR conference as "facing the threat of failure even before it opens," largely due to the high-profile US boycott threat. The threat was magnified by events only a week before, when the US delegates had stunned international arms control negotiators in Geneva by announcing they were walking out of the germ warfare negotiations.

Eleventh-hour fears that the US would make good on its threat, and UN and European pressure to ensure a successful conference with the US on board, finally trumped the earlier language debates. While fights over language continued even as the conference convened in Durban, the final text of the Declaration contained no reference to the Zionism is racism equation (or indeed any mention of Zionism), and none of the other references US officials had found so offensive. One clause stated simply that "the Holocaust must never be forgotten." A separate clause "recogniz[ed] with deep concern the increase in anti-Semitism and Islamophobia in various parts of the world, as well as the emergence of racial and violent movements based on racism and discriminatory ideas against Jewish, Muslim and Arab communities." In the only two paragraphs specifically referring to the Israel-Palestine conflict, the Declaration stated:

> We are concerned about the plight of the Palestinian people under foreign occupation. We recognize the inalienable right of the Palestinian people to self-determination and to the establishment of an independent State and we recognize the right to security for all States in the region, including Israel, and call upon all States to support the peace process and bring it to an early conclusion;

> We call for a just, comprehensive and lasting peace in the region in which all peoples shall co-exist and enjoy equality, justice and internationally recognized human rights, and security."

In the only specific reference to Israel-Palestine in its entire Program of Action, the Conference called for

> the end of violence and the swift resumption of negotiations, respect for international human rights and humanitarian law, respect for the principle of self-determination and the end of all suffering, thus allowing Israel and the Palestinians to resume the peace process, and to develop and prosper in security and freedom.

The Declaration was hardly an example of "hateful language," as Colin Powell dubbed it. Democratic Congressman Tom Lantos, a Holocaust survivor, backer of uncritical US support for Israel and a member of the US delegation in Durban condemned those he said "have made a go of hijacking the conference for propaganda purposes." It appeared, however, the actual language was not Washington's real concern. Certainly the US views any effort to address Israel's occupation of Palestine in a UN or other global arena with a jaundiced eye, as a step onto the slippery slope of internationalizing the conflict. But in this instance, US concern was equally, or perhaps even much more, focused on paragraph 166 of the WCAR document's section on "Remedies, Reparations, and Compensation." In that clause, the conference "urges States to adopt the necessary measures, as provided by national law, to ensure the right of victims to seek just and adequate reparation and satisfaction to redress acts of racism, racial discrimination, xenophobia and related intolerance, and to design effective measures to prevent the repetition of such acts." That represented a step on a slippery slope of an entirely different type: providing international legitimacy to demands for reparations for the victims of slavery and their descendants (whether to individuals, countries, or institutions), from the countries who profited so enormously from the slave trade of the last half a millennium.

Europe was equally uneasy with the reparations language, particularly because other parts of the document referred to the damage wrought by colonialism in the same light as that of slavery. Europe had no intention of paying reparations for ravaging much of the world during its colonial conquests. But, unlike the US delegation, which refused even to engage in serious debate over the question, Europe finessed the issue. It ultimately accepted the language of the resolution, and responded in language of its own that simultaneously recognized historical responsibility for colonialism and slavery in the abstract, and deflected contemporary responsibility for reparations. In a document issued two weeks before the WCAR convened in Durban, the European Commission stated that it "regrets" slavery and the slave trade, and that "some effects of colonialism" also caused suffering and that any such act must be condemned. The EC then described its "determination to honour this obligation and to accept its responsibility," but limited any concrete accountability to individual responsibility to remember the past.[24] The US was not prepared to accept even such a diplomatic dodge. On September 3, both the US and Israeli delegations to the conference packed up and left Durban in a high-profile fit of diplomatic pique.

The contrast between Europe's determination (however cynical) to keep the conference alive and Washington's insistence on not only pulling out but attempting to discredit the entire process was stark. One administration official in Washington, hoping for some kind of international cover, said they anticipated that Australia, Canada and Britain would follow suit,[25] but copycat walkouts did not occur. The Bush administration won kudos for its walkout among mainstream media and the majority of powerbrokers and policymakers at home, but condemnation for its actions abroad.

Writing several months later, after September 11 had largely pushed the drama of the World Conference Against Racism off the agenda, African scholar Mahmood Mamdani provided some historical context for the US move.

> Official America has a habit of not taking responsibility for its own actions. Instead, it habitually looks for a high moral pretext for inaction. I was in Durban at the World Congress Against Racism (WCAR) when the US walked out of it. The Durban conference was about major crimes of the past, about racism, and xenophobia, and related crimes. I returned from Durban to listen to [National Security Adviser] Condoleezza Rice talk about the need to forget slavery because, she said, the pursuit of civilized life requires that we forget the past. It is true that, unless we learn to forget, life will turn into revenge-seeking. Each of us will have nothing but a catalogue of wrongs done to a long line of ancestors. But civilization cannot be built on just forgetting. We must not only learn to forget, we must also not forget to learn. We must also memorialize, particularly

monumental crimes. America was built on two monumental crimes: the genocide of the Native American and the enslavement of the African American. The tendency of official America is to memorialize other people's crimes and to forget its own, to seek a high moral ground as a pretext to ignore real issues.[26]

The UN High Commissioner for Human Rights, former Irish President Mary Robinson, said she regretted the walkout but insisted the conference would go forward. "We must persist in our endeavors," she said. "The victims of racism, racial discrimination, xenophobia and related intolerance demand this of us."[27]

The South African government, hosts of the Durban conference, deplored the walkout as "unfortunate and unnecessary." As Palestinian ambassador to South Africa, Suleiman al-Herfi, described the US decision, "It's a pretext: the Middle East is 5 percent of the document; they don't want to give reparations for slavery, or condemn it.... It's a great pity. They themselves are confirming their isolation. They weren't able to impose their point of view... so they quit."[28]

Palestine, South Africa, and the United Nations were not the only international critics of the US walkout. Sharp critiques came from Europe, Asia, and elsewhere as well. Australia's former foreign minister, Gareth Evans, criticized the US for its potential walkout even before Washington made good on its threat, saying that the conference "should not be derailed."[29] The international human rights organization Amnesty International said that "by walking out in the middle of the conference, the US is letting down the victims of racism on all sides."[30] Among most critics, the unifying thread remained the US disdain for global opinion and the go-it-alone unilateralism that had become so prevalent in US power centers.

And then came September 11, and the criticism stopped.

TWO

LONG BEFORE: THE US IN THE MIDDLE EAST

The suicide hijackers of September 11 were apparently recruited in Pakistan, coached in Afghanistan, organized in Hamburg, and trained in Florida and the American midwest. But change in the Arab Middle East was their primary purpose. So US policy in that region remained central to the September 11 crisis. For Osama bin Laden, the key *raison d'être* for his al-Qaeda had always been to purify Saudi Arabia of its corrupt and insufficiently Islamic monarchy—which meant first ridding the kingdom of the polluting presence of US troops who protected the royal family. Coming in a distant second, seemingly as almost PR-driven afterthoughts, were the more widely popular issues of Israel's occupation of Palestine and the impact of US-imposed economic sanctions on Iraqi civilians.

The US response to September 11 included threatened and implemented expansion of the anti-terrorism war to countries around the world, from the Philippines to Malaysia to Georgia and Colombia, all far from the Arab world. Central to all US planning, however, was how to carry out this war to stabilize the Middle East in defense of US interests. The strategic considerations shaping Washington's response directly paralleled bin Laden's own regional concerns. That response reflected the three pillars of US strategy in the Middle East that have remained unchanged since the mid-1960s: oil, Israel, and stability. To understand how those considerations operated before and after September 11, and to understand why implementation of those policy goals angers so many people in the region, it is necessary to go back much further in history.

Direct US interest, involvement, and intervention in the Middle East is a relatively recent phenomenon. Although the region's strategic and economic importance in the world was known for centuries, significant interaction with the region was not a characteristic of the early years of the US. Colonization and control of the Arab world was left largely to European and neighboring empires—the Ottomans, French, and British.

By the end of the 19th century, that began to change. The US had eliminated the last vestiges of Native American resistance at home along with much of the Native population, and it had largely recovered from the ravages of the Civil War. The Monroe Doctrine was firmly in place; the US had consolidated its westward expansion to the far shore of North America and was eyeing Spanish colonies in the Caribbean, the South Pacific, and elsewhere. Its economy was thriving; the US was ready to go seriously global.

At that time, the region that stretched from Egypt and the Mediterranean coasts of Palestine and Syria, east through Mesopotamia (Iraq) to the very border of Iran, and south through the Arabian peninsula to the Yemeni port of Aden, had been under the control of the Ottoman empire for 400 years. When World War I broke out, the US fought with the British, French, and Russian empires against Germany and the Ottoman and Austro-Hungarian empires. Even during that period, Washington, however, remained only an emerging player; its rise to dominant power in the Middle East was years in the future. The Western effort to wrest control of the region away from the Ottoman Turks, primarily through alliances with local Arab leaders, was largely orchestrated by Britain and France. Even before the war ended, Britain and France began secret lines-in-the-sand negotiations aimed at dividing up the Arab lands once the Ottomans, as expected, were defeated. The US watched but played little part.

Britain allied itself with the Grand Sharif of Mecca, who agreed to lead an Arab revolt against the Ottomans in return for a British promise to make him ruler of an independent Arabia after the war. Simultaneously, however, Britain and France, concluded their secret negotiations with the 1916 Sykes-Picot Agreement dividing the anticipated post-Ottoman Arab world between themselves. Making everything even more complicated, at the same time they were promising the Arabs independence and secretly plotting with France to keep control of the region for Europe, the British took a third contradictory position. In 1917, they announced the Balfour Declaration, promising the Zionists, whose movement was mobilizing

Jews in Europe, Russia, and elsewhere, that Britain would "view with favour the establishment in Palestine of a national home for the Jewish people" after the war. It was pretty clear that not all the promises could be met. Nevertheless, the US remained largely on the sidelines in the region as its European allies consolidated their positions.

AFTER THE WAR

After the war, the defeated Ottoman rulers were overthrown and a secular Turkish state was established in Turkey, led by Mustafa Kemal. Elsewhere, relying on the terms of the Sykes-Picot Agreement, British control of Egypt was made official; London took over Transjordan, Palestine, and Iraq, while France took control of Syria and Lebanon. The Arabian peninsula also remained a British protectorate. That arrangement, dating from 1915 when London backed Ibn Saud's rebellion against Ottoman rule, would remain in place until Saudi Arabia's nominal independence in 1924. Similarly, London created a monarchy to rule Iraq under its protection, until Iraq was granted independence in 1932. (At the same time Britain carved out Kuwait from Iraq to ensure continuing British access to oil and ports; the little oil emirate would not gain its independence from Britain until 1962.) Meanwhile, in Persia the 1907 Anglo-Russian agreement dividing the country into spheres of influence was dissolved after the war and Persia was recognized as independent. The new Soviet Union officially renounced all claims to the country in 1921, but Persia remained largely under British control. In 1921, Reza Khan overthrew the Qajar dynasty and four years later crowned himself the new Shah of what would soon be called Iran, under the dynasty name Pahlavi.

Once the European powers agreed on the division of land in the Middle East, the Sykes-Picot Agreement was submitted to the League of Nations for approval. Turning to the League to legitimate colonial control meant little more than a formality. In fact, it was the bilateral provisions of Sykes-Picot that set the terms for Europe's colonial domination of the region for the next two decades or more.

Partly in response to Woodrow Wilson's Fourteen Points and their emphasis on the right of self-determination, the European victors of the war went through the motions of trying to find out the wishes of the peoples who had lived so long under Ottoman domination and who now chafed under European control. The British and French established an Inter-Allied Commission ostensibly to survey the population, but its work was inconclusive and few were surprised that it failed.

Wilson then began a campaign for greater influence in the Middle East. Having sided with the winning alliance in World War I, the US was now well-positioned to begin challenging the European powers, demanding a share of international economic and strategic influence. And it could do so under the guise of Wilsonian support for ending colonial empires— after all, many people believed the United States of America had never been a *real* colonial power. Despite the 1823 Monroe Doctrine's claims to Latin America, and the US conquests of the Philippines, Puerto Rico, and Cuba after the Spanish-American War of 1898, the US was never popularly understood as having an empire of its own. Wilson's approach to international affairs was rooted in his understanding that classic colonialism no longer represented the wave of the future. US policy soon turned to rely instead on unofficial and unacknowledged influence to win and maintain control of dependent governments, compliant populations, and accessible resources in the former colonies.

Due largely to isolationist currents in the Senate, the US did not join the post-WWI League of Nations. But Wilson, known as the father of self-determination, still played a major role in the drafting of its Covenant, so it is significant that the founding document never mentioned self-determination. Further, at the post-war Versailles Conference in 1919, US representatives never objected to the notion that the victorious allied powers had a perfect right to take over colonies once ruled by their defeated opponents.[1]

During the Versailles discussion of the Middle East, the Zionist movement, empowered by Britain's endorsement in the Balfour Declaration, pushed for conference approval of their goals. The intelligence section of the US delegation issued an internal report that proposed transforming all of Palestine into a Jewish state that would be placed under a British mandate. This was in stark contrast to the assessment Wilson got from his own legal adviser, David Hunter Miller, who said that "the rule of self-determination would prevent the establishment of a Jewish state in Palestine."[2] While the diplomats continued their work in Versailles, Wilson's own position was articulated on March 2, 1919 in Chicago, completely abandoning any pretense of a commitment to self-determination of an existing population. Although only about ten percent of the Palestinian population was Jewish, Wilson was instead "persuaded that the Allied nations, with the fullest concurrence of our own Government and people, are agreed that in Palestine shall be laid the foundations of a Jewish Commonwealth."3

Two months after that statement, in May 1919, Wilson dispatched an American delegation, the King-Crane Commission, to Syria, Lebanon, and Palestine with a mandate to consult local populations and determine what the preferred post-Ottoman settlement would look like. The commissioners, taking their work far more seriously than their European predecessors, based their approach on the Anglo-French Declaration of November 9, 1918, which made a commitment to "the complete and definite freeing of the peoples so long oppressed by the Turks, and the establishment of national governments and administrations deriving their authority from the initiative and the free choice of the native populations."4

Much of the American team's work focused on assessing local opinions of the Balfour Declaration. The Commission found that, although they had started their work "predisposed" to favor the Zionist movement, the "actual facts in Palestine" led them to oppose London's plan for allowing virtually unlimited immigration of European Jews into Palestine. Their report indicates that "in the Commission's conferences with the Jewish representatives... the Zionists looked forward to a practically complete dispossession of the present non-Jewish inhabitants of Palestine."5

The commissioners noted President Wilson's own Independence Day speech of July 4, 1918, when he outlined his goals for the Great War:

> The settlement of every question, whether of territory, of sovereignty, of economic arrangement, or of political relationship, [must be] on the basis of the free acceptance of that settlement by the people immediately concerned and not on the basis of the material interest or advantage of any other nation or people which may desire a different settlement for the sake of its own exterior influence or mastery.6

The commission also recognized the danger of Palestine becoming an entirely Jewish state. Because Palestine was sacred for Muslims and Christians as well as Jews, "one effect of the extreme Zionist program would be an intensification of anti-Jewish feeling both in Palestine and in all other portions of the world which look to Palestine as the Holy land."

That part, at least, certainly proved to be true.

THE WORLD WAR II YEARS

London's defense plan for the Middle East required more troops than Britain had available, so it needed to recruit assistance from the Arab armies in the region. Although Britain had backed massive Jewish immigration into Palestine up until this point, it issued a White Paper in 1939, in which it promised to restrict Zionist immigration. The Zionist leadership was furious because they knew that without extensive immigration to increase the small Jewish community already there, they had no way of creating a viable Jewish state in Palestine. Official British support for the Zionist effort to create that state was eroding as London turned to win Arab support for the war effort. From the vantage point of the Zionist leadership, a new patron of their state was needed.

Even before the war, Zionist leaders were looking to the US. David Ben-Gurion, one of the key founders of Israel, was convinced that the US should play that role:

> For my part, I had no doubt that the center of gravity of our political efforts had shifted from Great Britain to America, who was making sure of being the world's leading power and where the greatest number of Jews, as well as the most influential, were to be found.[7]

US Zionist organizations grew in influence as they expanded to include many American Jews once opposed to Zionism. They came to support the movement as the only viable response to Hitler's genocide and the American anti-Semitism that kept most Holocaust survivors out of the US. As the movement came to represent a majority position within the Jewish community, it simultaneously gained influence among US policymakers.

By 1942, at the height of the war, an international Zionist conference was held in New York. It was held not long after Hitler's tactics turned from expelling all the Jews from Germany to mass extermination of millions of Jews along with Communists, Roma, gays, Slavs, and many others deemed "unfit." For the first time, the Zionist movement called explicitly for a Jewish state in Palestine. Support for Zionism skyrocketed among Jews all over the world—not least because the nations fighting against Hitler, including the US, still showed little more than rhetorical concern for Hitler's Jewish victims. In 1943 the US did nothing to provide support to the Warsaw Ghetto uprising, in which Jewish fighters held off the Nazi attack for six months before being slaughtered. In 1944 the US refused to bomb the railroad tracks the Nazis were using to ship Jews to the gas chambers at Auschwitz, saying it would require "the diversion of considerable air support essential to the success of our forces" and would be of "doubtful efficacy."[8] Saving Jews was deemed by the US a diversion from the primary task of defeating the German military.

THE ZIONISTS, THE OIL COMPANIES, AND WASHINGTON

From the time oil was discovered in the Middle East in the 1920s, French and British oil companies vied for influence in the region, while the new Soviet Union sought ties with oil-rich Iran. US oil giants prowled throughout the region as well, but the British still remained the most powerful player. Well into the 1930s, Britain had dominated Middle Eastern oil, and American companies controlled less than ten percent of the known oil reserves. In the early 1930s, however, enormous oil reserves were discovered in Saudi Arabia, setting the stage for the rapid—and destabilizing—transformation of an impoverished, largely nomadic region into a wealthy, at least partly modern, country. For a while there was serious conflict between the US and British oil companies vying for access to the Saudi crude, but the US quickly gained the upper hand—not least because during World War I Britain had gone deeply into debt to the US to finance its war efforts. The terms of the loans were stiff; essentially, Britain had mortgaged its empire to fight the war, so the US was well positioned to call in its debts. In 1933 the Saudi monarchy granted an exclusive concession for oil exploration to the Arabian-American Oil Company, or Aramco, a conglomerate of four US oil companies (Esso, Texaco, Mobil, and Socal). The concession marked the beginning of the US rise to dominance in the region, a trajectory that would be consolidated with World War II.

The war transformed America's power and position in the world. The US paid a high price in soldiers' blood (although lower by far than its allies) but had escaped the massive civilian casualties and the physical, economic, and social destruction the war left behind in Europe. The French and British economies, infrastructures, and colonial empires, lay in ruins, as did their sense of power and international influence. The US had escaped the physical destructiveness of the European war, and was also the world's only

nuclear power. It was already challenging the Soviet Union in the first
battles of what would become the Cold War, but it was an uneven
battle. The Soviets had lost 20 million people in the war, and their
cities and countryside remained devastated. It was America's moment
to become the global superpower.

US President Franklin Roosevelt died on April 12, 1945, just before
the end of the war. When the war ended, the new president, Harry
Truman, had a big problem. Like the French and British, the US had
made contradictory promises to Arabs and Zionist Jews, all aimed at
shoring up allies for the US in the still-strategic post-war Middle East.
Truman had supported Zionism as a senator, although probably for
vote-getting rather than strategic purposes. But as president, he had to
weigh more important considerations—such as what the US oil
companies needed to consolidate their access to Middle East oil.

By the end of the war, US oil companies controlled 42 percent of the
known oil reserves in the Middle East—Socal, Esso, and Socony. Three of
the top five US corporations were giant oil companies involved in the
Middle East. Top officials of those companies filled key posts in the State
Department and Pentagon, and they were committed to see that the US
controlled the post-World War II Middle East and its vital oil supplies.
One aspect of the Marshall Plan aid project for Europe was that it created
a new market for newly-acquired US oil. Oil replaced coal as the key fuel
in Europe, and US control of vital petroleum consolidated its power; thus
Washington became the guarantor of European and Japanese access to oil.

The only opposition to this bold strategy came from within the
Middle East itself. Faced with US oil companies claiming rights to their
countries' oil, and US support for harsh governments in the region,
such as Saudi Arabia and the still British-controlled Kuwait, which
were both all too willing to use repression to help the US ensure
stability, Arab and other Middle Eastern nationalists began to oppose
the US presence, largely in the form of labor protests. In 1945–46,
strikes broke out among the Iranian oil workers. Later Iraq's oil workers
would follow suit. And in all the strikes, alongside the demand for
more control over their countries' resources, was the call to reverse the
motion toward creating a European Jewish state in Palestine.

When Rabbi Stephen Wise, leader of the American Zionist
movement, visited Truman only days after his inauguration, oil and
strategic interests were on the president's mind as much as support for

Zionism. President Truman believed, like many US policymakers, that a US-oriented, European-populated Jewish state in Palestine would provide a more trustworthy ally in the often volatile region than the sometimes undependable Arab regimes. It could serve as a junior partner in defending US interests; it could provide key on-the-ground logistical or even military support should US military involvement in the area be required; it could help maintain US and broader Western control of Middle East oil; and it could help make sure the Suez Canal and other key routes were protected and remained open to Western shipping. Crucially, as the Cold War was already heating up, it would be a vital bulwark in US efforts to block Soviet influence in the region, already emerging in Iran and elsewhere. And, lastly, it would help consolidate the support of America's active and vocal Jewish community, which was working feverishly to solve the problem of the European Jewish refugees. Just as crucially, right after the war, 75 percent of all Americans who had heard of Palestine supported the creation of a Jewish state there.

Supporting a Jewish state in Palestine seemed to Truman like a win-win situation. The only losers would be the local Palestinian Arabs, and, ultimately, opposition from that small and disempowered indigenous population, who had had little to do with the war and certainly nothing to do with the Holocaust, would be a small price for the Truman administration to pay for a very big gain in political and strategic interests.

BREAKING THE BRITISH BLOCKADE
& BREAKING THE BRITISH

By 1945 the US had consolidated its position as a major player in the Middle East. The war was over, but Europe was still awash with conflict. Although Britain still maintained some restrictions on Jewish immigration to Palestine, and Arab states still believed they would be granted the independence pledged to them in earlier British and French promises, Holocaust survivors filled the DP camps across Europe, waiting to go to Palestine, since Britain and the US did not want them.

Some of the Arab states, including Iraq, and later Syria and Lebanon, had indeed been set on track toward full independence. But Palestine was different. Britain still held the Mandate for Palestine, as well as the

League's Mandate for Egypt and Transjordan. Britain and the US knew that if Palestine were allowed to govern itself independently, large-scale Jewish immigration would be stopped overnight by the existing population, which was overwhelmingly Muslim and Christian Arab. Then Washington and London would still be faced with a massive problem of European Jewish refugees with nowhere to go. Independence was not, therefore, on the agenda for Palestine. But the British had a big problem. The conflict between the indigenous Palestinian Arab population and the rising numbers of European Jewish settlers was already rapidly escalating. Clashes were increasing. Something had to be done.

The US moved to play a much larger role in the region. Truman was diplomatically cautious but was eager to replace the British as the key outside regional power. He saw the creation of a European Jewish state in Palestine as a step toward a crucial potential alliance. Washington believed that eventually the Arab governments would come to accept such a state as a *fait accompli*. Back at home, the Zionist movement, now representing the vast majority of American Jews, encouraged this momentum. Although exploding industrial growth in the US resulted in the need for new workers, which might have led to a new welcome for Holocaust survivors, and the US Department of Labor announced that the US could easily absorb 400,000 new immigrants, the Jewish refugees were largely still excluded, mostly because existing anti-Semitism linked to growing anti-communism led to fears that the European Jews might harbor dangerous socialist ideas. Instead, public campaigns began across the United States to support mass emigration of the Jewish refugees out of Europe and into Palestine.

The two communities most directly affected were, however, hardly consulted. The Palestinian Arabs, faced with the threat of losing their land and their nation, were ignored. In what would become the famous slogan of Israel's creation, the new Jewish state was deemed "a land without a people for a people without a land." Palestine was hardly a "land without a people." Its population, in this case, was simply ignored. The second largely-ignored community was that of the Jewish refugees themselves. The displaced person camps were filled to bursting with German, Polish, French, Dutch, and many more Jews who had lost their families, their homes, and everything else in the Holocaust. In a report to the American Jewish Congress, Zionist organizer

Chaplain Klausner admitted that most of the refugees wanted to come to the United States. Instead, they were being offered refuge only if they went to Palestine. Klausner noted, "I am convinced that the people must be forced to go to Palestine."9

The campaigns worked. Editorial writers condemned Britain for its immigration quotas in Palestine. Americans sent over $130 million to Palestine to help transport more Jewish refugees. Anyone challenging Zionism in this atmosphere was quickly labeled anti-Semitic—but few challenged the anti-Semitism at the root of the US refusal to allow the Jewish refugees to come to America where they wanted to come in the first place. The US began officially pressuring Britain to lift all restrictions on Jewish immigration to Palestine. In 1945, Truman wrote to British Prime Minister Clement Atlee in support of the admission of 100,000 Jewish refugees to Palestine. Atlee reminded Truman that the US itself had promised the Arab governments it would consult with the Arabs on such issues. He said that such massive immigration threatened to "set aflame the whole Middle East."10

Washington and London finally established a joint Committee of Inquiry to go to Palestine and study the immigration question. The report they got from the Arab Office in Jerusalem was unequivocal. It said:

> The whole Arab people is unalterably opposed to the attempt to impose Jewish immigration and settlement upon it, and ultimately to establish a Jewish State in Palestine. Its opposition is based primarily on right. The Arabs of Palestine are descendants of the indigenous inhabitants of the country... and they claim the democratic right of a majority to make its own decision in matters of urgent national concern.11

The Committee's final report, in March 1946, supported the/ admission to Palestine of the 100,000 Jewish immigrants, but it rejected the proposal for a Jewish state and the idea that all Jews had an automatic right to go to Palestine. Britain tried to bargain: it would admit the 100,000 if the Zionist militias would disarm. Three months later, the Zionists responded by blowing up eight road and railroad bridges in Palestine. In July, the extremist Zionist militia Irgun blew up the British government's wing of the famous King David Hotel in Jerusalem, killing 80 people—Arab, Jewish, and British. Armed clashes flared between British soldiers and Zionist militias, and Palestine moved toward war.

The US kept up the pressure on Britain. In response, London

announced in early 1947 that it was turning its Palestine problem over to the new United Nations. In the guise of a United Nations settlement, Washington could call the shots in determining the future of Palestine, and Washington had already made clear it was on the Zionist side. Unlike its attitude toward the old League of Nations, Washington had embraced the UN and was from the beginning the most powerful member of the new organization. In 1947 the UN had only fifty-five member states. Most of the world's people still lived in colonies, denied independent governments and thus denied membership in the UN. And of those member states, most depended heavily on US aid to rebuild their war-shattered economies. Only four African states were included in the entire UN membership, and the nineteen Latin American member states were virtual colonies of the US.

The UN General Assembly created the UN Special Commission on Palestine to make a recommendation. UNSCOP had no African or Arab members. It reflected the needs of the British, most urgently, to get out of Palestine, and, in the longer term, the needs of the Americans to end the growing instability within Palestine and settle the Jewish refugee problem once and for all.

The United Nations proposal called for partitioning Palestine into two states, one Arab and one Jewish. The plan called for 55 percent of Palestine to become a Jewish state—although Palestine's Jews at that time amounted to only 30 percent of the population and owned only 6 percent of the land. More than 400,000 Palestinian Arabs lived in the area designated to become the Jewish state, almost as big as the Jewish population who lived there. The other 45 percent of the land was to become a Palestinian Arab state.

The US and its allies strongly supported partition. The Soviet Union, though it had long officially opposed Zionism, changed its position, thinking the creation of the two new states would weaken British colonial influence in the Middle East. The USSR and its allies voted for partition too. The vote was in the UN General Assembly, and a two-thirds majority was required. The decision would hang on the undecided states.

The November 1947 debate was sometimes harsh. The representative from the Philippines railed against the proposed plan:

> We hold that the issue is primarily moral. The issue is whether the United Nations should accept responsibility for the enforcement of a policy which is clearly repugnant to the valid nationalist aspirations of the people of

Palestine. The Philippines Government holds that the United Nations ought not to accept such responsibility.[12]

The Philippines, while nominally politically independent, was economically dependent on US aid, and its government relied on US backing. A phone call from Washington to the Philippine president led to a quick reversal. Two days later, the Philippine diplomat who had spoken out in the General Assembly was aboard ship back to Manila, recalled from his post. The Philippines voted for partition. The delegate from Siam (now Thailand), who voted against partition during the Committee hearings, was also recalled from his post. A telegram signed by 26 American senators with influence on foreign aid bills was sent to wavering countries. The president of Firestone Rubber Company, with major holdings in Liberia, pressured the Liberian government to support partition.

The US had made the decision to make the partition of Palestine and the creation of a Jewish state, which would be born already indebted to US support, its highest priority. Columnist Drew Pearson reported that "President Truman cracked down harder on his State Department than ever before to swing the United Nations vote for the partition of Palestine."[13]

THE BIRTH OF ISRAEL

Fighting between Jews and Arabs resumed in Palestine after Partition. In May 1948, Israel declared its independence, and the US was the first country to offer full diplomatic relations to the new state. The declaration of the new Jewish state brought several armies of surrounding Arab countries into the war in Palestine. Despite their larger numbers, the Egyptian, Trans-Jordanian, Syrian, and other forces were, however, soon defeated by the better-armed Israeli military, the new Israel Defense Forces (IDF), created out of a combination of the pre-state mainstream Zionist militias (the Haganah and Palmach) and the armed extremist "revisionist" Zionist groups (the Irgun and the Stern Gang).

A key goal of the Israeli fighters was to force the Palestinians off the land, to clear it of Arab residents in order to consolidate a Jewish presence. By the time the fighting ended, Israel controlled 78 percent of the land of Mandate Palestine, far beyond the 55 percent granted in the UN Partition Plan, and 750,000 Palestinians had been forced off their land and into exile. For years Israel claimed that the Palestinians fled because their leaders told them to. By the late 1980s though, with the declassification of wide-ranging documentation in Western countries and especially inside Israel, the new historians of Israel were able to rewrite their country's mythological historiography with truth. Basing his work on those new documents, Benny Morris, one of the first of that group, reported:

> Above all, let me reiterate, the refugee problem was caused by attacks by Jewish forces on Arab villages and towns and by the inhabitants' fear of such attacks, compounded by expulsions, atrocities and rumors of atrocities—and by the crucial Israeli Cabinet decision in June 1948 to bar a refugee return.[14]

The US position was that the Palestinian refugees should be permanently absorbed by the Arab states to which they had first fled, mostly penniless and in terror. When it became clear that those countries could not afford to provide for the enormous human needs, Washington supported the creation of the UN Refugee Works Agency (UNRWA), designed to provide food, health, and other basic needs to the Palestinian refugees. The US also voted in favor of UN Security Council Resolution 194, which granted the refugees the explicit right to return to their homes and receive compensation for their losses, but it made sure that, in keeping with Israel's insistence, no such Palestinian return was ever allowed.

The US moved to increase economic support for Israel, because Israel's new national economy faced severe challenges. By 1950 Israel imported ten times as much as it exported, and the military budget absorbed fully half the government's annual spending. In 1949 the US government decided that private donations to Israel would be tax-exempt, so that more Americans would donate large amounts of money. The Export-Import Bank lent Israel $100 million that same year. Israel also counted on increased political backing from the US. As the Cold War heated up and war broke out in Korea, the US was determined to consolidate its allies against any Soviet influence. Israel was now an important part of that anti-Soviet alliance, but it was new and small. The US was still not prepared to put all its Middle East eggs into Israel's basket; the oil-rich Arab and other Middle Eastern states remained high Cold War priorities. But as nationalist pressure on those governments increased, and the Soviets contended for influence in places like Iran and Egypt, divisions emerged between the US and its European allies.

IRAN, NATIONALIZATION OF OIL, AND THE US

Conflicts over oil policy emerged throughout the region. In Iran, the democratic nationalist Mohammed Mosaddeq rose to power in 1951 on a platform of nationalizing Iranian oil, dominated at the time by the British-controlled Anglo-Iranian Oil Company (now British Petroleum). After nationalization, Britain feared a precedent that could lead to other British losses in the region and enlisted the help of the United States in removing Mosaddeq from power. For Washington, this move provided enormously increased US influence in oil-rich Iran. In August 1953, the CIA engineered a coup in which Mossadeq was overthrown and the repressive and unpopular Shah Reza Pahlevi was installed in power. This US action laid the foundations for the next four and a half decades of a US-Iranian Cold War partnership characterized by widespread Iranian anger toward the United States. That partnership ended with the 1978 Islamic Revolution that removed the Shah's regime permanently, replacing it with the Islamic republic of the fiercely anti-American Ayatollah Ruhollah Khomeini.

SUEZ

In 1955 tensions between Israel and Egypt increased. Egypt hanged three Israelis charged with spying, and, in response, Israel attacked a military camp in the Gaza Strip, killing 36 Egyptian soldiers. The UN condemned the raid, and Egyptian President Nasser asked the US for arms. Washington, seeing an opportunity to further isolate the Soviets in the region, agreed to Nasser's request but added a condition: that Egypt sign the Baghdad Pact that had created the anti-Soviet Central Treaty Organization (CENTO) alliance the US had established in the Middle East.

Nasser refused. Instead, he negotiated with pro-Soviet Czechoslovakia for the needed arms, and he ignored the efforts of US Secretary of State John Foster Dulles to persuade him that Egypt was falling into communist hands. In July 1956 the US withdrew its promise of aid to help Egypt build the vitally needed Aswan Dam, which would have provided irrigation for much of Egypt's desert land. Britain and France applauded the US move, and the Soviet Union provided major backing for the dam.

The effort at intimidation backfired. On July 26, 1956, one month after the withdrawal of British troops, Nasser nationalized the Suez Canal, which had been under British control since 1875. In reclaiming Egypt's control of the canal, Egypt thus threatened long-standing Western domination of the crucial Suez shipping trade. Britain and France, hoping the US would continue its high-profile stance against Egypt, urged immediate military intervention. London wanted control of the canal back; Paris wanted to defeat Nasser for fear he was backing the nationalists in Algeria's anti-colonial revolution against France. The US, however, had a more sophisticated and long-range approach in mind, based on continuing economic pressure to bring Egypt to heel.

Britain and France were unwilling to wait. They contracted a secret alliance with Israel, and in October 1956 Israel invaded the Egyptian Sinai. Britain and France provided air and naval cover. But the US was not prepared to accept independent military actions by its now less-than-all-powerful European allies, with or without its regional favorite, Israel. Washington condemned the Israeli-French-British move. The Soviet Union, uneasy about a potential return of European colonial powers and eager to heighten Soviet prestige in Egypt and other key Arab countries, joined the condemnation. Working together for disparate reasons despite Cold War hostilities, Washington and Moscow urged the UN to impose a ceasefire. Israel continued to occupy territory deep inside Egypt for five months before it withdrew; the UN then stationed peacekeeping troops at the Strait of Tiran and in Gaza, who patrolled the border until 1967.

THE SIX-DAY WAR

Throughout the early 1960s, the US maintained its alliances with Arab regimes, most of which had become independent in the 1940s and 1950s. Governments in Lebanon and Jordan, fearing Palestinian guerrilla movements among the large refugee populations in their countries, helped Israel protect its borders. By the middle of the decade, however, nationalist sentiments were on the rise throughout the Middle East. The new government that came to power in Syria in 1966 declared it would no longer help protect the US and other Western oil companies in the region, and began a long battle with Aramco, the oil company that controlled the vast Saudi oil fields and was dominated by US oil giants.

Washington was worried. It was not only the $2 billion each year in profits to US oil companies from sales of Middle Eastern oil. Sixty percent of the fuel required by the massive US military machine in Viet Nam also depended on Middle Eastern oil. Further, US strategy toward its World War II allies and opponents in Europe and Japan was based on providing economic (Marshall Plan) and military (NATO) support that would simultaneously rebuild the countries and ensure that their militaries and economies remained dependent and squarely under US domination. Serving as guarantor of US access to oil was a key component of that strategy.

US fears grew as nationalist revolts in Yemen, South Yemen, and Oman, all bordering Saudi Arabia, took hold. A high-level US policy study concluded that Arab nationalism could spread to Lebanon, Jordan, and the Arabian peninsula. If it did, it would pose "a security crisis of major and possibly catastrophic proportions."[15] The US military was bogged down in Viet Nam, however, and sending US troops to shore up threatened allied governments in the Middle East did not seem possible. Something else had to be done.

In 1966 the US began providing Israel with new, advanced planes and missiles. Describing the new US strategy in the Middle East, James Feron wrote in the *New York Times* (11 June 1966): the "United States has come to the conclusion that it must rely on a local power—the deterrent of a friendly power—as a first line to stave off America's direct involvement. Israel feels she fits this definition."

Israel itself was facing a series of internal difficulties. Growing economic problems included high unemployment and rising taxes, the end of German reparation payments in 1965, decreasing sales of Israeli bonds, and diminishing numbers of new immigrants. There was even a large-scale Israeli exodus *out* of the country. So the possibility of Israel reaping the economic and military benefits of becoming the US watchdog in the region seemed like a win-win solution for both countries. After all, the enemies of the US oil interests were also the enemies of the Israeli government: Syria, the Palestinian guerrillas, Nasser, and other Arab nationalist forces in the region. Israel would punish their acts against both American and Israeli interests, and Israel counted on the US government to show its appreciation.

Palestinian guerrilla raids against Israel, begun in 1964, continued. Israel began attacks on Syria, claiming Damascus was behind the raids, even those that originated in other countries. In September 1966 Israel bombed Syrian targets, and the US stepped up its military equipment to

Israel. Israel's threats against Syria escalated, and the Syrian government took them seriously, signing a mutual defense pact with Egypt.

Over the next months hostilities increased between Israel and each of the surrounding Arab states. In April there were artillery exchanges between Israel and Syria. Israel launched a major tank and air attack on Syrian border villages; Israeli planes shot down six Syrian MiGs, and Israel penetrated as far as the Damascus suburbs. The US Sixth Fleet remained on maneuvers off the Syrian coast. Nasser publicly asked the UN to move its observers inside Egypt to the Israeli border, a move widely understood to be symbolic. The UN told him he could not ask for UN troop movement; his choice was only to demand complete removal of the UN troops, or to leave them where they were. Under pressure from other Arab governments and unwilling to back down, Nasser demanded the withdrawal of all UN troops from Egypt. Then on May 23, 1967 Egypt closed the Strait of Tiran to Israeli shipping.

The Pentagon predicted that the balance of forces was so one-sided that no matter who struck first, no combination of Arab forces would overcome Israel's superior military strength. Nonetheless, on May 25 the Pentagon sent battalions of marines to the Sixth Fleet in case they were needed to bolster Israel. By June 2, the date was set for Israel to teach Syria and Egypt the long-awaited lesson. But first Israel needed permission from the US. On June 4, even as Nasser was negotiating with the US representative in Cairo, President Lyndon Johnson telegraphed Defense Minister Moshe Dayan, and gave Israel the final green light. The next day, Dayan ordered the attack.

Israeli planes destroyed the entire Egyptian air force while it was still on the ground, uncamouflaged in eleven separate airfields. Egyptian troops in the Sinai desert, without air cover, were vulnerable targets, and thousands were killed and wounded. Syrian defenses crumbled, and the Jordanian army never even engaged in the fighting. The Palestinian resistance in Gaza and the West Bank, without serious assistance from any Arab armies, was unable to repel the Israeli forces, and Israeli troops occupied the last remaining parts of Palestine, the West Bank, the Gaza Strip, and East Jerusalem, within six days.

After the ceasefire, Israeli troops moved into Syria and captured the Golan Heights; 90,000 Golani Arabs were expelled. By the end of the war, Israel occupied Syria's Golan Heights, the Egyptian Sinai, and Palestinian East Jerusalem, the West Bank, and the Gaza Strip. Six hundred Israelis and 35,000 Arabs died in the fighting, 250,000 more Palestinians were forced into exile, and a million more were now under Israeli military occupation.

In the US, the war was presented as Israel heroically triumphing over the aggressive Arab Goliath. Support skyrocketed for closer US ties to Israel. Fundraising by pro-Israeli organizations, blood drives, and volunteer campaigns all soared. During the six days of the war, the United Jewish Appeal sold $220 million worth of Israeli bonds; American contributions for Israel in 1967 totalled $600 million.

The biggest gain for Israel was not, however, those individual contributions. Even more important was the new recognition in Washington of the role Israel could play. It was an acknowledgment of Israel as the regional police officer for US regional interests. A State Department memo noted:

> Israel has probably done more for the US in the Middle East in relation to money and effort invested than any of our so-called allies and friends elsewhere around the world since the end of the Second World War. In the Far East, we can get almost nobody to help us in Viet Nam. Here, the Israelis won the war singlehandedly, have taken us off the hook, and have served our interests as well as theirs.[16]

The reward for Israel was a flood of sophisticated weapons, including advanced Phantom jets. In the four years after the 1967 war, Israel would receive $1.5 billion in US arms—ten times as much as the total for the last twenty years. As for the US, the Soviet decision not to intervene in the war ensured US preeminence as the top outside power in the Middle East.

In 1951, the publisher of *Ha'aretz*, perhaps the most influential Israeli daily newspaper, had written:

> ...[S]trengthening Israel helps the Western powers to maintain equilibrium and stability in the Middle East. Israel is to become the watchdog. There is no fear that Israel will undertake any aggressive policy toward the Arab states when this would explicitly contradict the wishes of the US and Britain. But if for any reason the Western powers should sometimes prefer to close their eyes, Israel could be relied on to punish one or several neighboring states whose discourtesy toward the West went beyond the bounds of the permissible.[17]

After 1967 this US willingness to rely on Israel vastly expanded. Now, relations with the Arabs would be secondary to the emerging US-Israeli alliance.

There was, of course, a price to be paid. Protesters angry about US support for Israel stormed American embassies in Beirut, Amman, and Damascus. In Saudi Arabia, Aramco oil workers went on strike against the giant US company. Eight hundred Palestinians were deported from Saudi Arabia for anti-American activities. Within three months after the war, the premiere business magazine *Fortune* (September 1967) would report that "not since the Boxer Rebellion [in China] has there been as rapid... a revulsion against a foreign power as against the US in the Middle East."

The US had gained, however, a reliable regional surrogate, and the vastly increased aid from the US helped solve Israel's economic problems. It was the beginning of a beautiful friendship. The 1967 war alerted Pentagon strategists to Israel's military capacity, and Israel's wartime popularity among American policymakers and the public fueled a vast increase in the power and influence of the pro-Israeli lobby within US domestic politics. The two approaches converged to set the stage for an upgraded special relationship. The interests and decisions of the Pentagon, State Department, and White House remained dominant, but the fact that their Middle East strategy rooted US policy in the partnership with Israel, meant that the lobby's work bolstered, rather than challenged, traditional definitions of US national interests. That brought Congress into the mix, as members and candidates sought to capitalize on broad pro-Israeli sentiments. Certainly the pro-Israeli lobby had and retains the ability to channel large-scale financial and political support to carefully selected politicians. But it is the correlation between the goals of what is now known simply as "the lobby," and the overall direction of US strategic goals that give the American-Israel Public Affairs Committee (AIPAC)and its allies the status they retain today: that of one of the most powerful foreign affairs lobbies in Washington.

The composition of that core base of support for Israel in the US would change over time, as more right-wing Christian fundamentalists and other right-wing forces joined the predominantly Jewish activists in backing Israel and its expansionism. But the permanence of the broad US public support for Israel has remained immutable.

ISRAEL AND PALESTINE IN WASHINGTON'S COLD WAR
Officially, the US supported the international consensus that took shape in the UN after the 1967 war as the global organization sought

to reverse Israel's subsequent occupations. Resolution 242 began with a statement emphasizing "the inadmissibility of the acquisition of territory by war and the need to work for a just and lasting peace in which every State in the area can live in security." It called for "the withdrawal of Israeli armed forces from territories occupied in the recent conflict."

There were, however, two big problems. First, the Palestinians were referred to only in the context of a refugee problem; territorial rights and independence were limited to the existing states in the area. That meant that most Palestinians rejected 242 as insufficient to protect their rights. Secondly, while the French version spoke of Israel's responsibility to withdraw from "the" territories, the English version left out the crucial word "the" and instead required only that Israel withdraw "from territories." The result was a long-standing Israeli claim that its 1979 withdrawal from the Egyptian Sinai under the terms of the US-brokered Camp David Accords represented sufficient compliance with 242.

Despite voting for the resolution, the US never really backed the goal of 242 that most of the rest of the world supported—ending Israel's occupation. For years following the 1967 war, the UN voted over and over in favor of holding an international peace conference under the auspices of the UN, with all parties to the conflict (including the Palestine Liberation Organization, which emerged as a serious force after 1967) to solve the Israel-Palestine conflict once and for all. But the US always voted no, determined to keep the Israel-Palestine problem off the international agenda where Israeli interests would face much greater diplomatic challenges.

Instead, US diplomatic initiatives were devised to keep Washington in control. The first was the Cold War-driven Rogers Plan in 1969. It was designed largely to win Arab governments away from Soviet influence and into the US orbit. It offered Arab leaders the return of some occupied territory, in exchange for recognition of Israel. The Palestinians, however, would get nothing. Jordan was a major target. King Hussein was uneasy about the large and increasingly restive Palestinian refugee community in his country, and implementing the Rogers Plan would undermine Palestinian national claims. Another US goal was to woo Egypt away from Soviet influence by promising the return of Egypt's Sinai peninsula, then still occupied by Israel. Under significant pressure at home to win back the Sinai, Nasser agreed to the Rogers Plan in July of 1970.

Nasser's abandonment of his long-standing support for the Palestinians gave the green light to Jordan's King Hussein to go even further. Small-scale attacks by Jordan's army on Palestinian guerrillas in the refugee camps had been going on for some time, and tensions were high. On August 29, 1970, King Hussein also signed on to the Rogers Plan. The next day, Palestinian commandos hijacked three Western jumbo jets and flew them to the Amman airport. They allowed the passengers to leave, and then, when the king rejected their demand to halt attacks on the Palestinian camps, they blew up the empty jets.

Two weeks later, on September 15, King Hussein launched a major assault on the Palestinians in his country. In ten days, 5,000 people were killed and 20,000 wounded, most of them civilians. During the assault, naval ships from the US Sixth Fleet steamed toward the Mediterranean coast nearest Jordan. At the same time, a high-level meeting was held in Washington, involving the Israeli and Jordanian ambassadors, national security advisor Henry Kissinger, and top Pentagon and CIA officials. They planned an Israeli attack on the Palestinians, code-named "Operation Brass Strike," if the Jordanian attack proved insufficient to destroy Palestinian leadership in Jordan. Once the fighting ended, the US provided $35 million in emergency aid, mostly military assistance for rearmament, to Jordan. Soon after, the Palestinian guerrillas, their families, and many more Palestinian civilians, were forced into yet another exile, this time to Lebanon. King Hussein's position as a linchpin of US Middle East policy was now consolidated.

After the death of Nasser in September 1970, Egypt's new president, Anwar Sadat, began making strong peace overtures to the US, believing only Washington could pressure Israel to return the occupied Sinai. It quickly became clear that the US had little incentive to pressure Israel, since the Palestinians had now been expelled from Jordan and Egypt's embrace of the Rogers Plan meant calm on the Suez Canal. Sadat tried harder to please Washington; he ended land reform efforts, opened Egypt to Western investments, and allowed US oil companies to explore for oil and build pipelines. In 1971 he sent troops against a strike of 10,000 steelworkers at the giant Helwan Steelworks, and patched up relations with US ally Saudi Arabia. By the summer of 1972, Sadat went even further: he expelled the 15,000 Soviet military advisers from Egypt, providing Washington with an unmistakable sign of Cairo's intentions.

All of Sadat's actions, however, proved insufficient. Egyptian diplomats, even after the dramatic Soviet expulsion, received an icy reception in Washington and no action on Israel's occupation of the Sinai. On the other hand, when Israeli Prime Minister Golda Meir visited a month later, she returned from Washington with promises of new Phantom jets for Israel's air force. Sadat decided only a limited war could create the necessary pressure for an Israeli-Egyptian settlement.

VIET NAM, OIL, AND OCTOBER WAR

By the early 1970s, the strategic significance of the Middle East increased as US defeat in Viet Nam loomed. Oil companies became concerned that some of the more radical members of OPEC, the cartel of oil exporting countries, might attempt to limit Western, and especially US, access to their oil fields. Indeed some of the oil countries began to talk about nationalizing their oil and using the oil weapon against Israel and the US. Pressure mounted on the US government to reduce its backing of Israel to avert rising oil prices.

In May 1973 King Faisal of Saudi Arabia made clear to President Nixon and to Henry Kissinger that his country needed Arab allies to help defend US interests in OPEC, and that the king could not find such allies as long as the US backed Israeli occupation of Arab lands. US oil companies agreed. Kissinger, a longtime associate of the Rockefeller family of oil barons, agreed that changes were needed but was unwilling to risk a major collision with Congress by suddenly pressuring Israel to withdraw from the occupied territories.

As it turned out, the Egyptian and Syrian leaders were just then beginning plans for what they thought would be a limited war designed to create a crisis that could lead to more serious changes in political alliances and on the ground. On October 6, 1973, Egyptian troops launched a surprise attack across the Suez Canal into the Israeli-occupied Sinai, while Syrian troops stormed the Israeli-occupied Golan Heights. The fighting was intense, and Israel suffered heavy casualties. But as the fighting continued, the initiative shifted. Israel's air force attacked Damascus and attempted to reduce Syria's economy to rubble, bombing ports, factories, and oil refineries. On the Egyptian front, a massive US airlift provided crucial rearmament to the advancing Israelis.

Arab governments, even those traditionally allied with the US, were outraged. Led by Saudi Arabia's King Faisal, the Arab members of OPEC announced a 25 percent cut in oil production and an embargo on oil shipments to the US. That was bad enough, but then things got worse for Washington. Israeli troops were on the verge of encircling Egypt's Third Army and were threatening to destroy it. The Soviet Union, which maintained diplomatic relations with Egypt despite Sadat's expulsion of its military advisers, sent word to Nixon and Kissinger that Moscow would take measures to prevent that from happening. The threat of a US-Soviet confrontation, one which could have reached a nuclear showdown, on top of the oil embargo, was too much. On October 22 the US and Soviet Union jointly sponsored a ceasefire call and plan for US-Soviet sponsored peace talks in the UN Security Council, and Washington pressured a reluctant Israel to sign on. As Israeli Defense Minister Moshe Dayan admitted regarding his country's reliance on the US, "How can you oppose a country that sends you ammunition in the morning that you fire in the afternoon?"[18]

Despite the gas price increases faced by consumers in the west, US oil companies profited handsomely from the OPEC price hikes whose effects were at any rate felt more by Europe, Japan, and other countries. In 1973, the profits of Exxon Oil, one of the oil companies who owned Aramco, increased by 59 percent. Saudi Arabia's income grew too, and it became, along with the Shah-ruled Iran, an important customer for US arms. Until the US stepped in, however, Israel had not fared so well. The cost of the October war caused a major economic crisis in Israel, so Tel Aviv turned to the US for additional aid. In the first 25 years of Israel's existence, US government aid totalled about $3 billion in grants and credits. Now, in 1973, the US was considering providing $8 billion to Israel over the next four years. That shift would set the stage for at least the next quarter-century of US Middle East strategy— in which support of Israel would match protection of oil access as two of the three key goals.

THE US, THE ARAB GOVERNMENTS, AND— NOT QUITE—THE PALESTINIANS

The October War allowed the US to reopen negotiations in the region. The jointly-sponsored US-Soviet talks in Geneva collapsed almost as soon as they started, however, and their adjournment meant Henry

Kissinger could launch his famous shuttle diplomacy based on organizing separate agreements between Israel and each Arab government. The result, for the US and Israel, would be negotiations far more favorable to Israel, since Tel Aviv would be able to face each Arab country separately; against any Arab country Israel was far stronger. Negotiating with a unified Arab representation would have been far more difficult.

The fatal flaw in Kissinger's strategy, though, was that it ignored the Palestinians. Kissinger's approach focused on strengthening ties with Arab governments and dealing with the Palestinians only as refugees. Palestinian opposition to the US's Jordanian option of placing the Israeli-occupied West Bank under King Hussein's rule was virtually unanimous, and opposition spread around the world. One result was a major escalation in international support for and recognition of the PLO, culminating in Yasir Arafat's appearance in November 1974 at the United Nations General Assembly. The UN voted 105 to 4 to recognize the right of the Palestinians to self-determination and to grant the PLO observer status within the UN itself. Only Israel and the US, along with US-dependent Bolivia and the Dominican Republic, voted against the resolution. It was a major defeat for US policy.

CAMP DAVID

International opinion was never a major factor for Washington policymakers, especially in the Middle East, and the Kissinger strategy of excluding the Palestinians and negotiating only with Arab governments continued. In September 1975 the US brokered an agreement between Egypt and Israel. Israel promised to return part of the Sinai peninsula to Egypt, while Egypt signed a non-aggression pledge. Further, each country would reap heavy financial rewards: the US would grant Israel a $2.2 billion aid package (to be renewed on a yearly basis) that included nuclear-capable F-16 fighter jets; Egypt would be given half a billion dollars. The private agreement was later leaked to US newspapers: with the Israeli-Egyptian agreement in hand, Kissinger also assured Israel that the US would no longer pressure Israel to negotiate with Syria or the Palestinians.

Implementation of the accords stalled, however, with each side defining its responsibilities differently. On November 19, 1977, Egyptian President Anwar Sadat moved to break the stalemate. In an historic visit, the first by any Arab leader, he traveled to Jerusalem to address the Israeli Knesset. The US hailed the surprise visit as an important step, but many Arab leaders and most of the Arab populations were uneasy.

In his Knesset speech Sadat focused on the need for a comprehensive peace to end all wars in the Middle East. He spoke of the need for Israel to withdraw from all occupied Arab territories, including East Jerusalem, and to recognize the right of the Palestinians to regain their lost rights. Israel's rightist prime minister, Menachem Begin, however, saw things quite differently. While asserting that "everything was negotiable," Begin made clear that Israeli security was his overarching goal, that UN resolutions 242 and 338 did not require Israeli withdrawal from all the territories occupied in 1967 (especially not including the West Bank and Gaza Strip), that the Israeli settlements would remain in place and under Israeli jurisdiction, that Jerusalem would remained united under solely Israeli rule, and that Israel was not prepared to recognize the PLO—although it would consider some kind of autonomy for West Bank and Gaza Palestinians.

Negotiations continued after Begin paid a return visit to Egypt, but after some months Sadat broke off the talks. In response, the US moved in to take control of the diplomacy. Vice President Walter Mondale pledged that "my country will not fail to provide Israel with crucial military assistance, nor will we use that assistance as a form of pressure."[19] Secretary of State Cyrus Vance reiterated the pledge in testimony before the Senate Foreign Relations Committee only weeks before the Camp David conference, held when President Jimmy Carter summoned the two leaders to his presidential retreat in Maryland. Sequestered for thirteen days, Begin and Sadat finally emerged with the Camp David Accords in September 1978. Both sides, as well as their US sponsor, hoped other Arab countries would follow suit, and accept US-brokered bilateral agreements with Israel.

But it was not to be, as almost all the Arab states continued to hold out for broader regional goals. The Palestinians, too, opposed the Accords, seeing them as a surrender to Israeli power and an acceptance of the US-Israeli view that Middle East peace could be crafted without the Palestinians. Jordan's King Hussein, for example, condemned the Camp David Accords, claiming that Egypt's own interests lay in understanding that "the Arab world is a family," and called for comprehensive regional negotiations under United Nations auspices. The accords themselves were narrowly drawn, and it took six months more of US-Israeli diplomacy and the finalizing of significant economic, diplomatic, and military guarantees by Washington to Tel Aviv before a peace treaty was signed. Israel had been the main stumbling block. It was feeling the pressure of the Iranian revolution, which was in the process of ousting Tel Aviv's longtime ally, the Shah of Iran, and bringing to power the Islamist government of Ayatollah Khomeini, a longtime adversary of Israeli interests, perhaps threatening Israeli oil access. Carter pressed Egypt to guarantee Israeli access to Sinai oil, and the treaty was finally signed in March 1979. Within another year Israel and Egypt had exchanged ambassadors, and Israel withdrew from two-thirds of the Sinai Peninsula, returning it to Egypt. US policymakers were delighted, and President Carter shared the Nobel Peace Prize with his Egyptian and Israeli counterparts.

The ostensible next step of the Camp David process, agreement on arrangements for Palestinian autonomy, proved, however, more elusive. The US was unwilling to exert sufficient pressure to impose a settlement—and the fact that Israel and the US were negotiating with Egypt, rather than with the Palestinians themselves, made everything worse. Begin insisted that the Palestinians would have the right only to limited self-rule over the people but not the land, water, or other resources of the occupied West Bank and Gaza Strip. And whatever his own proclivities, Sadat knew that signing away Palestinian rights would thoroughly undermine his own rule, especially with the pressure of the Iranian turmoil pointing up his isolation in the Arab world. The autonomy talks sputtered on inconclusively. Increasingly isolated in his own country and throughout the Arab world for what was viewed as a betrayal of regional hopes by signing a separate peace with Israel and leaving the Palestinians to their fate, the Egyptian leader paid the ultimate price. On October 6, 1981, President Sadat was assassinated by a member of his own military, who saw him as a traitor to the Arab and Muslim cause.

THE US IN THE REGION: THE CARTER DOCTRINE
The US position as Israel's champion continued to isolate it from its other allies. In June 1980 the nine-member European common market issued its Venice Declaration. It reaffirmed Europe's commitment to

Israeli security and offered help to ensure that security, but went on to support the principle of Palestinian self-determination, condemn Israeli settlement policy (settlement construction and expansion continued throughout the Camp David process and after), and call for the PLO to be associated with the peace process. Washington reiterated its opposition to dealing with the PLO, and Europe retreated from active Middle East diplomacy.

There was another aspect of US-Israeli relations emerging as a major factor at the same time. The Iranian revolution, with its potential for regional power shifts and threats to US access to Persian Gulf oil, was soon followed by what was to become a decade-long war between Iran and Iraq. Pressures on the US mounted as, at the same time, the Sandinista revolution overthrew a long-standing US-supported dictatorship in Nicaragua, and a popular guerrilla war broke out against the US-backed government in El Salvador. Together, these factors led President Carter to craft his own "Carter Doctrine," in which he pledged to use force, if necessary, to defend US access to Gulf oil. The Middle East's crude, the President declared, was "our oil," and would be defended at all costs. Other Cold War-driven hot spots would be attended to as well, with a combination of a new Rapid Deployment Force, for which Carter reinstituted the long-dormant US military draft registration process, and a network of regional allies and surrogates to represent US interests around the world. One of the first actions of the Carter Doctrine involved sending advanced AWAC communications planes and F-15 fighter jets to Saudi Arabia in 1980 at the request of the king, who felt threatened by the overthrow of his former ally, the Shah of Iran.

Israel and its US supporters fought bitterly against Washington deploying the F-15s to Saudi Arabia. It was the first major public break between the pro-Israeli lobby and the foreign policy establishment, but in the end (by a very close vote in the Senate) regional stability and oil temporarily trumped Israel and the sale was approved—though with the condition that Israel's security not be eroded. Israel's ambassador to the US, Ephraim Evron, announced that his country would now expect increased US military aid to compensate.[20] That was fine with the US, and Israel was designated to play a key role in implementing the Carter Doctrine. It had both the willingness and the strategic capacity to intervene directly in crises in the Middle East, but as well in other Cold

War-driven crises then exploding in Nicaragua, Guatemala, Angola, Mozambique, and elsewhere. Israel's help was particularly useful for those instances in which the US was inhibited from intervening directly because of domestic political pressures.

In the meantime, events in the eastern part of the region were shifting the locus of US attention. The Iranian revolution had triumphed, the despised Shah had fled to sanctuary in the West, and Khomeini was remaking Iranian society in a newly Islamist mode. But the advanced weapons Washington had lavished on its once favored ally remained after the Shah was deposed. Islamist Iran and ruthlessly secular Iraq were now each poised to emerge as potential regional powers. Each had the requisite water, oil wealth, and large educated populations that would make such a position possible. Not surprisingly, competition between them escalated, and fighting over control of the Shatt al-Arab waterway soon erupted into full-scale war.

The US essentially wanted both sides to lose in the Iran-Iraq War, seeing the conflict as a means of depleting both countries' military and economic strength, and thus their ability as potential regional powers seriously to challenge US influence. Washington viewed Iran as militarily stronger and, therefore, to forestall a quick end to the war and a decisive Iranian victory, tilted significantly toward Iraq. Within a short time, the US was providing military intelligence, targeting information, loan guarantees, and access to advanced military technology (including the seed stock for biological weapons), to Saddam Hussein's government in Baghdad.

Israel, however, had long viewed Arab Iraq as a much more dangerous enemy than its former ally, non-Arab Iran under the Shah. Tel Aviv believed that Iraq could become the center of an anti-Israel Arab nationalist bloc. On June 7, 1981, Israeli Air Force pilots, in American-supplied planes, bombed and destroyed the not-quite-complete French-built Osirak nuclear power reactor outside of Baghdad. Iraq was a signatory to the Non-Proliferation Treaty (NPT), and had been allowing regular inspections of the reactor by the International Atomic Energy Agency. Nuclear-armed Israel (which has still never signed the NPT), used the excuse that the power plant could someday be used to produce nuclear weapons which might someday be used against Israel, and thus it had the right to destroy the reactor. The international community was outraged; Israel was claiming an unprecedented right to preemptively strike a potential future enemy. Even the US showed some concern; President Reagan told Congress that a "substantial violation" of the agreement mandating that US military equipment can be used only for defensive purposes "may have occurred."[21] But the US, threatening to use its veto, forced the UN Security Council to abandon any effort to impose sanctions, agreeing only to a resolution condemning the Israeli attack.

LEBANON'S CIVIL WAR

In the meantime, the civil war in Lebanon, begun in 1975, continued to escalate, drenching the country in bloody sectarian violence. For the US, the war was mostly about internal Lebanese struggles for power and resources between the various religious, political, and clan-based factions. But Lebanon also played a regional role: it was a key focal point in the Israeli-Palestinian conflict. With hundreds of thousands of Palestinian refugees living in Beirut and southern Lebanon, much of the governing, from schools and hospitals to licensing and legal systems, was taken over by the PLO. Palestinian guerrillas and Israeli troops also continued to trade rocket fire across the Israeli-Lebanese border. Since 1978, Israel had occupied a strip of southern Lebanon, in defiance of UN Resolution 425 calling on Israel to withdraw immediately and unconditionally. Instead, the Israeli Defense Forces (IDF) paid, armed, trained, and supported an anti-Palestinian Christian-led militia, the South Lebanon Army, in its occupied zone.

Israel saw the existence of the PLO as a major threat to the legitimacy of its occupation of Palestinian land, and much of Israel's anti-PLO strategy in Lebanon involved trying to turn the Lebanese against the Palestinians. They achieved some success, particularly among wealthier Lebanese who were disturbed by Palestinian influence in the South and in the poorer classes of Lebanese, who would form the backbone of Lebanese support for the Palestinian resistance movement. Israel's real goal though was to destroy the PLO infrastructure—social as well as military—in Lebanon, and to put in place a compliant, pro-Israeli regime in Beirut. When it appeared that Lebanon's civil war could drag on forever without those goals being achieved, Israel decided to move on its own. The influential military correspondent for *Ha'aretz* wrote on May 12:

It is not true that—as we tell the Americans—we do not want to invade Lebanon. There are influential forces, led by the Defense Minister which, with intelligence and cunning, are taking well-considered steps to reach a situation that will leave Israel with no choice but to invade Lebanon.[22]

First Tel Aviv needed to be sure its allies in Washington would approve.

Garnering US endorsement was a bit tricky. After all, the US-brokered ceasefire between Israel and the PLO in south Lebanon and across Israel's northern border had held for almost a year. There was no obvious provocation over which to justify a direct Israeli invasion as self-defense. In May 1982, Israel's Defense Minister Ariel Sharon went to Washington to meet with President Reagan's Secretary of State Alexander Haig. After a national security briefing, former President Jimmy Carter said that he was told that powerful people in Israel believe they "have a green light from Washington." Haig denied that was the case, but admitted "the Israelis had made it very clear that... at the next provocation they were going to react. They told us that. The President knew that." What lends the green light theory even more credence is the fact that during the first three months of 1982, while the invasion of Lebanon had to be in the planning stages, what the Pentagon called a "massive surge of military supplies" was transferred from the US to Israel.[23]

Then Israel created a new provocation. On June 3, a renegade, anti-PLO Palestinian faction attempted to assassinate Israel's ambassador in London. The British police immediately identified Abu Nidal's forces as responsible and revealed that PLO leaders were among the names on the would-be assassins' hit list. Although the PLO had nothing to do with the attack, Israel claimed it (the ambassador remained unhurt) provided a justification for war. Three days later the Israeli army invaded Lebanon in operation "Peace for Galilee," crossing the Litani River and moving almost as far north as Beirut, destroying the feeble resistance from local villagers and from United Nations peacekeeping troops swept aside in the assault. Israel remained in virtually uncontested control of the air and had overwhelming military superiority on land and sea. Beirut was besieged and subjected to merciless bombing for two months. Casualties were enormous. Hospitals were hit, and Palestinian refugee camps were levelled in the bombardment.

Israeli relied overwhelmingly on US-supplied planes, bombs, and other military equipment. Despite existing laws mandating that US military supplies be used only for defensive purposes, no one in Washington complained. In reference to a much-discussed photograph of Ronald Reagan looking somber as he greeted the Israeli prime minister during the invasion, the Washington correspondent of Israel's *Davar* newspaper wrote:

> Ronald Reagan played his part well....The [US] government is compelled to make a public show of a hard line toward Israel—in part to respond to public pressure and also to deflect the pressures from the Arabs—and to use the same opportunity to extricate itself from the image of a participant in the Israeli operation.... [Shamir was told to] finish quickly with this matter of West Beirut."[24]

The Reagan administration and Congress each tried to outdo the other in calls to raise US aid to Israel. Most significantly, military assistance continued to escalate. Military goods delivered rose 50 percent above 1981, and "Pentagon spokesmen confirm that these deliveries continued thorough June at a very high level... including 'smart bombs,' used with 'devastating' effect in Beirut."[25] Throughout June and July the siege of Beirut continued, with everyone in the city deprived of water, most food, electricity and safety. The bombing increased in early August, leading to a day of eleven solid hours of bombing on August 12. Condemnation poured in from around the world, and even the US issued a mild criticism of the bombing.

A ceasefire was soon reached. The US brokered the terms, which centered on the PLO leaving Beirut—its guerrillas, its doctors, its civilian infrastructure, its officials—everyone and everything would board ship heading for Tunis, almost as far from Palestine as you could get and still be in the Arab world. The US promised to serve as guarantor of Israel's promises of safety for the Palestinian civilians, primarily women, children, and old men, left behind in Beirut. US Marines were deployed as the centerpiece of an international force with a 30-day mandate to guard Beirut during the withdrawal of the PLO fighters.

THE END OF THE WAR, AND SABRA/SHATILA

On September 1, President Reagan announced a new peace initiative between Israel and the Palestinians, including a freeze on new settlements, limited autonomy for Palestinians in the West Bank and Gaza, and some version of a Jordanian solution, plus new economic and military aid for Israel. Israel, however, was not so happy about this approach, and the initiative remained stalled; in the West Bank, Israelis immediately inaugurated several new settlements. At the same time, Israel was having even more difficulties with the new president of Lebanon, Bashir Gemayel. Tel Aviv had expected Gemayel to be their man in Beirut, but Gemayel was emerging as a Lebanese nationalist instead.

On September 11, two weeks before the end of their official mandate, the last US Marines were withdrawn from Beirut. Three days later, Gemayel was assassinated. Within hours, Israel responded by invading the Muslim- (and formerly Palestinian-) dominated West Beirut. It was in complete violation of the agreement Philip Habib had negotiated with the PLO. After a few hours, Israeli Defense Minister Sharon announced that the Christian Phalangists, the most anti-Palestinian of all the Christian militias, would actually enter the Palestinian camps, rather than the Israelis themselves. The senior Israeli commander met with the top Phalangist leaders and told them, he said, "to act humanely, and not to harm women, children, and old people."

On Thursday, September 16, Israeli troops lit flares to light the way for their Phalangist allies to enter the Sabra and Shatila refugee camps on the outskirts of West Beirut. The massacre of unarmed children, women, and old men went on for three days. It resulted in the deaths of between 2,000 and 3,000 Palestinians, most of them left piled up or hastily buried in mass graves. The Red Cross later said it would be impossible to know the exact number who died.

There was no question that the Israeli soldiers knew what was going on inside—it was visible even without their high-powered binoculars, and the sound of machine-gun fire continued throughout the days and nights. Finally the US pushed Israel to withdraw the Phalangists. US Special Envoy Morris Draper told the Israeli officers: "You must stop the massacres. They are obscene. I have an officer in the camp counting the bodies.... They are killing children. You are in absolute control of the area and therefore responsible for that area."[26]

THE AFTERMATH

The Sabra-Shatila Massacre, as it quickly became known, transformed public perceptions about the war, especially inside Israel. Four hundred thousand Israelis, about 10 percent of the entire population of the country, marched in protest, and eventually Israel established a high-level commission of inquiry to investigate. (Among other things, it found Defense Minister Sharon to be "indirectly responsible" for the massacre.) In the US, revulsion quickly swung public opinion away from support of Israel. US officials spoke strongly against the massacres but refused to act on their words. The UN General Assembly voted 147 to 2 to condemn the massacres; the US joined Israel in voting against the condemnation. But many voices in the US pointed out that the massacres might not have happened if Washington had kept its word and kept its troops in Lebanon.

The Reagan administration's response was quick: the decision to send troops back to Beirut, just two weeks after they had been withdrawn, was made during the weekend of September 18–19, just as the massacre was ending. According to the Middle East specialist on the National Security Council, Geoffrey Kemp, it was "an emotional... response to a tragic event," influenced "by the feeling that the United States had assumed responsibility for the safety of the Palestinians and that our friends, the Israelis, had allowed the worst to happen."27

The 3,800 troops of the Multi-National Force, with French and Italian soldiers joining the Americans, returned to Beirut with awesome military power, and became the real power in the city. They were backed by an enormous naval armada filling Beirut Bay with American and French aircraft carriers filled with fighter jets, nuclear-powered destroyers and patrol boats speeding up and down the Lebanese coast. The US promised $105 million in aid to Lebanon by the end of the year.

The Lebanese civil war was not, however, over. Thirty-three Lebanese and foreign militias and armies still vied for control of the country; Israel's front lines nudged the outskirts of Beirut, Syrian troops still controlled large tracts of land, and the government of Lebanon was still dominated by the right-wing Phalangist Party, with close links to Israel. It welcomed the US, and the government and official Lebanese army became even more bullying and aggressive knowing they could count on American protection. As the tensions between various Lebanese factions heated up, Palestinian civilians (including many traumatized survivors of the massacres) were arrested or roughly interrogated. Attacks on the Israeli army increased throughout Lebanon, and kidnapping of Americans and other Westerners became more frequent.

In March 1983 small-scale attacks on the US and other Western forces began. Diplomatically, an ill-fated and already-stalemated

Reagan plan for Middle East peace collapsed even further when it was rejected by Jordan's King Hussein, who blamed its failure on the PLO. Then, on April 18, the US embassy compound was destroyed by a powerful car bomb, killing 63 people, of whom 17 were Americans, and wounding 100 more. According to British journalist Robert Fisk,

> Only days after the collapse of Washington's initiative on the West Bank, and at a time when the United States was still vainly trying to secure the withdrawal of Israeli and Syrian troops from the country, the bomb struck at the very heart of President Reagan's Middle East policy.[28]

The civil war intensified, with the Israeli-backed Phalangist government challenged by Syrian-backed Muslim, Druze, and secular militias. Cold War politics came into play, as the Soviet Union increased its support to Syria and the US took a harder line in backing Lebanese sovereignty under the existing Christian-based government. Israel withdrew its forces from the Chouf Mountains overlooking Beirut, and fierce fighting broke out there between the government and the Muslim-Druze militias. On September 19, exactly one year after the Sabra-Shatila massacre, the US military joined Lebanon's civil war. The warships of the American Sixth Fleet attacked, firing into the Chouf, aiming at the Druze who were operating near the tiny town of Souq al-Gharb. The giant battleship USS New Jersey led the attack, firing 2,000-pound shells the size of Volkswagens. Washington was now officially a partisan in Lebanon's civil war.

The fighting quickly increased, with other parts of the Multi-National Force drawn in. On October 23, the headquarters of both the US Marine Corps barracks and the French paratroopers were destroyed by a truck bomb; 241 American military troops and 58 French paratroopers were killed. The Italians, whose forces had not engaged in fighting, were not harmed.

The US and French troops surrounded their compounds with defensive walls. The fighting continued, and the US began air strikes from the carrier Eisenhower against Druze and Muslim militias above Beirut. Fighting increased again, and, on February 6, Reagan announced that the Marines in Beirut would retreat to their ships. The US mission to Lebanon was over.

BACK TO "PEACE PROCESSES" & "SPECIAL RELATIONSHIPS"

By 1985, Israel's partial withdrawal from Lebanon—Israel maintained its occupation of a nine- or ten-mile-wide strip of south Lebanon along the Israeli border—finally set the stage for the civil war to sputter to an inconclusive end. The UN's 1978 demand in resolution 425 that Israel withdraw "forthwith" from Lebanon would remain unfulfilled for another fifteen years, and the war itself would continue for another five. The withdrawal of US troops signalled a shift, however, in Washington's policy emphasis from Lebanon back to Israel and the occupied Palestinian territories. The PLO leadership was now banished to Tunis, far from its homeland, and Palestinians inside the territories began considering how to take more initiative on their own.

Throughout the early 1980s, the US had consolidated its strategic links with Israel. It was the height of the Cold War, and Israel was Washington's most reliable ally, or junior partner, in waging that war. Israel's military was involved in the training and arming of anti-government guerrilla movements in places like Nicaragua or Angola, and of repressive but pro-US governments themselves in countries as far afield as Guatemala and El Salvador, in the wars fought between US-backed and Soviet-backed forces. As Israel's role in US policy expanded far beyond the Middle East, US aid to Israel increased every year. It went from about $2.2 billion in 1982, to over $3.5 billion a year by 1986. The link between Israel's importance in foreign policy imperatives driven by Pentagon or State Department strategists, and the political backing for increased aid to Israel orchestrated through well-organized lobbies, made Israel the favorite ally of virtually everyone in Washington.

On the diplomatic front, Washington proposed several initiatives, all aimed at establishing some kind of partial autonomy for the Palestinians living under Israeli military occupation on the West Bank and the Gaza Strip. Some envisioned links with Jordan as well. But none broke new ground, and none was taken seriously. Israel continued to build and expand settlements in the occupied territories, and daily life for the Palestinians continued under the harsh rule of the Israeli army and Israel's "Civil Administration." Social, political, and economic conditions continued to deteriorate, and the US did little to respond or to pressure Israel to change its policies. As the occupation bit deeper and deeper into Palestinian lives and hopes, anger grew and tensions mounted. It was an uprising waiting to happen.

INTIFADA—THE CHILDREN OF THE STONES

In December 1987, twenty years into an increasingly pitiless occupation, Palestinian anger exploded into what quickly became known as the *intifada*—the uprising. The word in Arabic means to shudder or tremble, to shake off or shake out, to recover, or to jump to one's feet. The Palestinians chose "uprising" as the closest English equivalent, although they knew the word still missed some of the layers of meaning of the Arabic original.

What the world—including most Americans—saw was Palestinian children and teenagers confronting with barrages of stones the Israeli soldiers occupying their cities and towns and villages—day after day after day, arrests after beatings after arrests after beatings. The most important part of the uprising, however, was not the battle going on every day in the streets. The most important part went on *inside* Palestinian society itself, where the resistance "shook off" the passivity and fear that had so often characterized Palestinian responses to the occupation. Everything changed. Women became much more visibly active and played new leadership roles; young people challenged their parents in new ways; Israeli products were boycotted and local substitutes created; and a wide range of civil society organizations were created to figure out new ideas and to nurture new hopes. When the Israeli military ordered the universities or the schools or even the kindergartens closed, popular education classes were held in hidden rooms or under trees. When known leaders of the uprising were arrested by Israeli soldiers, new, often unknown, people stepped forward quietly to take their place. Everything was different.

The US hoped that the uprising would create a new generation of Palestinians outside of the PLO who would agree to talk with the US in a much narrower framework, who would not keep bringing up inconvenient things like international law and UN resolutions. US policy still prohibited talking to the PLO itself. But the uprising's leadership, who communicated with their own people through daily leaflets distributed through streets and marketplaces across the territories, made one thing very clear. Our diplomatic address, they told the world's press and the world's leaders, is in Tunis, with the leadership of the PLO. Every effort by the US to find an "alternate" leadership failed.

The Israelis responded with brutal repression. Israeli security agencies infiltrated and assassinated organizers of the intifada. Then-Defense Minister Yitzhak Rabin, later to win the Nobel Prize for Peace, famously called on his troops to "break the bones" of Palestinian youngsters to control rioting. In the summer of 1988, Jordan's King Hussein severed all administrative and economic ties with the West Bank, citing his move as an expression of support for the PLO. He reminded the world that "Jordan is not Palestine," dashing the hopes still floating around in Washington for a Jordanian solution to the Palestinian problem.

Then, on October 15, the PLO's parliament-in-exile, the Palestine National Congress (PNC), met in Algiers and declared an independent State of Palestine in the West Bank, Gaza, and East Jerusalem. The Palestinians controlled none of their own territory but, within a year, the new "state" had full diplomatic relations with more countries than Israel did. Shortly after, Washington supported a Security Council resolution condemning Israel for expelling Palestinians from their homes—a virtually unprecedented move for the veto-prone US. But not everything changed. In November, when Arafat was invited to address the UN General Assembly, the US refused to grant him a visa to come to New York to speak at UN headquarters. Unwilling to allow the US, host country or not, to dictate who the Assembly could invite, the entire membership and staff of the UN General Assembly, including translators, clerks, security guards, and assistants, as well as diplomats and their aides, packed up and traveled to Geneva to hear Arafat at UN headquarters there.

Building on the Palestinian peace initiative in that speech and aiming to end the US isolation of the PLO, Arafat formally recognized Israel, making official what had long been the PLO's unofficial support for a two-state solution. He also called for an international peace conference under the auspices of the UN. It was a breakthrough, but US officials monitoring the speech informed the PLO that the language was not clear enough in renouncing terrorism to allow the US to begin talks with the PLO. The press was recalled for a follow-up clarification based on the language Washington demanded. Within hours, US Secretary of State George Shultz announced his intention to open a dialogue with the PLO. It was the first break with Kissinger's 1975 commitment to Israel that the US would refuse to negotiate with the PLO.

TALKS ABOUT TALKS

The official opening of a US-PLO dialogue did not, however, lead to serious changes. Washington wanted the Palestinians to accept Israel's plan for elections in the occupied territories, from which the PLO would be excluded, and a narrow version of autonomy. The PLO refused and the talks stalled. Then in the spring of 1990, a marginal PLO faction attempted a military attack against Israel. It failed, but the US deemed the PLO's disavowal insufficient, and called off the talks altogether.

The world was already in turmoil as the Soviet Union slouched toward collapse. The Berlin Wall had fallen, and the Cold War was at its end. Many in the Middle East waited to see how the end of the global contention between the US and the Soviet Union would affect the regional version of that same battle. A few months later, on August 2, 1990, they saw the initiation of that shift. Iraq's military would invade and occupy tiny, wealthy, and oil-bloated Kuwait, and Washington immediately recognized the potential for ensuring the continuation of its global power status.

STORMING THE DESERT

The end of the Cold War presented a problem to the US. Without the Soviet Union as a visible competitor, it would be much harder for Washington to justify its aggressive assertion of regional power in the Middle East. Yet the vital US interests—access to oil, especially for US allies in Europe and Japan; defense of Israel; and stability to encourage investment and market development—remained. Iraq's invasion of Kuwait provided a new basis to reassert US dominance.

Iraq's invasion was a clear violation of international law, but it did not happen out of the blue. It came after a period of escalating tensions and threats by Iraq. In the longer run, it was triggered by long-standing competition between Iraq and Kuwait over oil. Kuwait is a tiny country with a tiny population, sitting on preposterously huge lakes of oil. It could afford to produce and export its oil slowly and still provide its citizens with unimaginable wealth. It also had large and varied investments in Western, oil-importing countries—so it shared the interests of the US, Europe, Japan, and other countries in keeping oil prices relatively low. Iraq, on the other hand, while also sitting on huge oil stocks, had a big country and a much larger population whose needs had to be met almost entirely through oil exports; its interests were in keeping oil prices and production quotas sky-high.

The US still maintained cordial relations with the Iraqi regime, although not as close since the end of the Iran-Iraq War in 1988. On July 25, 1990, the US ambassador to Iraq, April Glaspie, met with President Saddam Hussein. The US was aware, she told the Iraqi leader, of the inter-Arab tensions escalating in the region. "But we have no opinion on the Arab-Arab conflicts, like your border disagreement with Kuwait." It sounded, at the very least, like a yellow light. Seven days later Iraq invaded Kuwait.

The Gulf War, first called Desert Shield and then upgraded to Desert Storm when the US-led coalition attacked Baghdad in January 1991, transformed the Middle East. Early efforts by the Arab League and other regional actors to solve the crisis were rebuffed by Washington, which made clear it had no interest in a negotiated withdrawal from Kuwait, and would accept only a military defeat of Iraq.

Washington's determination to win a military victory was driven more by the end of the Cold War than by serious concern about the occupation of Kuwait. The Iraqi invasion, certainly a clear violation of international law, also provided a perfect pretext for Washington to reassert its role as global superpower despite the disappearance of its strategic challenger. How better to accomplish that than by "leading the world" to war? Negotiating an end to the Iraqi invasion, let alone encouraging a regional negotiating process to do so, would solve the immediate crisis but nothing more. "Liberating" the emirate through the fireworks of all-out war and restoring the Kuwaiti royal family to their thrones would provide a whole new justification for the US to reassert its role as a global superpower, despite the absence of a strategic contender. The US would lead an international coalition against Saddam Hussein, who was recast as the new Hitler.

President George Bush Senior had spent years as US ambassador to the United Nations during the Nixon administration, and he chose the global organization to orchestrate his new internationalization of the Iraq-Kuwait conflict. To make real his we-will-lead-the-world approach, the international support for a US war against Iraq had to appear unanimous. At first there was widespread support for US positions, since Iraq's invasion was a clear violation of international law. The Security

Council voted fourteen to zero (Yemen, the sole Arab country on the Council, abstained) to condemn the invasion. But condemnation was not enough, and resolutions imposing harsh sanctions were passed. From September on, US diplomats focused on winning unanimity in the Council to support a military campaign against Iraq.

By late November, even reluctant Council members had been bribed, threatened, and coerced to accept Washington's demand for a new UN resolution to authorize war against Iraq. More than two dozen nations, many of them under pressure, joined the Pentagon's anti-Iraq coalition authorized by the US-dominated Security Council but in which the UN had no voice. Countries that agreed, especially those on the Security Council, were rewarded: Colombia, impoverished Ethiopia, and corruption-ravaged Zaire were each offered new aid packages; Ethiopia and Colombia, long denied military aid suddenly won access to new weapons.

The US had worried that China might make good on its threat to veto the Security Council resolution authorizing war. So US diplomats asked China to name its price. Beijing, isolated since the 1989 massacre at Tienanmen Square, asked for and received a new package of long-term development aid and post-Tienanmen diplomatic rehabilitation in the form of a high-profile meeting between President Bush and China's foreign minister. That meeting was announced the day before the vote authorizing the use of force. The bribes worked: China abstained and the resolution passed.

In contrast, the US punished countries opposing the resolution: when the Yemeni ambassador voted against the go-to-war resolution, a US diplomat told him, "That will be the most expensive 'no' vote you ever cast," and three days later, the United States announced it was cutting its entire aid program to Yemen, the poorest country in the Arab world.

Once the resolution was passed, Washington demanded a halt to any diplomatic overtures to Iraq until the US-imposed deadline had passed. When Iraqi troops still remained in Kuwait after January 15, US and British planes launched around-the-clock attacks on Baghdad. The war was won largely through the six-week air war; the ground invasion of Iraq by US troops lasted only a few days.

AFTER THE STORM

When the war was over in mid-March, the occupation of Kuwait had ended, Iraq lay in ruins, and, with the Arab world split down the middle over support for Washington's war, the US had more power than ever in the region. With the simultaneous defeat of regional upstart Iraq and the collapse of the Soviet Union, US power appeared unstoppable.

First on the agenda was to show the Middle East and the world that the US could impose peace just as it had decreed war. The result was a US call for a Middle East peace talks—but not the international peace conference that the United Nations had long advocated. Instead, the US pressed Israel and the key Arab countries to agree to a high-profile but non-substantive multilateral conference to launch a new peace initiative. The substance would come after the conference in the form of separate tracks of bilateral negotiations. That meant that Israel would negotiate separately with Syria, Lebanon, Jordan, and the Palestinians (the PLO was still excluded).

The glittering Crystal Palace in Madrid was the site of the internationally-televised conference. Officially, it was sponsored jointly by the US and the Soviet Union. But the conference opened on October 31, 1991; sixty days later the quavering Soviet Union collapsed. The US, alone, was calling the shots. The conference heard voices well-known to the world—Presidents Bush and Gorbachev, Israeli Prime Minister Yitzhak Shamir. But it heard other, newer voices too—the Palestinian delegation, led by the respected Gaza physician Dr. Haidar Abdel-Shafi, presented a new, independent Palestinian voice. At the press conferences, Palestinian spokesperson Hanan Ashrawi and Israeli Ambassador to the UN Binyamin Netanyahu, soon to be Israel's prime minister, held the floor.

The Madrid talks quickly left the dazzle of the Spanish capital for bland State Department conference rooms in Washington. Talks between Syria and Israel bogged down over when Israel would withdraw from the Golan Heights and what Syria's "full peace" would look like. Lebanon's talks with Israel, largely derivative of the Israel-Syria agenda, stalled. Israel-Jordan talks went through the motions, but without serious negotiations on Palestine, there was little hope of a breakthrough. The Palestinian-Israeli talks, still without the PLO and officially held as a subset of the Jordanian talks, floundered on for more than a year. Ten inconclusive sessions of Washington negotiations led to nothing. Then suddenly, everything changed.

THE HANDSHAKE ON THE LAWN

In early September 1993, the secret negotiations between Israelis and Palestinians—this time including the PLO—taking place in Oslo, Norway, bore fruit. An interim agreement, dubbed the "Oslo Accords" was signed with great fanfare on the White House lawn by Israeli Prime Minister Yitzhak Rabin and PLO Chairman Yasir Arafat. President Bill Clinton, in one of his first major foreign policy triumphs, presided over the events, urging the two Middle East adversaries to a reluctant handshake.

Around the world, but especially among Palestinians and Israelis, hopes soared. The hyperbolic tone of US press reports and US government statements served to create the expectation that Oslo represented not only the end of the conflict, but the road to a new paradise where everyone would be free, wealthy, and happy. Unfortunately, it was not to be, and the chasm between the over-inflated expectations and the deteriorating reality brought bitterness, anger, and despair.

Oslo was based on the notion that all the problems between Israel and the Palestinians could be divided between easy ones and hard ones. The easy problems—prisoners, creation of the Palestinian Authority, economic assistance, creation of seaports and airports, etc.—would be negotiated over a five-year period. After that, relations would be so warm and fuzzy between the two sides that the hard problems, deemed final status issues, could be taken up. Those were the fundamentals: borders of a Palestinian state, the status of Palestinian refugees and Jerusalem, and what to do about Israeli settlers.

Oslo divided the West Bank into three categories of land in a Swiss cheese-like design. Area A, the main cities and comprising only 3 percent of the land, would be under full Palestinian control. Area B, mostly villages and towns and about 27 percent of the land, would be under Palestinian civilian authority, meaning schools and garbage collection, but would remain under Israeli security control. The vast majority of the land—70 percent—would become Area C, including the settlements, and remain under unchanged Israeli control.

One problem was that the ostensibly easy issues were not easy at all, and when the five years of interim negotiations passed and the opening of final status negotiations was extended two additional years to the year 2000, none of the interim goals had been met. The final status goals never even came into sight. The most important reason was that Oslo was not designed to end Israel's occupation—the text never even mentions the word. It was designed to protect Israeli interests, and to impose a new level of stability.

The Oslo process did accomplish a number of things. For Israel, most importantly, it brought an end to its isolation in the Arab world, and Arab businesspeople flocked to initiate trade with the more powerful and much more advanced Israeli economy. Oslo also provided Jordan with the necessary credibility to make the following year's Israel-Jordan peace agreement acceptable in the Arab world. It transformed the PLO from an enemy to a more-or-less compliant agent of Israel, who would administer the Palestinian population while Israel's hold on the land remained largely intact. And it renewed Israel's standing in much of the world, which had eroded as a result of its long occupations and human rights violations.

For the Palestinians, Oslo brought long-sought recognition of the PLO, despite the fact that it came only when the PLO was at its lowest ebb of power and influence. Second, for those Palestinians living in Gaza and most West Bank cities and villages, it meant that until 2001, at least, Israeli soldiers no longer occupied their very streets and houses; parents could send their children to school without fear they might be shot by soldiers stationed on the corner.

THE US AND OSLO

Washington did not directly orchestrate the Oslo process, but the negotiations and their result certainly reflected the US orientation toward what Middle East peace should look like; stability, rather than justice, would be its key component. Much of what the US gained from Oslo had to do with regional stability, in which high-tech-oriented and economically booming Israel, backed by the US, would emerge as the center of a Middle East free trade zone, taking advantage of the cheap labor and untapped markets available in the Arab world. Sponsorship of Oslo—even though Washington did not start it—also provided a great diplomatic and public relations boost to US policymakers. The photograph of Clinton, the emperor towering over his two vassal kings, urging Rabin and Arafat to shake hands with his own arms outstretched, became an instant hit around the world.

Within a year of the Oslo signing, Israel and Jordan signed a peace treaty, widely viewed as derivative of the Israeli-Palestinian peace process. For the US, consolidating ties with another already pro-American Arab state represented a significant step toward consolidating regional control.

On the ground inside Palestine conditions deteriorated rapidly. The soldiers were only redeployed out of the population centers, not withdrawn—and movement from the West Bank into Arab Jerusalem or Israel, or between Gaza and the West Bank, or even between Palestinian towns, remained tightly restricted and under Israeli military control. The closing off of the Palestinian territories from Israel, even from Arab East Jerusalem, meant economic crisis for the hundreds of thousands of Palestinians once dependent on low-wage jobs inside Israel. Unemployment and poverty soared, and Palestinian hopes plummeted. Inside Israel, divisions between secular and ultra-orthodox religious Jews rose to new heights. In 1995, the Israeli prime minister was assassinated by a young right-wing Israeli Jew. With Rabin's death, the US faced new difficulties. Suicide attacks by Palestinians killed dozens of civilians in Tel Aviv. Rabin's successor, Shimon Peres, who had orchestrated much of the Oslo process, was defeated. The rightist government of Binyamin Netanyahu came to power in Israel, committed to weakening or even ending the Oslo process. Settlement expansion increased, and the Israeli army imposed harsh internal closure within the West Bank and Gaza, during which Palestinians were even less able to travel. Negotiations between Israel and the PLO, difficult at best, ground to a halt in March 1996 when Israel began digging the foundation for a new Jewish settlement in Arab East Jerusalem.

In August of that year, Israel escalated its attacks against civilian targets in Lebanon, far north of its security zone, including one air assault that killed 106 civilians at a UN peacekeepers' center in the small village of Qana. Several Fijian peacekeepers serving with the UN were wounded as well. International condemnation followed, and the UN launched an investigation of the incident. The UN's report, issued some months later, documented the presence of an Israeli drone surveillance plane in the immediate area during the air strike, rebutting the Israeli claim that they had no way of knowing of the presence of civilians. US diplomats, maintaining their long-standing commitment to protect Israel from international censure, took on a major campaign in the UN to prevent the information from being released. Eventually, UN Secretary General Boutros Boutros-Ghali allowed the UN report, carefully edited but unmistakably damning to Israeli claims, to be made public. US officials were furious; their anger at the secretary-general was widely seen as strengthening then-Secretary of State Madeleine Albright's politically-driven campaign to deny Boutros-Ghali a second term.

After the Qana debacle, the Clinton administration continued its attempts to keep the Oslo process alive. High-level shuttle diplomacy, high-profile meetings between Netanyahu and Albright, as well as at the White House with the president, continued to fail. Facing scandals at home, the Clintonites escalated their efforts to achieve something that could be called Middle East peace—or at least a new round of photo-ops on the White House lawn.

IRAQ—STILL

By 1996, Washington was still in trouble in Iraq. Crippling US-imposed sanctions, orchestrated in the name of the UN but with only the US and Britain behind them, were killing Iraqi civilians, particularly children, in horrific numbers. Throughout the Middle East, Europe, and elsewhere, and even in cities across the United States, people were taking to the streets demanding an end to the sanctions. Some governments joined the protests, albeit quietly. The US and Britain were even more isolated in enforcing the so-called "no-fly zones" in northern and southern Iraq. Creation of the zones, and the bombing raids within them, were illegal, imposed by the two countries without any UN authorization. Several years later President Clinton would claim that the continual air strikes and bombing campaigns were legal, even necessary, because "enforcing the no-fly zone [is what] we're still bound to do under the United Nations resolution."[29] His claim may have reflected the belief of his former UN ambassador, later secretary of state, Madeleine Albright who admitted she viewed the UN as "a tool of American foreign policy."[30] But US tool or not, no such no-fly zones, and certainly no such lethal "enforcement," had ever been authorized or even mentioned in any UN resolutions.

Despite the bombings, and perhaps partly because of the economic sanctions, the Iraqi regime remained firmly in power. US-Iraq tensions were exacerbated in September 1996. The US responded unilaterally to an Iraqi military move into northern Iraq with a massive bombing campaign of unrelated targets in the south and center of the country.

The Iraqi regime's move was aimed at shoring up one of two feuding Kurdish factions and re-establishing its dominance in the northern no-fly zone, which had become a US-British protectorate. A key Iraqi goal was to eliminate the CIA-created resistance beginning to take shape there; following Baghdad's incursion, over 6,000 Iraqis, most linked to CIA-backed organizations, were evacuated to the US, along with the CIA officers themselves. At that point Washington said it no longer needed new UN resolutions to justify its assaults on Iraq.

In the meantime, economic sanctions continued to wreak havoc on the Iraqi population. Ninety percent of Iraq's income came from oil exports. With the sanctions prohibiting all oil sales, lack of access to even basic food and medicine soon reached catastrophic levels for the once largely middle-class population. Repair of the country's water, electrical, and oil systems, and other infrastructure, devastated in the 1991 bombing campaign, stalled. By 1996 negotiations between the UN and Baghdad led to creation of a limited "oil for food" plan, which allowed Iraq to export oil, but with all revenue remaining in the hands of a UN-run escrow account in Paris. Iraq would have no control over or access to its own money, but would be allowed to purchase food, medicine, and other limited items under strict UN supervision. With the Sanctions Committee reflecting Security Council power relations, the US and four other permanent members of the Council maintained a veto over every individual contract—and the US often used it. By late 2001, five *billion* dollars worth of contracts were on hold, almost all of them by US directive.

Iraq's main problem, of course, was lack of money. The degradation of Iraq's oil pumping infrastructure, and lack of money to repair it, meant that the money from the oil being produced and sold was simply not enough to care for a population of 22 million Iraqis. And not even all of the limited oil-for-food funds were available for Iraq's beleaguered civilians. Thirty percent (later 25 percent) was deducted off the top for the UN Compensation Fund, which paid reparations to victims of Iraq's invasion of Kuwait. An additional 5 percent was deducted to cover UN costs. Repair of the country's battered infrastructure, let alone its war-battered population, remained simply out of reach. In the US, the continuation of Washington's 1990–91 demonization of Saddam Hussein and, by extension, of all Iraqis made it difficult to build opposition to the sanctions.

Nevertheless, opposition to the US-imposed sanctions did increase, aided immeasurably by the sequential, high-profile resignations of the first two assistant secretaries general of the UN assigned to be humanitarian coordinator in Iraq. Those moves, by Irishman Denis Halliday and German Hans von Sponeck, were followed by a qualitative expansion of the largely faith-based anti-sanctions movement, and put the US sanctions policy seriously on the defensive. By 1997, bolstered by broader opposition to the escalating US bombing of Iraq, a larger and more visible anti-sanctions movement took shape across the US, matched by much larger such movements in the Middle East, Europe, and elsewhere in the world.

Early in 1998, the US response to a standoff between the Iraqi government and officials of the UN Special Commission (UNSCOM) in Iraq over the scope of inspections moved dangerously close to full-scale attack. UN Secretary General Kofi Annan, negotiating an arrangement later accepted by the UN Security Council, headed off a US attack in a last-minute mission to Baghdad. But US disdain for the UN was once again at work. When the Council passed a resolution endorsing Annan's negotiated settlement, it included language stating that Iraq would face "severest consequences" if there should be a future violation. Virtually every Council ambassador came out of the meeting to tell the press that the language did *not* mean the US or any other country had the right to move unilaterally against Iraq. When US Ambassador Bill Richardson spoke to the press, however, he shrugged at his colleagues' concerns and said, "We think it does."

In Israel and Palestine, meanwhile, inconclusive negotiations and rapidly deteriorating social and conditions were setting the stage for greater hopelessness.

WYE BOTHER?

In the fall of 1998, Clinton summoned the top Israeli and Palestinian officials to the secluded Wye River Plantation outside of Washington for intensive negotiations modeled on Jimmy Carter's Camp David marathon. Netanyahu and Arafat, along with their entourages, dutifully trooped off to the bucolic riverside estate. Given the global hype emanating from White House and State Department briefing rooms and from bored journalists camped outside the estate, one would have thought that peace, or at least an end to Israeli occupation, was indeed at hand. In fact, Washington's goals were much narrower. The main issues at hand were whether Israel would agree to a redeployment of troops out of a tiny thirteen percent of West Bank land, and whether the Palestinians would agree to a new formulation of their security commitments. When agreement was finally reached, "Wye bother?" was the most common reaction.

The Wye negotiations did consolidate one key aspect of US involvement in the conflict—the centrality of the CIA as Washington's key instrument and influence in Israeli-Palestinian negotiations. CIA Director George Tenet participated directly in the Wye talks, and CIA officers were sent to work with the myriad of Palestinian security agencies established under Oslo. One result, of course, was the complete abandonment of even the pretense that the US-supported democracy and the rule of law by the minimally-empowered Palestinian Authority ostensibly governed the tiny cantons of the West Bank and Gaza granted to Palestinian control.

There was little reason for optimism, given the CIA's no-longer-secret history of aiding, or at least looking the other way, while the authorities it backed violently shredded the human rights of civilian populations from Pinochet's Chile to the Shah's Iran. The Wye agreement stated that security matters should be taken up with "due regard to internationally accepted norms of human rights." With the US commitment to such rights delegated to the CIA, it was not surprising then that there were few US concerns when Israeli military authorities continued their round-ups of Palestinians, almost 2,000 of whom were still held in Israeli prisons in early 2002.

For the Clinton administration, it was clear that the alliance with Israel remained by far the most important of the three pillars of US policy in the region. The White House was not prepared to consider spending any of its scandal-reduced political capital on exerting serious pressure on Israel to end the occupation. In fact, it was during the Clinton tenure that the very reality of occupation at the root of the Israeli-Palestinian conflict essentially dropped out of Washington's political discourse. Instead, reflecting the Israeli position, the US focus was on ending the violence in what amounted to a shift from the land for peace understanding of UN Resolution 242, to an official approach perhaps best characterized as autonomy (without land) for security (at least for Israelis). In the meantime, US aid to Israel remained close to four billion dollars per year, accounting for a full 25 percent of the entire US foreign aid budget.

BACK TO IRAQ

Despite the victory at the Wye Plantation, the Clinton administration remained beleaguered by escalating scandals. It turned its attention back to Iraq, where the US-backed UNSCOM inspection agency had become mired in scandals of its own. Despite Iraqi efforts to obstruct the most intrusive of UNSCOM's inspections, the UN-created agency had succeeded at finding and eliminating the overwhelming majority of Iraq's prohibited weapons systems. In early 1998, UNSCOM chief Richard Butler said that his team was satisfied there was no longer any nuclear or long-range missile capability in Iraq, and that UNSCOM was "very close" to completing the chemical and biological phases.[31]

Something else had emerged, however, in the press and in Congressional hearing rooms that summer. That was the revelation that UNSCOM inspectors, ostensibly working solely for the UN to find and destroy Iraq's WMD systems, were in fact busy installing what the *New York Times* called

> an American eavesdropping system so secret that only a handful of Americans, British, Australians, and New Zealanders had full access to it. This, understandably, led to tensions, notably between the Americans on one side and the Russians, the Chinese, and the French on the other.[32]

It turned out that UNSCOM inspectors had provided Washington and Tel Aviv with intelligence materials whose value lay not in helping to eliminate Iraq's prohibited weapons, but in overthrowing the Iraqi government. For example, they reported on such tidbits as the whereabouts of Saddam Hussein and his Republican Guards. Such unilateral spying activity of course violated UNSCOM's own mandate and other UN resolutions, none of which allow efforts to overthrow a government or assassinate any leader, however undemocratic. The equivalent would be UN teams, legally and publicly inspecting American nuclear facilities under international treaty, using their position to secretly wiretap classified communication among Secret Service agents responsible for the President's safety, and then providing that information to a country publicly committed to overthrowing the US government. In installing this system, UNSCOM and its US backers undermined the legitimacy and credibility of the United Nations itself.

The immediate pretext for the intensive four-day bombing campaign Washington launched against in Iraq in December 1998 was UNSCOM's late November report on its progress. Richard Butler's report was deliberately ambiguous, describing a few examples of Iraq's non-compliance with UNSCOM. The report recognized, however, that those isolated instances of defiance took place in a broader context of overall Iraqi compliance, stating that "the majority of the inspections of facilities and sites under the ongoing monitoring system were carried out with Iraq's cooperation." The accompanying International Atomic Energy Agency (IAEA) report was even less ambiguous. It stated unequivocally that Iraq "has provided the necessary level of cooperation to enable the above-enumerated activities to be completed efficiently and effectively." Butler's conclusions did not match his own report's facts. His report's finale was written in crisis mode, asserting unequivocally that "the Commission is not able to conduct the substantive disarmament work mandated to it by the Security Council." There was no mention in the conclusion of the inconvenient fact that his own report admitted that UNSCOM *had* been able to conduct "the majority" of its inspections.

US officials also ignored the IAEA's definitive statement of Iraqi cooperation. The IAEA report had particular relevance, since it followed a year-long assessment process that concluded that, while the agency could not prove the complete absence of such a program, it had found no evidence that Baghdad had any viable nuclear weapons program.

Washington responded immediately, ratcheting up the crisis rhetoric to match Butler's apocalyptic tone while ignoring his report's actual facts. A group of influential members of Congress, former Pentagon officials and other well-known defense experts wrote an open letter to Clinton, calling for a more active effort to provide military support to the "Iraqi opposition." US Central Command's former commander, General Anthony Zinni, scorned their plan as leading to a "Bay of Goats" in Iraq. They were widely dismissed as right-wing hawks trumpeting a failed cause; after September 11, 2001, of course, back in office and with axis-of-evil rhetoric on their side, their reprised ideas, unchanged, would be anything but marginal.

Two days before the report was made public, influential Democratic Senator Joseph Biden met with Butler at length at the US mission to the UN. Top Clinton officials admitted they knew the contents of Butler's report even before the UNSCOM chief presented it to the Security Council. Before the Council had even discussed the report, the US advised Butler to pull his inspectors out of Iraq. Claiming concern for his inspectors' safety, Butler confirmed it was at the suggestion of the US that he withdrew his inspectors, as well as those of the IAEA. Neither Butler nor his Washington backers showed the same consideration for the UN's far more vulnerable humanitarian workers, however. They were not notified of the impending attack, and about 300 international plus 850 Iraqi staff of UNICEF, the World Food Program, and other agencies spent the four days of bombing huddled in a windowless hallway in the basement of the UN's Baghdad headquarters.

The bombing campaign clearly had no international authority. US efforts to ground its latest assault in UN resolutions in fact showed how Washington violated those resolutions. Defenders of the US bombing referred to Resolution 1154, of March 2, 1998, the Council's endorsement of Kofi Annan's earlier negotiated settlement with Baghdad. The resolution stated that only the Council itself, not any individual government acting on its own, had the authority to "ensure implementation of this resolution and peace and security in the area." Despite that very clear language, US Ambassador to the UN Bill Richardson claimed that the resolution "did not preclude the unilateral use of force."[33] In tandem, State Department spokesman James Rubin insisted, "We don't see the need to return to the Security Council if there is a violation of the agreement."[34] And President Clinton himself asserted that if Washington alone was not satisfied with Iraq's compliance, the resolution "provides authority to act."[35]

Kofi Annan, in an unusual (though characteristically subtle) criticism of the US, responded to the beginning of the bombing with the statement that his thoughts "are with the people of Iraq and the UN's humanitarian workers." Not, significantly, with Washington's UNSCOM spies or with Washington's pilots.

Following the attacks, dubbed Desert Fox, US bombing in the no-fly zones increased. By the end of 1999 the United Nations had documented 144 civilian deaths as a result of those US raids—far lower than the casualty figures attributed to economic sanctions, but a significant direct consequence of US foreign policy nonetheless.

As the anti-sanctions movement continued its efforts, Congress continued its refusal to rein in the Clinton administration's harsh policy.

While members of Congress were mostly unwilling to go to Iraq to investigate the humanitarian catastrophe continuing there, a few members, mainly from the Black and Progressive Caucuses of the Congress, agreed to send staff aides to see for themselves. Five congressional staff prepared to travel to Iraq, while the Clinton administration launched a full-scale, multi-agency effort to dissuade, frighten, or threaten them into canceling their trip. Refusing to grant an official waiver and thus threatening arrest of the Congressional staffers for violating the US-imposed sanctions against travel to Iraq, the State Department only by accident admitted that the travel was not itself illegal, only the use of a US passport. At a joint State Department-CIA security briefing, officials warned the aides that they would be in danger in the streets because Iraqis hate Americans. Asked when he was last in the country, the hapless young CIA briefer sheepishly admitted he had never been to Iraq.

The White House intimidation failed, however, and the aides were able to report back to their members of Congress firsthand observations regarding nutrition, health, education, and other social crises endemic throughout Iraq. Their report acknowledged:

> the image of emaciated babies and malnourished young children ill or even dying in Iraq is by now well-known in the US. The staff delegation, visiting hospitals in Baghdad, Amara and Basra, found that reality unchanged, with most of these children dying from treatable diseases, usually the result of unclean water and exacerbated by malnutrition, for which basic medications and treatments are unavailable.

In the report, Assistant Secretary General Hans Von Sponeck, the UN's Humanitarian Coordinator in Iraq, provided a broad overview of the humanitarian crisis facing the country. He described "the less visible, less dramatic non-material side of the economic sanctions" impact. "Everything is tired," he said. "Iraq's social fabric is under serious attack."[36] Despite their findings, the congressional staff reports did not reverse or even slow the US policy trajectory of sanctions, bombings, and threats to overthrow the Iraqi regime.

In late December, while economic sanctions continued to devastate Iraqi civilians, the *New York Times* admitted that what it dismissively called the Desert Fox "fireworks" represented "the final retreat of the Clinton administration from a policy of making the United Nations the focal point of policy on Iraq."[37] Unabashed unilateralism and the complete disregard for the human cost had triumphed again.

OSLO'S COLLAPSE

Inside the occupied territories conditions continued to deteriorate. Israel's Labor government of Prime Minister Ehud Barak continued his rightist predecessor's penchant for settlement building, house demolitions, and other forms of collective punishment against the Palestinians. In Washington, the Clinton administration headed into 2000 severely diminished by private scandals. The possibility of election defeat for Clinton's Vice President Al Gore loomed large, and the possibility of reprising the PR extravaganza of the 1993 Oslo signing provided an irresistible lure.

Clinton moved into his most intense Middle East peacemaking posture, stroking and cajoling the partisans, micromanaging his team's efforts to bring the faltering Oslo talks to some kind of fruition. By summer, that meant summoning Barak and Arafat back to Washington for another marathon summit. This one would be held at Camp David itself, the presidential retreat in the Maryland mountains, where Jimmy Carter had presided over the Israeli-Egyptian negotiations more than two decades earlier.

Clinton's plan was to leapfrog over Oslo's sequential division between interim and final status issues and force the two sides to plunge headlong into the difficult questions of statehood and borders, Jewish settlers, Palestinian refugees, and Jerusalem. Clinton spent long days and nights with the negotiators, leaving only for a truncated two-day trip to the G-8 summit in Okinawa. The two weeks of exhausting, round-the-clock negotiations were intensified by the electoral pressures facing both Clinton and Barak. When the marathon was over, the official post-summit statement issued jointly by the Palestinian, Israeli, and American sides called the talks "unprecedented in both scope and detail."

In the end, the talks failed anyway. The collapse of the Camp David talks, followed quickly by the electoral defeat of Ehud Barak and his replacement by the arch-rightist Ariel Sharon, sent Palestinian hopes further into a downward spiral. The Clinton administration, followed largely uncritically by the US media, placed the blame for the failure squarely on the Palestinian side. Barak's offer, the pundits claimed, was far more generous than any Israeli government had ever offered before. That was certainly true. It was also, however, profoundly irrelevant.

The problem was one of standards. Judging an Israeli offer solely against earlier Israeli offers was quite beside the point. It would also be pointless to weigh the offer solely against Palestinian demands. The relevant scale should have been those of the Geneva Conventions, UN resolutions, and the requirements of international law. And by those combined standards, Barak's offer was far from adequate.

No document emerged from Camp David II providing a definitive look at what was on the table. The parties had agreed to accept a make-it-or-break-it process, so any compromises offered would be made on the basis of "we offer this only if we get agreement on everything else." Any such compromises would no longer be binding once the summiteers went home. But from news reports at the scene, the plethora of deep-background leaks from participants on all sides, and a few after-the-fact analyses by former officials who participated in the talks, US and otherwise, some things are clear.

The Camp David II talks were not based on ending Israel's occupation and returning to the border of June 4, 1967, before Israel occupied the last 22 percent of Palestinian land. The talks were instead predicated on the understanding that something called a Palestinian state would indeed be created. Barak offered to withdraw from Gaza and from a significant amount of territory of the West Bank—reports ranged from 90 to 97 percent of West Bank land. Israel would continue to control a swathe of the West Bank's Jordan valley. All the settlements in Arab East Jerusalem would remain unchanged and under Israeli sovereignty and control. The large settlement blocks in the West Bank would remain intact, annexed to Israel with "equivalent" tracts of Israeli land, likely barren desert near Gaza, turned over to the Palestinians in exchange. A few settlements in the center of the West Bank, including only about 20 percent of the settlers, would be evacuated. And beyond the settlements, much of the land that would remain in Israeli military hands would comprise the vast, still-expanding network of settlers-only roads, bridges, and tunnels that crisscross the West Bank, dividing the land into tiny, separate Palestinian cantons.

As the Israeli journalist Amira Hass described it in *Ha'aretz*,

> the majority of the settlements... would remain intact, situated in an area that is of the utmost strategic importance to the texture of the West Bank. The largest and most consensual (within Israeli public opinion) of the settlements, for example, Ma'aleh Adumim, is one that chops the West Bank in half; and don't think that acrobatics and juggling with roads and

tunnels is going to change this fact.... Even if the "Israeli generosity" were
to mean remaining with only Ma'aleh Adumim, Ariel and the Etzion Bloc,
the roads to these settlements would be patrolled by Israeli soldiers. How
then can anyone assume that a Palestinian could see himself as being
independent in his own state, when the simplest of journeys to work or to
visit his family would involve daily encounters with foreign soldiers?[38]

And the borders and settler issues were supposed to be the easier ones!

The truly intractable problems were those of Palestinian refugees and
Jerusalem. That those would be the deal-breakers was no surprise to
anyone. They were the most difficult because the Israeli position on
these issues was grounded largely in religious, ideological, and
emotional claims, far from the requirements of international law.
Finally, there was the question of the vast power inequality between the
two sides. On the question of the Palestinian refugees, Israel held all the
power—it held the land of the 419 villages destroyed during and after
the 1948 war, from which 750,000 Palestinians were expelled. The
Palestinians, on the other hand, had no cards to put on the table;
instead of power, they had only their five million or so exiles (including
the 1948 and 1967 refugees and all their descendants). And the US, the
most powerful of all, accepted the vast disparity of power between the
Israeli and Palestinian sides, as if Camp David were a level playing field
on which an honest broker could referee a fair game.

Human rights, UN resolutions, and international law were
abandoned in the Camp David talks. After the 1948 war, the United
Nations had passed Resolution 194, mandating compensation for the
Palestinian refugees *and* assuring their legal right to return home. The
UN made Israel's own membership in the world body contingent on
Israeli acceptance of 194 and the rights it granted to the Palestinians.
Resolution 273 of May 11, 1949, welcoming Israel into the UN,
established that the new state's entry was based on Israel's
representations regarding its ability and willingness to implement 194.

The Palestinians' right to return to their homes, despite more than a
52-year delay in realizing that right, should have been recognized as no
less enforceable at Camp David (or before), and no less compelling
than the right to return home of the Albanian Kosovars (in whose
name the US led NATO into war). It should have been seen as no less
than the right of Rwandans returning home from the Congo, or East
Timorese going home from Indonesian refugee camps.

In fact, as Susan Akram and others have noted, the Palestinian right of return has an even stronger legal basis. Resolution 194 (which the US and every other UN member state except for Israel itself voted to reaffirm each year from 1949 until 1994) was consciously designed to provide privileged protections for Palestinian refugees. Those special rights were not granted to other refugees, whose rights are determined solely by broader international laws—that is, the Universal Covenant on Human Rights and the Geneva Conventions.[39]

Yet Israel specifically rejected the "right" of return, maintaining that allowing the Palestinian refugees to come home would change the demographic balance of the Jewish state. The claim is accurate: if all the exiles returned home, it would more than double the percentage of Israel's current Palestinian population, now about nineteen percent. But concern over resulting changes in the ethnic makeup of the country is not an acceptable basis for rejecting international law and Resolution 194. The equivalent would have been a post-war Rwandan government refusing—and the US backing its refusal—to recognize the right of indigenous refugees to return home because of fears it would somehow change the Hutu-Tutsi demographics.

Israel did offer a "humanitarian compromise" at Camp David II, allowing a small number of Palestinians to return home based on an Israeli-controlled family reunification program. But it continued to reject the terms of 194, the Palestinian *right* of return, and it denied any Israeli legal or moral responsibility for the refugees' plight. At most, one rumor held that Ehud Barak's team offered a passive-voice recognition that "pain was caused" to the Palestinians—as if such pain fell from an unforgiving sky.

Rights such as the right of return are absolute. But implementation of that right is remarkably negotiable. Compromise remained possible, but only a compromise based on recognition of the right of return as a real, fundamental right—not a compromise based on the assertion of Israel's raw and asymmetrical power. Real compromise is certainly possible in determining how the right of return will be implemented. Certainly not all Palestinian refugees will ultimately choose to return at all. And the return of those who do choose to go home could be organized over time to minimize rather than exacerbate disruptions to existing Israeli lives in the areas. Palestinian refugees might agree to return to their lands around their original villages but leave negotiable exactly which plots of lands would be reclaimed. Refugees could work with Israeli officials to ensure an orderly rather than a chaotic return. The starting point for compromise, however, had to be Israeli acknowledgement of some responsibility for the refugee crisis. Instead, at Camp David, Israeli intransigence and refusal to recognize any Israeli accountability and US backing for that intransigence, ensured that no compromise was possible.

On Jerusalem, Barak reaffirmed Israel's long-standing "red line," that Jerusalem must remain undivided and under sole Israeli sovereignty. But the Palestinian side also had its red line, including the right to share Jerusalem, making it the capital of a Palestinian state with full Palestinian sovereignty over Arab East Jerusalem. With continued Israeli sovereignty over West Jerusalem, that would make for what Palestinians describe as "two capitals, one city."

Instead, the Israelis offered only what they called "administration-plus." They offered the Palestinians only municipal administration of a few neighborhoods, while maintaining Israeli sovereignty and control over all of Arab East Jerusalem. Senior sources in Barak's office were quoted as saying the Palestinians "are not yet ready to accept the hard decisions that are required."40 Those hard decisions would have required abandoning their long-held dream of East Jerusalem as the capital of an independent Palestinian state—not to mention forgetting the international law prohibiting Israel's continued occupation of it—in return for the illusion of Palestinian sovereignty.

The talks foundered. Israel floated small cosmetic concessions. One would have expanded Israel's municipal borders of Jerusalem to include three small Palestinian villages outside the city. Then the Palestinians would be offered some modicum of authority over the villages, one of which, Abu Dis, would be declared the capital of a Palestinian statelet. Palestinians would be allowed to call the dusty hillside village Jerusalem, "al-Quds" in Arabic. The only problem was that everyone knew that Abu Dis was not Jerusalem, and redrawing municipal borders could not make it so.

Israel also offered to allow Palestinians to administer their own municipal services in scattered parts of East Jerusalem. The Palestinians could collect their own garbage and replace their own streetlamps—but Israel's police would still be in charge. Barak apparently even offered the right to fly a Palestinian flag over al-Aqsa Mosque in Jerusalem's old city, and a safe passage to the Muslim shrine so that Palestinian leaders could travel from their capital without seeing Israeli soldiers. After so many years of Israeli military occupation though, symbolic authority was not enough. Jerusalem was more than a collection of religious sites: it was and remains a living city, with real urban populations not only in Jewish West Jerusalem but in Arab East Jerusalem as well—a city long recognized as the national, cultural, political, and commercial center of Palestinian life.

Israel's claim of sovereignty over all of Jerusalem was based on a 3,000-year-old history and, more significant in today's world, on Israeli power, the right of might. Israel's annexation of East Jerusalem was never recognized by the US or the rest of the world community. In Resolution 242, the UN reaffirmed the illegality of holding territory by force, declaring that after the war occupiers must withdraw. East Jerusalem was not exempt.

In 1991, in the run-up to the Madrid peace conference, US letters of assurance to the Palestinians stated clearly that East Jerusalem was part of the occupied territories of 1967, and that Israel's annexation was illegal. But under US sponsorship, the Camp David talks almost a decade later took precisely the opposite position. The Clinton administration treated Israel's 1967 military occupation of Arab East Jerusalem as a permanent reality, which might be revised somewhat but did not necessarily have to be overturned. In essence, Washington revised the old saying that possession is nine-tenths of the law to say that for Israel in Jerusalem, possession is all.

That final sense of hopelessness, of being abandoned by the international community, set the stage for the second uprising, the al-Aqsa intifada, that erupted at the end of September 2000. And because of the US insistence—both official and media—that the failure of Camp David was solely the responsibility of the Palestinians, it is important to note the words of President Clinton's Special Assistant for Arab-Israeli Affairs, Rob Malley, once he left the White House. He wrote:

> [W]e often hear about Ehud Barak's unprecedented offer and Yasir Arafat's uncompromising no. Israel is said to have made a historic, generous proposal, which the Palestinians, once again seizing the opportunity to miss an opportunity, turned down. In short, the failure to reach a final agreement is attributed, without notable dissent, to Yasir Arafat. As orthodoxies go, this is a dangerous one.... [I]t fails to capture why what so many viewed as a generous Israeli offer, the Palestinians viewed as neither generous, nor Israeli, nor, indeed, as an offer. Worse, it acts as a harmful

constraint on American policy by offering up a single, convenient culprit—Arafat—rather than a more nuanced and realistic analysis.[41]

Shortly after Camp David, at the end of September 2000, Israel's right-wing opposition leader General Ariel Sharon staged a deliberate provocation. With Barak's permission, Sharon, accompanied by over 1,000 Israeli soldiers, marched onto the Haram al-Sharif, the Noble Sanctuary, site of the third holiest place in Islam, in Jerusalem's Old City. The Palestinian response was angry though relatively restrained, but, the following day, stone-throwing Palestinian youths were met with a hail of lethal gunfire. Six died, some on the steps and some actually inside the al-Aqsa Mosque; the response became the second uprising.

In the first fifteen months of the second intifada, 887 Palestinians were killed by Israeli troops, helicopter gunships, F-16 fighter jets, or settlers, almost as many as the 1,000 or so Palestinians killed during the entire six years of the first intifada. Two hundred thirty-nine Israelis were killed during the same period. In that time, nearly 25,000 Palestinians were injured, many of them critically and many of them children. That figure represents almost 1 percent of the entire Palestinian population in the occupied West Bank and Gaza Strip.[42]

Talking about Russian human rights violations in Chechnya, State Department spokesperson Richard Boucher recognized a key reality: "The lack of a political solution and the number of credible reports of massive human rights violations, we believe, contribute to an environment that is favorable toward terrorism."[43] He might have said the same about Israel and the Palestinians. In 2001 violence continued to spiral out of control, as settlement expansion, house demolitions, and widespread closures and curfews continued as features of Israel's occupation practice. Israeli tanks took up positions in towns ostensibly under full Palestinian Authority control. Israel's policy of assassinating Palestinian political and alleged military leaders in attacks that often caused the deaths and injuries of many other Palestinians as well came under widespread international condemnation. The Australian television program *Lateline,* for example, began a segment on the Israeli killings with the question "Self defense or assassination?" Reporter Chris Clark moved quickly to answer his own question.

> Now to the question of Israel's state-sanctioned assassinations. When an
> Israeli helicopter hovering over the West Bank last Tuesday launched a

missile attack on the headquarters of the Hamas resistance in the town of Nablus, it killed two senior Hamas leaders and six other people. Palestinians and many international observers described the attack as political assassination. The Israeli government, endorsing the attack in the face of widespread international criticism, denied it was an "assassination" and urged the world's media to use their preferred formulation—"targeted killings"—an unfortunate choice of words when two of those blown apart by the missiles in that "targeted killing" were young brothers aged ten and seven.... So how does Israel justify its policy of assassinations?[44]

But these targeted killings, as Israel and its allies primly defined them, brought from the US only a mild expression of concern.

Despite growing global criticism for running away from difficult issues in the preparations for the World Conference on Racism in Durban that summer, President Bush continued to keep the US out of serious Israel-Palestine negotiations. Talks stumbled, and various plans to revive a diplomatic process came and went. None were implemented, and none held out any promise of ending the occupation. In the middle of the summer Israel took over and re-occupied Orient House, long a center for Palestinian diplomats to meet their European and other international counterparts in Jerusalem. By chance the German Foreign Minister Joschka Fischer was in the region, and he moved quickly to seize the diplomatic moment to invite both sides to Berlin for a new round of talks. European foreign policy chief Javier Solana was in the region as well, attempting to broker a new ceasefire. Neither were close to succeeding on an entirely new European-led peace process, but their initial responses to the crisis, moving on their own without direct US involvement, portended a slight bit of hope that a new arena for negotiations might yet be found.

That was August. Things looked just slightly optimistic. Perhaps the talks would be in Europe. Perhaps South Africa, emerging powerfully on the world stage following the Durban conference, would take the lead to return Israel-Palestine diplomacy to the international arena and to the UN, out from under Washington's unilateral control. Just perhaps.

Then came September 11.

THREE

The Response: The Empire Strikes Back

When the planes hit the World Trade Center and the Pentagon on September 11, the Bush administration responded by heading into what European security chief Chris Patten would later call "unilateralist overdrive."[1] Within 24 hours, President Bush announced that the attacks were "more than acts of terror. They were acts of war." Not just any war, he told reporters assembled in the White House Cabinet Room, but a war that "will be a monumental struggle between good and evil. But good will prevail." To carry out that war, Bush said, would rally the world.[2]

The world's leaders and the world's governments did not object. To the contrary. Before September 11, outrage had been rising among French intellectuals over whether the US hyperpower was behaving like a sovereign of an empire. Before September 11, Russia was audibly objecting to US threats to abandon the ABM treaty. Before September 11, Europeans and others had begun cautious efforts to punish Washington's lack of accountability to the international community through such moves as stripping the US of its seat on the UN Human Rights Commission. But by 10 A.M. on that September Tuesday, all those already hesitant moves came to an abrupt stop. Instead, governments cheered and much of the world stood by as the US asserted the rights of empire. "Nous sommes tous les Américains," proclaimed *Le Monde*'s September 13 headline in Paris. We are all Americans.

Within days NATO had, for the first time in its history, invoked Article Five of its Charter, identifying the attacks as attacks against all its members, the precursor to playing a military role. But there would be no NATO role; the Pentagon had it well in hand. The immediate mobilization of military force in Afghanistan, despite the ultimately symbolic involvement of several other countries' armed forces, demonstrated unequivocally not only American power in its own right, but the vast gap between US military capacity and that of any other country or any other group of countries.

President Bush announced in January that US military capacity would be built up to wage his new war, "whatever it takes, whatever it costs."[3] In fact, the strategic gap between the US and the rest of the world shown in the response to September 11 was so vast that no immediate emergency spending alone could have created it—it must already have been under way. The $48 billion addition to the Pentagon budget requested by the Bush administration in January 2002 by itself was more money than any other country spent on its military—and that was on top of the existing $379 billion military budget.[4] In US terms alone, it was by far the biggest defense increase since the Cold War.[5]

What emerged from September 11 was the largest, most powerful mobilization of US force—military as well as political—in history. It set in motion what the influential editor of *Newsweek International,* Fareed Zakaria, called "a new era of American hegemony."[6] It was a thoroughly militarized unilateralism, one that legitimized, even glorified, the use of US military force anywhere in the world, with the unchallengeable expectation that the world would join the crusade. It demonstrated quickly that while Washington's rhetoric identified September 11 as an attack on the whole (at least civilized) world, the US in fact had no need for the rest of the world to respond.

People, of course, did respond. Around the world people were shocked by the events of September 11 in New York and Washington. The brutal assault was televised in real time, then re-shown over and over again in lurid and horrific detail. The targets may have been the symbols of US global economic and military power, but those whose charred bodies fed the flames that day, those whose families continue to mourn, those who lost their already precariously low-income jobs were ordinary people, rich and poor, from dozens of countries around the world. The human carnage and the broader human toll remained incalculable. At the human level, the world was united in shock—at the scale, the audacity, the cruelty of the attacks. Only Americans, however, were also surprised, as distinct from shocked. While everyone in the world may have been shocked that such an act could occur, only Americans seemed astonished that such an act might be contemplated or attempted.

The surprise itself might have been anticipated. For a country that prides itself on openness, Americans have a remarkably narrow world view. Most Americans had never considered that there might be people around the world who blame the US government—and Americans themselves—for ongoing devastation and for immediate crises in countries on the other side of the globe.

INNOCENTS AT HOME?

Pre-September 11 Americans were not "innocent" of the carnage that US policies had wrought or ignored in so many countries, as much as they were ignorant of that carnage and of their government's decisions responsible for it. Prior to the events of September 11, many, perhaps even most, Americans paid little attention to global events, not even to the actions of their own government around the world. Beyond the broadest and most general concerns, few international developments reached the center of US public discourse in recent years, while newspapers and television stations slashed their news budgets and shut down bureaus around the world.

Certainly many Americans recognized that global warming and the AIDS pandemic represented serious threats to their own well-being. But few went on to recognize the disproportionate US responsibility for causing global warming, or the impact of US neglect and criminally low levels of foreign aid that made solutions to the AIDS crisis in Africa and elsewhere vastly more difficult. Despite congressional claims to the contrary, large majorities of Americans continued to support the United Nations; but few even knew about, let alone challenged, the fifteen-year-long US refusal to pay its dues, or the ruinous consequences to the global organization of that budget shortfall. However sharp the occasional polemics, post-Cold War elections rarely turned on candidates' foreign policy differences.

For most of 2001 Americans retained their illusions. One was that most US actions in countries around the world could best be nobly described as "nation-building" or "democratization"; another was that the US foreign aid budget was generous and that its purpose was to help the poorest of the world's poor. Most were unaware that the US pays only 0.1 percent of its GNP in foreign aid—lower by far than all the other wealthy countries.[7] Few Americans know that 25 percent of every year's foreign aid budget goes to Israel, one of the wealthiest countries of the world. Few Americans considered that US policies abroad might be viewed as anything other than friendly, helpful, and benign by the people who lived outside the US, and who were the targets of those policies.

This ignorance bred surprise when September 11 happened, and the surprise created two very different phenomena of national psychology. First was the need to recalibrate American identity in light of the sudden recognition—new, for many—that not everyone in the world saw America as Americans like to think of themselves and their country—as generous, fair, democratic, and open-minded. Second was coping with the loss of a key component of pre-September-11 American national identity: the century-old assumption of American impunity, born of geography and oceans, and now combined with the arrogance of unchallenged power. For generations Americans believed themselves immune from any repercussions of their government's actions. Nothing US policymakers did around the world would ever have any serious consequences on their lives at home. Raining bombs on Iraq, claiming Persian Gulf petroleum to be "our oil" as President Carter memorably described it, providing massive military aid and diplomatic support to Israel's occupation, or imposing crippling sanctions on Iraqi civilians would never, in the popular mind, have any impact here at home.

Somehow most Americans never learned the lesson of an earlier September 11—in 1973. On that day, the US backed a military *coup d'etat* against the democratically-elected government of President Salvador Allende in Chile. In the brutality that followed, General Augusto Pinochet's military government murdered or "disappeared" 3,000 Chileans and several foreigners, and imprisoned and tortured thousands more. Those chickens came home to roost in Washington in 1976, when the exiled former Chilean ambassador to the United Nations, Orlando Letelier, and his young American colleague at the Institute for Policy Studies, Ronni Moffitt, were murdered by Pinochet's agents on the streets of Washington, DC. It remained, for years, the worst act of international terrorism ever committed in the United States. Too few Americans, however, learned the lesson. As a result, besides the universal shock, far too many Americans were surprised by the attacks of this September 11.

THE BUSH DOCTRINE—THE "NEW" FOREIGN POLICY

Public support in the US for ever-expanding war in Afghanistan and beyond seemed to be rooted in the sudden sense of individual vulnerability that accompanied the loss of national impunity. If "we" go after "him" (given the individualized, bin Laden-specific propaganda), the logic seemed to go, my family and I will be safe. It was in that context that self-defense and anti-terrorism took hold as the new twin justifications of US foreign policy. This framework quickly supplanted not only the anti-communism of the Cold War and George Bush Senior's New World Order, but laid to rest as well the global interventionism masquerading as multilateralism that lay at the heart of the Clinton foreign policy.

People around the world reacted with massive outpourings of human compassion for the victims of the attacks, even from those who held some sympathetic understanding for the attackers' perceived motivations. But those human responses to horrifying human tragedy had little to do with the strategic considerations that drove Bush administration decision-making. When press accounts reported that as early as the evening of September 11 Bush had already decided to respond with war and told his advisers that he saw the attacks as an opportunity, it was consistent with the already-evident hallmarks of his still-new presidency. Even before his administration had come to power, Bush's soon-to-be-appointed Secretary of Defense Donald Rumsfeld told the president he believed that US military power was needed "to help discipline the world."[8]

That discipline would come in two ways. Internationally, the US would use its new-found victim status to rationalize a strategy based on asserting the right of self-defense, a right which Bush would redefine from the careful, limited language of the UN Charter to reflect a new vision of an infinitely expandable, unilaterally determined, limitless war. An international coalition would be created, but its member countries were to have no illusion that they had decision-making power; the coalition's role was to bolster US strategic decisions, not to participate in making them.

At home, the president's discipline would be imposed on the legislative branch. Congress would be granted the barest modicum of collaboration. President pro-tem of the Senate, Robert C. Byrd, (Democrat, West Virginia), told his fellow members that President

Bush "didn't want" a declaration of war, though he might be interested in a resolution supporting the broad use of force. Clearly the preference was not rooted in fear that the Congress might deny the Bush team the endorsement of virtually anything requested; rather, the decision appears based on a determination to avoid even the appearance of Congressional approval being required for what was already envisioned a White House war.

Bush administration discipline would already be evident in Congress' first official response to the crisis. On the morning of September 13, the Senate voted to approve the administration's "Authorization for Use of Military Force." Hours later, the House of Representatives endorsed the same bill. The bill gave the president a virtually unlimited mandate to

> use all necessary and appropriate force against those nations, organizations, or persons he determines planned, authorized, committed, or aided the terrorist attacks that occurred on Sept. 11, 2001, or harbored such organizations or persons in order to prevent any future acts of international terrorism against the United States.

The reference to preventing future acts certainly indicated that no restraints were envisioned; Bush's Pentagon now had congressional authority to use its power in preemptive attacks anywhere for an unlimited period of time.

Read closely, there was language in the resolution's text that could be defined as limiting presidential options. Most particularly, the use of military force to prevent future terrorist acts was authorized only against "such nations, organizations or persons" that had also already planned, committed, or aided the attacks of September 11. In other words, it was not technically an unlimited authorization to deploy US troops or warplanes to prevent *any* "future acts of international terrorism against the United States." Read by the rules of strict constructionism, the authority was granted only to use the military to prevent those future acts of terrorism that might be contemplated by the very same group of perpetrators. But given the mood in Washington in those early post-September 11 days, there was clearly no intention to impose any limits at all on the president's ability to wage as wide a war as he and his military and political advisers chose. Among the 535 legislators, there was only one vote against the blanket authorization: Oakland/Berkeley's lone brave Congresswoman Barbara Lee. Weeks after September 11, Congress continued what the *Washington Post* called its "uncharacteristic acquiescence to President Bush's decision to go to war in Afghanistan and his strategy for winning it."9

The effort to impose discipline on an unruly world would come to be known as the Bush Doctrine—expressed in the president's Wild West-style threat that "you're either with us, or with the terrorists." Governments around the world scrambled to remake their image in American eyes, transforming themselves from distastefully authoritarian regimes held publicly at arm's length by a virtuous State Department, to vigorous allies clamping down on opposition movements (especially, though not necessarily, if Islamist-oriented). If they suddenly discovered their opposition movements to be homegrown versions of al-Qaeda terrorists, they had a good shot at a White House photo-op. Self-defense now shaped Washington's new definition of what had once been self-righteously (if hypocritically) condemned as human rights violations.

The officially narrow language of the Congressional resolution may have played some part in the ability of sundry governments eager for US troops, training, arms, and money—or impunity from human rights charges—to suddenly discover links between their own troublesome oppositionists and Osama bin Laden. In the Philippines, for example, the violent but tiny Abu Sayyaf gang of criminal thugs on one southern island was upgraded by Pentagon fiat (parroted by much of the US media) to new status as the just-discovered Southeast Asian branch of al-Qaeda.

There was a rush to join the US crusade even before it was clear just what it was that other nations were joining. Seventy-six governments granted landing rights in their countries for US military operations. Twenty-three governments offered bases for US forces involved in offensive operations. Most of these governments got something in return for joining the US anti-terrorism coalition. Russia expected and got a free hand in Chechnya, as did China in its restive Muslim border regions, both Pakistan and India in and around Kashmir (at least until their regional conflict threatened to spill out of control), Turkey in its Kurdish southeast, and Uzbekistan throughout its territory. Perhaps most overtly (though not in the first days of the crisis), Israel's General Ariel Sharon was given a public green light by the Bush administration to further brutalize the population of occupied Palestine. Around the world, spin-doctors justified allied governments' human rights violations and repression by denying the basis for finger-pointing—after all, don't we have the same right to self-defense that the US is using in Afghanistan?

How did the Bush administration determine that countries were joining "with us" and not "with the terrorists?" *New York Times* veteran hawk and wordsmith William Safire provided one answer, citing a passage of dialogue in a Sherlock Holmes story:

> "Is there any point," asked the Inspector, "to which you would like to draw my attention?" "To the curious incident of the dog in the nighttime." "The dog did nothing in the night-time." "That was the curious incident," remarked Sherlock Holmes.

For Safire, the fact that "diplomatic dogs are not barking all over the world" was evidence of international acquiescence to Bush's power-driven unilateralism. Safire, of course, liked it. "This welcome silence is a form of grudging assent, and is the first major achievement of George W. Bush's first year as president."[10]

That silence of the diplomatic dogs was certainly true for the first months after September 11. The silence was audible from the first hours after the attacks. No one was quite sure what Bush's war "between good and evil" would look like, where it would be fought, or who would be on the other side. No country wanted to risk being tarred by the with-the-terrorists brush, which helped consolidate the absence of international opposition as White House decisions became known.

China provided a good example. The first major foreign policy crisis of the Bush administration in the early months of 2001, saw Beijing and Washington locked in an antagonistic duel over the downed American spy plane and the death of the Chinese fighter pilot. China's rhetoric was tough and uncompromising, and the crisis saw new saber-rattling before a diplomatic standoff in which the US blinked first. Contrast that with the next spying incident involving China. In January 2002 (post-September 11 this time) news emerged that the Boeing 767 plane China had purchased for use by President Jiang Zemin was riddled with spy gadgets within its luxury fittings. The story broke on the front page of US newspapers, but, on the record, the Chinese government refused even to confirm or deny the report—and maintained a tight-lipped refusal to challenge Washington's espionage.

SELF-DEFENSE

When the US called the UN Security Council into special session on the morning of September 12, only slightly more than 24 hours had elapsed since the planes hit the Pentagon and the World Trade Center, just a few miles south of UN headquarters. Smoke still poured from the WTC site, casualty figures were still unknown, and wildly exaggerated rumors of tens of thousands of deaths still flew. Many thought the convening of the Council meeting foretold a US decision to work collaboratively, and collectively, with the rest of the world, a decision to abjure earlier Bush tendencies toward unilateralism and automatic military responses.

Article 51 of the UN Charter seemed precisely drafted to deal with just such a scenario. It recognizes the inherent right of a nation under attack to use force to defend itself against an armed attack—but only until the Council takes necessary steps to deal with the conflict and to maintain peace and security. Convening the Council so quickly after the attacks seemed to portend a US plan to engage the United Nations and the international community as a whole to respond to this massive crime against humanity. There was no fear that anything the US proposed might be rejected; a US request for creation of a new special anti-terrorism tribunal, backed by a new international police enforcement unit whose first mandate would be the identification and capture of the perpetrators of the attacks—all would have been welcomed with enthusiasm. Given the immediate collapse of opposition to US hegemonic power in the wake of the September 11 attacks, it is certain that even a US request for UN authorization for a coalition-based or even unilateral military strike would have been accepted.

But the US-drafted resolution did none of those things. Resolution 1368 recognized the right of self-defense in an introductory clause, but authorized no use of force, whether by UN Blue Helmets or by anyone else, and was not passed under the auspices of Chapter VII of the UN Charter, a prerequisite for any consideration of military force. The resolution called on all states "to work together urgently to bring to justice the perpetrators, organizers, and sponsors of these terrorist attacks and stresses that those responsible for aiding, supporting or harbouring the perpetrators, organizers, and sponsors of these acts will be held accountable." It went on to call on "the international community to redouble their efforts to prevent and suppress terrorist acts including by increased cooperation."

The Council discussion leading up to the passage of 1368 was characterized by both unanimity of condemnation, and unanimity of support for creating precisely the kind of cooperation needed for what the French ambassador called a "global strategy" to deal with terrorism. Jamaica's Ambassador Patricia Durrant, in words similar to other Council ambassadors, called on the Council to ensure that "the masterminds, and those in collusion with them, must be brought to justice, and the global community must demonstrate a solid front to "defeat terrorism."[11] Bringing perpetrators to justice and using global cooperation to do so were the consistent themes of the discussion; launching a war half a world away from the still-flaming ruins of the World Trade Center was not on the agenda.

The US position in the UN was compromised at that time by the absence of a Permanent Representative or ambassador from the US. The Bush administration's nominee, John Negroponte, had yet to be confirmed by the Senate. There was widespread opposition to his appointment, based largely on his history of covering up human rights atrocities committed by US allies during Central America's Contra wars, during his 1980s stint as US ambassador to Honduras. Passage of Resolution 1368 was orchestrated instead by James Cunningham, a career State Department diplomat assigned to the UN mission.

In less than an hour, Resolution 1368 was passed unanimously and with enormous emotional fervor; in an unprecedented show of solidarity, the fifteen Council ambassadors stood to cast their votes in favor of the resolution, rather than simply raising their hands. But the US-drafted text was deliberately limited, not taken under the explicit authority of Chapter VII of the UN Charter. Instead, the Council Resolution concluded by expressing "its readiness to take all necessary steps to respond to the terrorist attacks of September 11, 2001, and to combat all forms of terrorism, in accordance with its responsibilities under the Charter of the United Nations." Finally, the Council decided "to remain seized of the matter."

What the resolution did *not* do was authorize military force. Expressing "readiness to take all necessary steps" is a far cry from actually taking any specific step, including the authorization of force. The resolution did not identify what the Council believed to be "necessary steps." The limits of the resolution were clarified further by the crucial concluding language that the Council "remain seized" of the issue. In UN diplo-speak, that means the subject remains on the Council's agenda and under Council jurisdiction, to be revisited as necessary.

Washington's refusal to put before the Council a resolution explicitly authorizing military force reflected a very conscious strategy of unilateral power assertion. The Bush administration's problem was not that Council support would have been difficult to obtain. Unanimity of endorsement for anything the US asked for was a virtual certainty. Rather, the challenge for Washington was to craft a resolution that would put the UN and the Council governments on record supporting the US, without seeming to acknowledge the Security Council's right to confer or withhold legal authority to wage the still undefined war that Washington was already planning. From that vantage point, Resolution 1368 fit the bill admirably.

Without, however, such an explicit Council mandate, when the Council had indeed met and endorsed a response, the US war in Afghanistan lacked legal authority. Launched weeks after the New York and Washington attacks, against uncertain targets of unproven responsibility with inevitable and disastrous civilian consequences, Bush's war remained a serious violation of international law and the UN Charter. The creative US claim of what amounts to a new concept of preemptive self-defense is not a concept within the UN Charter or international law. One could argue that such a claim may indeed apply to collaborative international law enforcement operations to prevent future crimes, especially such horrific crimes against humanity, but it does not fall within the deliberately restrictive confines of the legal use of military force in the UN Charter.

Relying on Resolution 1368 to legitimize the US war simply does not work. The Charter language describes the right of unilateral self-defense only *until* the Council can take over. In this instance, there was no problem of the Council being unable to meet or of an unacceptably long delay between the armed attack and the relevant meeting. There was not even a problem of the Council deciding it was unable to accede to the US request for action or authority. To the contrary, this meeting was held only 24 hours after the attack with the full participation of every member state, and was voted for unanimously, without any changes, in less than one hour. As soon-to-be Ambassador Negroponte later described it, "this was no instance where the United States had to lobby for votes. Among all the issues and problems the UN confronts, global terrorism clearly was the new priority. Humanity was appalled; solidarity was complete."12 If the US chose not to ask for authorization for its chosen military response at the Council meeting, it cannot then rely on what Article 51 allows a country to do before the Council acts. A military attack after a meeting that could have authorized any number of responses but did not do so because the country under attack did not request such a response would not constitute lawful self-defense, and would simply be outside the bounds of Article 51.

One could argue, perhaps, that while 1368 did not provide any authorization, the follow-up resolution, 1373, passed two weeks later under Chapter VII authority, did so. Negroponte, whose pre-September 11 stalled ratification slid through the Senate quickly as part of the post-September 11 do-not-challenge-the-president mood that struck the Congress, seemed to assert just such a claim several months later. Speaking to an audience of would-be diplomats at Georgetown University, he tacitly acknowledged that Resolution 1368 had no authorizing significance.

> The single most powerful response the UN could take came on September 28, when the Security Council passed Resolution 1373, instructing all member states to review their domestic laws and practices to ensure that terrorists could not finance themselves or find safe haven for their adherents or their operations.13

The situation of complete support in the UN for US initiatives had not changed. Two weeks after 1368 had passed, again the US could have presented the Council with a comprehensive plan and request for authorization for its chosen response, up to and including the use of military force. Even if one accepts Negroponte's view that the Council resolution passed on September 12 was insufficient to respond to the terrorist acts of the day before, Washington could have used the new resolution put before the Council on September 28 to answer the challenge. But again the US chose not to do so. Instead, it put before the Council a resolution which, while taken under the terms of Chapter VII, was largely limited to economic measures to cut terrorists' access to funds. It did not call for any use of military force. Negroponte called the new resolution "the most powerful response the UN could take." If it were not powerful enough, if the US believed military action was required, the US certainly had the time, the resources, and the international support to draft a stronger resolution calling for such action under international imprimatur. If the resolution was indeed powerful enough, its Council-mandated actions regarding efforts to cut financing and protection for terrorists should have sufficed in implementing the needs of self-defense. Under the terms of Article 51 of the Charter, the resolution's terms should have replaced Washington's unilateral plans for military action. Instead, little more than a week after the second resolution was passed, the US launched its air war over Afghanistan.

The US violation of the UN Charter was in two parts. First, and most important, the right of unilateral self-defense is not unlimited. If, for instance, the US had been able to scramble a fighter jet to shoot down the second hijacked plane before it hit the World Trade Center, that would have been a perfectly legal unilateral use of military self-defense. Launching a full-scale war, defined as one without an identifiable end point, across the globe against speculative targets, with the inevitable result of economic and human devastation for civilian populations, does not fall within the ordinary definition of self-defense.

Secondly, the Charter language in Article 51 is very explicit regarding the responsibility of the country asserting the right of self-defense to consult and involve the Security Council in responding to an armed attack. In an October 2001 analysis of the international law factors involved in the US response to the September 11 attacks, the legal director of the British human rights organization Interights described how

> self-defense under the Charter… is clearly permissible only as a temporary measure pending Security Council engagement. If measures of force are initially justified, as necessary and proportionate self-defence, they may still fall foul of the law if they are coupled with a subsequent failure to engage the Security Council.[14]

In other words, even if an initial military attack in the name of self-defense were deemed lawful, the US would be in violation if it later refused to return to the Council for discussion, involvement, and approval for further action.

Throughout the first months of the US war there was little criticism from governments around the world. A few hesitantly expressed hopes for a break to allow food supplies to be sent in; there was an occasional wish for a Ramadan pause in the bombing. But certainly no government stood ready to challenge the US strategy of full-scale military assault on Afghanistan to answer the attacks of September 11. It is sadly likely that, given the fear of challenging Washington that prevailed at the UN, a US request for United Nations authorization for that war would have won immediate approval. The US violation of the UN Charter was not even necessary.

Going to war was the chosen US response. It was not inevitable, but a carefully selected strategic choice. From the beginning the war was not aimed at identifying specific perpetrators (the main ones, of course, were already dead) and bringing them to justice in an international or even a US national tribunal. The stated goal was to wipe out the al-Qaeda network led by Osama bin Laden and to destroy the Taliban government in Afghanistan that had given them refuge. From the beginning the war would be explicitly defined in the apocalyptic, unlimited, global terms that came to characterize Bush's war against terrorism. "Our war on terror begins with al-Qaeda," Bush announced. "But it does not end there. It will not end until every terrorist group of global reach has been found, stopped, and defeated." With the expansion of the war beyond al-Qaeda to all global terrorists, and the no-holds-barred language of "either you are with us or you are with the terrorists," the president set the stage for what later would come to be called (improbably for this internationally untutored neophyte) the Bush Doctrine.

The initial call to war preceded by many weeks the provision of actual evidence against al-Qaeda; the early justifications for the war were limited to assertions of responsibility without clear evidence. When an evidentiary dossier was finally made public, it came not from US officials at all but from a British white paper excerpted in the US press.

THE SPEECH

The lack of evidence did not halt, or even slow, Washington's war juggernaut. Just over a week after the attacks, President Bush addressed a joint session of Congress. His demeanor was serious; jokes about which names he would mispronounce quickly faded. Some of his language was powerful, even soaring. "Tonight we are a country awakened to danger and called to defend freedom," he said.

If Bush's speech styled itself after the rich cadences of Churchill rallying Britain, its substance was closer to the aggressive bullying of the wild west and the OK Corral. His message to the US military was short and clear: "Be ready. I've called the armed forces to alert and there is a reason. The hour is coming when America will act and you will make us proud." It was impossible to deploy the military against the immediate perpetrators, who of course were already dead, and it was not yet clear what country or countries would be considered targets by virtue of proximity to the perpetrators' supporters. But already Bush's war cry—"be ready"—resonated as the lodestar of American response.

In his speech Bush promised to answer the many questions Americans were asking. His answers were telling. He began with, "Americans are asking 'who attacked our country?'" He spoke of "the evidence we have gathered that points to a collection of loosely affiliated terrorist organizations known as al-Qaeda." He described his view of who they were, their "fringe form of Islamic extremism," and where they were. Thousands of them, he claimed, in more than 60 countries. But he provided none of the evidence he claimed to have.

He noted that "Americans are asking 'How will we fight and win this war?'" But his answer was only the swaggering promise to use every weapon available in the US arsenal. There was no explanation of strategy, only the warning of what the coming war would *not* be. It would not look like Desert Storm, with a quick victory and liberated ground to crow over. It would not be like Kosovo, without a single American casualty. It would not be (in an unspoken dig at Clinton) a war of quick retaliation and isolated air strikes.

What *would* the coming war look like? Americans should expect:

> a lengthy campaign unlike any other we have ever seen. It may include dramatic strikes visible on TV and covert operations, secret even in success. We will starve terrorists of funding, turn them one against another, drive them from place to place until there is no refuge or no rest. And we will pursue nations that provide aid or safe haven to terrorism.... From this day forward, any nation that continues to harbor or support terrorism will be regarded by the United States as a hostile regime.

All of which is to say that the war will look like anything we want it to look like, and we are not going to tell you, the American people, how we will fight and win it. Nowhere in the oratory did we hear what winning would look like, or how we would know when we had "won." Nowhere did we hear a commitment to actually finding and bringing to justice—to trial, somewhere—those individuals who may have had actual responsibility for the events of September 11, as opposed to declaring war on the entire country where they had taken refuge. It was as if F-16 fighter jets and B-52 bombers could be deployed as bounty hunters in this new frontier.

Nowhere did we hear a plan to engage other nations in the planning or the strategizing—only a threat that any country that did not come on board Washington's coalition, accepting whatever its plan turned out to be, would be treated as a hostile regime, presumably to face the same punishment as the terrorists themselves. Nowhere did we hear a plan to engage the United Nations in a global effort to find the perpetrators; in fact, we never heard the words United Nations at all. There were references to other countries, but only to "ask every nation to join us. We will ask and we will need the help of police forces, intelligence services, and banking systems around the world." Nowhere did we hear of asking for ideas or for collaboration; we heard only the demand for uncritical acceptance of *our* plan, *our* strategy.

The discussion of other nations was shaped by a thoroughly ideologically-driven agenda reflecting the Bush administration's commitment to worldwide dominion. "This was not just America's fight. And what is at stake is not just America's freedom." But the discussion did not then turn to the essential internationalism that would make possible a serious response to a horrific crime against humanity and begin the process of changing the conditions that would continue to give rise to terrorism in the future. Bush turned, instead, to the Manichean division of the world, claiming that "this is civilization's fight.... the civilized world is rallying to America's side." Those who are not with us, then, are not only with the terrorists, they are outside the bounds of civilization.

The call for a coalition reflected the still-unresolved debate within the administration over the best approach to maintaining US global hegemony. Was US power best protected by operating through US-created coalitions of the willing (or not so willing), or by asserting the use of unilateral military force with the expectation that the rest of the world would simply fall into line? Bush's September 19 speech demonstrated a remarkably agile negotiation between the two positions: on the one hand, the aggressive join-us-on-our-terms-or-face-our-wrath approach was designed to satisfy the fiercest unilateral instincts of the most hawkish elements of the administration. On the other hand, the reassuring rhetoric of "the civilized world... rallying to America's side" provided at least a symbolic concession to those pragmatists in and out of the administration concerned about the consequences of going it alone. It was a balance that would continue throughout the early months of the Afghan war: the most extreme assertion of raw unbridled power would be softened by iconic references to global participation and the images of international cooperation. But neither position took seriously the possibility that other nations might have legitimate and valid opinions and independent strategic approaches of their own—or that nations might have the right to diverge from or even (gasp!) oppose US war moves.

President Bush next reminded the world that "Americans are asking 'Why do they hate us?'" The very question reflected the ideological edge to Bush's approach. He assumed that all Americans shared his definition of who "they" are, as well as sharing a common understanding of just who "we" are. The "they" in this context did not refer simply to the perpetrators of the September 11 attacks. "They" were the undifferentiated masses of humanity over "there" who hate. Exactly whom or what they hate was not specifically identified. US policies in the Middle East? US policymakers who impose their will through the exercise of raw power? American foreign policy as a whole? The American people?

Of course in the charged environment of post-September 11 Washington, there was little doubt who "they" were: Arabs and Muslims, mainly but not solely in the Middle East and South and Central Asia, and maybe some sneaky ones right here at home. "They" were Afghans and Palestinians, Saudis and Somalis, as well as a troublemaking contingent among Malaysians, Indonesians, Pakistanis, and Filipinos, although most of those populations, we were to understand, want to actually be like us. The identity of "us," in fact, was equally clear. "Us" was Americans; the category might include some Muslim or Arab-Americans, but probably only those who loudly and affirmatively proclaimed their hatred for "them."

When Bush came to answering his "Why do they hate us?" query, things got even more interesting. The fundamental basis of his answer focused on the question of democracy.

> They [the terrorists] hate what they see right here in this chamber, a democratically-elected government. *Their* leaders are self-appointed....

They want to overthrow existing governments in many Muslim countries, such as Egypt, Saudi Arabia, and Jordan.

Somehow Bush's key speechwriters missed the irony of blaming terrorists for having self-appointed leaders, when his three favored Arab governments, approvingly dubbed "moderate" Arab states, are classic examples of self-chosen, self-perpetuating regimes. Pro-US Saudi Arabia and Jordan are two of the world's last old-fashioned the-king-is-dead-long-live-the-king absolute monarchies. Egypt's president has remained in office for more than twenty years, "elected" over and over again in what Human Rights Watch called "no-choice"[15] balloting.

The speechwriters missed the boat. With the perpetrators dead, it will probably never be possible to know the complex web of illusions, religious zealotry, resentment, anger, and other motivations that set the deadly hijackings in motion. The question Bush and his advisers *should* have asked was not why the perpetrators hate us, but why it was that so many people in so many disparate parts of the world, even including those who mourned the human losses of September 11, thought maybe the attack was not such a bad idea. That would have been, and still remains, possible to answer, and, in the long run of history, its answer is of far greater import than the particular motivations of the nineteen suicide flyers of September 11.

UNDERSTANDING THE DISCONTENT

Answering that question brings us much closer to the impact of US global policy around the world. Although the hijackers themselves were largely middle class and educated, with relatively privileged access to the globalized goods and services of the modern world, those few who cheered and those many more who secretly applauded the deadly attacks were disproportionately found among the poorest, most disenfranchised, powerless, and hopeless of the world's peoples. The British journalist Robert Fisk wrote of "the crushed and humiliated people" in whose name the hijackers claimed to speak. Comprehending who those people are, and what role US policy might have in making or keeping them crushed and humiliated, would go very far in the effort to understanding why people support such horrific acts. And understanding that is a key step toward ensuring such events never happen again.

The resentment is not aimed at America or Americans in some general sense. Contrary to Bush administration and media pundits, it is not democracy that is hated. In fact, it is America's support for regimes in the region that *deny* democracy to their people that fuels Arab anger. It is not even American power *per se*. Rather, it is the way that American power is used in the Middle East that has caused such enmity.

This does not mean that if Western control of oil exploitation in Central Asia, and US support for the Israeli occupation of Palestine and for repressive and corrupt regimes elsewhere, were all to end overnight that there would never again be an act of terror. It does mean, however, that future anti-US terrorists would have to act in much greater isolation, without public support, without a popular base. In the long term that means the threat of terrorism against American targets would be qualitatively reduced. It is not a coincidence, after all, that Osama bin Laden in his public statements began emphasizing the plight of Palestinians living under Israeli occupation and the impact of economic sanctions on Iraqi civilians only after the September 11 attacks. Neither of those two issues was a major priority for him before the attacks, even if they were fundamental for many of his supporters. Appealing to those concerns, however, of far wider significance to virtually all Arabs and most Muslims than the more limited goal of overthrowing the Saudi monarchy, was a shrewd tactical move that significantly raised the level of public support for bin Laden's goals, if not always for the specific acts for which he was held accountable.

US POLICY AND ITS DISCONTENTS

One needs to examine US policy with the goal of identifying what aspects of that policy, and especially its secondary (even if anticipated) consequences, are the central issues generating public opposition around the world. From that vantage point, there are two sets of policy approaches, regional and global, that come to the fore. In the Middle East and South Asia, the regions most directly relevant to and affected by the events and aftermath of September 11, those issues start with US support for Israel's occupation of Palestinian land. Knowledge of the provision of billions of dollars in US military and economic aid to Israel; the vast Israeli purchases of US military equipment; and the use of US-made F-16s, helicopter gunships, and anti-tank missiles against Palestinian apartment buildings, refugee camps, villages, and towns, are all far more widely known in the Middle East than in the US itself. Washington's use (and threat of use) of its Security Council veto to prevent international observers from being sent to the occupied territories is far more common in the media and therefore familiar to people in the Middle East than those dependent on the US press.

Most fundamentally, perhaps, there is a widespread understanding outside the US, not only in the Middle East, that the relationship between Israel and Palestine is that between occupier and occupied, and that the issue to be addressed is not simply the violence, but how to end occupation. For observers of those policies outside the United States, the uncritical nature of US support for Israel leads quickly and inexorably to the angry view that the US shares responsibility for that occupation. For US policymakers, support for Israel includes a complex web of geostrategic, military, and economic considerations. Supporting Israel's occupation is not necessarily the conscious goal of the US—but Israel's maintenance of its illegal occupation is of little concern to Washington. If Israel decided its occupation had become a strategic liability and it was time to end it, the US would congratulate Tel Aviv. But as long as Israel continues its occupation, the US has been prepared to go along—and inevitably is held responsible for the brutality that accompanies any military occupation of another people's land.

Regarding Iraq, outside the US the human devastation caused by economic sanctions (whatever the separate depredations of the Baghdad regime) is widely known and condemned, particularly in Europe but most powerfully in the Middle East. While Secretary of State Powell may claim that "we have succeeded, because we stopped the talking about Iraqi children,"16 people in the region are aware that as long as the children are still dying there is no victory beyond public relations. Crucially, while the economic sanctions are imposed in the name of the United Nations, it is widely known and understood around the world—but with greatest emotional consequence in the Arab Middle East—that only US-UK insistence keeps the sanctions stranglehold in place. Again, Washington is held accountable for the deaths of hundreds of thousands of Iraqi civilians, many of them children, as a result of economic sanctions.

In 1996 when Madeleine Albright made her famous "we think the price is worth it" remark regarding the death of half a million Iraqi children as a result of sanctions, her callousness actually reflected a clear political decision. Killing children was likely not the primary goal of US-Iraq policy. But the reality of that secondary consequence, weighed against the perceived strategic advantage of maintaining sanctions, was something Washington was prepared to live with, and even to defend. In fact, as early as January 1991, just one week into Desert Storm, a Defense Intelligence Agency document entitled "Iraq Water Treatment Vulnerabilities" acknowledged that destruction of Iraq's water purifying equipment and supplies would "result in a shortage of pure drinking water for much of the population. This could lead to increased incidences, if not epidemics, of disease."17 A second document, dated January 22, 1991, identified the diseases that would result from the bombing of water systems: they would include E.coli, salmonella, and others, affecting, the DIA noted, "particularly children." Why then, is anyone surprised when people throughout the region hold the US responsible for those deaths, and that some charge genocide?

Finally, the legacy of Washington's long years of backing repressive, often corrupt, absolute monarchies throughout the Arab Middle East resonates strongly in public sentiment toward the United States. For example, while relatively few in the Middle East share Osama bin Laden's view that the Saudi monarchy is insufficiently Islamic, vast numbers believe the Riyadh royals to be corrupt, self-serving, and interested far more in maintaining their family's power than in bettering the lives of their subjects. Others' rage is fueled by the absolute control the House of Saud maintains in the kingdom, where women are legally prohibited from driving, traveling alone, or making ordinary decisions about their own lives without the permission of a male relative. Throughout the region, it is common knowledge that US backing for the absolute monarchy is itself absolute, that the call for democratization that shapes US policy toward so many other countries is virtually absent regarding Saudi Arabia, Kuwait, the United Arab Emirates, and most other Gulf states. Saudi Arabia has for years been the top purchaser of US military equipment and hardware. In 2001, the UAE, that tiny collection of Gulf sheikdoms with a total population significantly less than that of Chicago, was the first country to be provided with the most advanced fighter jet in the US arsenal, the F-18.

Since the end of the Gulf War in 1991, the US has maintained troops, bases, warships, fighter jets, and more in virtually every country in the area, helping to keep in power and abjuring criticism of the repressive regimes in favor of pragmatic diplomacy and joint military training exercises. Osama bin Laden was hardly the first to call for getting US troops out of Saudi Arabia; democratic opponents of the Saudi monarchy in and outside the kingdom had long raised just such a demand with a very different goal in mind. Maximizing the monarchy's ability to withstand popular demands for democratic reform was probably not Washington's primary goal in making the kingdom a forward military base and crucial oil provider. No one in Washington would likely have complained if the royal family had suddenly decided to cede power to a newly-elected parliament, to enfranchise women along with other citizens, or to lift the gender-based segregation imposed on half the Saudi population. But the kings and their brothers and sons made no such offer, and the repressive discrimination (however assuaged by oil wealth) remained in place, and the US was happy to accept that too. So why are we surprised when some in and around Saudi Arabia blame Washington for empowering the monarchy enough for it to stand up to the popular will?

Throughout the Middle East and Central Asian regions, people watch. They watch as overarching US power moves inexorably and immutably into their part of the world, ensuring that unpopular and discredited governments remain in power, and propping up the wealthiest sectors in their societies for the purpose of joint ventures and shared oil exploitation, ignoring the vast disparities of wealth and poverty that remain. It is not only the poorest who view the US with resentment and anger; it is those whose lives are defined by political and economic disenfranchisement, marginalization from decision-making in their society, and lack of voice to challenge their lot. It is those who are hopeless, who see those few in their own societies with wealth and power tied to their US counterparts, and who realize they have no hope of reaching that position. It is the hopeless who cheered when the jets crashed into the World Trade Center and the Pentagon, even as they mourned the dead and feared what would come to them in return.

AND GLOBALLY...

Beyond the specifics of US strategy in the Middle East and surrounding regions, there is a particularity to US foreign policy that engenders antagonism around the world, from Washington's closest European and Canadian allies to the poorest countries of the impoverished global South. More than any single policy or even set of policies, that is the arrogance with which US policy is imposed—with international law dismissed, UN requirements ignored, and internationally supported treaties abandoned. While the US demands that other countries strictly abide by UN resolutions and international law, and threatens or imposes sanctions or even military assault in response to violations, it holds itself accountable only to a separate law of empire which applies to the US alone.

Every empire in history has created its own set of laws for managing its far-flung possessions and colonies. Thucydides wrote of how Athens governed Mylos, the island that resisted Greek colonization, according to an entirely different set of laws than those governing the metropolitan center. The Roman empire largely followed suit, with one set of laws for Rome itself, another for its far-flung possessions. The Ottoman, Russian, and British empires did much the same thing. Finally, toward the end of the 20th century, having scaled once unimaginable heights of military, economic, and political power, it was Washington's turn.

This American-style law of empire exuded extraordinary arrogance, the arrogance of absolute power unchallenged by any other global force. The US demanded that every other country sign on to UN-brokered treaties and other international agreements, while exempting itself from any such responsibility. The arrogance was evident in Washington's rejection of the International Criminal Court in 1998, its refusal to sign the 1997 Convention against anti-personnel land mines, its failures on the Convention on the Rights of the Child, the Law of the Sea, the Comprehensive Test Ban Treaty, and more. It was also sharply apparent in the dramatic abandonment throughout the 1990s of Washington's 1990–91 Gulf War assertion (however cynical or tactical) of the need for United Nations endorsement to confer legitimacy on fundamentally unilateral interventions.

In the context of September 11, US arrogance takes the form of hypocrisy. The US purports to champion democracy as the linchpin of US foreign policy, while continuing to prop up governments famous for denying any hint of democracy to their own peoples. And then President Bush claims the September 11 attackers were motivated by hatred for American democracy. We may not know for sure the exact motives of the architects of the September assault. But it is a pretty good bet that the fury of those who cheered them on—in Saudi Arabia, in Indonesia, in Gaza, in Uzbekistan—was fueled not by hatred of American democracy, but at least in part by American support for far-flung governments denying their people the same democracy the US claims to stand for.

Those governments were among the clearest beneficiaries of the US response to September 11. But they were by far not the only ones to sign on. As the nascent pre-September 11 resistance to US hegemony screeched to a halt that Tuesday morning, presidents, prime ministers, parliaments, and kings went into competition overdrive to see who could be the first ally, the strongest supporter, the most reliable partner to board Washington's war train. Coalition-building was in the air.

FOUR

MOVING TOWARD WAR:
A COALITION OF COERCION

The kind of coalition George Bush and his advisers had in mind had little in common with our normal understanding of that word—implying cooperation, mutual decision-making, power-sharing, and teamwork. The actual Bush response to the September 11 attacks, "you're either with us or you're with the terrorists," the basis of what would soon become known as the Bush Doctrine, gave the lie to any such understanding.

For this administration, unilateralism remained the underpinning of every strategic plan. That included redefining the very essence of coalition to reflect Washington's unquestioned commitment to unilateral control of decisions and power in determining how to respond to the September 11 attacks. Within hours of the attacks, the US did put in place a process of creating a coalition—but it was not a coalition of the willing; rather it was a coalition of coercion. Giving other nations a choice was not on the Bush agenda.

Nor was paying attention to the United Nations. The Security Council and General Assembly votes of passionate but undefined solidarity with Americans were followed by two weeks of uneasy silence toward the unilateral approach of the US. Then, in a major speech to the Assembly on September 24, Secretary-General Kofi Annan sounded a cautionary note. He identified the attacks as having "struck at all our efforts to create a true international society," and went on to call for the world, through the United Nations, to "respond to it in a way that strengthens international peace and security—by cementing the ties among nations, and not subjecting them to new strains." Focusing on the need to make the United Nations the central player in a global response, he went on to note that "this Organization is the natural forum in which to build such a universal coalition. It alone can give global legitimacy to the long-term struggle against terrorism."

Annan did not explicitly criticize Washington's plan, by then very clear, to respond to the terrorist attacks with a call to war; he did not call on the US to seek Council approval for the use of force, as would be required under Article 51 of the UN Charter. But he did provide a very different answer than the Bush administration to the fact that "the attack of September 11 was an attack on the rule of law—that is, on the very principle that enables nations and individuals to live together in peace, by following agreed rules, and settling their disputes through agreed procedures." For the Secretary General, the response to that attack should mean "reaffirming the rule of law, on the international as well as the national levels. No effort should be spared in bringing the perpetrators to justice, in a clear and transparent process that all can understand and accept." Annan concluded by urging the world to

> respond by reaffirming, with all our strength, our common humanity and the values that we share. We shall not allow them to be overthrown. Let us uphold our own principles and standards, so that we can make the difference unmistakable, for all the world to see, between those who resort to terrorism and those who fight against it.

It was soaring language. But the Bush administration had no intention of acceding to international will or international law. Responding to Annan's speech, a State Department official told the *Washington Post*, "The United States welcomes a more active UN role as long as it does not interfere with America's right to use military force....we don't think we need any further authorization for what we may have to do to get at the people that murdered American citizens."[1] It appeared Madeleine Albright's famous "the UN is a tool of American foreign policy"[2] position had successfully made the transition to the new Bush White House.

Bush Junior clearly had no interest in obtaining UN support or even an imposed UN credential for its plans; it was already moving on its own. Colin Powell, flying back to Washington from Peru within hours of the attacks, told reporters on his plane the goal would be to find the perpetrators and bring them to justice. But that pragmatic focus, with the implied reliance on a law-enforcement, rather than war-based approach, was quickly squelched. Others had different ideas.

Within the administration and in right-wing circles surrounding it, the September 11 attacks provided a new set of justifications for long-standing policy prescriptions. George Shultz, secretary of state in the Reagan administration, said states harboring terrorists had better "look out." Richard Perle, a Pentagon strategist in the Reagan years and now chair of the semi-official Defense Policy Review Board in Bush Junior's administration, was clearer.

> I believe this will now be the catalyst that causes a significant change in our policy toward terrorism, and that change should be to hold responsible governments that support terrorism. It's been our policy to hold individual terrorists accountable rather than the governments who support them and that policy has failed.[3]

(When information soon surfaced regarding the September 11 hijackers having trained to fly the jumbo jets at various US commercial flight schools, Perle may or may not have regretted his next remarks, which called for military action against governments providing such help to the terrorists. "This could not have been done without the help of one or more governments. Someone taught these suicide bombers how to fly large airplanes. I don't think that can be done without the assistance of large governments. You don't walk in off the street and learn how to fly a Boeing 767.")

In the first days after September 11, mainstream media accounts included references to experts—often unnamed and/or paraphrased—warning of the difficulties and lack of effect of using military attacks to respond to terrorism. Various early analyses included references to the failures of the Reagan administration's attacks on Libya, the Clinton administration's revenge strikes in Sudan and Afghanistan, and more. But as the Bush administration consolidated its call to war, those cautionary voices were largely relegated out of mainstream discourse.

Once his call to war was issued, Bush warned the nation that this war would not look like Desert Storm. His implication was that we should not expect to see the Gulf War's popular video-game images (however disingenuous) of supposedly smart weapons hitting supposedly limited military targets with supposedly limited "collateral damage." This time around we might still be seduced with new weapons with even higher IQs than those deployed in the Gulf War, but we shouldn't expect to see those grainy 1991-era black-and-white cockpit video clips on our televisions. Media coverage of this "war in the shadows" would be far more restricted even than the constrained access journalists fought for in Desert Storm.

In important ways, though, Bush Junior's war did reflect key aspects of his father's situation of a decade before. Like the international response on August 2, 1990 following Iraq's invasion of Kuwait, the initial condemnation of the terrorist attacks on New York and Washington was virtually unanimous and was truly reflective of governmental (and most of civil societies') positions around the world. And like his father's "Guns of August," Bush Junior's immediate announcement of a Wild West-style military response to the attacks was far from unanimously supported. The announcement engendered caution and skepticism, if not outright opposition, across the globe. Both Presidents Bush used the actual international unity that existed on one issue—condemnation of Iraq's invasion in 1990, of the September 11 terrorist attacks in 2001—to provide political cover for their *imposed* agreement on coerced coalitions in support of goals that went far beyond the original unified condemnation.

Both Bushes *chose* to mobilize a global force in response to, respectively, Iraq's invasion of Kuwait and the September 11 attacks on the World Trade Center and the Pentagon. Neither scenario was necessitated by circumstances, and both presidents had a range of other options. Bush Senior rejected, for instance, allowing the Arab League to deal with what was initially an inter-Arab regional conflict. His administration gave the regional organization 48 hours to respond to the Iraqi invasion, and, when that proved insufficient for these widely disparate leaders to agree on a plan, Bush announced he was sending the troops.

At that time, the real reason for Bush Senior choosing war had far less to do with the particularities or significance of Iraq and Kuwait, both of which had been allies of the US. Rather, along with ensuring continued US access to oil, the war reflected Washington's perceived need to demonstrate to the world that, despite the imminent collapse of the Soviet Union, the US remained very much a superpower with strategic power and global reach. Making an announcement of that fact would be ineffective; action—war—on a global scale would provide a far better demonstration. The UN was quickly identified as the venue of choice for assembling enough endorsements to link this thoroughly unilateral move to an "international coalition." Such a mandate would give credence to the new post-Cold War position of the US as leading the world in a new fight for freedom.

Rather than mobilizing a truly international collaboration based on justice and international law, Bush Junior chose war as well. Instead of following a course designed to identify, find, and bring to trial, perhaps in a newly-created international tribunal, the actual perpetrators of the horrors of September 11, Bush preferred war. He did, however, recognize the political value, even if he denigrated the strategic importance, of crafting something that would look like a coalition. This time, though, the United Nations would be kept entirely out of the loop. When the UN Security Council convened the morning after the September 11 attacks, the US-drafted resolution carefully avoided asserting Council, or indeed any UN, authority to organize and execute the world's response to the dramatic crimes against humanity committed in the United States. For its part, the Council put itself on record as being prepared to take any steps required to respond and, in the meantime, contenting itself with strong condemnation of the acts and expressions of condolence and solidarity for the American people.

No longer would a Bush in the White House rely on an official (even if dubiously achieved) credential from the UN to authorize its actions wherever in the world it chose; it would claim instead the mantle of self-defense. What Bush Junior really relied on, was a newly strengthened commitment to US unilateral power, however international the partnerships and alliances appeared.

Although they differed on the UN, both Bushes put creation of a coalition in whose name America could orchestrate a global crusade on top of their agenda. When Bush Senior chose the United Nations as his instrument of choice, he chose from a wide array of time-tested diplomatic tools including bribes, kickbacks, and punishments to win adequate, even if not unanimous, Security Council endorsement for a US war against Iraq. China, for example, after threatening to veto a use-of-force resolution, was offered the reward of long-sought resumption of long-term development aid and post-Tienanmen Square diplomatic rehabilitation. Washington offered both, and China abstained instead of using its veto. Impoverished Council members, including Ethiopia and Zaire, were offered new economic aid packages from Washington, access to World Bank credits, and, in some cases, refinancing of International Monetary Fund grants or loans. New military packages were dangled in front of Ethiopia, long denied military aid because of its war with Eritrea, and also offered to war-wracked Colombia.

Then there was the Yemen precedent. The sole Arab country on the Security Council in 1990, Yemen had only recently been reunified after a punishing civil war. Its still-fragile government could not risk alienating half of a badly-divided Arab world by voting to endorse an invasion by the United States of another Arab country, whatever the circumstances. Yemen voted against the US military response to Iraq. As soon as the Yemeni ambassador put down his hand, a United States diplomat at his side said, "that will be the most expensive 'no' vote you ever cast." The remark was broadcast—deliberately or not—over the UN's sound system and quickly relayed to capitals around the world. Three days later the US cut its entire aid budget (a paltry $70 million) to Yemen, the poorest country in the Arab world. The message was heard far beyond Aden; those who refuse to toe the line on an issue deemed crucial to the United States would pay a heavy price.

Bush Junior explicitly sidelined the UN. Nevertheless, when other nations heard Bush Junior's threat that "you're either with us or you're with the terrorists," it is likely that Yemen's lesson precedent was still on the minds of diplomats and government officials.

THE RUN-UP TO WAR

The debate over the necessity (or lack of necessity) of military coalitions was a long-standing one in and around the Pentagon. During the Clinton administration, Pentagon officials spent large amounts of time cultivating close ties with their counterparts around the world. "Military engagement" was the popular term of the day. In the absence of a defined global antagonist, small-scale military deployments were common, and made easier if prior military relationships already existed. The heads of the various regional commands were sometimes charged with behaving like the pro-consuls of an earlier era of empire, when representatives of the sovereign held overweening power in far-flung colonies.

When Bush came to power, Secretary of Defense Donald Rumsfeld voiced a different view. "I'm tired of hearing about engagement," he reportedly told his commanders. But that was before September 11. Once the military mobilization was under way, it appears Rumsfeld changed his views. "Indeed, several of the commanders came to town feeling that the events of the past six months have proven them right and Rumsfeld wrong," wrote one pair of journalists. "More important, they felt that the defense secretary and others in the Bush administration have quietly if grudgingly come around to their view."[4]

Warm and fuzzy relations between the Pentagon and military

officials around the world did not, however, mean automatic enthusiasm for the US war. The weeks between the September 11 attacks and the launching of the US war in Afghanistan on October 7 provided an eerie parallel to the August 2–November 29 period at the United Nations in 1990, when all countries united to condemn Iraq's invasion, but at first refused to endorse the rapid escalation of military response that Washington had in mind. Bush's September 20 speech heightened the unease already spreading in response to the warmongering tone of his earlier pronouncements.

Much of Europe, especially, was caught between the desire to stand by the US to respond to its attack and fear that the US reaction would lead to a far more dangerous spiral of war. In Britain, Tony Blair continued his role as Washington's First Friend. He sat with Laura Bush during the September 20 speech, and the president welcomed him saying, "America has no truer friend than Great Britain." Elsewhere in Europe support for the soon-to-be-launched US war was not so clear. Meeting with President Bush on September 18, Chirac said France stood "in total solidarity" with the US, but pointedly disagreed with Bush's formulation: "I don't know whether we should use the word 'war'," he said.[5] On September 19, the day before Bush's speech, a German parliamentarian from the opposition PDS party insisted, "It must be possible—even in Germany—to warn of an escalating cycle of violence without being called anti-American."[6] Across Europe, intellectuals, parliamentarians, other politicians and activists grappled with the conflict between support for the victims of the September 11 attacks, and unease ranging toward outright opposition to the emerging US military response.

In England, too, not everyone was happy. Tony Blair's ratings did not drop significantly with his embrace of the Bush strategy, but not everyone was pleased. One British analyst wrote in the influential Times of London: "Our Prime Minister should spend less time with his shoulder glued to President Bush's and more time applying it to the wheel back home." A Daily Telegraph cartoonist showed Blair boarding "Royal Air Force One."[7]

The disconnect between Washington's official demand for unconditional international military and political support on the one hand, while repeatedly asserting the "right to act unilaterally despite the expressions of support"[8] on the other hand, only increased the international hesitation. The basis of Washington's demand was the new level of militarized unilateralism that took the Bush administration beyond its preexisting trajectory of one-sided acts involving rejected treaties, abandoned negotiations, or neglected international institutions. It was clear that immediately after the terror attacks of September 11, Bush and his advisers were preparing to vastly expand the US military presence around the world; a coalition would be convenient, but was far from necessary.

NATO's nineteen-member alliance voted the day after the attacks to invoke the mutual defense language in Article Five of its Charter, regarding the attack on the United States as an attack on all NATO member states. From the start, Secretary of State Powell made clear, however, that the US did not view the alliance as having a direct role to play or imposing any constraints on Washington's military decision-making.[9] Shortly afterward, the US sent NATO a shopping list of specific requests, including unlimited access to ports, airfields, other military venues, and airspace; use of early-warning aircraft; replacement of US troops rotated out of Balkan peacekeeping assignments, and more. All the requests were immediately granted.

On a country-by-country level, the potential success of long shots such as Bulgaria and Romania in joining NATO received enormous boosts because of the anti-terrorism war. Instability and political unease among Central Asian governments meant that the United States needed to line up bases much farther from Afghanistan. The Black Sea region, particularly Bulgaria and Romania, emerged as a key staging area for US wars in Afghanistan and potentially in Iraq, and those countries consolidated new partnerships with the Bush administration. Both governments offered Washington unconditional access to their airspace, bases, ports, and all other military facilities. Both sent troops to participate in Balkan peacekeeping operations specifically in order to free up US troops for transfer from Bosnia or Kosovo to the Afghanistan front. Air tankers based in Bulgaria flew missions to refuel bombers and fighter jets in Afghanistan, and the *Washington Post* identified a Bulgarian military airport on the Black Sea as "a de facto US base with about 200 Americans stationed there."

Going even further, Sofia and Bucharest refurbished ports, airfields, and other facilities with what the *Post* called "the implicit promise that if the United States wishes to use them in future campaigns, including

possible strikes against Iraq, they are available for the asking."
According to the Romanian foreign minister, Mircea Geoana,
"September 11 transformed the Black Sea into a natural
springboard.... The next time when [the US] asks for support, or needs
support, Bulgaria will be an excellent ally."

The US did not officially announce an end to its ongoing concerns
about economic corruption or rampant repression against the Roma
(gypsy) peoples in both countries, but diplomats familiar with the
NATO accession process noted that the generous Bulgarian and
Romanian offers "have not gone unnoticed in Washington."10

Even with such eager levels of unanimous support from NATO and
its wannabes, however, Washington did not even pretend that the
Alliance would be involved in decision-making. And not everyone in
NATO was pleased with these developments. At a global security
conference in February, a German legislator asked "our American
friends to bear in mind that the core of the international coalition
against terrorism is NATO. It can't be that you can act on your own
and we trot along afterwards."11

It appeared, however, that Washington expected precisely that. And it
appeared that NATO was prepared to accept those terms, whatever the
Americans did or did not bear in mind. Back in October, before the
launching of the US war in Afghanistan, the alliance's Secretary-General
Lord Robertson had already acknowledged that it was "open to the
United States to act on its own."12 What the Pentagon wanted, and got,
was access to NATO's military facilities and its unconditional military
support, without having to consult or collaborate on any of its decisions.
As the *New York Times* noted just days before military strikes began:

> in submitting just a shopping list to the alliance instead of looking for a
> NATO-led operation, the United States gains strategically without
> becoming bogged down in the often cumbersome decision-making
> processes of a 19-member organization. Military experts said some
> American requests like permission to fly over allied territory and to stop in
> any port for refueling could greatly enhance military effectiveness. At the
> same time, however, America remains relatively free to make military
> decisions on its own.... Although Washington obviously wants the NATO
> stamp of approval... the United States was quite unlikely to ask NATO
> itself to join in the operations.... "This is great support for the US and
> reflects great trust in President Bush's leadership," said R. Nicholas Burns,
> the American ambassador to NATO."13

Unilateralism still reigned in Washington, NATO or not.

No European government, and almost none anywhere else, came out clearly against what was rapidly becoming an inevitable war. At the public level, though, there was widespread unease—and significant opposition—toward what was widely perceived as the US pushing the rest of the world into backing a unilaterally chosen war. Germany reflected the divergence between public and official positions. Public opinion had long opposed deployment of the German military outside the country, even closer to home. Even at the height of the Kosovo crisis, in March 1999, a poll in *der Spiegel* magazine indicated 76 percent of Germans opposed to using German troops in Kosovo, and only nineteen percent supported the idea. One month later, despite having less than one in five Germans behind them, German bombers joined the US-led NATO assault on Kosovo and the rest of Serbia. So it was unlikely that Bonn would hesitate to join Washington's war in Afghanistan, when public support for German participation had increased to about 58 percent by early October 2001.

THE MIDDLE EAST RESPONDS
In a few places elsewhere in the world, there was even more hesitation regarding support for Washington's war. Throughout the Arab world, public opposition to a US war was widespread and formidable. Every regime in the region faced a population angry and relatively unified against such a prospect. Virtually every government in the region faced significant crises of legitimacy, and each was aware that failure to speak against a looming US war against Muslims in Afghanistan would further delegitimize them in the public eye. At the same time, however, virtually every government in the region was—to varying degrees—dependent on the US—either for economic reasons like Jordan, or military ones like Saudi Arabia, Kuwait, or the little Gulf states, or for both economical and military reasons like Egypt.

Governmental responses differed largely according to the level of dependency on the US and of popular outrage. The Egyptian leader and close US ally, Hosni Mubarak, facing massive public opposition, cautioned that the US should think twice in considering a military response, and urged that "countries not be punished for the acts of individuals.... The world has a proposal of making a coalition for fighting terrorists, but I could tell you very frankly it's too early to think of this."14

King Abdallah of Jordan hedged, not endorsing a war but offering full support of his government in finding al-Qaeda. (It was probably not a coincidence that ratification of the US-Jordan free trade agreement was still pending in the Congress at that time.) Elsewhere in the Middle East region, government opposition went a step further. Sheik Zaid bin Sultan al-Nahayan of the United Arab Emirates warned that a coalition could only work if the US did not rely on double standards. He called on Washington to stop "the terrorist Israeli actions in the occupied Palestinian territories."15

In Israel, to the contrary, some initial reactions to September 11 were almost gleeful, hoping that the US government and Americans would finally understand what Israel faced. Israeli government officials were blunt. Defense Minister Binyamin Ben Eliezer, elected to lead the Labor Party in the last days of 2001, gloated that in the first days following September 11 "we have killed 14 Palestinians in Jenin, Kabatyeh and Tammun, with the world remaining absolutely silent."16

Prime Minister Ariel Sharon also went on the diplomatic offensive. Sharon feared a repeat of the Gulf war diplomacy of 1991, when the US, concerned about maintaining Arab participation in the anti-Iraq coalition, urged Israel to avoid retaliation even when hit by Iraqi scud missiles. To head off such a scenario and make clear that Israel would not, this time, agree to stand on the sidelines, Sharon pulled out all his rhetorical stops. He warned the US in heated language evoking Hitler and World War II:

> I call on the Western democracies and primarily the leader of the free world, the United States: Do not repeat the dreadful mistake of 1938 when enlightened European democracies decided to sacrifice Czechoslovakia for a convenient temporary solution. Do not try to appease the Arabs at our expense. This is unacceptable to us. Israel will not be Czechoslovakia. Israel will fight terrorism.17

In the first weeks after September 11, it appeared that General Sharon's fears were almost justified. The Bush administration, after months of absolute refusal to engage in any new diplomatic efforts (although Washington's $4 billion subsidy to Israel and its uncritical protection of Israel in the UN and other international arenas remained unchanged) suddenly began to talk about new efforts to get peace talks going. Bush sent retired General Anthony Zinni, former chief of the US Central Command (the region including Iraq), as his special envoy to Israel, ostensibly to help implement a ceasefire between Israel and the Palestinians. The rhetoric began to shift; Secretary of State Powell and Bush himself began hinting about a new US policy in the Israel-Palestine conflict. It was understood that it would be more generous to the Palestinian side.

In back-to-back speeches by Bush and Powell, first at the UN General Assembly and soon after at a Kentucky university, the new policy emerged from the shadows. It turned out, unsurprisingly, to be a new spin of an old policy. The only new thing was the use of words long unspoken by US officials. At the UN General Assembly meeting delayed by September 11 to early November, Bush actually uttered the word "Palestine." Powell went further, saying "the occupation must end." Actual US policy, however, remained unchanged.

THE GLOBAL PLAYERS—RUSSIA AND CHINA

Key strategic countries were guarded in their responses to the US war preparations. They raised no specific disagreement with the US, except to add a reminder or two of extraneous issues that should perhaps be considered (the Russians, for example, urged that evidence be given a chance), and generally were willing to go along. For countries like Russia and China, their own bilateral relations with the world's sole remaining superpower remained far more important than what the US did in other parts of the world. And if becoming putative allies in the aftermath of September 11 provided an opportunity to reconsolidate and strengthen Russian-American or Sino-American relations, so much the better. On top of that, if the US were handing out goodies to its new allies, like an end to annoying human rights criticisms, everybody might be happy.

Although the Russian President Vladimir Putin warned that any military reaction must rely on solid evidence linking the targets specifically to the crime, he also said the international community should punish "evil." It was left to an influential parliamentarian, Aleksei Arbatov, to identify a clearer Russian view. He acknowledged a consensus of "total moral support" for the US and even for the struggle against terrorism, but he went on to distinguish that moral support from absolute endorsement of Bush's war. He pointed to a strong humanitarian need "not to resort to massive strikes, to nonselective actions which are unjustified from the moral point of view, to avenge the death of thousands of innocent people with the deaths of tens of thousands of other innocent people."[18]

Whatever the feelings of the Russian people or of the Duma, it was clear that Putin saw the events of September 11 as an opportunity to strengthen relations with the Bush administration. Moscow would acquiesce to, if not enthusiastically join in, the extension of US reach into Russia's very backyard, the formerly Soviet Central Asian republics and Afghanistan, the regional lodestone of US-Soviet contention during the last years of the Cold War.

In return, Russia hoped for several things, including the possibility that the US might hold back on NATO expansion, already intended to reach the very border of Russia by absorbing the former Soviet Baltic republics of Latvia, Lithuania, and Estonia. Washington was not prepared to go that far. But the US did signal a new willingness to overlook Russian atrocities in Chechnya. It was not as if Washington ever took its claimed human rights concerns very seriously. But post-September 11 it soon became clear that Russia would be given essentially a free pass to impose collective punishment on civilians and abandon even the pretense of the rule of law in the disputed province.

According to Amnesty International:

> [I]n the Russian Federation there was increasing talk by those in positions of power or influence of using the worldwide "war against terrorism" to solve the Chechen question. Several government officials have drawn a close link between Osama bin Laden's organization and the Chechen fighters, stating that Chechens had been trained by Osama bin Laden. Following the events on 11 September, Russia increased pressure on Georgia to extradite Chechen fighters.[19]

Following a template that would emerge in numerous other countries, new and heightened allegations were raised regarding links between Chechen separatists, some of whom had undoubtedly committed their own human rights horrors, and Osama bin Laden. Given the rapidly globalizing demonization of bin Laden, such links acted as precursors to virtual impunity for anything done against the Chechen population.

Before September 11, Russia still tended to consider Uzbekistan, Kyrgyzstan, Kazakhstan, Tajikistan, and Turkmenistan part of its own sphere of influence. It was perhaps a sobering reflection of Russia's view of its own position vis-à-vis power in the world that it accepted with hardly a whimper the construction of US military bases and what looked to be the permanent deployment of US troops and planes in every one of the five formerly Soviet Central Asian republics.

Russia had also pressed hard to prevent NATO's expansion from including countries on Russia's own borders before September 11. But with the assertion of Washington's post-September 11 global reach, the ascension of the three Baltic republics, Latvia, Estonia, and Lithuania to the top of the NATO wannabe list, as well as the sudden improvement of the chances for membership of Bulgaria and Romania, was accepted with hardly a *nyet*. Of course the post-September-11 diminished importance of NATO itself, in a world suddenly shown to have such an extraordinary disparity between unilateral US military power and that of any other countries, may have softened the blow. Another mitigating factor would be Moscow's new invitation to join "NATO-20"—officially the NATO-Russia Council, a largely ceremonial club composed of the nineteen NATO members plus Russia, an occasional grouping that would discuss some similar issues, but not have power over the ordinary NATO of nineteen members. It amounted, essentially, to the military version of the "G-7 plus" or "G-8," groupings of the seven wealthiest economies of the world (those of the United States, Britain, Japan, France, Germany, Italy, and Canada) who felt compelled to embrace symbolically post-Soviet Russia in a gesture of inclusiveness and stability.

By the middle of November, when Bush hosted Putin at the White House and then at his ranch in Crawford, Texas, the tone of the meeting was warm and fuzzy. Secretary of State Powell, praising the "unprecedented cooperation Russia has given us since September 11," noted that Putin "was the first foreign leader to call President Bush and not just to offer sympathy and condolences, but to offer help, to align Russia with us in this new campaign against terrorism."[20] It was, for Putin, as close as anyone other than Tony Blair could get to being dubbed "no truer friend" of Washington's.

Similarly, China said little to challenge Washington's assertion of global power, seeing the post-September-11 circumstances as an opportunity to rebuild the relations with the Bush administration strained since the spy plane incident of early 2001. One week after the attacks, President Jiang Zemin called the leaders of France and the UK, both of whom were soon to meet with Bush. He told Blair and Chirac that "any military action against terrorism" should be based on "irrefutable evidence and should aim at clear targets so as to avoid casualties to innocent people." When he telephoned Putin the same day, the two leaders discussed working together and with the UN to "develop a mechanism for fighting terrorism."[21] China's foreign ministry went further, saying that it would support military retaliation only if the action was consistent with the UN Charter.[22]

China, however, was on the verge of joining the World Trade Organization (WTO), a long-sought achievement scheduled to come to fruition in December 2001. Beijing sent its Foreign Minister Tang Jiaxuan to meet with Secretary of State Powell on September 21, followed by a delegation of Chinese counter-terrorism experts. Both the US and the Chinese described the meetings as designed to enhance cooperation between the two countries.

The thorny question of Taiwan, let alone long-standing Chinese repression of the predominantly Muslim population of the Uighur region in China's northwest, did not come up. Official linking of separatist tendencies among the Uighurs with the charge of terrorism as some Chinese officials had recently done, paralleled the post-September-11 global propaganda approach of redefining every opposition movement operating in a US-allied country (especially if Islamist-oriented) as a local arm of bin Laden's al-Qaeda network. A calmer relationship with a newly tolerant Washington was, however, highly prized in China, with its role in the WTO and other international positions still being consolidated; acquiescing to an otherwise distasteful US war was likely considered a small price to pay.

Global public opposition remained strongest in the Arab Middle East and other Islamic countries. But governments all over the world continued to waiver, balancing the need at least to appear accountable to public opinion with their overweening dependence on, and resulting reluctance to criticize, the United States. Significant numbers of people throughout Europe still had qualms about the now-imminent US war, and many were opposed outright to it. Governments, however, from the stalwart UK to the newest NATO wannabes eager to show their anti-terrorism vigor to win favor in Washington, showed little hesitation in joining Washington's bandwagon once specific requests came in and the air war was launched on October 7.

NUKES IN THE NEIGHBORHOOD

One of the key exceptions to that balancing act was Pakistan. Almost immediately after the attacks of September 11, US-Pakistani relations were transformed. From a suspect country led by a general who had seized power in a military coup just two years earlier, still languishing under sanctions imposed because of Pakistan's 1998 nuclear testing, Pakistan suddenly became one of Washington's closest allies in George Bush's anti-terror war. During the 1980s, Washington had imposed a partial arms embargo against Pakistan because of its then-nascent nuclear program. The embargo was never designed to punish Pakistan seriously, because of its long-standing role in supporting the US-backed anti-Soviet war in Afghanistan. In fact, the United States, particularly during the Reagan years of anti-Soviet "Contra wars" around the world, had found in Pakistan's powerful Inter-Services Intelligence (ISI) agency the perfect conduit for training, arming, and supporting the anti-Soviet guerrilla organizations across Afghanistan. Those organizations, those arms, that training would, of course, soon give rise to civil war, the Taliban, and Osama bin Laden's al-Qaeda network.

Before September 11, though, that historical trajectory was not of particular concern to the US—nuclear weapons *were* a big concern. The earlier embargo imposed in the 1980s had clearly not prevented Pakistan's inexorable march toward nuclearization, a process made inevitable once India, then under a Hindu fundamentalist government, provided the taunting example. US arms restrictions were significantly tightened after Pakistan tested its first nuclear bomb on May 28, 1998, just two weeks after India's May 11 test.

India's and Pakistan's nuclear tests, in Pokharan and Chagai respectively, were rooted in different motivations and political trajectories. A right-wing Hindu-nationalist party, the BJP, with a long commitment to making India a nuclear weapons power, governed in New Delhi. It had announced its intention to test a nuclear weapon only one day after taking office. While its claimed goal was to achieve higher levels of international credibility and influence for India, it was widely understood that the BJP's actual goal had far more to do with the ideological assertion of Hindu superiority both within India (vis-à-vis its large Muslim minority) and on a global scale. Pakistan, smaller, poorer, and weaker of the two South Asian neighbors, justified its own nuclear test generally in the context of deterrence against the better-armed and much larger Indian military. For some of the most militant Islamists in and out of government, however, going nuclear would also be an assertion of Islamic power; Pakistan's would be the long-denied Islamic bomb.

The consequences of the two tests were far more similar than the rationales. In both countries, the enormous expenditures required for nuclear weapons testing further impoverished large populations. Pakistan faced a more severe impact from the US sanctions imposed on both countries because, as a consequence of greater poverty, it was far more dependent on international aid that was cut in the aftermath of the tests. Both countries ended up paying a heavy economic price. And in both countries the military and nuclear arms complexes gained political and economic power at the expense of more democratically-oriented social forces.

At the regional level, the nuclear tests further intensified the simmering conflict over Kashmir, transforming that longtime battleground into a site of potential nuclear exchange. In fact, exactly one year after the nuclear tests, fighting erupted again over control of the divided Kashmir province. The rapid intensification of the military conflict provided a frightening portent to a nuclear might-have-been.

Writing in the *Times of India* as the Kargil fighting erupted, the Indian scholar and anti-nuclear campaigner Praful Bidwai wrote:

[The] high-profile air strikes with their high-risk escalation potential testifies to the same flaws [as the nuclear tests]. One year after Pokharan-II, these put a huge question mark over nuclearization's claimed gains. The Bomb has comprehensively failed to raise India's stature, strengthen our claim to a Security Council seat, expand the room for independent policymaking, or enhance our security. India stands morally and politically diminished: a semi-pariah state to be equated with Pakistan, and periodically reminded of Security Council Resolution 1172 [which condemned the nuclear tests and called for both India and Pakistan to end their nuclear weapons efforts]. Most Third World countries see India as contradictory: a nation that for 50 years rightly criticized the hypocrisy of the Nuclear Club, only to join it; a country that cannot adequately feed its people, but has hegemonic global ambitions. Our neighbors, crucial to our security, see us as an aggressive, discontented state that violated its own long-standing doctrines without a security rationale.

After prolonged talks with the US, in which we put our "non-negotiable" security up for discussion, India remains a minor, bothersome, factor in Washington's game-plan as a non-nuclear weapons-state. South Asia's nuclearization has enabled Washington to grant Pakistan what Islamabad has always craved, and which New Delhi had always denied it, viz parity with India. Today, India and Pakistan act like America's junior partners."[23]

Those junior partners, hamstrung by the economic and military sanctions still in place after the nuclear tests, had yet to consolidate their potential bonds with the United States. After September 11, both Pakistan and India saw an opportunity to repair their still somewhat strained relations with Washington. In India, key policymakers made an effort toward what Bidwai described as, "forging a special relationship of proximity and 'partnership' with the US, to the exclusion of (and at the expense of) Pakistan.... Equally significant [was] India's offer of full cooperation in identifying, tracking down and bringing to book the concerned terrorists."24

In return, India brought to the table a long catalog of requested military purchases. On its wish list were combat aircraft, advanced light helicopters, communication and surveillance platforms, spare parts, and radar. "We are at the beginning of a very important arms sales relationship," Robert Blackwell, US ambassador to India, recently told Agence France-Presse."25 Touring India during his rally-the-world tour in November 2001, Secretary of Defense Rumsfeld announced the United States had resumed its military-to-military relationship with India, ties that had been all-but-severed after the 1998 nuclear tests. Rumsfeld vowed to back India's fight against Pakistan-backed guerrillas in Kashmir and said he and his Indian counterpart, George Fernandes, "talked about terrorism in the broadest sense. We talked about terrorism that has affected both our countries."26

While India made considerable moves toward strengthening its relationship both with the US and with Israel, seeing Tel Aviv as a natural ally in the struggle against "Islamic terrorism," it was Pakistan that gained far greater advantages. The military regime in Islamabad immediately announced its decision to align itself unequivocally on the side of the United States in the professed effort to wipe out the Taliban regime and al-Qaeda. This was a complicated tightrope for Musharraf and his minions to walk, given the power and influence of pro-Taliban forces within Pakistan's ruling circles, as well as the authority and long history of the semi-autonomous ISI intelligence agency as key state sponsor of the Taliban. The stability of the military junta remained fragile for some time.

The rewards, however, were great. In return for Musharraf's unstinting support, the new direction of Washington's Pakistan policy soon became clear. Within the first days after September 11, Bush asked Congress to waive existing military aid restrictions to countries he deemed vital to the US war effort. Congress quickly complied, and both Pakistan and its nuclear-armed rival, India, were among early beneficiaries. Once the overall US arms embargo to Pakistan was eased, Apache helicopter gunships arrived in Islamabad along with millions of dollars in direct aid for border patrols and other internal security purposes. General Musharraf also took the opportunity to request access to 28 advanced F-16 fighter jets that Pakistan had purchased and paid for during the heyday of its US alliance in the 1980s, but which the US had withheld as part of the early punishment for Pakistan's nuclear program.[27] US concerns about the military coup that had overthrown a civilian, more-or-less elected government in Pakistan and Congressional restrictions on supporting governments whose head of state had been overthrown were themselves overthrown, and Islamabad's military government was embraced.

SPECIAL FRIENDS

Later in the war, President Bush would single out Pakistan, along with another Central Asian former pariah, Uzbekistan, for special praise as "friends" of America in the battle against terrorism.[28] Maybe there was still "no truer friend" than Britain, but these once-ignored Central Asian governments were turning out to be favored allies indeed.

Uzbekistan quickly jumped to the head of the queue of former Soviet republics near Afghanistan looking for US sponsorship in return for joining Washington's anti-terrorism crusade. Like its neighbors—Turkmenistan, Tajikistan, Kazakhstan, and Kyrgyzstan—Uzbekistan was impoverished and isolated. For Uzbek President Islam Karimov, the September 11 attacks provided a new opportunity to redefine his domestic opponents as terrorists on a par with those who had destroyed the World Trade Center and attacked the Pentagon. Much of the political opposition in Uzbekistan functioned in the context of mosques and religious activity outside the government-sponsored network of official mosques. On October 9, 2001, Karimov appealed to his population for greater vigilance against global terrorists.

> Above all, we should look directly at the ugly face of the terrorist threat, denounce it and call it by its own name. Indifference to, and tolerance of, those with evil intentions who are spreading various fabrications, handing out leaflets, committing theft and sedition in some neighborhoods and who are spreading propaganda on behalf of religion should be recognized as being supportive of these evil-doers.[29]

It was a remarkably broad brush Karimov used to paint leaflet distribution as supporting global terror.

The US State Department itself had described Uzbekistan in 2001 as

> an authoritarian state with limited civil rights.... The police and the NSS [National Security Service] committed numerous serious human rights abuses. The Government's human rights record remained very poor, and it continued to commit numerous serious abuses. Citizens cannot exercise the right to change their government peacefully; the Government does not permit the existence of opposition parties. Security force mistreatment resulted in the deaths of several citizens in custody. Police and NSS forces tortured, beat, and harassed persons....[30]

But none of that history was mentioned when Karimov, whom the same State Department report identifies as having been "chosen president in a 1991 election that most observers considered neither free nor fair," visited the White House in March 2002. The meeting took place within hours of Bush's speech singling out Uzbekistan as a "friend" of the United States.

Instead, when Uzbekistan first came to US public attention in the second month of the Afghan war, its dismal human rights record was not on anyone's agenda in official Washington. Instead, the focus was on Uzbekistan's proximity to the embattled city of Mazar-e-Sharif on Afghanistan's northern border that made it a useful entry point for humanitarian supplies. At the time of the fall of the Taliban in Mazar-e-Sharif, the Uzbek government refused to open the border crossing, fearing hoards of starving, bomb-ravaged Afghans would stream across in search of bread and safety from the fighting. Eventually it did allow truckloads of United Nations and other humanitarian supplies to cross the border river, but continued to deny refuge to fleeing Afghans.

Tashkent was not so reticent, however, when it came to providing the Pentagon all the help it requested. For that, its reward was not in the form of Afghan mouths to feed, but something far more valuable for the Uzbek regime. According to a Pentagon spokesperson, after September 11, Tashkent allowed the United States to make use of its intelligence and its strategic location. In return, the US gave Uzbekistan "non-lethal" military equipment (transport vehicles and night-vision goggles among others) and an increase in aid for military training. Bush also requested $40.5 million in economic and law-enforcement assistance for Uzbekistan in 2002, up from $5.9 million in fiscal 2001.[31]

Some may have believed that US economic aid, police training, or other forms of support would serve to diminish at least some of the Uzbek torturers' enthusiasm. But a May 8, 2002 report by the United Nations Committee Against Torture, issued two months after Bush's cozy identification of Uzbekistan as a special "friend" of the US, indicated otherwise. The report, by ten independent experts conducting the periodic review mandated for compliance with the UN Convention Against Torture (which Uzbekistan signed in 1995), detailed "numerous, ongoing and consistent allegations of particularly brutal acts of torture by law enforcement personnel." It cited the "numerous" convictions based on confessions, and called on the Uzbek government to review prior "convictions based solely on confessions... recognizing that many of these may have been obtained through torture or ill-treatment."[32]

Washington's post-September 11 coziness with Uzbekistan and its Central Asian neighbors provided a three-part advantage for the Bush administration. In the immediate crisis, they were convenient staging grounds for military strikes against Afghanistan. Eager to overcome decades of isolation and poverty, governments in each country found it convenient to welcome varying combinations of US troops; planes for bombing, transport, and refueling; new bases and airfields constructed by US military engineers; US access to airspace and existing military facilities, and more. Within the first few weeks of the US mobilization toward war, the Pentagon had military forces in or on their way to Uzbekistan, Tajikistan, Kazakhstan, Turkmenistan, and Kyrgyzstan, countries that had hardly made it into the spell-checkers of major US newspapers prior to September 11. In return, these governments acquired money, new military assistance, and higher profiles in US strategic calculations—which often translated into US-granted impunity for long-standing human rights violations.

At the end of March, a Kazakh opposition leader sought refuge in the French embassy in Almaty, evading arrest on charges of "abuse of power" including, according to the country's interior minister, organizing unauthorized demonstrations and meetings. The US embassy expressed "surprise and concern," and said "the actions suggest an effort to intimidate political opposition leaders and the independent media."[33] Neither the embassy nor anyone in Washington, however, called for any shift in US policy toward the petro-rich and strategically positioned country.

Second, in the medium term, the Central Asian republics played a collective role similar to that of Arab Gulf states after the US-Iraq war of 1991. At the end of that war, for the first time there were US troops, planes, ships, airfields, or bases stationed in most Arab countries, from thousands of troops on the ground in Saudi Arabia, to naval base access in Bahrain, to airbases in Kuwait, and more. Public opposition or not, virtually all the Gulf sheikdoms were prepared to accept a direct, overt US military presence on their ostensibly sovereign territory. In the run-up to the Afghan war in 2001, by late October moves were already under way to replicate that changed reality in Central Asia.

The temporary deployments of US forces set the stage for creating permanent US bases; maintaining permanent forward deployments; and stationing permanent troops, planes, and other military equipment across the strategic Central Asian region. The expansion of US power in the post-Soviet independent states of Kazakhstan, Kyrgyzstan, Tajikistan, and Uzbekistan was in the process of consolidation less than a month after the US war began. By early November, when improvements in Uzbekistan were already under way, Defense Secretary Rumsfeld visited Tajikistan. A US military team followed, assessing the repairs that would be required to bring the sprawling Kolyab airbase near Dushanbe and several other bases up to speed for US bombing and supply runs. Their Tajik visit was the second, after Uzbekistan, in a regional shuttle that would then take them to Kyrgyzstan and Kazakhstan as well, all aimed at establishing a potentially permanent US military presence in the resource-rich countries surrounding Afghanistan. Political issues were not a problem; Rumsfeld had gone to Moscow before his own visit to Tajikistan and received immediate approval from Defense Minister Sergei Ivanov to take over the Soviet-built bases there.[34]

Russia may have once viewed the region as part of its own backyard, part of its historic sphere of influence and therefore off-limits to the US military. No longer. China may have been uneasy with US troops deployed just across its borders—not only in Pakistan but in Tajikistan, Kazakhstan, and Khyrgyzstan too. Nevertheless, Beijing remained quiet as the Pentagon's influence—and its people and weapons— quickly spread in the surrounding countries.

And third, in the long term, the critical question of oil rises to the fore. Since the industrial revolution created large-scale dependence on petroleum fuels, access to oil has always played a major role in shaping the priorities of US foreign policy. It was the driving force for early US contention with British and other foreign powers in the early 20th-century Middle East, and oil was the basis for intensive US intervention, economic, political, and military, in Saudi Arabia, Iran, and, later, Iraq and Kuwait. Ensuring its own ability to act as guarantor of its competitors' access to Gulf oil was one of the key reasons for the US decision to mobilize a global conflagration in response to Iraq's invasion of Kuwait in 1990.

OIL, OIL EVERYWHERE

The Gulf states are not, however, the only source of large oil deposits. Along with Russia itself, Central Asia and the Caspian basin, made up of the Caspian Sea and the countries surrounding it, Azerbaijan, Iran, Turkmenistan, Kazakhstan, Turkey, and Georgia are sitting on enormous oil and natural gas reserves. Other than Russia's, these reserves remain largely untapped. On the day before the September 11 attacks, the *Oil & Gas Journal* reported that Central Asia has twenty billion barrels of undeveloped oil reserves, and 6.6 trillion cubic meters of natural gas.[35]

The problem for those countries has not been the lack of resources, but rather the problems of poverty and location. Newly independent after the Cold War and the collapse of the Soviet Union, they have insufficient resources to exploit their gas and oil reserves on their own. Because they are landlocked, they are dependent on neighboring states for transporting the oil and gas out to the rest of the world. And because the Central Asian countries spent three-quarters of the 20th century as part of the Soviet Union, it is not surprising that the existing pipelines head north and west into Russia. Western oil companies have long coveted access to the rich potential profits of the Central Asian oil and gas fields as well as control of the transit arrangements.

Long-standing Russian domination of Caspian and Central Asian oil production remained a major stumbling block to those Western oil company plans. Before September 11, the US Energy Advisory Board website outlined the US policy goals regarding energy resources in this region:

[They] include fostering the independence of the states and their ties to the west; breaking Russia's monopoly over oil and gas transport routes; promoting western energy security through diversified suppliers; encouraging the construction of east-west pipelines that do not transit Iran, and denying Iran dangerous leverage over the Central Asian economies.[36]

The still-untapped oil reserves in Kazakhstan, Kyrgyzstan, Tajikistan, Turkmenistan, and Uzbekistan are estimated to be worth up to $2 trillion. Six of the biggest US oil companies—Unocal, Total, Chevron, Pennzoil, Amoco, and Exxon—have all plowed money into exploiting oil fields throughout Central Asia.[37] But the oil giants still face the problem of getting the oil out of oil-rich but market-deficient Central Asia and on its way to lucrative markets to the east in China, Korea, and Japan, and to the west in Europe, and maybe on to the US as well, all without giving Russia the upper hand.

Afghanistan, as it turns out, is the only country in the neighborhood without significant oil deposits of its own and is perfectly situated geographically as a crucial transit point for Central Asian crude. A US government Energy Information Fact Sheet, published in September 2000, one year before the World Trade Center attacks, is very clear:

Afghanistan's significance from an energy standpoint stems from its geographic position as a potential transit route for oil and natural gas exports from Central Asia to the Arabian Sea. This potential includes proposed multi-billion dollar oil and gas export pipelines through Afghanistan.[38]

Since 1979 Afghanistan had been wracked by war. From 1996 on it was under the control of the Taliban, the al-Qaeda-backed government that would become the target of the US war after September 11. Before the World Trade Center and Pentagon attacks, the US did not, however, have such a problem with the Taliban. As Vice President Dick Cheney recognized in 1998 (during his private sector years in between his stints as secretary of defense and Vice President of the United States), "the good Lord didn't see fit to put oil and gas only where there are democratic regimes friendly to the United States."[39]

Cheney was right about Afghanistan and the other Central Asian states not being paragons of democracy. Finding governments in the region who would be "friendly to the United States"—and making sure the US treated them as friends—did not, however, seem to be too much of a problem. During Dick Cheney's five years as CEO of the Halliburton Oil Services company, he served on the advisory board of

Kazakhstan's state oil company along with executives from Chevron and Texaco. Bush's Undersecretary of Commerce for Economic Affairs Kathleen Cooper is a former chief economist for Exxon-Mobil. Together, Chevron-Texaco and Exxon-Mobil are among the biggest investors in Kazakhstan's famed Tengiz oil field.[40]

The collaboration helped the two sets of American oil companies accomplish a stated US goal of challenging traditional Russian domination in Kazakhstan. The two mergered giants joined a complicated partnership with Russia and Kazakhstan, along with Oman, to build a pipeline from the Tengiz field in Kazakhstan to Russia's Black Sea port of Novorossiisk. And it all took place during the ten-year tenure of Bush administration National Security Adviser Condoleezza Rice on the board of Chevron. Chevron-Texaco thanked Rice for her advice in that period by naming an oil tanker after her.[41]

The economic potential for US oil interests in this region thus remained strong. In 1998 the *Amarillo Globe-News* reported that Cheney told oil executives that "the current hot spots for major oil companies are the oil reserves in the Caspian Sea region."[42] It should have been no surprise then that the oilmen and oilwomen of the Bush administration would continue their efforts to protect US access to current and future Central Asian oil and gas even as they prepared to wage war across the country they had hoped would soon begin service as a giant oil transit hub. After the September 11 attacks, the Bush administration began casting around for the right person to protect those interests. Zalmay Khalilzad, on staff at the National Security Council and a special adviser to the president on Afghan policy, fit the bill admirably.

A November 2001 article in the *Washington Post*, described a bit of the Bush envoy's history.

> Four years ago at a luxury Houston hotel, oil company adviser Zalmay Khalilzad was chatting pleasantly over dinner with leaders of Afghanistan's Taliban regime about their shared enthusiasm for a proposed multibillion-dollar pipeline deal. Today, Khalilzad works steps from the White House, helping President Bush and his closest advisers in attempts to annihilate those same Afghan officials. From his perch as a member of the National Security Council and special assistant to the president, the Afghanistan native is one of the most influential voices on Afghan policy.[43]

The oil company Khalilzad had advised was Unocal. In the mid-1990s Khalilzad worked as a risk assessor on behalf of Unocal, analyzing the viability of the natural gas pipeline Unocal and its partners were planning across Afghanistan. Unocal had already gotten the Taliban to sign on. And why not? According to Khalilzad, writing on October 7, 1996, just as the Taliban was sweeping to victory in Afghanistan's civil war and five years to the day before his boss launched a massive war against Taliban-ruled Afghanistan

> [the] Taliban does not practice the anti-US style of fundamentalism practiced by Iran. We should... be willing to offer recognition and humanitarian assistance and to promote international economic reconstruction.... It is time for the United States to reengage [the Taliban.]44

By the end of 1999, Khalilzad had slightly, only slightly, changed his tune. "Change the balance of power.... [and] create a military stalemate" was part of his first recommendation to the White House, drafted as part of a major set of proposals for a new US policy. The sixth, and last, recommendation was for the White House to

> appoint a high-level envoy for Afghanistan who can coordinate overall US policy. The envoy must have sufficient stature and access to ensure that he or she is taken seriously in foreign capitals and by local militias. Equally important, the special envoy must be able to shape Afghanistan policy within US bureaucracies.45

Two years later, on December 31, 2001, Khalilzad's appointment as special envoy to the new Afghan regime was announced. The White House announcement did not mention his history with Unocal.

The Central Asian region where Bush's oil-company-cum-White-House would soon wage all-out war, was still unstable. But the region's oil and gas wealth made it irresistible. And Dick Cheney was not the only former official of the Bush Senior administration who returned to the oil industry and used the combination of his diplomatic and oil industry clout to negotiate for access to Central Asian oilfields and exploration rights. Those negotiating with Turkmenistan, Kazakhstan, Azerbaijan, and Uzbekistan included Bush Senior-era Secretary of State James Baker, former National Security Advisor Brent Scowcroft, and former Chief of Staff John Sununu, as well as former Secretary of Defense Dick Cheney.46

Then there was Afghanistan. As the respected *World Press Review* pointed out, the "United States was slow to condemn the Taliban in the mid-1990s because the Taliban seemed to favor US oil company

Unocal to build two pipelines across Afghanistan."47

Bush Junior operatives were very close to the action. In 1996, when the Taliban triumphed in the inter-warlord war raging in Afghanistan, the US oil company Unocal continued negotiations with the new rulers over plans for a thousand-mile long trans-Afghan oil pipeline and a parallel natural gas pipeline almost as long. The Taliban had no diplomatic relations with the US, but Unocal flew Taliban ministers to Texas and flew their own corporate officials to Afghanistan for negotiations.48 No one in Texas and virtually no one in Washington had anything to say then about the Taliban's treatment of women, about its imposition of harsh medieval laws mandating punishments of amputation and death by stoning, about its destruction of Afghanistan's rich cultural heritage, or about its denial of health care and education.

In fact, once the Soviet Union collapsed and Afghanistan's war lost its Cold War cachet, no one in Washington was paying a great deal of attention to anything happening in Afghanistan, unless it had to do with pipelines. As the noted Pakistani journalist and author Ahmed Rashid put it:

> [The] United States walked away from Afghanistan in 1989, after the withdrawal of Soviet troops from that country. Washington allowed two allies, Pakistan and Saudi Arabia, to run with their own proxies—first Gulbuddin Hekmatyar, who destroyed most of Kabul with rocket attacks in 1993, and then the Taliban.... The United States has failed to give adequate political support to successive special representatives of the UN secretary-general who for the past decade have been trying to make peace in that blighted land. In 1994–96 the Clinton administration supported Pakistan and Saudi Arabia's military and financial aid to the Taliban.49

In 1998, at the height of the Taliban's power, it looked as if the pipeline deal were to be completed. But concerns remained regarding the stability of Afghanistan and the ability of the oil companies actually to build and protect the pipeline. After the US sent cruise missiles against Afghanistan, in retaliation for bin Laden's involvement in the bombings of the US embassies in Kenya and Tanzania, Unocal quietly shelved the project.

Access to Central Asian, Caspian Sea, and potentially even Russian oil remain, however, central to US global energy policies. As of March 2002, Russia surpassed Saudi Arabia as the biggest oil producer in the world—with production rising to seven million barrels per day. While

Saudi Arabia remained the biggest exporter of oil, given Russia's much larger domestic market, it lost the position it had held for more than a quarter of a century as the biggest producer.[50]

Such production capacity could become a key component ensuring Russia greater influence in the global economy—particularly if its production levels continue to rise and exports begin to rise as well. And because Russia is not a member of OPEC, the oil exporters' cartel, it is not subject to the production-limits discipline that other producers, led by the Saudis, have imposed on themselves. Even before the 1990–91 Gulf crisis, Saudi Arabia kept production in check, keeping oil prices stable between about $22 and $25 per barrel. Kuwait and other US-backed Gulf states accepted production limits too, but it is primarily the huge Saudi production power that determines prices and availability.

Rising levels of political and economic discontent and the potential for instability in Saudi Arabia, already major considerations for US strategists casting their eyes toward other, possibly more reliable sources of oil, could also push Russia toward making oil export a greater priority. Such a trajectory could mean that Russia will work harder to rebuild its relationships with and control over oil production and export in the newly independent former Soviet republics. For the same reason, that might make the effort by US oil companies to consolidate their access to and relations with the state-run oil industries in places like Kazakhstan and Uzbekistan—as well as Afghanistan—even more urgent.

The 1998 report of Cheney's talk to oil executives in Amarillo, Texas about the importance of Central Asian oil stated that the "potential for this region turning as volatile as the Persian Gulf, though, does not concern Cheney.... 'You've got to go where the oil is,' he said. 'I don't worry about it a lot.'"[51]

After September 11, one assumes Vice President Cheney began to worry about it a lot.

THE WAR AT HOME

When Bush Senior began his war preparations against Iraq within the first hours after Iraq's invasion of Kuwait in the summer of 1990, he had to move aggressively and quickly to demonize Iraqi leader Saddam Hussein. After all, until the moment of that invasion, Iraq under Saddam Hussein had remained a cozy ally of the US—unpleasant, perhaps, but no more so than other unsavory alliances Washington had cultivated throughout the Cold War. Military intelligence for the war against Iran, even the seed stock for biological weapons, all were provided by the United States to Baghdad for over a decade, even after the Iraqi military's later much-talked about use of chemical weapons against Iranian troops and Iraqi civilians in 1988. Turning on this erstwhile ally could be embarrassing, so the massive "Saddam is Hitler" propaganda offensive was launched immediately.

Bush Junior's public relations efforts were slightly easier; Osama bin Laden's name was already generally associated with terrorism and bad guys in most American minds. Bin Laden's roots, on the other hand, first in US-allied Saudi Arabia, and later throughout the 1980s as organizer and financier of the US-backed anti-Soviet Afghan *mujahedeen*, as well as his Taliban partners' origins with Pakistan's US-backed ISI intelligence agency, were mostly forgotten. In the United States especially, where historical memory is remarkably short, that national amnesia made going to war against "him" even easier.

After September 11 there was no doubt that the vast majority of Americans supported Bush Junior's call to war. Few had considered or been presented with any other options. The choices most people were aware of could be boiled down to "should we go to war, or should we let them get away with it?" Possibilities of justice-based solutions, empowering international institutions or creating new ones to answer new needs, or treating the attacks as a crime against humanity to be dealt with by international legal efforts—none of these possibilities was taken seriously in the mainstream discourse.

And yet, since the September 11 attacks, faith-based, peace, trade union, and other activists around the country gathered precisely to articulate different responses to the horrific destruction, responses that would not be grounded in war. Much of the emerging response focused on international law, the need for a new international court, empowered and backed by a newly-created international police agency, made up of police forces from the region to cooperate on identifying and bringing to trial the real perpetrators of the attacks. Some of the critique was rooted in a sense that, in the absence of a clear and identifiable alternative strategy, the words of Hippocrates should guide us all: First do no harm. While there were varying alternatives discussed, there was agreement that the war, already seemingly inevitable, was wrong. It would not lead to justice, it would kill innocents and destroy an already-ravaged country; it would engender future terror.

If one looks at history, earlier US military responses to terrorist attacks bear two things in common: one, they all kill, injure, and/or render even more desperate some number of already-impoverished innocents; and two, they don't work to stop terrorism. In 1986 Ronald Reagan's military bombed Tripoli and Benghazi to punish Libyan leader Muammar Ghadafi for a discotheque explosion in Germany that killed two GIs. Ghadafi survived, but several dozen Libyan civilians, including Ghadafi's three-year-old daughter, were killed. And still, just a few years later, came the Lockerbie disaster, for which the US implicated the Libyan government.

In 1998, responding to the attacks on US embassies in Kenya and Tanzania, US bombers hit bin Laden's training camps in Afghanistan and an allegedly bin Laden-linked pharmaceutical factory in the Sudan. It turned out the factory had no connection to bin Laden (its owner sued the United States for damages), but it was the only provider of vital vaccines for children growing up in the profound scarcity of central Africa. And whoever might have been killed, and whatever might have been destroyed in those primitive camps hidden deep in the Afghan mountains, attacking them obviously had no impact on the propagators of the attacks of September 11, 2001. In fact, while it appears the training camps were empty when they were hit, journalists later reporteded a significant increase in anti-US, pro-bin Laden sentiments among local Afghans who lived in close proximity to the bombing targets.

Within days after the September 11 attacks, the media was reporting demonstrations planned on 105 college campuses in 30 states.[52] Washington DC's first demonstration against the looming war was held on September 24, a small rally in Lafayette Square. The justice-not-war forces gained strength with the emergence of new allies—family members of victims of the September 11 attacks, who were troubled, sometimes deeply angered at the prospect of war.

Phyllis and Orlando Rodriguez's son Greg was killed in the World Trade Center. They wrote an open letter to President Bush, urging him to rethink his planned reaction to the September 11 attacks.

Your response does not make us feel better about our son's death. It makes us feel worse. It makes us feel that our government is using our son's memory as a justification to cause suffering for other sons and parents in other lands. It is not the first time that a person in your position has been given unlimited power and came to regret it. This is not the time for empty gestures to make us feel better. It is not the time to act like bullies. We urge you to think about how our government can develop peaceful, rational solutions to terrorism, solutions that do not sink us to the inhuman level of terrorists.

An accompanying letter to the *New York Times*, that *Times* editors chose not to publish, circulated widely on the internet.

We cannot pay attention to the daily flow of news about this disaster. But we read enough of the news to sense that our government is heading in the direction of violent revenge, with the prospect of sons, daughters, parents, friends in distant lands dying, suffering, and nursing further grievances against us. It is not the way to go. It will not avenge our son's death. Not in our son's name.... Let us not as a nation add to the inhumanity of our times.

On October 7 a wide coalition known as "New York Not in Our Name" came together for a quiet vigil and an angry protest at the war that was soon to come. Among the endorsers of the demonstration was the janitors' union, local 32BJ of the Service Employees International Union (SEIU), 26 of whose members had died in the World Trade Center. Others participating included members of Local 100 of the Hotel Employees and Restaurant Employees Union, 43 of whose members died in the Windows on the World restaurant in the World Trade Center; 400 others lost their jobs when the WTC collapsed. Led by Nobel peace laureates Adolpho Perez Esquivel and Maired Maguire, they met for a vigil at Times Square and marched under police escort to Union Square, just a few miles north of what was now known as "Ground Zero," to commemorate the victims and demand that no more victims be killed in their name.

Shortly before the speeches began, the organizers behind the stage received word by cell phone that the first US bombs had fallen on Afghanistan. Bush's war against Afghanistan—soon to become a global "war against terrorism"—had begun.

FIVE

THE BATTLE IS JOINED:
AND THE WORLD STANDS SILENT

The war that George Bush would wage in the name of fighting terrorism would transform US power around the world. No longer the sole remaining superpower of the post-Cold War era or even the proud unilateralist power of the early Bush administration, the US response to September 11 took the form of a massive mobilization of military, strategic, and diplomatic power. A *New York Times* columnist called the post-September 11 United States a "Modern Day Rome."[1] But never before, not in the ancient Persian Empire of Cyrus the Great, not in the eras of the Roman, the Ottoman, the British, or the Portuguese empires, had the colossus of any existing imperial center so thoroughly dwarfed the combined capabilities of the rest of the world.

US military power had been strategically unchallenged since the last years of the Soviet Union before its official collapse on Christmas Day 1991. Since that time (as well, certainly, as during the military competition with the Soviet Union), the US had more or less routinely deployed troops, armed regional allies, and maintained conventional military and nuclear superiority—all as a matter of right. In 1990, relying on what one dismayed UN official called "raw power" to obtain Security Council authority for its move, the US had mobilized its largest military force since Viet Nam to storm the Iraqi desert.

But never had the world seen such a combination of unilateral military might with unyielding diplomatic pressure and untrammeled strategic reach. Former British Prime Minister Margaret Thatcher, who famously inspired Bush Senior with the words, "Now don't go wobbly on us, George," on the eve of the Gulf war, could not be happier. Dismissing concerns about earlier neglect of Afghanistan as "trite," she recognized with appreciation that "it is best that the United States,

137

as the only global military superpower, deploy its energies militarily rather than on social work. Trying to promote civil society and democratic institutions is best left to others." Evaluating Bush Junior's performance after September 11, she noted approvingly how the US "has proved to itself and to others that it is in truth (not just in name) the only global superpower, indeed a power that enjoys a level of superiority over its actual or potential rivals unmatched by any other nation in modern times." And that is a good thing, according to the Iron Lady. Offering her own "advice to a superpower," she admonished:

> as long as America works to maintain its technological lead, there is no reason why any challenge to American dominance should succeed. And that in turn will help ensure stability and peace....The good news is that America has a president who can offer the leadership to do so.[2]

One might forgive Thatcher her quasi-maternal tone of pride in Bush; her endorsement of untrammeled US power, while not unexpected, is not so easy to forgive.

The United States would not even seek the illusion of a United Nations seal of approval this time around. Relying on the claim that self-defense has no limits, the Bush administration "rallied the world," as the President put it, through a naked threat that brooked no question. Every government knew the choice: "You're either with us, or you're with the terrorists." Every government knew the consequences of its choice: join the US crusade on US terms, or face the possibility of being the target of the crusade after that. Within weeks there were thousands of US troops in and surrounding Afghanistan, 500 on a "training mission" in the Philippines, 150 assisting Yemen in going after terrorists, as well as overt threats against Iraq, Somalia, and other countries. The noted French analyst Dominique Moisi said the war in Afghanistan "shows that the hyperpower is even more powerful than we had thought."[3]

Washington's unmistakable message was: we have the power, and, since becoming the world's most powerful victim on September 11, we have the moral *right* to extend our global reach, our troops, our bombs, and perhaps even our nukes, anywhere in the world that we choose. George Bush put it clearly: "whatever it takes, whatever it costs," we will wage this war.[4] And we won't ask and won't tell anyone, whether target governments or our own people, when we choose to do so.

This was a unilateralism more powerful and more widely militarized than any that had gone before. It saw a kind of marshalling of global force, herding the suddenly compliant governments of the world into line to launch, with international support but absent international collaboration, a lethal battle against one of the poorest, most isolated nations on earth.

On the first day after September 11 the *Washington Post* lamented that following what it called "the black-and-white clarity" of the Great War and the Cold War, "the bloody muse of history now gives us the Gray War, a war without fronts, without armies, without rules."[5] The reference was to the attacks in New York and Washington, but when the US first launched its war in Afghanistan, it was itself far from a clearly-defined war. At first it was an unstoppable, one-sided bombing campaign launched by the US (with some help from eager Britain) against a country whose population was already one of the most desperate in the world. Only after the bombing began did the Northern Alliance reemerge as a military force challenging the Taliban military and al-Qaeda with their own quotient of the surplus arms left over from the long years of US-backed anti-Soviet and civil wars.

The initial bombing was, however, sufficient to win widespread international acclaim for Bush's war. Existing supporters applauded, the fence-sitters climbed down, those who had hedged their support stopped waffling, and the few opponents largely shut up. Some believed that other governments welcomed Bush's war mainly as an optimistic response to Washington's initial post-September-11 call for an international coalition to answer the terrorist attacks. That is, having just spent the previous seven months angry at the Bush administration's abandonment of the Kyoto protocol, its rejection of the ABM treaty, and its insistence on building a fatuous weapons shield, other governments heard the call for a coalition—any kind of coalition—as something to be embraced.

Maybe. But perhaps more likely was the possibility that most governments were simply afraid to say no to the United States. Shocked by the ferocity of the September 11 attacks and intimidated by the resulting increase in power and the appearance of invincibility of Washington's unilateral reactions, rebuffing the US was simply too fraught with danger.

Whatever combination of fear and hope motivated the response, official support for the US bombing raids materialized immediately. Across Europe tentative backing turned into enthusiastic cheerleading within hours of the first bombing raids. In Brussels, the European Union expressed "full solidarity" with the US-British attacks. The European Commission President, Romano Prodi, said "all Europe stands steadfast with the United States and its coalition allies to pursue the fight against terrorism."[6]

German Chancellor Gerhard Schroeder expressed his government's support "without reservation," and said Germany's solidarity with the US was "unlimited." As the US bombers headed for Afghanistan, French President Jacques Chirac pledged that French troops would participate directly in the military campaign. "The fight against terrorism is complex and without mercy," Chirac said. He added that "at this stage" French vessels were already involved with the operation.[7] In Rome, rightist Prime Minister Silvio Berlusconi put Italy on high alert and sent troops to set up concrete barriers at the entrance to a major NATO base. Agence France Presse quoted Berlusconi saying, "Italy is on the side of the United States and of all those who are committed to the fight against terrorism," even as hundreds of protesters marched through Rome denouncing the US attack on Afghanistan.[8] Italy joined Germany and Britain in urging Washington to accept the offers of allied military support, mostly to little avail.[9] Canadian Prime Minister Jean Chretien announced that Canada would provide military support to join the American force and that military units were being called up.

Russia offered the Pentagon intelligence, access to Russian airspace, and weapons to arm the Northern Alliance.[10] Russia's foreign ministry issued a statement applauding the US strikes and linking them to Russia's own campaigns. "The time has come for decisive actions to fight this evil," the statement said, read on Russian television. "Terrorists wherever they are—in Afghanistan, in Chechnya, the Middle East, or the Balkans—should know that they will be brought to justice." Referring to Russia's providing arms to the Northern Alliance and the Russian military advisers then in Afghanistan, the deputy chairman of the Duma's defense committee bragged that "Russia de facto is participating in the military actions against the Taliban."[11]

Japan endorsed the air strikes, and Japanese Prime Minister Junichiro Koizumi launched a campaign within the parliament for a new law allowing Japanese military participation in the US war. The move was strongly opposed by Japan's large peace constituency, who argued that it violated the Japanese constitution's rejection of war as a national right and its ban on sending Japanese "Self-Defense" forces abroad. The new legislation allowed Koizumi to send a fleet of two destroyers and a supply ship carrying four helicopters and 700 troops to the Indian Ocean to carry out noncombat support for the war.[12] China, while urging that "military strikes on terrorism should be targeted at specific objectives, so as to avoid hurting innocent civilians," gave cautious support to the US air strikes, stating that it "opposes terrorism of any form."[13]

The expansion of US military domination around the world proceeded at breathtaking speed. This was not the careful months-long deployment of ultimately half a million troops that characterized Bush Senior's war against Iraq a decade earlier. This was the fast-paced consolidation of the global transmission of US power—a military force that needed no nation's help and no coalition's approval in waging its global war. Even Great Britain, whose leader personified unequivocal support for the US war, had to beg for weeks before the United States would agree to allow it to lead a UN-mandated peacekeeping force to be deployed in Kabul. Washington only accepted the proposal to create the peacekeeping force after London agreed that the US Central Command would maintain supreme command authority over the international troops.[14] US troops would not, of course, participate in the peacekeeping force—they were far too busy fighting their anti-Taliban war to be bothered with protecting Kabul. But Washington would maintain ultimate control nonetheless.

One of the early policy casualties of the Afghan war was the so-called Powell Doctrine. Promulgated when the secretary of state worked in his earlier incarnation as chairman of the Joint Chiefs of Staff, the principle asserted that US forces should be used only when they had full political support and a clear exit strategy. Then, if the use of force was needed and those requirements met, the force should be overpowering and massive. The doctrine reflected Powell's experience in Viet Nam, when US strategists refused to acknowledge that Vietnamese nationalist forces had beaten the technologically superior US troops, and instead blamed Washington's political elite for hobbling the military and engendering insufficient public support.

Accepting that set of assumptions led Powell to his initial opposition to going to war against Iraq in 1990–91 and, once the decision to use force was made, his insistence on an enormous troop build-up in the Gulf before the US began its war.

The illusion of a coalition war melted quite rapidly. As the military campaign in Afghanistan escalated and US troops on the ground played a much broader and deeper direct role in the fighting, the Pentagon continued to rebuff offers of support. By the end of the year, as the French Institute for International Relations' Moisi put it, "the coalition-building looks like a diplomatic fig-leaf, allowing the US to pick what she wants, when she wants, if she wants, from her allies."

The head of the International Peace Academy in New York and former Canadian ambassador to the UN, David Malone, described the actions of the United States in equally blunt terms, but tried to put a more sympathetic gloss on his assessment. The US "is not operating multilaterally," he said. "Rather, it might be described as practicing smart unilateralism, just as it has used smart weapons to gain military dominance."15

NOT SO SMART WEAPONS

The support of other governments for Washington's war remained strong. Yet murmurs of unease about the US as the hyperpower, about military unilateralism, and about taking allies for granted, began to surface once again. The murmurs grew louder as the early reports of civilian casualties and looming humanitarian catastrophe in Afghanistan began to surface.

For all their hype, the newest generation of computerized "smart" weapons turned out to be responsible for an awful lot of dead civilians. Most of the time the weapons themselves worked exactly as they were programmed to. But serious problems emerged when high-flying bomber pilots relied on often inaccurate, incorrectly processed, or deliberately misleading information to program these "smart" weapons. The location of supposedly military targets was often obtained from outdated Soviet-era maps from which newer residential, commercial, medical, or other facilities were simply missing. The claimed identity of alleged al-Qaeda or Taliban forces targeted for air strikes was often a jumble of ignorance, speculation, and deliberate efforts by local residents or warlords to gain power over rivals by feeding false information to US special forces guiding the pilots. The combination made the computer-driven smart weapons just as deadly to civilians and friendly forces as old-fashioned dumb gravity bombs.

The high levels of civilian casualties, initially only hinted at by mainstream media outlets in the United States, also reflected a more fundamental problem. According to University of New Hampshire Professor Marc W. Herold, who compiled the first comprehensive survey of civilian casualties by monitoring a wide range of international press sources, a more sinister reality was at work. The high level of civilian casualties, his report indicates, is best explained by

> the apparent willingness of US military strategists to fire missiles into and drop bombs upon heavily populated areas of Afghanistan. A legacy of the ten years of civil war during the 80s is that many military garrisons and facilities are located in urban areas where the Soviet-backed government had placed them since they could be better protected from attacks by the rural mujahedeen.... But the critical element remains the very low value put upon Afghan civilian lives by US military planners and the political elite.

Herold documented (including only verifiable and comprehensively cross-checked sources) 3,767 civilian casualties just in the first eight and one-half weeks of the US attacks on Afghanistan.[16]

Reports of civilian casualties began in the first hours of the United States' bombing (though not in the US press). An October 8 Reuters news agency article published in UK newspapers included an interview with a sixteen-year-old from Jalalabad who said he had lost his leg and two fingers in a missile strike on an airfield near his home the day before. The boy, named Assadullah, was an ice cream seller; he was interviewed in a Peshawar hospital. "There was just a roaring sound, and then I opened my eyes and I was in a hospital," he said. "I lost my leg and two fingers. There were other people hurt. People were running all over the place."[17]

From the beginning there were clear efforts on the part of the Pentagon to portray the Afghan war as limited to military targets and more humane than any war in history, with the US military careful to avoid civilian casualties. Just hours before publication of the Reuters report of the young boy who may have been among the first civilian casualties, US Secretary of Defense Donald Rumsfeld and his British counterpart, Geoff Hoon, told reporters the air raids had been entirely successful, hitting only military targets. Rumsfeld said "every single target which the coalition forces hit was a military target."[18]

In fact not every target hit was military. The issue of civilian casualties and targeting "mistakes" emerged with much higher-profile coverage after the October 9 US attack on a United Nations office in Kabul that served as headquarters for the UN's mine-removal teams in Afghanistan. Four UN employees were killed, and the program's work was seriously set back. After that, in most of the world, "bombing mistakes have been reported almost daily."[19] Not in the US press, though; coverage remained uneven largely until early February 2002, when a shift occurred from shorter news articles chronicling some of the individual incidents of civilian casualties and related "mistakes," to more analytical pieces looking seriously at patterns.

By October 30, the UN High Commissioner for Refugees, Ruud Lubbers, called on Washington and London to exercise "self-restraint" in the bombing in order to prevent more civilian casualties. He said:

> If this goes on, with more and more civilians killed, I don't think it will help to say "okay, let's break for two days or two weeks." We need to get self-restraint. I do hope that those who are planning military action will understand that it has to be targeted at ending terrorism, and at those who protect terrorists, and that it should not become a war against Afghans.[20]

From the beginning, though, Pentagon sensibilities were running high. Eager to maintain at least a veneer of legitimacy in the claim that its war was against terrorism, not against Muslims, the growing dossier of civilian dead and injured and attacks on non-military targets represented a major challenge. New evidence piled up regarding bomb raids that hit civilians in cities and towns across Afghanistan. On October 23, Pentagon spokeswoman Victoria Clarke admitted that Navy fighter jets "accidentally" dropped a 1,000-pound bomb near a senior citizens center in Herat, in northern Afghanistan. She acknowledged that the senior residence might in fact be the building that Pentagon officials originally described as a "military hospital." Clarke's disclosure came only a day after her boss, Secretary of Defense Rumsfeld, categorically denied Taliban claims that a hospital was hit in Herat. "We have seen repeatedly things that are not true put out by the Taliban," he said. "We have absolutely no evidence at all that would suggest that [the reported hospital bombing] is correct. I'm sure it's not."[21]

US reports of civilian casualties did continue, even if sporadically. A *Washington Post* headline read, "Villagers Describe Deadly Air Strike," reporting on a bomb which killed 25 villagers, all civilians, on October 22.[22] The *Post* ran another story a month later: "At Hospital, Villagers Tell of US Bombing" in which the death toll in villages southwest of Jalalabad reached 150 in four days of US air strikes that began November 30; 36 seriously injured people, many of them children, were admitted to Jalalabad's Public Hospital Number One.[23] The *New York Times* also reported back from the civilian war front: "In Village Where Civilians Died, Anger Cannot Be Buried" told how the tiny fifteen-house hamlet of Madoo was obliterated by US bombs, killing 55 people.[24] "An Afghan Village Where Errant Bombs Fell and Killed, and Still Lurk in Wait," brought the news of 30 villagers in Charykari killed by what they believe was a B-52 payload.[25] In the "Plaintive Afghan's Plea from Community: Stop the Bombing," the bearer of letters addressed to Presidents Bush, Musharraf, and Putin, as well as to UN Secretary General Kofi Annan and other world leaders, explained that "the terrorists and the leaders are still free, but the people are dying and there is no one to listen to us. I must get to President Bush and the others and tell them they are making a terrible mistake."[26]

The casualty tolls were, as the *Washington Post* carefully described them, "certain to complicate the administration's efforts to portray the campaign as a war against terrorists and not against Muslims."[27] Those efforts were clearly set back when US bombers dropped two 500-pound bombs on the Kabul studio of the Arabic-language television network al-Jazeera on November 13. Al-Jazeera, based in Qatar, was widely known for its unfettered news and public affairs coverage, including freewheeling talk shows that even featured criticism of various Arab regimes, something unprecedented in the Arab world. The network went on the air via globally-accessible satellite in 1996, but most Americans had never heard about it until after September 11. From that time on, it became known in the United States for its broadcast of videotapes of statements by and interviews with Osama bin Laden. For Arabic speakers around the world, however, al-Jazeera, which remained the only television network to operate in Kabul throughout the period of the crisis, became a lifeline for immediate footage of the effects of the US bombing on Afghan civilians and the already-collapsed infrastructure of the country. While high-ranking members of the Bush administration including Secretary of Defense Rumsfeld and National Security Adviser Condoleezza Rice were interviewed on al-Jazeera's programs as well, US officials made their displeasure unmistakably known and pressured the television network, fruitlessly, to censor its broadcasts of bin Laden.

The day after the bombing of al-Jazeera, the spokesman for the US Central Command, Colonel Brian Hoey, said that US aircraft dropped the bombs on the al-Jazeera building based on "compelling" evidence that the facility was being used by al-Qaeda. At the time the bombs were dropped, Hoey said, "the indications we had was that this was not an al-Jazeera office."28

For a brief time, the US had somewhat less to worry about regarding the mainstream press. Public opinion in the United States remained sky-high in support of Bush's war, and the press tread cautiously on anything remotely resembling criticism. At the end of the first month of the war, the *New York Times* ran an article regarding Bush administration efforts "to try to influence Islamic opinion." It included a rather straightforward description of the media campaign, the hiring of a special PR-savvy ad executive to run the Pentagon's information war, and how concern about civilian casualties was eroding support in Europe. The article noted how difficult the US effort was to win public support in crucial Islamic countries:

> [W]ith lingering resentment in the Arab world about America's superpower status, support for Israel and cultural dominance, countering the Taliban's information offensive has not been easy. The United States says its intense air attacks are necessary to destroy the terrorist network and topple the Taliban government, and it has stressed that it is trying to avoid civilian casualties and is not at war with the Afghan people. But the specter of bombs falling on an impoverished country that has been ravaged by war for more than two decades has been used by the Taliban to foment opposition to Americans.29

The *Times'* assumption seemed to be that while European support for the war dropped because of civilian casualties, in the Arab world it was only because of the Taliban's "information offensive" that the US propaganda war did not work.

Certainly policymakers in the United States were particularly concerned about public opinion in the Arab Middle East, Central Asia, and elsewhere in the Islamic world. But it was not only Arabs and Muslims who were concerned, angry, and even outraged over the increasing reports. One particularly damaging pair of attacks, both from the vantage point of actual civilian destruction and of causing further erosion of international support for the war, was on a large Red Cross complex in Kabul. On October 16, US planes bombed a warehouse and other buildings used by the International Committee of the Red Cross (ICRC). The Pentagon said at the time it was unaware that the site was an ICRC complex. It even sent a military official to Geneva afterwards, to the headquarters of the ICRC, to prepare a detailed review of all Red Cross structures in Afghanistan to ensure they would be kept off any future target lists. But no sooner had the review been completed, than the Pentagon struck again. Ten days after the first bombing, two Navy fighter-bombers and two B-52s returned, in two waves over the same carefully mapped Red Cross center, the second wave in bright daylight just before noon. It dropped satellite-guided bombs "that wrecked and set ablaze warehouses storing tons of food and blankets for civilians."[30] One of the B-52s missed the complex altogether, instead hitting a residential neighborhood nearby. The Pentagon said it "sincerely regret[ted]" the attacks.

EAT YOUR LAND MINES, BOYS AND GIRLS

Just a few days after the second Red Cross debacle, the Pentagon faced one of its most embarrassing revelations. Even before the war began, humanitarian catastrophe was endemic in Afghanistan. Twenty-three years of war, abandonment by Cold War-era sponsors who left behind only weapons, culminating in five years of harsh Taliban rule, all spelled disaster for Afghanistan's 23.5 million people. Exacerbating that cumulative crisis was a three-year drought, the most severe in recent history. The drought, combined with massive refugee flows within and outside the country, meant that food shortages had risen to catastrophic proportions. In the year 2001, some 900,000 people had been driven from their homes prior to September 11, and the UN had already warned of impending famine.

The food shortage became even worse after September 11. With George Bush's first announcement that the United States was going to war against Afghanistan in retaliation for the suicide bombings in New York and Washington, major aid organizations, on whom 5.5 million or more Afghans depended for basic subsistence food, began to withdraw their international staff in anticipation of bombing. The UN's local Afghan staff largely remained at their posts, but the overall situation was compounded by Taliban efforts to cut communication between the UN's local staff and the regional headquarters in Pakistan. As the international staff pulled out in response to the security threat, food shipments into the country stopped as commercial trucks and drivers for the most part disappeared, similarly unwilling to risk being caught on Afghan roads under US bombing that could begin at any moment.

In the early weeks of the bombing, a major US propaganda exercise involved air drops of military-style individual food packets over isolated parts of Afghanistan. Experts in humanitarian crisis assistance were unanimous that such drops were not only expensive and logistically difficult, but that, in additioin, they did virtually nothing to address even the most immediate consequences of the near-starvation conditions prevailing throughout much of Afghanistan. The drops became the butt of a lot of jokes about propaganda food and more. But then the food packets caused a really serious public relations debacle.

Pentagon officials grudgingly admitted that in a major bombing raid on October 22 in the village of Shaker Qala near Herat in western Afghanistan, US bombers dropped cluster bombs, each containing 202 bomblets powerful enough on their own to damage tanks and kill people. In Shaker Qala, the cluster bombs killed nine civilians and injured fourteen others. On average, seven percent of cluster bombs fail to detonate on impact; instead, they lie on the ground ready to explode at the touch of a farmer's foot or a child's curious hand. They become the equivalent of anti-personnel land mines, which were banned and declared illegal after an international campaign to prohibit their manufacture and use. (The United States was one of the few countries who refused to sign the Ottawa Treaty banning land mines, which kill about 26,000 people every year.) Since their widespread use by American forces in Viet Nam, cluster bombs had also been the target of similar US and international abolition campaigns because of their disproportionate impact on civilians. According to a Human Rights Watch estimate, there are 1.2 million unexploded bomblets in Iraq and Kuwait, left over from the US air campaign in 1991. In 1995 the United States prohibited the use of cluster bombs in Bosnia because of the danger to civilians. Yet, four years later, in 1999, US and allied NATO planes dropped more than 1,765 cluster bombs on Yugoslavia.[31]

The fact of using the cluster bombs themselves was not, however, what caused the greatest embarrassment. Instead, it was the bombs' links with the airdropped food packets. Those military meals, 960,000 of which were dropped by US planes, were single-day rations designed for one person with a "nutritionally depleted system." They included such well-known Afghan favorites as peanut butter; radio broadcasts stated they were full of nutritious Halal food, in keeping with Islamic dietary laws. On the outside of the packets, convenient labels read "This is a food gift from the people of the United States of America" in English, Spanish, and French, all very useful languages for the largely illiterate Afghan villagers. And the packets were wrapped in heavy duty, designed-to-survive-a-plane-crash indestructible bright yellow plastic. [32]

But even this was not the really embarrassing part.

The real embarrassment was that the food packs turned out to be the exact same bright yellow as the cluster bombs being dropped at the same time by other US planes. Radio broadcasts in Persian and Pashto announced:

> Attention people of Afghanistan! As you may have heard, the Partnership of Nations is dropping yellow Humanitarian Daily Rations… In areas far from where we are dropping food, we are dropping cluster bombs. Although it is unlikely, it is possible that not every bomb will explode on impact. These bombs are a yellow color… Please, please exercise caution when approaching unidentified yellow objects in areas that have been recently bombed."[33]

On November 1, the Pentagon announced that it would change the food packets to blue. "It is unfortunate that the cluster bombs—the unexploded ones—are the same color as the food packets," said General Richard Myers, chairman of the Joint Chiefs of Staff. He admitted the possibility that Afghan civilians might confuse a desperately anticipated meal with an unexploded cluster bomb. "Unfortunately, they get used to running to yellow," he said. He did not, however, know how long it would take to change the colors. "That, obviously, will take some time, because there are many in the pipeline." In a press conference with Secretary of Defense Rumsfeld, General Myers also announced that the US did not intend to suspend the use of cluster bombs.[34]

However cynical the varying propaganda exercises, growing unease about the reports of the attacks on civilian targets may also have been part of the Pentagon's decision to revise its handling of the press. Pressure from news agencies was already on the rise from the first weeks of the war; it was clear that the restrictions imposed on the media in

Afghanistan and elsewhere were far more severe even than the tight controls imposed during the Gulf War. Reporters were not allowed to travel with military units, were kept away from the fighting— sometimes even threatened at gunpoint by US soldiers when trying to get near the front— and were provided only the barest sanitized and vague information. Rumsfeld had set the terms for tight restrictions at the very beginning of the war, claiming it was required because of the nature of a war against terrorism; he had threatened legal action against Pentagon officials who might leak information.

By early December the pressure was high enough that the Pentagon felt compelled to apologize. Its December 6 letter to major news organizations noted:

> the last several days have revealed severe shortcomings in our preparedness to support news organizations in their efforts to cover US military operations in Afghanistan.... [W]e intend to provide maximum media coverage with minimal delay and hassle. That has not always been the case over the last few days, particularly with regard to the coverage of dead and wounded returning to the Forward Operating Base known as Rhino.[35]

The incident referred to involved the Pentagon's decision to confine in a warehouse the few reporters grudgingly allowed access to the front-line base, while three dead and nineteen wounded US troops were brought in to the base. The reporters were prevented from speaking with the survivors, their doctors, or their rescuers. It was presumably not a coincidence that the closely-held secret casualties were the result of a "friendly fire" incident.

Pentagon unease regarding public awareness—especially international awareness—of the civilian casualties was also part of the motivation for the decision to establish the short-lived Office of Strategic Influence. The OSI, a plan worthy of the best of Orwell and Dr. Strangelove combined, would have been officially responsible for feeding false information to the international press. Pentagon officials reported the OSI was given a large budget for propaganda operations, including such things as leaflet drops advertising rewards for Osama bin Laden's whereabouts, or radio scripts designed, according to Rumsfeld, "to counter the lies that this was a war against the Afghan people or a war against Muslims, which it wasn't."[36] Once news of the new office leaked to the press, it had little hope of survival. Even before its demise was officially announced, there was enough embarrassment in the Defense Department that major newspapers covering the story actually ran headlines such as the *New York Times'* priceless "New Agency Will Not Lie, Top Pentagon Officials Say."

The demise of the not-quite-comic OSI hardly meant the end to Pentagon propaganda efforts. Immediately after the launch of US air strikes in Afghanistan, the White House had initiated an office called the Coalition Information Center. It was designed to ensure that the key allies of the moment—then Britain and Pakistan—would be kept in line and on message with the US soundbite of the day. Directed by the White House, the CIC would coordinate the public output of every part of the Bush administration as well—the Pentagon, Justice Department, State, Treasury, Voice of America, and more. That office—and the work of coordinating global propaganda—remained untouched when OSI was brought down by the untimely leak.

THE OPPOSITION GROWS

Within the first month of the war, unease began to surface, some of it from countries whose own governments had been among the first and most eager to join the United States' crusade. Cracks appeared in the previously unmarred surface of international governmental compliance with US plans.

In Germany, for instance, despite Chancellor Schroeder's "support without reservation" and "unlimited solidarity" with Washington's war, the German public, parliament, and even the coalition government itself were filled with reservations and limitations. Certainly Schroeder's position reflected the undeniable public support that was emerging for ending Germany's post-war reticence regarding use of its troops abroad. The taboo had been broken in Kosovo and Serbia in 1999, when Germany sent bombers as part of NATO's war in Yugoslavia. Afghanistan, however, was much farther away, outside of Europe and beyond NATO, so the new expressions of public support this time around were significant. But they were not unanimous. In an early November poll, a bare 51-percent majority of the population agreed with Schroeder's "unlimited solidarity" with the US, and 58 percent of eastern Germans and 76 percent of supporters of the Greens were opposed.37

Four days after the United States' bombardment of Afghanistan began, Schroeder spoke in the parliament in defense of sending troops to join the US war. "The willingness to provide security through the military is an important declaration for Germany's allies," he said. It "means a new self-conception of German foreign policy.... Germany needs to show a new international responsibility." He even parroted some of President Bush's language: "We did not want this conflict.... But we will take on this battle against terrorism—and we will win it."38 Just a few weeks later, with the bombing at its height, Schroeder offered the Pentagon 3,900 German troops, including an elite special forces unit and 800 troops with the special Fuchs tanks specially configured for use in chemical warfare situations.39

Schroeder had made the troop commitment without, however, the parliamentary approval required for deploying German troops outside of NATO territory. And within Germany's parliament, support was far from unanimous. While the opposition Christian Democrats supported Schroeder's Social Democrats in joining the war, the junior coalition partner, the Greens, were divided. Shortly after the US bombing of Afghanistan began, Green parliamentary leader Claudia Roth had called for a bombing pause. Another Green party leader, Fritz Kuhn, said he preferred "critical solidarity" with the United States rather than Schroeder's version of "unlimited solidarity." In a bitter conference just before the bombing began, supporters of the government position beat out the historic pacifism of the Greens—but just barely.

When Schroeder took the deployment issue to parliament on November 16, he linked it to a vote of confidence for the governing coalition. It was a tactically shrewd, but thoroughly cynical move; there was no doubt that, with support from the opposition parties, Schroeder would easily have won a strong majority to endorse his deployment decision. He knew, though, that major Green opposition from within his government would weaken his coalition, so he forced the Greens to choose between staying in power and keeping their principles. He won the vote of confidence with 336 votes, just two more votes than the simple majority needed. Only a last-minute, save-the-coalition switch by four Green legislators who were opposed to the war but who wanted to keep the Greens in the government, pushed Schroeder over the edge to win what the *New York Times* called his "game of chicken" with his coalition partners.40 The only undivided parliamentary opposition to Germany's participation in the war came from the Party of Democratic Socialists, whose origins are in the former East German Communist Party.

THE WAR EXPANDS AGAINST…?

As the war in Afghanistan raged on, it became clear that the United States faced a much more difficult military task than many had anticipated. The analogies of the fighting, if not the politics, seemed closer to Viet Nam than to Iraq, with guerrilla forces capable of seizing and holding high ground, living in hidden caves, and melting away when large conventional attacks loomed. Military tactics shifted, with much greater on-the-ground roles for US special forces providing crucial backing for the anti-Taliban—but divided and ambiguously led—Northern Alliance forces. Within months, the initial goal of getting Osama bin Laden and/or the equally elusive Taliban leader Mullah Mohammed Omar had been largely replaced by the broader effort to bring down the Taliban and destroy the al-Qaeda network.

Destruction of the Taliban was largely achieved with the fall of Mazar-e-Sharif, the Taliban's strategic northern stronghold, on November 9, the fall of Kabul on the 13th, and the Taliban surrender of Kandahar in the south on December 6. US bombing attacks and ground operations shifted to the Tora Bora range, amid military and media speculation that Mullah Omar was being held somewhere near Kandahar and reports that US troops were close to capturing the al-Qaeda leader. "Allied Forces Say They've Cornered Osama bin Laden," a front-page *New York Times* headline enthusiastically trumpeted on December 14. What would replace the Taliban remained uncertain, as the UN-sponsored but largely US-controlled Bonn meeting of Afghan leaders and exiles struggled to agree on a governing structure throughout December.

By the end of the year, the war's focus on "getting" Mullah Omar and Osama bin Laden had faded from the public agenda. The nature of the military war in Afghanistan changed as intense bombing campaigns and US special forces operations took place in region after region where al-Qaeda or Taliban forces were thought to be taking refuge. Expansion of the war beyond Afghanistan took center stage in both American and international discussion. And the determination of the United States to move unilaterally regardless of international public opinion became even stronger. The Powell Doctrine of all-out—but rare—use of military force seemed to diminish in the face of a war which, regardless of failure to accomplish its initial bounty-hunter aims, seemed possible to "win" (however that might be defined in Afghanistan) with a lot of planes but only a few special operations forces armed with the highest high-tech equipment. The bodies were virtually all Afghans; US casualties were almost non-existent, and those few were mainly the result of accidents or "friendly fire" incidents.

Britain's *The Guardian's* correspondent in Washington, Julian Borger, described the increasing gap between Powell's viewpoint and that of the rest of the Bush administration.

> [Powell's] influence and his advocacy of multilateral solutions to US foreign policy challenges had appeared to be on the wane even before September 11, and he was emerging as a lone voice in an instinctively unilateralist administration. After the terrorist attacks, however, he seemed suddenly to be the indispensable man, as Washington scrambled to build coalitions to support its war on terrorism. Now the wheel has turned full circle. The Pentagon triumphed with only a few body bags. Grave warnings from the State Department that the war would trigger uprisings across the Islamic world have been proved groundless. The bombing of Afghanistan even continued through Ramadan without much controversy. America's sense of interdependence with the rest of the world, which seemed so profound on September 12, is now an uncomfortable memory in the Bush administration. As the defense secretary, Donald Rumsfeld, pointedly told a gathering of policy wonks in Washington, "The mission determines the coalition. The coalition must not determine the mission."[41]

By mid-November it was clear that US concerns about maintaining the coalition had faded. The military campaign was going very well, in terms of routing Taliban fighters out of mountain caves and hamlets and keeping US casualties to a bare minimum. The Pentagon clearly had little need for the coalition.

Ending weeks of speculation, the United States boycotted a November 11 United Nations conference on disarmament designed to encourage ratification of the 1996 Comprehensive Test Ban Treaty (CTBT). Although the United States was one of 161 countries that had signed the treaty during the Clinton years, the Bush administration made clear on taking office it had no intention of even submitting the treaty to the Senate for ratification, viewing it as a potential impediment to plans for a Star Wars-style missile shield. Since implementation of the treaty requires ratification by the 44 signatories considered capable of developing nuclear weapons, including, of course, the United States, Bush's rejection of ratification linked the US with the rest of the rejection front, including China, India, Pakistan, North Korea, and Israel.

Speaking at the opening session of the UN conference, Secretary General Kofi Annan told the delegates, "We have a precious but fleeting opportunity to render this troubled world a safer place, free of the threat of nuclear weapons. We must not let it pass."[42] Letting it pass, though, was precisely what the United States intended. Rejection of the CTBT represented a major victory for supporters of a long-standing Pentagon effort to end limits on the US nuclear arsenal. And in the Bush Junior era of increasing tension between State Department pragmatists who recognized the need at least to pretend to operate mulilaterally and defense hawks committed to untrammeled military unilateralism, it was a clear win for the Pentagon. By November 15, Bush and Russian President Putin concluded their talks on reducing nuclear stockpiles and arms control after Washington's abandonment of the ABM treaty; no agreement was reached. Other nations, especially in Europe, were outraged, but no international criticism seemed to reach Washington.

When the General Assembly's annual special session featuring heads of states convened weeks late at the UN's headquarters in New York, President Bush used the opportunity to say the long-expected magic words of US/Middle East diplomacy: he referred to "Palestine" living side-by-side with Israel in a two-state solution. The event was widely viewed as part of the United States' campaign to maintain support from the Arab world in the anti-terror coalition, but there was no corresponding shift in US actions toward Israel, such as revoking its veto in the Security Council to prevent international observers from being sent to the occupied territories. During the same UN session, despite urging from Saudi Arabia, Bush continued his symbolic affront to Palestinian leader Yasir Arafat, refusing to meet with him while both were at the UN in New York.

One item on the UN's agenda was the need for international peacekeeping forces in Kabul and elsewhere in Afghanistan. The need was clear; the security situation, not only in Kabul but throughout the rest of the country, remained tense. Warlordism had prevailed before Taliban rule suppressed it, and the phenomenon returned with a vengeance on the heels of the retreating Taliban troops. The Northern Alliance itself, a fractious grouping barely worthy of the term "alliance," was only one of several contending forces, and was itself led by figures long associated with some of the worst depredations of the pre-Taliban civil war in Afghanistan. Even before the fall of Kabul, reports surfaced regarding torture and execution of prisoners taken by the Northern Alliance as its troops moved into Taliban territory.

The *Times* described the Alliance soldiers "celebrat[ing] with executions" their move toward Kabul.

> Near an abandoned Taliban bunker, Northern Alliance soldiers dragged a wounded Taliban soldier out of a ditch today. As the terrified man begged for his life, the alliance soldiers pulled him to his feet. They searched him and emptied his pockets. Then, one soldier fired two bursts from his rifle into the man's chest. A second soldier beat the lifeless body with his rifle butt. A third repeatedly smashed a rocket-propelled-grenade launcher into the man's head.... Two hundred yards away, the soldiers who had minutes earlier shot the older man searched the possessions of a motionless Taliban soldier on the ground. After emptying his pockets, a soldier fired a burst from his rifle into the man. The soldiers moved on quickly, showing no emotion.... Looting was widespread. Alliance soldiers, who have received extensive backing from the United States, plundered Taliban bodies and bunkers, stealing shoes, bags of sugar, flashlights and anything else that they could find.[43]

By December 4, the Bonn meeting settled on the US-backed Hamid Karzai, a talented former Unocal consultant who spoke fluent English and charmed the international press, to lead the interim government. The plan was for the interim government to rule for six months, during which time plans for selecting a *loya jerga*, or grand council, would be finalized. The council would then rule for two years, in preparation for country-wide elections.

Karzai was a Pashtun, a crucial feature given the need to win over Pashtun sympathies because that ethnic group had provided the base of support to the Taliban. The largely Tajik-led and Uzbek- and Hazara-backed Northern Alliance was less than thrilled with Karzai's selection, given the primacy of those ethnic groups in routing the Taliban, but careful handouts of cabinet positions assuaged major potential opponents.

The United States, maintaining a major military assault throughout Afghanistan that eventually settled on the Shah-i-kot valley in the east, had no interest in helping to create, let alone providing troops for, an international peacekeeping mission. But neither did it want to empower the United Nations to do so. Instead, as the Taliban rout from Kabul came closer, Colin Powell called for the creation of a "coalition of the willing," to be led by Muslim states. He said that

Turkey, Bangladesh, and Indonesia had offered forces, saying it would be better to have Muslim countries "than one of the big-power nations coming in to do it."[44] His hesitation appeared, however, to include only the biggest of the "big-power" nations; the United States was too busy bombing Afghanistan to participate, but it would be wannabe "big-power" Britain who eventually won US approval to lead the force.

By early January a small British-led international peacekeeping force was in place in Kabul, but the rest of the country languished under increasingly active warlords. Karzai himself said that the delegations of local leaders he was receiving "keep asking for a larger number of international security forces... to be deployed in other provinces, other cities of Afghanistan. As need arises, we might ask for that." He did not, however, make that request, and he went out of his way to tell the press that he had not asked the United States to request a bombing halt. In so doing, he was giving additional credence to the Bush administration's special envoy, Karzai's former colleague at Unocal, Zalmay Khalilzad, who noted that even though the bombing was causing civilian casualties

> you have to weigh the risks of ending the conflict prematurely with the costs of continuing it. I have no doubt, on balance, that we will continue until we achieve our goals. ... We do not target civilians, but civilians unfortunately do get affected, even killed," Khalilzad went on. "War is a very imperfect business.[45]

Indeed.

It was not surprising that as Washington left behind even the pretense of commitment to an international coalition, in the rest of the world there was a parallel return to the unease with and even criticism of Washington's unilateralist trajectory. The criticism rose again as the United States made clear its intentions regarding the prisoners it was holding from the Afghan war.

By mid-December, the Bush administration had announced that it was sending the prisoners United States and allied Afghan forces had captured in Afghanistan to a prison camp at the US naval base in Guantanamo Bay, Cuba. It was, as Secretary of Defense Rumsfeld described it, "the least worst place" available. Other possibilities, including Guam (whose residents complained of security fears), and US ships at sea (deemed too small), were dismissed as inadequate. The key criteria was to ensure that the detainees remained under US jurisdiction, but to make sure they did not reach US territory.

That would have complicated the situation enormously because the United States Constitution guarantees everyone, even accused terrorists, inalienable rights including fair trials and the right to confront one's accusers, among others. Fundamentally, presence within US territory would give the detainees access to US courts, and that, according to Bush administration legal strategists, was to be avoided at all costs.

Then things got even worse. On January 18 Pentagon officials announced that those taken prisoner on the battlefields of Afghanistan would not be considered prisoners of war, thus subject to the protections of the Third Geneva Convention, which identifies the rights of prisoners of war. The Conventions, first signed in 1949, remain what the *New York Times* called "the world's most revered accords, garnering signatures of 189 countries, a number exceeded by only one treaty."[46] (Although the *Times* noted that that one treaty, the Convention on the Rights of the Child, had been signed by more countries than the Geneva Conventions, it did not mention that the United States, along with Somalia, were the only two countries who refused to ratify the children's protection statute.)

Rather than being deemed POWs, the prisoners would be held under a vague status of "unlawful combatant," assertedly undeserving of the Geneva Convention protections. Violating the United States Army's own rules, the non-POW status of the prisoners would be determined in advance for the entire group without separate hearings. The Army rules themselves "require that all persons taken into custody by US forces during a conflict be treated as prisoners of war, 'until some other status is determined by a competent tribunal.'" Clearly, as constitutional legal scholar Michael Ratner noted

> all combatants—Taliban, al-Qaeda and others—captured on the battlefield in Afghanistan must be treated at first as POWs, until their status can be decided by a competent tribunal. These fighters won't necessarily receive POW status. Some people have argued that al-Qaeda fighters may not qualify as POWs if they did not wear distinctive marks identifying them or obey the laws of war; others have argued similarly about the Taliban. But the facts are not established, which is why US Army regulations require a 'competent tribunal' to judge each individual case fairly. [47]

Even before the official denial of POW status, opposition was growing to the clear violation of the Geneva Convention's protections inherent in housing the prisoners in open-air cages, the reported instances of forcibly drugging prisoners during their flight to Cuba, and the use of blindfolds and shackles during the flight and within the high-security camp. The forced transfer of the prisoners from Afghanistan, where they were captured, to detention half a world away, itself raised questions of dubious legality. The administration at first refused to provide a list of the detainees, or even their countries of origin or citizenship. Human rights advocates, as well as many concerned with how captured US military personnel in conflicts around the world might be treated if captured by opponents, were outraged. Then administration spokespeople went further, announcing that the detainees would be tried in military tribunals which might be held in secret, from which they would have no right of appeal to a civilian court, in which they might be convicted by a less than unanimous decision, and in which they might be sentenced to death.

International opposition was on the rise. British Prime Minister Tony Blair was blasted by his own party as well as the opposition when he defended the military tribunals in parliamentary debate. UN High Commissioner for Human Rights and former President of Ireland, Mary Robinson, warned that "we risk the values that we have fought to preserve" if the prisoners were denied their rights as POWs under the Geneva Convention. The Paris-based International Federation of Human Rights Leagues, one of a number of human rights organizations that had supported or stood silent in response to the US anti-terror war, said that the treatment of prisoners without the required protections could turn into "a mere parody of justice."48

Things got worse for the United States position. Faced with the possibility of the death penalty for the prisoners, something the European Union and its member states had outlawed years before, Europe made clear it would go beyond trying to protect its own nationals who might get caught up in the Afghan war. European countries would also stick to their ordinary position of refusing to extradite to the United States anyone who might face the death penalty, accused terrorist or not. Europe was not about to abandon one of its most intensely felt principles. The European Union's commissioner for external affairs, Chris Patten, picked for the job on the heels of his applauded toughness in handling Hong Kong's transfer to China, said that mistreatment of the prisoners or the death penalty, would result in the United States "losing international support and losing the moral high ground."49

Even in Britain, Bush's best friend Blair was in trouble. "This is more than just the predictable left-wing crowd," said one knowledgeable British analyst. "Blair has a big problem at home if those Brits [in detention] are mistreated. He is genuinely worried about what Rumsfeld has in mind."50

Secretary of Defense Rumsfeld was unmoved. In an hour-long Pentagon news conference, he condemned critics of the prisoners' treatment as "isolated pockets of international hyperventilation."51 Answering British critics on the BBC, he said, "I do not feel even the slightest concern about their treatment. They are being treated vastly better than they treated anybody else."52 On another occasion, Rumsfeld dismissed the detainees' right to the protections of the Geneva Conventions on the grounds that "these people are committed terrorists," as if the Conventions were not a right but some kind of privilege available selectively only to Boy Scouts and Mother Teresa.53

NATO allies were concerned about Bush's rejection of Geneva Convention coverage for the detainees. Britain and France told US officials they might not turn over to the US Taliban or al-Qaeda fighters that their own troops might capture in Afghanistan. Shortly afterward, Spain announced it would not turn over to the US eight suspects it was holding whom the US wanted for September 11-related and other terrorism activity, because they could face the death penalty if convicted. Italy indicated it would withhold similar cooperation. These two examples are particularly significant because in 2001 and 2002, both Spain and Italy were led by rightists closer to the Bush administration than to most western European leaders.

Even the International Committee of the Red Cross, whose mandate includes monitoring implementation of the Geneva Conventions, issued a rare public criticism of the United States' approach, stating its views were "divergent" from those of Washington.54

Pressure grew even within the administration. First Powell alone, and then Powell and Rumsfeld in a rare display of unity, asked that a formal announcement be made that even if they were not designated as POWs, the prisoners would be covered by the Geneva Conventions. Within a couple of weeks, the Bush administration had shifted its position. Taliban prisoners would be officially covered by the Geneva Conventions according to the new regulations, but al-Qaeda prisoners would not. Even for the Taliban prisoners, however, it was an incomplete reversal. The new position provided the detainees with formal coverage by the Geneva Conventions but did not designate them POWs. That meant that certain additional rights, such as repatriation after the end of the conflict, might still be denied.

International reaction to the military tribunals went far beyond concern about the treatment of individual European citizens, even beyond the death penalty issue. The treatment of the Afghanistan detainees put back at center stage the long-simmering issue of American hypocrisy and double standards, especially on human rights issues. Since the Nuremberg trials and the 1948 Universal Declaration of Human Rights, the United States has taken the lead in holding other countries accountable for human rights violations. In international forums, and domestically as the basis for granting or denying eligibility for US aid, human rights was always an issue Washington used to hammer others; its own violations were ignored and would-be critics quickly slapped down.

Human rights abuses had, however, continued unabated in the United States, ranging in recent years from racial profiling, denial of voting rights to whole communities of people of color, inhumane conditions of imprisonment, racially-determined prison sentencing, all the way up to the death penalty. Every member state of the European Union has long rejected the death penalty as a holdover of more barbaric times, so for many Europeans state-sponsored executions in the United States remained the key indicator of US brutality and indifference to human life.

Before September 11, 2001, things had begun, just a little bit, to change. Fed up with growing US unilateralism in the first months of the new Bush administration and angry over the United States' cavalier abandonment of the ABM treaty, their boycott of the test ban treaty discussions, and their walking away from the Kyoto Protocol on global warming, Europe finally took the unprecedented step of voting the US off the UN's Human Rights Commission. It was a small, but important signal of growing anger.

After September 11, criticism of American unilateralism was cut short for a while. But then, Washington's dismissal of the United Nations, the global bullying of "you're either with us or with the terrorists," and the taking for granted of allies while belittling their offers of assistance, all had the effect of rebuilding the layers of anger.

Anthony Lewis, the former columnist for the *New York Times,* described how the issue of the Guantanamo prisoners "touches a profound resentment abroad at what many see as an American tendency to lecture others about international standards while refusing to comply" with those standards itself.[55]

The treatment of the detainees at Guantanamo brought an inevitable comparison between US human rights rhetoric and US human rights practice. Under the former, human rights served as a convenient diplostick to beat up competitors (like China), challengers (like Russia), or domestic political annoyances (like Cuba). Under the latter, human rights concerns were something to be waived in the interests of protecting long-standing human rights-violating allies (like Saudi Arabia, Israel, Colombia, or Turkey), or equally egregious but newfound post-September 11 friends (like Uzbekistan or Romania).

As the year drew to a close, foreign affairs analyst Fareed Zakaria noted:

> America leaves 2001 more powerful than at the start of the year. Within three months, from a standing start, it toppled a government 7,000 miles away in the most inhospitable terrain on earth—the mountains and caves of Afghanistan—defeating tribes that had beaten back the British and Soviet empires. And it did this largely from the air and suffering few casualties. No other country could do this. No other country in the history of the world has done this."[56]

It remained to be seen whether those "tribes that had beaten back the British and Soviet empires" were indeed defeated this time around. But the United States had certainly demonstrated to the world its capacity to do what no earlier empire had ever accomplished.

Soon after 2002 dawned, as international outrage grew regarding the treatment of the Guantanamo detainees, and as the ferocity of B-52 carpet-bombing gave way to broad-scale special forces operations in the Afghan mountains, the Philippines, and Yemen, US allies, both close and arms-length, began to voice new concerns regarding what would happen next. Iraq, and whether the US intended to justify a new war for "regime change" in Baghdad with the rhetoric of anti-terrorism, remained at the center of the debate. Uncertainty whether Washington would engage in serious consultation with its allies, or would continue to make its go-it-alone decisions, underlay the growing international unease.

SIX

EXPANSION: THE AXIS OF EVIL AND BEYOND

A s the first months of Bush's war ground on, inconclusively, and international opposition started to reemerge, cautiously, even some supporters of the war began to raise new questions. "Who hijacked our war?" asked a *San Francisco Chronicle* columnist.

> A month ago I knew why we were fighting. You knew why we were fighting.... So what happened to that gutsy war of bringing the World Trade Center and Pentagon killers to justice? Who hijacked that clear-eyed, all-American front of September-to-January and left our leaders mouthing this "axis of evil" line? Who hijacked the firefighters' war of righteous outrage and got us reciting this weird mantra about Iran, Iraq—and North Korea, of all places?[1]

In fact, of course, the war was never about bringing anyone to justice; it was about conquest and the mushrooming of US global power, all in the name of righteous vengeance. But certainly for the first couple of months, the White House and the Pentagon succeeded in keeping media and public attention on message with clearly identified targets: this war was about payback, about getting Osama bin Laden and Mullah Mohammed Omar. The F-16 noose was tightening around the targets, no bomber pilots were shot down, and New York City Mayor Rudy Giuliani was voted *Time* magazine Person of the Year. That was all before Bush's "axis of evil" speech.

Only after the collapse of Taliban control of Afghanistan's cities, the installation of a tenuous interim regime in Kabul, and the increasingly public rise in the number of US and allied casualties, did the Pentagon's spin control weaken, and the war began to look much murkier. The fighter jets and bombers went on bombing, but it was no longer so clear what their targets were. They were joined on the ground by Special Forces, and suddenly there were hundreds, and then thousands, of US ground troops leading allied (more or less) Afghan troops in a much messier kind of war, prowling for bad guys in the bombed-out caves of the Tora Bora Mountains. A US transport plane crashed in Pakistan, for reasons that remained obscure. The number of known civilian casualties in Afghanistan rose above the total number of victims of the World Trade Center (even if much of the American media did not report it). And none of those escalating numbers of dead, wounded, homeless, and desperate in Afghanistan seemed to include anyone named Osama bin Laden or Mohammed Omar.

On Christmas day of 2001, the commander of the United States campaign, General Tommy Franks, spoke to sailors aboard the aircraft carrier USS Theodore Roosevelt and said that US forces would continue to search the Tora Bora caves for Osama bin Laden "until we satisfy ourselves that he is there and dead."[2] Except it seemed he was neither there nor dead. By early January the Pentagon announced it would no longer provide regular updates on the manhunt. Bush himself pretty much stopped talking about the effort to find bin Laden and Omar. His staff insisted that the new, bin Laden-less language did not reflect a particular decision. As one of Bush's close aides admitted however, "there's not a lot to be gained by talking about them." Especially, the *New York Times* writer noted—deadpan—"when they appear to have escaped."[3]

The fact that the Pentagon had somehow lost track of the central targets of the manhunt that supposedly underlay the entire United States war in Afghanistan did not, however, bring about even a pause in the ferocity of the fighting. When the ground fighting in Tora Bora was finally deemed fruitless, attention shifted to the Shah-i-kot Mountains in eastern Afghanistan. But the bomber-assisted search-and-destroy missions failed to find any evidence that bin Laden or Mullah Omar were there either (or dead). By mid-April, Pentagon officials were sheepishly acknowledging that bin Laden had likely escaped the Tora Bora encirclement.

At first, the Pentagon claimed that half of the 600–700 Afghan guerrillas involved in the fighting of "Operation Anaconda" around Shah-i-kot had been killed. Later, when reports emerged of 8 American soldiers killed, over 30 injured, and a number of allied Afghan troops killed and injured, US officials also "spoke of 500–600 guerrillas killed, almost as many as had been earlier estimated to be involved in the whole conflict." The tallies of local Afghan commanders allied to the

US differed. By the time the fighting died down in mid-March, and US forces were calling their work a "mopping-up" operation,

> one leading Afghan commander took the view, however, that substantial numbers of guerrillas may have successfully moved out of the area. There were also reports that some of those captured during the fighting were actually local farmers rather than guerrillas from other parts of Afghanistan or from abroad.[4]

Reports also soon surfaced about large numbers of putatively pro-Taliban guerrillas streaming across the Afghan border into the Pashtun-dominated areas of Pakistan long outside the control of the central government in Islamabad.

The unmistakable implication was that the US war, that "clear-eyed all-American" war, was no longer so clear, and that victory was not necessarily anywhere in sight. As Paul Rogers, professor of peace studies at Bradford University described it, if those reports were right:

> [then] the war in Afghanistan stretches into the spring and summer... [and] then the rate at which President Bush's "war on terror"extends to other parts of the world may be slower than anticipated. This has considerable political implications as unease grows in Europe and outright opposition develops in the Middle East.

International support for the war remained intact, but as it became clear that Afghanistan was only stage one of a much larger war contemplated by Washington, concern grew and some of the more tentative supporters began to waffle. Soon, Bush's late-January "axis of evil" speech would reshape the trajectory of Washington's war from bounty-hunting in Afghanistan, to threatening invasions, overthrowing of governments, and military attacks in countries across the globe.

First, however, other international crises, in South Asia, in Latin America, and especially in the Middle East, crept closer to center stage. As the end of the year approached, it became more difficult for the Bush administration to convince the rest of the world that the attacks of September 11 themselves, horrific as they were for the United States, somehow had transformed the entire world.

ACROSS A NUCLEAR BORDER

In India, an armed attack on the parliament in New Delhi on December 13, in which fourteen people—five attackers and nine Indian security guards—were killed, quickly led to a major escalation in Indo-Pakistani tensions. After September 11, the two nuclear antagonists had reached a kind of uneasy truce in their conflict over disputed Kashmir. US efforts to recruit and keep both New Delhi and Islamabad within its anti-terrorism front had largely tamped down the simmering war.

But the relations were not problem-free. In the first day or two after the war in Afghanistan began, the Pakistani leader, General Pervez Musharraf, publicly claimed he received "definite assurances" that the military operation in Afghanistan would be short; Bush contradicted him directly, thus undermining Musharraf's effort to co-opt Pakistan's popular opposition to the war. Bush even used the growing Pakistani anger as the basis for asserting that only the United States really had the right to have an opinion. "I understand people's willingness to protest," he said in Washington after Musharraf's speech. "But they should not protest the decisions our coalition [sic] is making, because it is in the best interest of freedom and humankind."5 The Bush administration also added several Pakistan-based groups to its list of terrorist organizations. Nevertheless, Washington still welcomed Pakistan as a key "friend" in backing the war in Afghanistan, rewarding it for cooperation by lifting sanctions and dramatically raising the level of aid.

Regarding India, Bush envoys worried that rising anger in India toward Pakistan's sponsorship of military attacks across the Line of Control in Kashmir would lead to an escalation of the conflict, so they spent most of their time urging restraint. The Hindu nationalist leadership in India remained uneasy about the rapid warming of Washington's relations with Pakistan, and its mood softened only when the administration expressed its willingness to open long-blocked military equipment sales to India, with Secretary of Defense Rumsfeld announcing that his goal was "to strengthen the military-to-military and defense ties between our two countries, which I think are so important."6 In fact, on the same day as the attack on India's parliament, a US aircraft carrier arrived offshore near Bombay for unprecedented joint exercises with the Indian military.7

The underlying issues had not, however, disappeared, and the December 13 attack in New Delhi sent things into a new spiral of escalation. India was convinced that two Pakistan-based organizations, Lashkar-I-Taiba (Army of the Pious) and Jaish-I-Muhammad (Soldiers of Muhammad), were responsible for the attack on the Parliament and asked Pakistan to crack down on them. Pakistan proposed a joint investigation instead, which India rejected, and pressed India for evidence against the groups.

One week later India's government recalled its top envoy to Islamabad and suspended bus and train service between the two South Asian neighbors. It was the first time in 30 years that top diplomats were recalled, a crisis indicator not seen since the war of 1972 that led to the creation of Bangladesh. Both countries mobilized troops near the Line of Control, and the rhetoric grew increasingly heated. Announcing the diplomatic recall, India's deputy foreign minister, Omar Abdullah, said, "We are not going to sit back and let Pakistan walk all over us." He said his government faced "overwhelming public pressure to take hard action" against Pakistan. Claiming that India wanted to avoid all-out war because of the threat of nuclear escalation, he warned, "Every time there is an attack like this, the thread that holds us back gets thinner and thinner."[8]

Five days later, India test-fired the newest version of its nuclear-capable Agni II missile. Prime Minister Atal Bihari Vajpayee denied the test was designed as a political statement or aimed against Pakistan, but the foreign ministry in Islamabad called it provocative. "The test comes at a time of tensions when the Indian forces are massed on our borders," the statement said. "We hope the international community will take note of this Indian behavior which is prejudicial to the pursuit of stability in our region, especially during the current situation."

The United States responded with a mild rebuke; Secretary of State Powell said:

> I would just as soon they had not performed that test at this time of high tension, but I don't think it will inflame the situation particularly....I remain pleased that both sides are looking for a diplomatic solution, and we will continue to work with the Indian government and the Pakistani government to find a way forward that does not lead to a conflict on the subcontinent.[9]

India, which eagerly defines its relationship with the United States as a tie between the world's two largest democracies, has long harbored resentments about US double standards toward Pakistan. Washington's relations with Islamabad have been closer than those with India, as well as more strategic, harking back to the Cold War days when Pakistan was a pliant ally whose Inter-Services Intelligence agency served as a convenient conduit to funnel money to the anti-Soviet *mujahedeen* in

Afghanistan. In those days, India maintained close Soviet ties and was a leading proponent of non-alignment, viewed with suspicion in Washington. More recently, when General Musharraf seized power by overthrowing a more-or-less elected civilian president in Pakistan, Washington (and its own less-than-elected president) barely murmured a word of protest.

In the days following the December 13 attack in New Delhi, Indian politicians fumed over the United States demand that India be patient in responding to Pakistan, the perceived harborer of those responsible for the raid. As American bombs rained down on Afghanistan, it seemed reasonable for Indians to ask why only the US should be allowed to respond militarily to those who attack it. "I do not know how many people have been bombed in Afghanistan, and still the bombing continues," George Fernandes, India's defense minister, told the *Wall Street Journal.* But "when it happens to us, we are supposedly not giving chances to others."10

By January 11, the head of India's army declared directly that his military was completely ready for a large-scale conventional war with Pakistan, and he was prepared to use a nuclear strike if Pakistan used a nuclear weapon first. If attacked by a nuclear weapon, he said, "The perpetrator of that particular outrage shall be punished so severely that their continuation thereafter in any form of fray will be doubtful." Answering another question, he said, "We are ready for a second strike, yes," and, in case there was any doubt about the sufficiency of India's nuclear arsenal, "Take it from me, we have enough."11

Despite India's bluster, Washington's post-September 11 courting of allies in the region and its push for a narrow focus on the global war on terrorism served to shift a key aspect of the Indian-Pakistan conflict in Islamabad's favor. India, by far the larger, wealthier, and more powerful of the two countries, remained committed to keeping the Kashmir conflict regional, excluding outside powers. For Pakistan, for the opposite set of factors, internationalization of the conflict was a long-sought goal that had remained elusive. India, however reluctantly, had come closer to acquiescing to making international involvement in the conflict a reality when it threatened to ask the United Nations to intervene in forcing Pakistan to arrest members of the militant organizations India believed were behind the parliament attacks. But active engagement between the two junior members of the nuclear club and the United States effectively put Kashmir on the international agenda as well, regardless of India's wishes. New Delhi was not pleased. As the *Wall Street Journal* noted, "India may allow the US to play an informal mediating role behind the scenes, but not much more."[12]

When Secretary of State Colin Powell announced his intention to travel to the region in mid-January, his prime goals were to keep India cool and to keep Pakistan on board the global anti-terrorism campaign. In that context, neither unease about staying so chummy with a military-led government in Pakistan that had seized power from an elected leader, nor fears about the human rights violations and dangers to the Muslim community rampant in India's new "anti-terrorism" laws, were high on Washington's list of concerns. India and Pakistan could keep their nukes, face off against each other's armies in the Vale of Kashmir, and cut diplomatic or transportation ties—as long as they both accepted the primacy of their roles in the US war against terrorism.

Both Islamabad and New Delhi seemed quite willing to accede to the US demands. At the request of the United States, General Musharraf made a strategic decision to privilege his new alliance with the US over public opinion in Pakistan by declaring his intention to crack down on Muslim organizations that factions of his government had long tolerated and supported. Similarly, the usually bellicose Hindu nationalist government in India made the decision to prioritize its newly-cozy military ties with the United States, and answered Pakistan's assertions with a calm, measured response.

By January 13, on the eve of Secretary of State Powell's visit to the region, President Bush had called both General Musharraf and India's Prime Minister Atal Behari Vajpayee. He thanked them for their help in reducing tensions, and he declared that despite the hundreds of thousands of troops massed on the border, despite the nuclear arsenals, despite everything, the situation that Colin Powell a week early had identified as a crisis had now reached a "plateau."[13] Everything would be okay. Washington was in control.

How long that control would hold as tensions continued to escalate, remained uncertain. In April, US displeasure with General Musharraf mounted when the Pakistani leader refused to allow full-scale American military operations in the more-or-less lawless tribal areas of the country adjacent to the Afghan border. An early May attack in Indian-controlled Kashmir, which New Delhi blamed squarely on Pakistan, killed 30 Kashmiris. By mid-May the Indian leader would extol the hundreds of thousands of Indian troops arrayed along the Line of Control across from similar numbers of their Pakistani counterparts to be prepared for the ultimate sacrifice. And some US strategists returned to earlier assessments that the grave threat of new war loomed larger between the two nuclearized south Asian giants than anywhere else in the world. For Washington, however, the anti-terrorism war still trumped everything else.

GOING GLOBAL

In his January 2002 State of the Union address, Bush laid down new markers for friends and foes alike:

> America will always stand firm for the non-negotiable demands of human dignity: the rule of law; limits on the power of the state; respect for women; private property; free speech; equal justice; and religious tolerance. America will take the side of brave men and women who advocate these values around the world, including the Islamic world, because we have a greater objective than eliminating threats and containing resentment. We seek a just and peaceful world beyond the war on terror.

It was not clear how those ringing commitments would stand up against the realities of life in countries ruled by governments allied with the United States after September 11. Life under the absolute monarchies of the Middle East where the "rule of law" was limited to the whims of kings and princes? The torture awaiting Uzbek and other prisoners in countries where "religious tolerance" was limited to followers of the state-sanctioned version of religion?

Few pundits, however, and even fewer power-brokers felt the need to challenge the hypocrisy that underlay Bush's claims. Debate centered instead on modalities and approaches—how and when to attack Iraq, which newly-allied Central Asian countries would be most useful for US air bases, and which would be better for army troops.

In the meantime the Pentagon expanded its direct reach, increasing the number of soldiers deployed in the southern Philippines to "train" Filipino troops hunting down the Abu Sayyaf gang of thugs. It was a scenario eerily similar to early Viet Nam, where US troops ostensibly limited to "training" their Asian allies were soon participating in and then running the war. And some in Washington seemed to like it. "US Eyes

Military Assistance For Yemen: Counter-terrorism Aid to Philippines Cited as a Model," read a *Washington Post* February 28, 2002 headline.

Also in February, the *New York Times* and *Washington Post* ran parallel headlines announcing deployments of US troops to the former Soviet republic of Georgia. The Pentagon suddenly decided that the bandits of the Pankisi gorge in the Caucasus mountains in northeast Georgia had, like the 80–100 kidnapping criminals of Abu Sayyaf, suddenly taken on the global significance of being an arm of al-Qaeda and international terrorism. Those who knew the region well knew that the Pankisi valley area had been known as the Gorge of Bandits, or similar names, for over 400 years. Nevertheless, as a headline in London's *Guardian* sarcastically noted, "Bush Sends in 200 Crack Troops at a Cost of $64 Million to Tackle a Few Dozen Militants." US and some Georgian officials claimed:

> [A]mong the Chechen gangsters, drug dealers, kidnappers, refugees and fighters of the notoriously lawless gorge, there lurks a tight-knit network of Middle Eastern militants connected with Osama bin Laden. The Americans suspect that there are at least 10 and up to 80 militants from Saudi Arabia, Jordan and Algeria in the gorge. Some have been there for years, more have arrived since September 11.

Sending 200 troops and spending $64 million to go after perhaps fewer than a dozen "militants" seemed just about right in Washington.

Not everyone in the area was even convinced of the presence of the alleged terrorists. The *Guardian* article went on to note that European officials in Tbilisi agreed that Islamic missionaries from the Middle East were in the Pankisi villages, but were less convinced of the presence of al-Qaeda members.

> "There was a clear influx of what the locals call Wahhabites in 1999–2000," said one diplomat in Tbilisi, referring to missionaries propagating the austere Saudi Wahhabi Islamic credo. "They brought aid, charity, powerful communications equipment. They're very active, preaching, taking control of the population. They built a mosque. They're still there."
>
> "We haven't seen a single international terrorist here," said Altangil Turkiashvili, the Georgian regional police chief in the town of Akhmeta, 20 minutes south of Duisi. "But there are some Wahhabites."[14]

For the Bush administration there was clearly little or no difference.

SOUTH OF THE BORDER

In Latin America, governments already dependent on the support of the United States competed with each other to see which could take a stronger anti-terror stance. Barely a week after the September 11 attacks, the Organization of American States voted to activate its mutual defense treaty in response to the terrorist acts. The 1947 accord requires members to view an attack from outside the region as an attack on all member states and to participate in a joint defense. Just before September 11, Mexico had launched a nascent effort to scrap the treaty, with President Vicente Fox calling it "obsolete and useless." At that time the Bush administration had agreed on the need for modernizing the treaty, an anachronistic product of anti-communism and the Cold War, but after September 11 the United States reversed itself, calling for immediate activation of the Rio Treaty along with all other mutual defense treaties.

For a brief moment the Mexican government held to its position; Fox issued a statement saying the Rio Treaty was "not the ideal mechanism" to respond to the September 11 crisis. A day later, however, on the eve of the OAS vote, Mexican Foreign Minister Jorge Castaneda said he had told Secretary of State Powell that "if this [treaty] is important to you, despite the fact that we do not like it, and we do not think it is the proper way to go, we will go along with it."[15]

Nicaraguan political analyst Alejandro Bendaña, director of the Center for International Studies at the University of Nicaragua, noted:

> in Latin America, Governments are outdoing each other in out-condemning the September 11 events. In El Salvador and Nicaragua and Colombia, there is an opportunistic inclination on the part of governments to link their opposition movements, particularly ex-guerrilla organizations that are now legal parties (Nicaragua's FSLN and El Salvador's FMLN) or in Colombia the FARC and the ELN, with international terrorism.[16]

In fact, in the run-up to the fall 2001 election in Nicaragua, the United States backed a broad electoral campaign aimed at discrediting the opposition Sandinista Front (FSLN) party by highlighting its alleged links to "terrorist governments" in Libya, Cuba, and Iraq. One television ad by the governing and US-backed Liberal Party included a photo of Osama bin Laden among a rogues' gallery of ostensible enemies; a voice-over warned, "if they could vote in Nicaragua, they would vote for Daniel Ortega," the Sandinista candidate and former president.

Former Sandinista and Vice President of Nicaragua, Sergio Ramirez, warned of the consequences if the United States failed to heed the Cold War lessons of its Central American alliances as it cultivated new friends in Central Asia.

> The United States dealt with people like [Chilean junta leader General Augusto] Pinochet or [Nicaraguan dictator Anastasio] Somoza for reasons of national security and allowed them to do what they wanted because they were struggling against Communism. But that guarantee against Communism resulted in greater internal wars and deaths among our own people.[17]

In fact, there was little indication that the US had learned any of those lessons. Quite the contrary. In the wake of September 11, Guatemala's military sought increased aid for a presidential security team that has been linked to political assassinations and human rights abuses. El Salvador passed legislation consolidating presidential control over intelligence, and sent 400 troops and police to take over the international airport, barring 200 workers from their jobs. Honduras, long the base of operations for the anti-Sandinista Contra rebels backed by the United States, applied for tens of millions of dollars in additional US military aid.

The hypocrisy of US definitions of terrorism remained a hot topic in Nicaragua. Throughout the 1980s, the Contra guerrillas sought to destroy the Sandinista revolution that had toppled the Somoza dictatorship in that country and, in doing so, committed numerous terrorist acts against Nicaraguan civilians and the nation's economy. In 1986 the World Court ruled against the United States for Washington's role in the Contras' mining of Nicaragua's harbors. But the United States dismissed the ruling, claiming it did not recognize the Court's jurisdiction. Remembering those times, the Reverend Miguel d'Escoto, the former Sandinista foreign minister, noted, "If the US likes you, you're a freedom fighter. If they don't like you, you're a terrorist."[18]

Argentina's economic crisis exploded just before Christmas 2001. After four years of drastic recession and unemployment reaching almost twenty percent, the government's desperate decision to restrict bank withdrawals served as the last straw. Massive political demonstrations erupted, and the government cracked down. Within a few days, the government collapsed, and an interim government made the decision to default on Argentina's $155 billion foreign debt. It was the largest such public bankruptcy in history, but as Argentina quickly lost its privileged position as poster child for the International Monetary Fund (IMF)'s shrinking constellation of success stories, the new government had nothing to offer the population to mitigate the economic breakdown, and it soon collapsed.

Argentina's collapse was not directly related to the September 11 crisis or the United States' war on terrorism. Nevertheless, the Bush administration's virtually exclusive focus on its anti-terror crusade contributed to their hands-off approach to Argentina. According to Sarah Anderson, director of the Institute for Policy Studies' Global Economy Project:

> We can't assume that if 9/11 hadn't happened that the Bush administration would have rushed to Argentina's rescue. Bush Treasury officials were already pushing for an end to the massive bailouts that characterized the previous administration. On the other hand, it's clear that the terrorist attacks pushed Latin America off the radar screen. For example, in a February 1 address at the World Economic Forum, Colin Powell called for stronger measures to combat the "poverty, despair, and hopelessness" that he said were the breeding ground of terrorism. But not once did he mention the crisis then raging in Argentina.[19]

Among Latin American countries, the impact of Bush's global crusade emerged most directly in Colombia. That war-torn nation had become one of the top recipients of US support; US aid to Colombia was more than $1.5 million each day, making Colombia the third highest recipient of US aid (after Israel and Egypt). Under the terms of the Clinton administration's Plan Colombia, Washington officially limited the aid to Colombia's drug war, prohibiting assistance to the government's brutal counter-insurgency campaign against leftist guerrillas. In practice, though, the restrictions were often violated, and the government tried to erase any distinctions between the two parts of its military campaign.

After September 11, however, and in the context of a global crusade against terrorism, the Bush administration was able to go public in its endorsement of the Colombian government's military assault against the Revolutionary Armed Forces of Colombia, or FARC. On February 20, following a series of bad-faith actions on both sides, Colombian President Andres Pastrana ordered his troops to retake the swath of land that had been granted to the FARC years earlier as part of the on-going peace process. Senior US military officials accompanied Pastrana on his triumphal trip to San Vicente del Caguan, capital of the formerly rebel-held territory. "This is no mission, we're just here visiting," said Col. William Graves, commander of the US Military Group in Bogota, adding that he was invited by the Colombian army. "We're just here seeing what's going on."20

The government's effort to reoccupy the rebel zone came just as State Department officials were debating whether to recertify Colombia's human rights record as sufficiently acceptable to warrant additional aid. Human rights organizations and other critics urged de-certification because of the Colombian military's continuing links to right-wing paramilitary forces responsible for murdering thousands of civilians. The Bush administration, however, praised Pastrana's move against the FARC and it immediately announced it would begin sharing military intelligence and expedite shipping replacement parts for the about 50 military transport helicopters that were already in the aid pipeline.

At the same time, the Colombian president discussed with both Powell and Rumsfeld the possibility of changing the rules for the use of military aid. Pastrana wanted official approval to use the money and weapons provided by the United States for his war against the FARC, without having to claim it was part of an "anti-drug war." In late March, the Bush administration asked Congress for an increase in military aid to the Colombian government and a lifting of the earlier counter-narcotics and human-rights-based restrictions on that aid.

According to Sanho Tree, Colombia expert at the Institute for Policy Studies:

> When the escalation in US aid was debated under the Clinton administration, many of us in the NGO community warned of mission creep from counter-narcotics into counter-insurgency. That mission creep turned into mission gallop. The conjunction of the Bush administration's appointment of ultra-right wing Otto Reich as Assistant Secretary of State for Western Hemisphere Affairs with September 11th gave the administration a new way to push for military aid to Colombia—the global war on terror. By repeatedly denouncing the guerrillas as "narco-terrorists," the administration hoped to merge the drug-guerrilla-terror wars into one. 21

Few in Washington seemed prepared to question the Bush administration's request for increased aid to Colombia. In spring 2002, the House of Representatives passed an emergency supplemental spending bill that included a multi-million dollar appropriation for protection of the Colombian oil pipeline—effectively crossing the line into counterinsurgency. According to Adam Isacson of the Center for International Policy:

> [T]he administration is looking for a blank check, almost a Gulf of Tonkin resolution, allowing it to do whatever it wants in Colombia without any conditions or oversight. This is well beyond what Ronald Reagan enjoyed in El Salvador, where Congress limited the number of advisors and required at least the fiction of human rights improvements.[22]

Fiction was an apt description of Washington's next diplomatic debacle—as in "stranger than...." In mid-April, a group of army officers tossed the fiery, populist president of Venezuela, Hugo Chavez, out of office and into a prison cell. The events bore all the hallmarks of classic US-backed military coups common in Latin America a generation earlier. Chavez held a solid, mid-list position on Washington's enemies' roll, less for his domestic policies than for his friendship with Cuba's Fidel Castro and his determinedly normal ties with Iran, Iraq, and other states demonized by the United States. While Venezuela maintained a disciplined membership in OPEC (meaning it accepted the cartel's oil quotas), Caracas had long provided a significant amount of oil to the United States. The military's coup plotters, pro-business and opposed to Chavez's populist social welfare programs, included several who had had contact with Otto Reich, who had been the ambassador to Venezuela before joining the Bush State Department.

The White House had sneaked Reich into his position through a recess appointment made when it became clear the Cuban-American arch-enemy of the Cuban revolution would not win Senate approval. His reinstatement in government signalled a new level of activism in the region for the Bush administration. Reich had a long and devious history in the United States' propaganda efforts during the Contra wars in Central America throughout the 1980s. As assistant to Contra puppet-master Oliver North in the Reagan White House, Reich ran the semi-clandestine Office of Public Diplomacy, an unlamented propaganda precursor to the Pentagon's stillborn Office of Strategic Information twenty years later.

Reich had served as ambassador to Venezuela during the arms-for-hostages Iran-Contra scandal of the late 1980s. His tenure was a tendentious one, not least because of Venezuelan and other regional concerns regarding Reich's undisguised anti-Cuba agitation. Among other things, Reich paid particular attention to a Cuban-American terrorist jailed in Venezuela,Orlando Bosch, imprisoned for the 1976 sky-bombing of a Cubana Airlines passenger plane, killing all those aboard, including most of Cuba's national fencing team and an American peace activist.[23] Reich's notice paid off; during his term as ambassador, the Venezuelan government released Bosch from prison. Bosch immediately moved to the Miami area, where he was soon pardoned by Bush Senior. Bosch continued to brag about his terrorist activities, including the downing of the Cubana flight, to all who would listen. Somehow, however, even after September 11 brought terrorism and terrorists back to center stage, Bosch's exploits did not seem to attract attention from Miami's FBI field office.

In mid-March 2002, Otto Reich was sworn in to his top State Department position. At the ceremony, Reich intoned:

> Since September 11, exactly six months ago today, we are more determined and indivisible than at any time since World War II. Whether they are terrorists in Afghanistan or Colombia, or despots in Baghdad or Havana, anyone trying to impose tyranny over the mind of man has earned our eternal hostility.

Bringing down planes and killing everyone on board would seem to have been part of Reich's lexicon of those deserving "eternal hostility"—unless the plane and most of the passengers were Cuban. That small distinction would apparently make Orlando Bosch—if not necessarily a hero—then at least not a terrorist, in Otto Reich's eyes.

THE AXIS OF EVIL

The impact of Bush's anti-terrorism war in Latin America, despite the havoc it wreaked in Argentina and elsewhere, remained, in global terms, largely a sideshow. The big top remained centered around the Middle East/South and Central Asian arc of crisis. And while the main event, militarily, was under way in and around Afghanistan, Bush used his January 29, 2002 State of the Union address to redefine the war, its venue and its scope. In a speech linking Iran and Iraq, long and bitter enemies, and, inexplicably, North Korea, Bush pointed to an "axis of evil" whose targeting would reframe the nature and the parameters of his crusade far beyond the war of vengeance then in process against the Taliban and al-Qaeda in Afghanistan.

Going further, Bush held up the vision of "tens of thousands of trained terrorists [who] are still at large. These enemies view the entire world as a battlefield, and we must pursue them wherever they are." There are "thousands of dangerous killers, schooled in the methods of murder, often supported by outlaw regimes, [who] are now spread throughout the world like ticking time bombs," against whom "our war against terror is only beginning." It was a breathtaking assertion. In one speech the president charted a new, global war of unlimited scope against virtually infinite enemies across boundless venues.

In the immediate term, Bush's speech set out a new justification, beyond terrorism, for the United States waging a war. First priority remained the war against al-Qaeda—to "shut down terrorist camps, disrupt terrorist plans, and bring terrorists to justice [sic]." Bush carefully avoided speaking the name of Osama bin Laden, no doubt to avert reminders that al-Qaeda's leader remained alive and busy, at least in video production, his whereabouts unknown to Pentagon targeters or to Washington's bounty-hunting Afghan allies.

There was little question that Bush's State of the Union address was also crafted to shape a long-term vision of the war that had been set in motion within hours of the September 11 attacks and articulated in the president's September 20 speech four months earlier. Under ordinary circumstances, Bush would have faced a daunting challenge. His first address to the joint houses of Congress a year earlier, little more than a month into his presidency, reflected an almost triumphant response to positive conditions his administration had had little hand in fashioning. On February 27, 2001 he exulted that the US could boast of "blessings: a balanced budget, big surpluses, a military that is second to none, a country at peace, technology that is revolutionizing the world."

Facing the overcrowded chamber on January 29, 2002, those "blessings" were largely out of reach. The budget was no longer balanced; big surpluses had disappeared; the military was deployed and fighting in venues scattered around the world, despite the fact that the key targets of the military campaign were still alive and at large; the country faced a war without borders and without end; and four of the products of the US technological revolution had been seized and turned into weapons of mass terror turned against American targets.

But these were not ordinary times. Despite the recession, which had officially socked in by the spring of 2001, despite the government's inability to find the perpetrator behind the anthrax attacks of the fall, despite the Pentagon's failure to capture bin Laden or Mullah Omar, Americans remained in the president's corner. White House approval ratings had never been higher. And Bush knew that maintaining a high level of fear among Americans would tamp down any nascent nay-saying that might begin to question the legitimacy of a war without end against enemies without names.

Identifying a second military-strategic priority, beyond the immediate anti-terrorism war, therefore had a domestic political component as compelling as the global assertion of strategic reach that lay at the heart of Bush-Cheney-Rumsfeld ideology. It might have been enough to target Iraq alone. Baghdad had long been at the center of the right wing's militarist aspirations, and the ideologues in the Bush camp, Cheney, Rumsfeld, and Richard Perle at the Pentagon's Defense Policy Board, and especially Rumsfeld's deputy Paul Wolfowitz, carried decade-long portfolios as advocates of military strikes against Iraq. The demonization of Saddam Hussein that marked the build-up of domestic support for Operation Desert Storm in 1990–91 (designed to overcome the legacy of a decade-long alliance between the US and the Baghdad regime) had long since spilled over to a popular demonization of Iraqis and Iraq itself.

The Evil Axis countries were not necessarily carrying out terrorist acts, but they were "regimes that sponsor terror," who "seek chemical, biological or nuclear weapons," and whom the United States must keep "from threatening the United States and the world." In Bush's lexicon, they were:

> arming to threaten the peace of the world. By seeking weapons of mass destruction, these regimes pose a grave and growing danger. They could provide these arms to terrorists, giving them the means to match their hatred. They could attack our allies or attempt to blackmail the United States. In any of these cases, the price of indifference would be catastrophic.

There was not, we were told, any new evidence of such potential attacks. In fact, to the contrary, "some of these regimes have been pretty quiet since September the 11." The link with the anti-terrorism framework of Bush's expanding war was a tenuous one. Even Iraq, by far the most demonized, and the "Axis country" most directly threatened with US invasion or military assault, was credited with only a paltry lexicon of terrorist acts even by the US State Department's own reckoning. Its April 2001 Report on Global Terrorism acknowledged that Iraq "has not attempted an anti-Western attack since its failed plot to assassinate former President Bush in 1993 in Kuwait." Given the Bush administration's focus on Iraq as a danger to the US and its allies, that acknowledgement clearly should have undermined the credibility of the claimed Iraqi link with terrorism. Targeted political assassination is hardly considered a legal means of political discourse (except by Israel), but Iraq's bungled assassination attempt hardly stands alone. US policymakers also apparently decided to abandon their earlier prohibitions against targeted murders, with the CIA's acknowledged but failed May 6, 2002 effort to assassinate Washington's once-favorite Afghan *mujahedeen,* Gulbaddin Hekmatyar, in a missile strike outside of Kabul.24

Whatever the crimes of the Iraqi regime against its own population, and they are legion, the State Department's charges of those Iraqi actions simply do not fulfill the United States' own definition of international terrorism. Ambassador Francis X. Taylor, coordinator for counter-terrorism in the State Department, identifies terrorism as "when I see innocent civilians being killed indiscriminately for political reasons." Iraq, he said, "has not renounced terrorism as a policy and that's why they're still on the [State Dept. anti-terrorism] list."25

The problem was that "non-renunciation" seemed to be all that the United States had. Even the State Department's own description of Iraqi terrorist activity offered no actual international examples of "innocent civilians being killed indiscriminately for political reasons" by Iraq, only unconfirmed cases of Baghdad's "anti-dissident activity overseas." The only evidence of an Iraqi threat to the "US Government-funded Radio Free Europe/Radio Liberty (RFE/RL), which produces Radio Free Iraq programs and employs expatriate journalists," for instance, was the fact that police in Prague provide protection to its offices.

In another example, the State Department report described the hijacking of a Saudi Arabian Airlines flight to Baghdad in 2000, admitting that "the origins of... the hijacking were unclear." The report acknowledged that Iraq promptly returned the passengers and plane to Saudi Arabia, but it went on to contend that the Iraqi regime's decision to rebuff a Saudi request for the extradition of the hijackers constituted an example of terrorism. The report stated:

[T]he Iraqi regime readily exploited these terrorist acts to further its policy objectives. Disregarding its obligations under international law, the regime granted political asylum to the hijackers and gave them ample opportunity to ventilate in the Iraqi Government-controlled and international media their criticisms of alleged abuses by the Saudi Arabian Government, echoing an Iraqi propaganda theme.

Given the legacy of the United States' welcome of Orlando Bosch, proud murderer of the Air Cubana passengers blown up in-flight in 1976, Washington's claim that Iraq's hijacker welcome not only violated international obligations but itself represented a kind of terrorism, was a particularly egregious example of American hypocrisy.

In fact, the United States never quite succeeded in making the terrorism link work as the justification for moving toward war against Iraq. Although the legacy of demonization of Iraq was strong enough that moves toward war would be largely accepted, if not welcomed, by most Americans, enormous efforts were expended to find and prove a link between Baghdad and the attacks of September 11. The efforts failed, however; despite work by legions of US and Israeli intelligence officials, no connections could be found.

A serious problem for those working so diligently to find an Iraq-al-Qaeda link, was the inconveniently well-known fact of long-standing antagonism between Osama bin Laden and Saddam Hussein. According to the *New York Times:*

[S]hortly after Iraqi forces invaded Kuwait in 1990, Osama bin Laden approached Prince Sultan bin Abdelaziz al-Saud, the Saudi defense minister, with an unusual proposition.... Arriving with maps and many diagrams, Mr. bin Laden told Prince Sultan that the kingdom could avoid the indignity of allowing an army of American unbelievers to enter the kingdom to repel Iraq from Kuwait. He could lead the fight himself, he said, at the head of a group of former mujahedeen that he said could number 100,000 men.[26]

Even if that claim were inflated, bin Laden's hostility toward the ruthlessly secular Iraq remained evident.

Much television time and many newspaper column inches were expended analyzing an alleged meeting between one of the lead September 11 hijackers, Mohammad Atta, and an Iraqi intelligence official in Prague in the summer of 2001. First, Czech officials reminded the press and eager government officials that they had no evidence of what was discussed, that it may well have been a discussion of an attack on Radio Free Europe/Radio Liberty, but there was no evidence of discussion of an attack on the United States. Then, further infuriating the voracious audiences in the US, Czech officials backtracked even further, casting doubt on whether such a meeting had ever occurred at all.

By May, the Bush administration itself had to admit they had no evidence to support the notion of a link between Saddam Hussein and the September 11 attacks. Even the FBI and CIA conceded they had no evidence of any Prague meeting between Mohammad Atta and any Iraqi intelligence official.

It was not a good day for the blame-Iraq-for-everything crowd.

That group had not, however, been gunning for Saddam Hussein for over a decade, both in and out of office, with nothing to show for it. They had been urging, not to say demanding, a military strike to overthrow the Iraqi leader since the end of Desert Storm in 1991. September 11 was simply one more in the lexicon of reasons, and Bush's "Axis of Evil" speech in January reflected the multiplicity of their reasons and rationales.

Bush admitted that Iraq and its evil partners "have been pretty quiet since September the 11." Going to war against Iraq was still high on the president's things-to-do list though, so a rationale beyond terrorism would have to be found. Luckily for Bush's Iraq ideologues, that part was easy. The mantra of "weapons of mass destruction" remained fixed, a long-standing and convenient focal point for anti-Iraq mobilization. Thus Bush's State of the Union address returned to the threat of Baghdad and its WMD programs, with just the added fillip of potential/possible/hypothetical links to future/prospective/maybe terrorists.

Bush went on to say, "Iraq continues to flaunt its hostility toward America and to support terror." Okay, so the State Department could not come up with much evidence of any actual terrorism that Iraq actually supported, and the president did not cite any details, but hopefully no one noticed. Then came, the "Iraqi regime has plotted to develop anthrax, and nerve gas, and nuclear weapons for over a decade." Well, Baghdad hardly had to "plot" to develop anthrax; the highest-quality seed stock for anthrax germs (along with those for botulism, e-coli, and a host of other deadly diseases) were shipped to Iraq by a US company, legally, under official US Department of Commerce license, throughout the 1980s. According to the Senate

Banking Sub-Committee Report of 1994, shipments of biological germ stock continued well into 1989—despite US knowledge of Iraq's use of internationally-banned poison gas weapons against Iranian troops and Kurdish civilians a year earlier.

Which brings us to Bush's next line. "This is a regime that has already used poison gas to murder thousands of its own citizens— leaving the bodies of mothers huddled over their dead children." Absolutely right. Baghdad's Anfal campaign against Iraqi Kurds, including the use of internationally-outlawed poison gas, was brutal and murderous (and was exacerbated by Baghdad's battle against Iranian troops operating in Iraqi Kurdistan). Significantly however, the Anfal campaign and Iraq's use of poison gas weapons all took place while Baghdad, under Saddam Hussein, was a close ally of the US, which viewed Iraq's war against Iran as a useful check on the rising power of the then-new Islamic Republic of Ayatollah Khomeini. As was the case in so many other instances of United States-backed dictators brutally repressing their own people, despite occasional voices of concern in Congress, official Washington did nothing to stop the atrocities of its oil-rich ally in Baghdad. The Commerce Department continued to issue licenses authorizing the American Type Culture Collection, an internationally known germ distribution center outside of Washington, to send high-quality germs to Iraq.

Iraq's chemical weapons materials came largely from Germany and other European countries. But the United States did have some direct involvement in Iraqi chemical weapons attacks. A February 2002 *Newsweek* article featured interviews with five former Iraqi generals whom various US officials were promoting as the potential leadership of Iraq after a US-backed attack had successfully overthrown Saddam Hussein. The article said:

> One general interviewed by *Newsweek* made no bones about his use of chemical weapons. General al-Shamari commanded nine divisions in the Iran-Iraq War before he defected in 1986. (Now 56, he runs a small restaurant in northern Virginia.) He says he carried out Saddam's orders to gas the Iranians, firing chemical weapons from howitzers. The impact was devastating. "It created a state of chaos," said al-Shamari. Given that he was miles from the target, how did he know that? From US intelligence. "We got information from American satellites," said al-Shamari. (A former CIA official confirmed that the United States, which was backing Iraq against Iran, provided intelligence to the Iraqis. "Included in that, I'm

sure, would have been some feedback, intended or unintended, to the
Iraqis on their use of chemical warfare," said the official.[27]

Next in Bush's speech came, "This is a regime that agreed to
international inspections—then kicked out the inspectors. This is a
regime that has something to hide from the civilized world."
UNSCOM, the UN Special Commission or arms inspectors did
indeed leave Iraq in December of 1998. But they were not "kicked
out." Rather, recall that UNSCOM officials were notified by the
Clinton administration that massive bombing, what would be called
Operation Desert Fox, was about to be launched over Baghdad and
elsewhere in Iraq. The inspectors left the country for their own safety.

Once the bombing ended, it surprised no one that Iraq refused to
allow the UN inspectors (who had admitted sharing intelligence
information with US and Israeli spy agencies) to return, but that is a
very different story than kicking them out. As for having "something
to hide," Iraq may or may not have viable scraps of chemical or
biological weapons material left after UNSCOM's years of inspections,
but it is highly questionable whether any viable weapons programs
remain. As early as February 1998, UNSCOM chief Richard Butler
had already said that his team was satisfied there was no longer any
nuclear or long-range missile capability in Iraq, and that UNSCOM
was "very close" to completing the chemical and biological phases.[28]

Washington, however, knew all about biological weapons and having
something to hide. In November 2001 Washington walked away from
multilateral negotiations over implementation of the germ warfare
treaty. The reason was its refusal to accept exactly the same kind of
international inspections of American pharmaceutical and
biotechnology facilities as those whose rejection by Iraq brought threats
of a new war.

Since the inspectors left at the end of 1998, there has been little
credible new information regarding Iraq's current WMD capacity. A
small stream of defectors, understandably eager to sell their stories to
western asylum officials and increase their value to western intelligence
agencies, continued to emerge with grandiose tales of still ongoing
WMD programs. But without inspectors on the ground, it remained
impossible to verify their claims. The defectors' stories validated only
the urgency of getting UN inspectors back into Iraq, and into countries
and across borders throughout the arms-glutted region. A vital missed

opportunity—in what passed for diplomacy regarding Iraq in the decade or more since the Gulf War—was the lack of any serious effort to implement Article 14 of Security Council Resolution 687, which originally imposed sanctions. It identified the resolution's efforts to disarm Iraq's WMD programs as "steps toward the goal of establishing in the Middle East a zone free from weapons of mass destruction and all missiles for their delivery and the objective of a global ban on chemical weapons." Given the responsibility of the United States for the massive arms glut across the Middle East (Saudi Arabia alone is by far the biggest purchaser of US military hardware), it is perhaps not surprising that Article 14 is not the part of the sanctions resolution that US officials most like to talk about.

The intensity of anti-Iraq sentiment in the United States meant that historical accuracy was never high on the public or media agendas when it came to responding to announced or implicit US threats. So no one examined too closely or delved too deeply into what was real and what was propaganda regarding the relevance of attacking Iraq in a so-called "anti-terrorism" war. In fact, Bush administration strategy for going to war against Iraq had as much, perhaps even more, to do with domestic political imperatives—finishing Bush Senior's unfinished war and placating the Republican right-wing—as with consolidating US control over oil and the restive Middle East. September 11 had done nothing to change that.

One of the top cheerleaders for a military strike against Iraq, longtime neo-conservative William Kristol of the hawkish Project for the New American Century, testified before the Senate Foreign Relations Committee on February 7, 2002. "Removing Saddam Hussein and his henchmen from power," he said, "presents a genuine opportunity—one President Bush sees clearly—to transform the political landscape of the Middle East." Leaving aside the question of whether the president of an administration sharply divided over the efficacy if not the legitimacy of going after a foreign head of state actually did see that clearly, one must be tempted to ask of Kristol, Who appointed you God? Or, at least, who appointed you, a non-official American pundit, to oversee the transformation of a political landscape half a world away?

US military unilateralism, no longer the sole provenance of official power centers, was indeed running amok.

ABM—LITE

This moment was also the right time for Washington to consolidate its new relationship with Russia. After being slapped down by Bush when Bush announced his unilateral abandonment of the Anti-Ballistic Missile Treaty, Putin said that, while the ABM treaty was a cornerstone of international security, its abandonment "does not threaten [Russia's] national security." [29] Bush was now ready to reorchestrate strategic ties with the no-longer-a-superpower-challenger in Moscow.

In May 2002 Bush and Putin agreed to sign a new treaty calling for significant reductions in each side's strategic nuclear arsenal. They would reduce each side's 6,000 or so strategic nukes by about two-thirds. At the same time, NATO welcomed Russia into a new structure, the NATO-Russian Council, in which Moscow would participate as a full and equal member.

As Andreas Zumach noted in Berlin's *die Tageszeitung,* "during the time of the Cold War such agreements would have been celebrated as 'breakthroughs for disarmament,' and as a step toward détente which would benefit the whole world. But today no such thing can be said. Quite the opposite." The problem was not only that the agreement kept in place more than 2,000 nuclear weapons on each side, far more than would be needed to wipe out virtually the entire world. More than that, however, its price was what Zumach called "the elimination of the last Russian resistance to the strategic military projects of the Bush administration." [30]

Putin meekly accepted the Bush administration's missile defense plan, as well as the Pentagon's pipe-dreams of taking advantage of the end of the ABM treaty to create new "tactical" nuclear weapons. Russia also accepted the United States demand that the nuclear reductions come in the form of storing decommissioned weapons, not destroying them. Thus Washington, with its vastly superior military infrastructure, could keep all the warheads it wanted, claiming to use them only for spare parts, testing, or whatever, and still get credit for denuclearization, while Russia's impoverished military would face the bitter choice of either inadequate storage, or expensive and strategically inequitable destruction of their weapon stock. The only sop to Russian demands was the United States agreement that the accord would take the form of a treaty, rather than a mere handshake between the two leaders as Bush had urged.

Similarly, the NATO-Russian agreement transformed the relationship between the Cold War enemies into one of polite subordination. The form of a Council in which Moscow had an equal voice would obscure the reality of NATO's expansion to the very border of Russia and its consolidation within broader foreign policy goals of the United States. Certainly the trajectory was already under way prior to September 11, but there is little question that the aftermath of those attacks, including renewed US interest in oil and gas, air space, and military personnel and bases in Georgia and the former Soviet Central Asian republics that Russia had until then counted within its sphere of influence, reshaped the US-Russian relationship to Moscow's detriment.

On the eve of Bush's May 2002 Moscow summit with Putin, Stanford University professor Michael McFaul noted, "In many ways, the big issues of US-Russia relations and Russia's relations with the West have been decided."[31] Particularly after September 11, those issues were decided solely in Washington's favor.

The withdrawal of Russia's pre-September 11 veto threat over Iraq sanctions in the Security Council provided another indicator of the profound imbalance in the new relationship. Public opposition to a new US war against Iraq remained unchanged throughout the world—in Russia, in Europe, in the Arab world, and elsewhere. Bush's "axis of evil" speech had fallen on deaf ears outside US borders. Off the record, Russian diplomats, like their European and Arab counterparts, scorned Washington's claimed justifications for attacking Iraq, but when forced to choose between long-standing oil and financial ties to Iraq, and maintaining crucial relations with the world's sole superpower on an issue of self-defined vital importance to Washington, Moscow faced an easy decision. If Washington chose, against virtually unanimous international public and official opposition, to wage a new war against Iraq, Russia was not likely to stand in its way.

WAGGING THE DOG: IRAQ IN US POLITICAL LIFE

Public calls to expand the war to Iraq continued to escalate. Official statements reiterated official Washington's belief that, just as there was no need for UN authorization for a military response to the September 11 attacks, any future attack on Iraq would be orchestrated unilaterally too, sidelining the global organization.

In mid-December, Congress voted 393 to 12 to brand any Iraqi rejection of new arms inspectors a "mounting threat" to US security, thus ratcheting up the call for a new war. Many in Congress, as well as other policymakers and pundits, by then accepted as gospel the once marginalized claim that because of September 11, Iraq should be attacked—despite the absence of any Iraqi link to September 11. Why? Because Iraq was a state with some assumed future unconventional weapons potential, which could provide WMD material to some unknown and unidentified terrorists at some point in the unspecified future. (Presuming, that is, that if Osama bin Laden were the chosen recipient, he had by that time repudiated his earlier eagerness to send 100,000 troops to war *against* Iraq.)

Throughout the post-September 11 period, what remained unchanged in US-Iraq policy was the maintaining of crippling economic sanctions that had already been responsible for the deaths of hundreds of thousands of Iraqis, most of them children and others of the most vulnerable sectors. In the two years prior to September 11, 2001, the direct cause of death among Iraqi children had shifted—no longer were children dying of starvation; instead their deaths came from easily treatable diseases carried by unclean water, diseases which were not treated simply because there was not sufficient medicine or hospital equipment to do so.

Under the US-imposed sanctions regime, Iraq was allowed to export oil. The money for the oil, however, was deposited in a UN-controlled escrow account in Paris rather than being sent directly to Iraq. When Iraq wanted to purchase hospital equipment or other supplies, the proposed contract was sent to the UN's "661 Committee," so named for the Security Council resolution that created it, which then examined the contract and either approved it or put it "on hold." As a member of the committee, the United States had veto power over every contract, and by the spring of 2002 over $5 billion worth of contracts were being held up, almost all of them by US decision.

The United States did not, of course, veto all contracts. Less than three months before September 11, the *Washington Post* reported that during Vice President Cheney's years as the chairman and CEO of the Halliburton oil services company, the corporation "held stakes in two firms that signed contracts to sell more than $73 million in oil production equipment and spare parts to Iraq." During the 2000 presidential campaign, Cheney acknowledged that Halliburton

> did business with Libya and Iran through foreign subsidiaries. But he insisted that he had imposed a "firm policy" against trading with Iraq. "Iraq's different," he said.... Two former senior executives of the Halliburton subsidiaries say that, as far as they knew, there was no policy against doing business with Iraq. One of the executives also says that although he never spoke directly to Cheney about the Iraqi contracts, he is certain Cheney knew about them.[32]

Selling oil equipment to Iraq may have helped make Cheney rich, but the UN sanctions regime under which that equipment was sold resulted in a completely distorted Iraqi economy. In the first five years of the oil-for-food program's operation, beginning in March 1997, the escrow account took in over $52 billion of oil revenue. Of that, about $33 billion was contracted for food, medicine, and other supplies (including some oil equipment), but only $21 billion worth of goods actually arrived in Iraq.[33] The $5 billion on hold represents more than ten percent of the entire available income. (Not all the oil-for-food income is available to Iraq at all. The money arriving in the Paris account is only what is left over after 25 percent off the top is deducted to pay compensation to Kuwait and other victims of Iraq's invasion of Kuwait, and an additional four percent or so is siphoned off to pay the costs of the UN programs in Iraq.)

With a population of 22 million people, that oil-for-food system brought in somewhat less than $200 per Iraqi per year. With such economic straits, there were inevitably insufficient funds to rebuild and rehabilitate Iraq's bombed-out water treatment system. Even before September 11, public awareness regarding the impact of sanctions had continued to rise in the United States, even more so in Europe, and with growing outrage across the Middle East. In response, Colin Powell made the replacement of the existing sanctions with a new "smart sanctions" arrangement a cornerstone of his State Department's approach to Iraq policy. Throughout the first months of the Bush administration in 2001, a new US-proposed sanctions arrangement was under discussion in the Security Council. Officially the proposal was designed to loosen some restrictions on importing food and other goods, while tightening the semi-clandestine oil shipments out and consumer goods in over Iraq's long and porous borders.

In fact, it was a spin-driven proposal, intended primarily as a public relations ploy to undercut growing regional concern about the dire conditions facing Iraqi civilians under sanctions. As originally endorsed by Powell, the new arrangement would only have tinkered with the sanctions' impact, not reversed them. Bringing in additional consumer goods, the linchpin of Washington's so-called "smart sanctions" proposals, simply did not have the capacity to change substantially life in Iraq. After September 11, however, it became clear that Washington no longer felt compelled to respond even with spin to global concerns regarding the impact of sanctions.

The UN Security Council decision of early November reflected this new post-September 11 reality. During the earlier negotiations, Russia (which was owed billions in Iraqi debts) had indicated it believed it was time to lift the economic sanctions. Moscow wanted to allow the reconstruction of Iraq's economy, in the context of the return of UN weapons inspectors to Iraq. But after September 11, it was clear Russia was not prepared to challenge US insistence on maintaining sanctions.

After the November decision, the United States took off the table the original "smart sanctions" proposal that Russia had threatened back in the spring to veto. Looking for a way to link a revised sanctions approach with gaining regional support for a military build-up against Iraq, Washington sent envoys to Iraq's neighbors to test the waters. With Syria on the Security Council, Washington had to tread lightly. It soon became clear though that if the border-tightening efforts were dispensed with, there would be little regional opposition, except in public opinion-driven statements, to continuing some kind of revised economic sanctions. Negotiations turned on the technical question of whether the new arrangement would feature a list of potentially dual-use items requiring special inspection while everything not on the list would be approved automatically (the Russian approach), or a list of limited pre-approved goods to be allowed in, with anything not on the pre-approved list subject to the 661 Committee's inspection and potential veto (Washington's preference).

On May 14 the Council voted for Resolution 1409, imposing the new sanctions arrangements with the Goods Review List at its center. Like its "smart" predecessor, it was largely crafted for spin purposes. Under the new arrangement, contracts for anything on the list of several thousand items, supposedly only those having "dual use" military value, would automatically still go to the UN's 661 Committee. Anything not on the list would still have to be approved, but it would be done by UN secretariat officials, with the assumption that everything would be allowed in. One small result might be that contracts for basic food, some medicines, and some other consumer goods might get approved and into Iraq more easily and in somewhat larger quantities. Of course the needs-special-approval list still included such basic items as cargo trucks and fast computers for inventory control.

The far more serious problem that 1409 did not address was that the Iraqi economy would remain completely stalled and under UN control with all the restrictions on investments. No major investment in new oil production was allowed. Even if it were, no oil company was going to risk large-scale (read: multi-billion dollar) investment in oil futures knowing that at any moment the 661 Committee might reverse itself and suddenly deny said oil company the right to repatriate its profits.

The continuing impact of Iraq's shattered economy on the population as a whole was also not addressed by 1409. Baghdad's inability to rebuild its economy meant the continuation of skyrocketing unemployment rates, up to 70 percent in some areas, and the denial of income to most families. The consumer goods that might increase under the "smart sanctions" would not be accessible to the majority of Iraqis, most of whom were impoverished. Social indicators, including child labor, health, and education would remain dramatically worse than pre-sanctions levels.

On the other hand, the sanctions-driven, black-market profiteering appeared to be increasing, so even luxury goods were visible in some markets—but again, the vast majority of Iraqis had no money to buy any of them. The money coming into Iraq from smuggled oil sold to Turkey, Jordan, and Syria was estimated at somewhere between $1 and $2 billion per year. Yet even if every dollar were directed to civilian use (and while some of it in fact was so used, certainly most was siphoned off for maintaining Iraq's military and the ruling elites' comfortable lifestyle) those funds would remain completely insufficient for civilian needs. Economic sanctions, revised or not, would ultimately help keep Saddam Hussein in power and Baghdad's black marketeers in luxuries.

When the Security Council vote was taken, it was unanimous. Moscow agreed to accept the new arrangement, saving face by getting the United States to agree to the Russian, rather than American version of how the list would work. The only somewhat discordant note came from Syrian Ambassador Mikhail Wehbe: "It's high time to lift the sanctions," he said. He added that it was incomprehensible that the Council continued to impose sanctions on Iraq for an unlimited period of time.34 Nevertheless, Syria voted in favor of the resolution anyway, claiming that it did so to facilitate a diplomatic resolution of the Council's stand-off with Iraq. In fact, the Syrian decision probably also had something to do with the new resolution's silence on the continuing export of low-cost Iraqi oil to Syria, allowing Damascus to sell its own smaller oil supplies on the international oil market.

If the United States did mount a major new assault against Iraq (US bombing of the no-fly zones continued unabated after September 11), it would do so without international public support—facing, in fact, widespread international opposition. But that did not mean it would do so alone. While public opposition, certainly across the Arab world but throughout Europe as well, was fierce, official opposition was more cautious, with one eye on public opinion and the other cast firmly in the direction of Washington. This was, after all, post-September 11, and there was not a government across the globe, especially in the strategic Middle East, that could afford to risk appearing cavalier with a Washington priority as high as going after Saddam Hussein.

Washington was not, however, taking any chances. On April 22, the Bush administration succeeded in ousting Jose M. Bustani, the Brazilian director of the Organization for the Prohibition of Chemical Weapons. Bustani had been unanimously reelected with the United States' support in 2001, but in February 2002 he was approached by US diplomats who demanded that he resign, and that he should not make their demands public. "They said they did not like my management style, but they said they were not prepared to elaborate," Bustani said. Bustani's refusal to step down led to an intense diplomatic show-down with the organization, in which the United States threatened to cut off funding of the OPCW until Bustani was gone. According to one European diplomat, "I think a lot of people swallowed this because they thought it was better for Bustani to be removed than have the US pull out and see the organization collapse."35

What the press reports largely ignored was the fact that the US decision to oust Bustani appeared tied to his efforts to persuade Iraq to join the umbrella of the OPCW, which would have brought Baghdad under international inspection for its chemical weapons programs. The United States, ostensibly concerned precisely about those CW programs, appeared uneasy because of concerns that OPCW inspections would call into question the US claims regarding Iraq's alleged weapons programs, and might therefore strip the United States of its justification for military strikes against Iraq because of Baghdad's rebuff of UN inspectors.

(Washington's willingness to play diplomatic hardball with threats to cut off funds and force the ouster of international directors was certainly nothing new. Only a week before Bustani was ousted from the OPCW, the United States and "at least one American oil company" had orchestrated the ouster of Robert Watson as chair of the Inter-governmental Panel on Climate Change.[36] He had been outspoken on the threat of global warming, and the Bush administration's anti-Kyoto, there's-no-such-thing-as-global-warming cabal found him an irritant.)

After the new Iraq sanctions resolution was passed, the *New York Times* editorialized, "Washington is now in a better position to lead the international debate on the future of the Iraqi regime without the distraction of accusations over humanitarian concerns."[37] It was an approach eerily similar to that of Colin Powell during his February 7, 2001 confirmation hearings in the Senate. At that time, the secretary of state-designate said that simply by announcing Washington's intention to craft a new model of a "smarter" sanctions regime, "We have succeeded, because we stopped the talking about Iraqi children, and instead are talking about weapons of mass destruction, not sanctions to hurt civilians." Like the *Times'* later disquiet about humanitarian concerns being a "distraction" from the more important issue of overthrowing the Iraqi regime, Powell's view was that a United States victory lay not so much in ensuring that no more Iraqi children were dying, but that no one was any longer *talking* about children dying. The United States could now debate "the future of the Iraqi regime" without any such distractions.

IRAQ AND THE REST OF THE WORLD

In the Arab world, the consequences of that debate were clear. Arab governments had to assess, on an almost daily basis, what level of instability might erupt at home if they acquiesced with—or even hinted at support for—a US military assault on Iraq. These regimes, most of them absolute monarchies, militarized one-party states, or repressive pseudo-democracies, had generally little concern about public opinion—until the possibility surfaced that such opinion might become mobilized and might threaten their stability in power. On the other hand, the kings, princes, and emirs remained all too cognizant of their fundamental dependence on the United States—whether for military reasons (like Saudi Arabia, Kuwait, and elsewhere in the Gulf), economic ones (like Jordan), or both (like Egypt). The unknown factor was whether—and when—Washington would demand that their dependents toe the US line on Iraq (though perhaps allowing them to do so without fanfare), and how high a price in domestic legitimacy they would be expected to pay. If that price included the fatal weakening—or even overthrow—of any of those regimes, all of which already faced severe crises of legitimacy, would Washington still insist?

In Europe the scenario was somewhat more complex. Public opposition to an attack on Iraq by the United States was clear and widespread; even stronger was public opposition to a European role in any such attack. But the issue was not nearly as high on the public agenda as in the Arab world, and European governments were somewhat diffident in their critique of Bush administration plans. No government embraced such military plans, but few were unqualified in their opposition, either.

Berlin's *die Tageszeitung* reported in January that, at Washington's request, Prague would send 350 soldiers to Kuwait, most of them from the Czech Ninth Special Chemical Weapons Unit, over the next two months. (This followed an earlier request by the United States ambassador in Prague, Craig Stapleton, to Czech Prime Minister Milos Zeman, back in November 2001.) On January 8 in Berlin, plans were revealed for sending German chemical warfare troops and specialized Fox tanks designed for chemical warfare in response to Washington's September request. Chancellor Gerhard Schroeder had recently reiterated firm opposition to expanding the war to Iraq, largely to keep his coalition with the Green Party intact. But the deployment was set to go ahead nonetheless.[38]

BACK AT HOME...

The movement of those small numbers of European troops and a few tanks was certainly not proof of actual, let alone imminent, US intent toward Iraq. Despite the troops moving toward the region, Europe still remained politically opposed to expanding the war. But the willingness of Germany and the Czech Republic to send troops and tanks, despite widespread public opposition within those countries, signaled that the Bush administration could allow its get-Iraq hawks to have their way with little concern for the consequences.

Even more significant was the ambiguity of elite opinion within the United States itself. Growing unease from a few influential members of Congress, including even House majority leader Tom Daschle, and former diplomatic and military officials, such as Admiral Eugene Carroll, former Ambassador to Saudi Arabia James Akins, and others, and continued pressure from a small but vocal anti-war movement, continued to raise the domestic political stakes for a war which all agreed would not be an Afghanistan-style walkover. (Given the failure by the United States, as of the beginning of summer 2002, to capture Osama bin Laden or other key leaders, it was a question whether the "quick victory" assessment of the Afghanistan war was appropriate even in Afghanistan.) Soon after the 2002 State of the Union address, the rhetorical focus of Bush officials shifted from Iraq to alleged terrorist threats in Somalia or Yemen. That, plus the increasing presence of military "advisers" in the Philippines in the campaign against Abu Sayyaf, gave credence to later administration claims that Iraq's rise to the top of the target list, if it happened at all, was unlikely until the following year. And even then, the clearer-thinking, less ideological of Bush's advisers grouped around Colin Powell appeared to be appropriately wary of the military challenges Iraq posed, as well as of the likelihood of greater international isolation should the United States go forward along that path.

Even if an invasion of Iraq by the United States or a US-backed covert operation involving Iraqi exiles waited until 2003, a swift, tough-looking bombing raid as a run-up to the November 2002 elections could certainly not be ruled out. As *Los Angeles Times* columnist Robert Scheer noted in early May:

> Clearly, Bush's preoccupation with Iraq has permitted the tail to wag the dog. Yet without the link to bin Laden's al-Qaeda, there is little excuse for

what would prove to be a very costly war, rejected by almost all of our allies as an irrational response to what remains of the Iraqi military threat. Bush's foreign policy is based on a fairy tale, the persistent if childish hope that all of our problems can be solved by one solid blow to the latest Evil Empire, now found in Baghdad. Someone needs to read the president a better bedtime story.[39]

Whether Colin Powell had such an effort in mind remained unclear. Certainly none of Washington's European or Arab allies were preparing for George Junior's story hour.

In fact, the single most significant check on US military ambitions in Iraq lay within the American military services themselves—not with the civilian leadership of the Pentagon, but the uniformed services. Secretary of Defense Rumsfeld, his deputy Paul Wolfowitz, the hawks grouped around them, and Richard Perle's quasi-official (but requiring no Senate confirmation) Defense Policy Board represented the hardest-line faction most consistent in demanding the overthrow/ assassination/head-on-a-stick of Saddam Hussein. But those top-ranking officers who would have to actually craft battle plans and lead their troops into combat had few illusions about just what was and was not possible in Iraq. However debilitated the Iraqi army's weapons capacity was after years of sanctions and air strikes that followed the military's near collapse in the 1991 war, it was still a large army, with at least a significant part grouped around the Republican Guard who remained relatively intact and well-armed.

A February 2002 Defense Intelligence Agency plan aimed to show what a military attack in Iraq by the United States would look like. A *Los Angeles Times* article described it:

[The plan] clearly presents toppling Hussein's regime as a challenge so formidable that only tremendous military resources could accomplish it.... When a prospective Iraq war strategy first circulated within a tight circle in CentCom [US Central Command, the military sector responsible for overseeing Iraq as well as Afghanistan] earlier this year, it called for a full-scale ground campaign with the goal of "regime change" in Baghdad. That was to be achieved by a combination of brute force and a hoped-for rising up of the Iraqi people and military commanders against Saddam. The plan, which seemed not to consider America's advantages and Baghdad's accumulated weaknesses, struck critics as simplistic and myopic. Three of the four subordinate commands within CentCom—the Air Force, the Navy and the Marines—took the unprecedented step of expressing alarm at a CentCom meeting at Ramstein Air Base in Germany last month.[40]

When a more detailed invasion plan was leaked in June 2002, it reflected further military unease regarding the efficacy of a covert operation to foment a coup d'etat against Saddam Hussein. While beginning with special forces operations, the plan acknowledged that up to 250,000 American troops would have to be deployed.

There was little doubt in the Bush administration that, when pushed, Turkey, a key ally needed for bombing base rights, would agree to launching US air strikes from its territory. After all, Turkey was recipient of the fourth-largest US aid package of any country in the world (having been displaced in third by Colombia). Yet as Ankara vacillated between private reluctance and public opposition to a new war against Iraq, the difficulty of relying on such a reluctant ally was not lost on military planners. Diplomatic pressure, including new negotiations with Turkey over what a post-Saddam Hussein arrangement would look like in the Kurdish areas of northern Iraq, matched the military discussions.

Similarly, Saudi Arabia would, when so ordered by its Washington protectors, no doubt accede to at least unpublicized or covert use of its massive air bases. But growing instability within the kingdom, rapidly increasing after September 11 and the revelations that fifteen of the nineteen hijackers were Saudi citizens, decreased Saudi Arabia's appeal as the Pentagon's high-tech air base and communications center it had been since the 1990–91 Gulf crisis. Indeed, in the months after September 11, Washington began the quiet and largely-unpublicized process of replicating key Saudi-based facilities in the assumed-to-be safer emirate of Qatar, a tiny thumb-shaped peninsula off the Saudi coast.

Three other points were crucial as well to the military critics' arguments. First, Iraq's population was overwhelmingly concentrated in the cities, throwing up the prospect of brutal house-to-house urban warfare, guaranteeing high American casualties and holding out the possibility of a protracted guerrilla war with overwhelming numbers of civilian deaths. Unlike Afghanistan, where al-Qaeda's foreign fighters based in the country provided the toughest opposition, Iraq's military would be fighting on their own land and defending their own homes. Even if many had little enthusiasm for fighting to defend the repressive regime in Baghdad, Iraq's home-country advantage would provide a formidable foe for the United States.

Second, once the war had begun, the domestic political stakes
would require the removal from power (at least) of Saddam Hussein;
this time around there would be no just-get-Iraq-out-of-Kuwait limit
to a military strike by the United States. Given the Iraqi president's
access to the highest levels of protection, bunkers, and hide-outs,
"getting Saddam" might prove far more useful as a slogan than as a
serious goal. The periodic embarrassment of Bush administration and
Pentagon officials questioned during the war on terrorism about the
whereabouts of the elusive Osama bin Laden would not be even close
to the political nightmare that would follow their failure to capture
or kill the Iraqi leader.

And third, overthrowing the regime would require a long period of
post-war occupation and, unlike in Afghanistan, that job would
inevitably fall directly to the United States. Eleven-plus years of
crippling economic sanctions had led to the flight of a large
percentage of Iraq's educated classes and the erosion to virtual non-
existence of Iraq's once-vibrant civil life. There was simply no
possibility that the internally divided and perpetually scrapping Iraqi
exile-based opposition (for there is virtually no organized internal
opposition) could take over and run the large and complex nation of
22 million people without a long-term American military, economic,
and political presence on the ground. Whether Americans—or even
the Bush administration—had the stomach for a protracted
occupation of a hostile (at least partly) Arab population remained a
serious question.

Despite those warnings, however, the danger of a new war by the
United States against Iraq could not be dismissed. In January 2002,
Henry Kissinger weighed in as cheerleader for an Iraq operation. In the
Washington Post, Henry Kissinger wrote:

> Creating an appropriate coalition for such an effort and finding bases for
> the necessary American deployment will be difficult. Nevertheless, the
> skillful diplomacy that shaped the first phase of the anti-terrorism
> campaign would have much to build on. Saddam Hussein has no friends
> in the gulf region. Britain will not easily abandon the pivotal role, based
> on its special relationship with the United States, that it has earned for
> itself in the evolution of the crisis. Nor will Germany move into active
> opposition to the United States—especially in an election year. The same
> is true of Russia, China, and Japan.[41]

The coercive power of Washington's post-September 11 projection of military power and the widespread fear of other governments to stand up to Washington's unilateral intentions was not lost on the architect of so many earlier examples of just such scenarios.

Whatever the uncertainty within the administration regarding the advisability, feasibility, and timing of an attack on Iraq, by the end of March military preparations for a US military strike on Iraq were well under way. In the Gulf region and Central Asia combined, in an arc reaching from Saudi Arabia in the west to Pakistan in the east, US military personnel more than tripled from less than 25,000 before September 11 to nearly 80,000. By March 30, CBS news reported that "in Kuwait—at Iraq's door—the number of American troops has nearly doubled, from 5,500 to about 10,500, since September 11, defense officials said. Most are support personnel who keep planes flying and food flowing to troops in the field." The article was titled "Iraq Attack Inching Closer?"

By mid-April, after a slowdown in anti-Iraq pronouncements, Bush resumed his drumbeat. In a speech at the Virginia Military Institute, he told cadets:

[A] small number of outlaw regimes today possess and are developing chemical and biological and nuclear weapons. In their threat to peace, in their mad ambitions, in their destructive potential and in the repression of their own people, these regimes constitute an axis of evil and the world must confront them.[42]

This time around he did not spell out the members of the Axis of Evil Club, but the focus on Iraq was unmistakable.

Despite the efforts of Bush's ideologues, throughout the spring of 2002 the pragmatic wing of the administration appeared to retain the upper hand. The violence in occupied Palestine and inside Israel itself spiraled further and further out of control, making the United States effort to win regional support for a strike against Iraq an almost impossible goal. Arab leaders, their populations surging into the streets in long-prohibited demonstrations against Israeli assaults and Washington's uncritical backing, paraded through Washington urging, begging, and beseeching the Bush administration, Pentagon officials, members of Congress, the press, and almost anyone who would listen, please not to attack Iraq. At least not while Palestine was burning and Arab populations, already angry at their own rulers for a host of long-standing grievances, were prepared to turn on anyone allied with those backing the occupying army that had turned Jenin into a living grave.

Even Tony Blair, long considered Bush's most reliable ally, pulled back from his earlier support of a military attack by the United States to oust Saddam Hussein. In early April, in the run-up to a high-profile visit to Bush's Texas ranch, Blair's advisers announced that the prime minister was carrying with him a dossier ostensibly detailing Iraq's crimes. The announcement recalled Blair's similar role in early autumn as the public voice of evidence of Osama bin Laden's and al-Qaeda's responsibility for the September 11 attacks. In that instance, the Bush administration adamantly refused to publicize their alleged evidence, supposedly to avoid having to risk intelligence sources or other classified material going public.

This time round, the plan was for Blair to carry to Texas a British-drafted bill of particulars justifying a military strike against Iraq. But as the suicide bombings increased inside Israel, and as the Israeli military invasions and re-occupations of Palestinian cities and refugee camps that began on March 29 generated so much anger throughout the Arab world and beyond, Blair reneged on his plan. He announced a delay in releasing the written case against the Iraqi leader, and said that the way to proceed regarding Iraq "is a matter that is open."[43]

Before the Pentagon's more detailed covert-operation-plus-maybe-invasion plan was leaked in early summer, President Bush did not seem willing to risk his post-September 11 sky-high popularity ratings by launching a war that could fail. The Pentagon's own General Anthony Zinni, after all, later a top Middle-East envoy for the Bush administration, memorably said that a military effort to overthrow Saddam Hussein would turn Iraq into a "Bay of Goats" (See Chapter Two). Not the best legacy for an election year. It was certainly possible that by bracketing the arch-evil Iraq with Iran and North Korea, two countries which were widely understood not to be the target of military assault, Bush gave himself some degree of political cover if he should choose the least reckless course against Baghdad. There was a strong likelihood that the leaked Pentagon document confirming military planning, but focusing on the viability of a covert operation utilizing Special Forces, may have come from those in the administration opposed to full-scale invasion, but who were determined to prove they would still be tough on Iraq. On the other hand, with military planning well under way and the Pentagon's civilian ideologues still trumpeting the necessity of going to war, the possibility of a much larger-scale assault on Iraq loomed as a frighteningly real prospect.

ISRAEL AND PALESTINE

All of the politicking and in-fighting within the administration and inside the Pentagon regarding whether and how to mobilize a military strike against Iraq paled in the face of what would become the biggest obstacle to such an attack by the United States. It erupted a thousand miles west of Baghdad, in Israel and the occupied Palestinian territories.

The second intifada, or uprising, that began in September 2000 after the collapse of the Camp David summit and the collapse of the Oslo-driven hopes of Palestinians, was escalating through much of Bush's pre-September 11 presidency. Settlement construction, house demolitions, and long-term closures of towns and villages with resulting unemployment, were all on the rise. Incidents of Palestinian resistance to occupying soldiers and settlers continued, Israel's military forces throughout the West Bank and Gaza increased their firepower, and Palestinians were dying in higher numbers. More Israelis, too, were dying; many of them were occupation soldiers or armed settlers, but—significantly—Israeli civilians, inside Israel itself, began to be counted among the victims.

The Bush administration's flip-flopping over its Middle East policy, especially about Israel-Palestine, continued. In the first months of its term, the Bush administration adopted a policy of keeping up the aid to and diplomatic protection of Israel, but keeping their heads down and their hands off peace talks. This was not terribly surprising—this was, after all, an administration whose economic and political power was thoroughly enmeshed in the oil industry. Israel slid out of first place.

Certainly the existing close ties between the United States and Israel did not disappear. Nevertheless, despite the continuity of $4 billion or so in military and economic aid, and a continued use or threat of use of UN vetoes and walk-outs to protect Israel in the United Nations, the Bush policy became known as "disengagement." Europe, Arab states, and others around the world began crying for "greater engagement," as if Washington's billions in aid, the protective vetoes, and the diplomatic privileging of Israel did not constitute intimate engagement. What was needed, of course, was not *more* engagement, but an entirely different kind of engagement. And that was not on Bush's Middle East agenda.

Immediately after the World Trade Center attacks, the Bush administration appeared to distance itself from Israel. The need for maintaining Arab and Islamic government support in Bush's new "anti-terrorism war" trumped the former warm and fuzzy embrace of Israel, although US economic and strategic backing remained quietly unchanged. Fearing exactly that reaction, Israeli spokespeople launched a near-frenzied campaign of linkage, claiming unparalleled unity with Americans as victims of common terror and common Arab/Islamic enemies.

The *New York Times'* Clyde Haberman, writing within hours of the attack on the World Trade Center, weighed in on Israel's behalf. On September 12, he wrote:

> Do you get it now? It is a question that many Israelis wanted to ask yesterday of America and the rest of the finger-pointing world. Not in a smart-alecky manner. Not to say, 'We told you so.'...The American criticism of Israel has been sotto voce. But it is there. And in this Black September, after the worst act of terrorism in history, the question arises from Israelis...Do you get it now? It was simply a question for those who, at a safe remove from the terrorism that Israelis face every day, have damned Israel for taking admittedly harsh measures to keep its citizens alive.[44]

Similarly, Israeli Prime Minister Ariel Sharon called the World Trade Center and Pentagon attacks an assault on "our common values." He declared, "I believe together we can defeat these forces of evil." For his part, asked what the terrorist attack on the twin towers in New York and the Pentagon in Washington meant for Israel, former Prime Minister Benjamin Netanyahu blurted out, "It's very good." Then, editing his words, he added, "Well, not very good, but it will generate immediate sympathy." He predicted that the attack would "strengthen the bond between our two peoples, because we've experienced terror over so many decades, but the United States has now experienced a massive hemorrhaging of terror."[45]

(Later, fearing a Bush administration shift away from a clear embrace of Israel to seek Arab support for its anti-terrorism war, Sharon would accuse the United States and the West of "appeasement," conjuring up images of Neville Chamberlain's acquiescence to Hitler.)

Overall, however, the Israeli effort to link its occupation of Palestine with the looming anti-terrorism war of the United States did not work very well beyond the punditocracy and Israel's own American supporters. By November, both Colin Powell's speech at the University of Kentucky in Louisville and Bush's own UN General Assembly address paid more attention to words the Palestinians and—more strategically—Arab governments and their restive populations wanted to hear. Bush's call for a "state of Palestine" and Powell's assertion that "the occupation must end" appeared to herald a new, maybe even even-handed, approach of US diplomacy.

But this approach was not to last. The Bush administration was prepared to weather Israel's displeasure, and that of Israel's backers in the United States, as long as winning Arab compliance was at the top of its regional agenda in the now-primary anti-terror war. For a while the administration appeared unconcerned with the escalating violence in Israel, appearing to believe, against all evidence, that Palestine could burn and somehow the crisis would stay contained and US alliances in the region would not be harmed.

BACK TO THE "PEACE PROCESS"

Then, at about the same time that keeping a coalition together became less important in Afghanistan (about the time when major cities under Taliban rule were falling and the need for regional support diminished), the tactical pendulum swung back and Washington returned to its more traditional public embrace of Israel and Sharon. The shift came in an announced plan to "re-engage" in the "peace process." The first messenger was General Anthony Zinni, whose two earlier visits at the end of 2001 had ended in failure (one after a suicide bombing and one following the discovery of the shipload of arms en route to Palestine ostensibly from Iran).

When Bush made his State of the Union speech, he deliberately and explicitly included the Palestinian organizations Hamas and Islamic Jihad, as well as the Lebanese resistance movement Hezbollah, in his litany of "terrorist" organizations. The point was not so much to signal a new direct campaign by the United States against those groups. Rather, the US sought to pressure Iran, backer of several of the groups, as well as the Palestinian Authority, the putative "government" in whose territory two of them operated, as "sponsors" of terror or governments "harboring" terrorists. In addition, the message regarding the Palestinian Authority in particular was widely seen as a green light to Sharon. It was a signal that anything he did to the PA would be viewed in Washington as a legitimate attack on a "government" (however disempowered) that was harboring terrorists—a direct parallel to what the United States was doing in Afghanistan.

By February, however, Iraq had reemerged as a central feature of US regional efforts. The stakes were going up and a new round of regional shuttling was required to lay out the requirements and lay down the law to Washington's Arab allies. General Zinni was not quite high enough in the administration hierarchy for this one, so into the breech stepped Vice President Dick Cheney, an experienced Middle East hand from his years as secretary of defense in the Bush Senior administration.

In fact, the Vice President had carried out a virtually identical Middle East regional roundup once before—on the eve of the Gulf War more than a decade ago and for a similar purpose: to ensure Arab and broader regional (read: Turkish) support for a new strike against Iraq. In the wake of September 11, with dependent and already compliant Arab regimes almost falling over each other to climb on board the Bush anti-terrorism train, the administration seemed to anticipate Cheney's job would be a pushover. Sure, there might be some unease in the palaces over how Arab populations were raging over the rapidly deteriorating crisis in the West Bank, but it was assumed that however much they twitched and weaseled, Washington's Arab allies would stand reluctantly with Washington.

As it turned out, Cheney's job was not quite so easy. While there was little doubt that at the end of the day the Arab kings, emirs, princes, and presidents would indeed do as their patron ordered, public opinion throughout the Arab world had hardened not only against Israel and its occupation, but against its global backer, the United States. Arab governments, already facing severe crises of legitimacy, would pay a very high price for their alliance with Washington. Israel's military escalation in the occupied territories afforded what seemed to provide an easy dodge for the Arab royals looking for a way out of supporting an attack on Baghdad: "How can you even talk to us about supporting an invasion or overthrow campaign against Iraq when Palestine is burning and you are doing nothing?"

Some time before Cheney's Air Force Two took off, someone in Washington realized what was about to happen, so General Zinni was sent back to the region. His mandate had not changed and there was little chance he would succeed, however that elusive word was defined (a ceasefire, a diminution of violence, whatever), but that was okay. His real role had far more to do with developments in Arab capitals than it did in Jerusalem and Ramallah where he began a shadow shuttle. Zinni was Cheney's political cover. "What do you mean we're doing nothing— we're sending General Zinni!" was the Vice President's new mantra.

As it turned out, that plan did not work either; while Arab regimes were still likely to cave in to pressure from the United States when it was finally exerted, shaky governments were simply not willing to concede prematurely and risk further destabilization or even potential threats to their regimes. One *Washington Post* article reported on Cheney's next-to-the-last stop in the Arab world, Bahrain:

> Crown Prince Salman bin Hamad al Khalifa made clear that Arabs have little patience for considering a strategy to confront Iraq with pictures of Palestinians killed during clashes with Israelis that continue to dominate newscasts and front pages across the region. "The people who are dying today on the streets are not a result of any Iraqi action," he said at a joint news conference with Cheney. "The people that are dying today are dying as the result of Israeli action. And likewise, the people in Israel are dying as a result of action in response to those actions that are taken. So the perception of the threat in the Arab world really focuses around that issue and we are preoccupied by it, deeply so."[46]

Cheney's trip fizzled, and the Vice President's response was to try to re-spin a new rationale for his trip, denying that winning regional support for striking Iraq was his goal at all. "I sense that some people want to believe that there's only one issue I'm concerned about or that somehow I'm out here to organize a military adventure with respect to Iraq," he told reporters in Bahrain, "That's not true."

Then it was Secretary of State Powell's turn. Following Cheney's failed trip, the Bush administration had called a brief time-out in the new game of engagement. Pundits played the Washington version of Kremlinology, trying to read tea leaves and photo-ops to judge who was up and who was down in the Bush entourage. The early splits that had characterized the administration were still in place: once shaped by policy disagreements over Iraq, the division between the Powell pragmatists and the Rumsfeld/Wolfowitz ideologues now played out over Palestine. Should any US official higher than an acting assistant deputy under-secretary of something ever sit in the same room with

Yasir Arafat? Could any US official criticize anything that General Sharon did since he was fighting terrorism just like the United States was doing in Afghanistan?

The press focused largely on the messenger. Was General Zinni simply too far down in the hierarchy to have the requisite clout with Sharon and/or Arafat? Would Bush send General Powell, ratcheting up the four-star factor? What was largely left out of the debate was the reality that it was not the messenger but the message that would determine the success or failure of the mission. Zinni failed not because he was not of high enough rank, but because he had no mandate to seriously dictate terms to Israel.

As it would turn out, though, neither did Powell.

Before the decision was made to send the secretary of state back to the region, the situation on the ground turned even grimmer in March. Following a rash of deadly suicide bombings inside Israel, including one on the first night of the Jewish holiday of Passover in which 26 Israeli Jews, including children, were blown up as they sat down to a Seder dinner, Israel invaded and re-occupied cities, villages, and refugee camps across the occupied West Bank. The March 29 assault was by far the largest operation of the Israel Defense Forces (IDF) since the Lebanon war of 20 years earlier. And the brutality and destruction of the assault matched that of 1982.

It was an unprecedented action, destroying the last vestiges of Oslo's mythology of Palestinian authority in the major population centers across the West Bank. IDF troops punched into Ramallah, Bethlehem, Nablus, Jenin, Tulkarem, and tiny villages in between with tanks, helicopter gunships, armored bulldozers, and F-16s. It looked, said UN Secretary General Kofi Annan, like "a conventional war." Israel claimed its goal was to find and arrest terrorists, but the military strike was designed to punish the entire Palestinian population for the actions of a few unaccountable extremists.

At that point Bush himself jumped into the fray. In a major speech in the White House Rose Garden on April 4, he announced he would send Powell to the region and outlined a vision, if a bit skimpy and more than a bit blurry, of what a peaceful settlement might look like:

> This could be a hopeful moment in the Middle East. The proposal of
> Crown Prince Abdullah of Saudi Arabia, supported by the Arab League,
> has put a number of countries in the Arab world closer than ever to

recognizing Israel's right to exist. The United States is on record supporting the legitimate aspirations of the Palestinian people for a Palestinian state. Israel has recognized the goal of a Palestinian state. The outlines of a just settlement are clear: two states, Israel and Palestine, living side by side, in peace and security.

It was not, of course, anything remotely resembling a hopeful moment. Referring to the Saudi/Arab League proposal, Bush conveniently ignored the inconvenient fact that the prince had called for Arab recognition of Israel only following a complete Israeli withdrawal to the 1967 borders. The United States may have been on record supporting Palestinian aspirations, but everything Washington was doing, before as well as after September 11, only helped prevent those aspirations from becoming reality.

If a Palestinian state had not been achieved, Bush said, Yasir Arafat had only himself to blame:

> The situation in which he finds himself today is largely of his own making. He's missed his opportunities, and thereby betrayed the hopes of the people he's supposed to lead. Given his failure, the Israeli government feels it must strike at terrorist networks that are killing its citizens.

Israel's actions might "run the risk of aggravating long-term bitterness and undermining relationships that are critical to any hope of peace," but, despite that, Bush would not criticize Sharon's assault, except to remind Israel "that its response to these recent attacks is only a temporary measure."

For long-term thinking, the words were all there: Israel must stop settlement activity, and "the occupation must end through withdrawal to secure and recognized boundaries...." Four days later Bush said he told Sharon, "I expect there to be withdrawal without delay." He talked the talk of serious pressure; but he refused to walk the walk.

Bush's only action against Israel was limited to sending Powell back to the region; there would be no pressure on Israel through use of any of the myriad of tools available to the president. There would be no cut in the billions of dollars in military or economic aid to Israel; no brake on the pipeline of military equipment the IDF was using against civilians; no reversal of the veto in the Security Council preventing the deployment of international protection or even observer forces.

Given the lack of any action to match the strong words, it should have surprised no one that Sharon paid little attention. As veteran *Washington Post* columnist Mary McGrory described Bush's posture, "the leader of the free world lolled in a lounger in Crawford, Texas, and told Sharon to go to it."[47] For anyone who still harbored some optimism regarding Bush's intentions, the harsh reality was made clear in the timetable. Powell would go to the region, but he would take his long sweet time getting there. Arriving first in Morocco, several days after Bush's speech, its young king welcomed Powell with the question "Why are you here; why aren't you in Jerusalem?"

Powell traveled at a languid pace, first from Morocco to Madrid to convene the "Quartet" of Russia, the European Union, and the UN, along with the US, then on to Jordan and to Egypt, until finally arriving almost a week later in Jerusalem. It was, without doubt, a week-long green light for Sharon's assault on the cities, villages, and especially refugee camps of the West Bank. It was a green light for the horrors of Jenin, which soon joined Qibya, Gaza, and Sabra/Shatila in the lexicon of Sharon's war crimes.

The situation was explosive enough that the usually cautious UN Secretary General Kofi Annan called on the international community to create a multinational force under the terms of the UN Charter's Chapter VII, authorizing the use of military force to protect Palestinians in the occupied territories. He said he did not favor an official UN force of Blue Helmet peacekeepers, but rather a "coalition of the willing," made up of member states of the UN, who would have, he hoped, a "robust mandate." The Security Council, presumably anticipating a US veto, ignored his proposal.

When Powell returned, President Bush welcomed him home with the astonishing claim that the goals of the United States had been met and that the trip was a success. All was well with the world. It was an Alice in Wonderland moment, with Bush announcing straight-faced that "I do believe Ariel Sharon is a man of peace" and "history will show [Israelis] have responded" to Bush's call for an immediate pull-out.

AFTER JENIN

Israel's attack in the Jenin refugee camp, in particular, showed the horrors of military occupation. Resistance to the occupying forces had been fierce in Jenin. Israeli tanks and armored bulldozers had crushed houses, cars, and even people trapped inside. Twenty-three Israeli soldiers were killed in the fighting. Over 50 Palestinians were identified, among a possibly even greater number of unknown dead, pulled from the moonscape-like rubble of what had once been a crowded warren of a camp. Twenty-two were civilians. Harsh debate broke out over whether the Palestinian claim of a "massacre" was accurate; Israeli officials accused anyone using the term of a "blood libel." Human Rights Watch, which sent in a forensic team, indicated in a preliminary finding (and urged a full international investigation) that they had not seen evidence of an identifiable massacre. That part was a lead story and made front-page headlines in the American press. Few media outlets, however, picked up on the human rights organization's first point: that numerous war crimes *had* been committed by Israeli troops.

The United Nations quickly took up the issue. The UN special envoy to the Middle East, Terje Roed-Larsen, called conditions in the Jenin refugee camp following the Israeli assault, "shocking and horrifying beyond belief.... It looks as if an earthquake has hit the heart of the refugee camp here." Larsen, who went into the camp with representatives of the Palestine Red Crescent and UNRWA, the UN's Palestinian relief agency, described "the large-scale suffering of the whole civilian population here. No military operation could justify the suffering we are seeing here," he said. "It's not only the corpses, [it's] children lacking food." Larsen called on the Israelis to give fuller access to the camp to aid agencies distributing food and water to the residents. Journalists accompanying Larsen reported the air filled with the stench of decaying corpses. An earlier report that day had indicated that two boys, ages six and twelve, had been pulled alive from beneath the rubble of their house at the camp. Palestine Red Crescent and other rescue officials, however, told journalists the boys were dead.[48]

According to the preliminary report of Physicians for Human Rights, who sent a forensic team into Jenin:

> Children under the age of fifteen years, women and men over the age of 50 years accounted for nearly 38% of all fatalities.... One out of three fatalities was due to gunshot wounds with vast majority sustaining fatal wounds of head, or head and upper torso. Eleven percent of the total fatalities were due to crush injuries in addition to a 55-year old male crushed by a tank in the township of Jenin.

Of the hundred-plus patients with gunshot and other traumatic injuries from the siege, whom the PHR team interviewed at the Jenin hospital, women, children under fifteen years, and men over the age of

50 years accounted for a total of over 50 percent of all admissions.[49]

Human Rights Watch investigators documented the deaths of numerous residents of Jenin camp. They included:

> fifty-seven-year-old Kamal Zghair, a wheelchair-bound man who was shot and then run over by IDF tanks on April 10 as he was moving in his wheelchair equipped with a white flag down a major road in Jenin; thirty-seven-year-old Jamal Fayid, a paralyzed man, who was crushed in the rubble of his home on April 7 after IDF soldiers refused to allow his family the time to remove him from their home before a bulldozer destroyed it; fourteen-year-old Faris Zaiben, who was killed by fire from an IDF armored car as he went to buy groceries when the IDF-imposed curfew was finally lifted on April 11.[50]

In one case study documented by Physicians for Human Rights, a patient with a severely fractured leg interviewed at the Jenin hospital was a 42-year-old Palestinian male. Their report read:

> Review of pre-surgery X-rays revealed shattered distal left tibia and fibula with compounded comminuted fractures. The fracture pattern was consistent with high velocity gunshot injury. During the interview the man related that he was a schoolteacher employed by UNRWA, teaching in an elementary school in a nearby village. His parents came to the [Jenin refugee] camp in 1948 and he was born and lived in the camp. He commuted to work every day. On the evening of April 4, 2002, when he went to the second floor of his two-story dwelling to get milk for his young child, he was shot, reportedly by an IDF sniper. The bullet struck his left leg above the ankle along the inner side and there was a dark hole on the outer surface of his left leg. According to this report, he collapsed and his wife dragged him down to the lower floor. He had no painkillers or antibiotics, but he applied a tight homemade bandage. He made many attempts to obtain help from the Palestinian Red Crescent and the Jenin Hospital but, because the camp was sealed off, no one could come to help him. He even begged an Israeli foot soldier to help him, showing him his UNRWA identity card. The soldier told him that if he needed help he should call Kofi Annan. After his house was demolished, he was allowed to go to Jenin Hospital by Red Crescent ambulance on April 11, 2002.

Secretary General Kofi Annan, appalled by the reports of his special envoy, called for an international investigation team to be sent. A draft Security Council resolution sponsored by the Arab Group called on Annan to investigate "the full scope of the tragic events that have taken place in the Jenin refugee camp." It also called on Israel to respect the 1949 Geneva Convention for protecting civilians in times of war, and called for "an international presence that could help provide better conditions on the ground."[51]

In the Council, however, those initial efforts to table a tough resolution condemning Israel's action collapsed. The United States immediately made clear it would veto a resolution with strong language or any enforcement clout. After days of squabbling, a weakened resolution was finally passed, supporting the secretary general's initiative in sending a fact-finding team to Jenin. Israel had earlier denied entry to UN High Commissioner for Human Rights Mary Robinson, who had assembled a team in response to a Commission decision to investigate the human rights aspects of the Israeli incursions into the West Bank. Along with Robinson, the high-profile team included former Spanish prime minister Felipe Gonzalez and the former secretary general of South Africa's African National Congress, Cyril Ramaphosa.

At first Israel indicated it would accept a UN team to investigate the crisis in Jenin. Foreign Minister Shimon Peres told the UN secretary general that Israel "has nothing to hide" and would welcome an investigation. But as soon as the Council voted to support the secretary general's effort to send a fact-finding team, Israeli opposition began. First were complaints about the composition of the team; it was to be led by Finnish president and experienced UN envoy Maarti Ahtissari, along with Sadako Ogata, former UN High Commissioner for Refugees, and Cornelio Sommaruga, former head of the International Committee of the Red Cross (ICRC). The team also included retired United States general William Nash, initially as a military adviser but raised to full participatory level at Israeli insistence, and Irish police official Peter Fitzgerald as police adviser. Israel wanted "anti-terrorism" experts to be added as well. Then Israel demanded the right to determine which Israeli witnesses would be allowed to testify and guarantees ahead of time that any witnesses would be immune for war-crimes prosecution that could arise from their testimony. Ultimately Israel made clear that it would not allow the fact-finding team to enter the country.

In recent UN history, there were precedents for such efforts. The most similar, of course, was Iraq, whose refusal to allow UN inspectors to return prompted the massive US bombing campaign of December 1998. But it was clear from the beginning that Israel would be handled very differently than Iraq. As Hanny Megally, executive director of the Middle East and North Africa division of Human Rights Watch, announced, "Suspects shouldn't be able to choose their investigators."[52] But Israeli rejectionism prevailed. And the United States provided Israel with protection in the Security Council, effectively preventing any Council action to hold Israel accountable, to impose some kind of sanction, or even to condemn the Israeli action. It was clear that the US decision to back Israel's refusal was part of a *quid pro quo.* The United States would back Israel's rejectionism in the Council in return for Israel's agreeing to the US proposal that Israeli troops end their siege of Yasir Arafat's compound in Ramallah and allow the Palestinian leader out of the putative house arrest under which he had been held for weeks.

The deal worked, and the Council issued only a mild statement of "regret" that the fact-finding team was not able to work. No blame apportioned, no condemnation imposed. On May 2, the UN secretary general officially disbanded his team, whose members had been cooling their heels in Geneva waiting for Israeli authorization.

Less than a week later, however, the issue moved to the General Assembly, which called on the secretary general to go ahead in producing a report on alleged war crimes in the Jenin refugee camp. The Assembly resolution, unlike the original Security Council call, also went beyond Jenin alone to condemn Israel's entire assault on Palestinian cities and towns and its refusal to cooperate with the original fact-finding team. While there was no expectation that Israel would cooperate in allowing in a new team, Annan indicated he would base his report on available information from other observers on the ground, and would ask Israel and the Palestinians to "provide information" regarding events.

After the standoff ended at Arafat's tank-encircled presidential compound in Ramallah, Israel's assault gradually wound down in parts of the West Bank, even as tensions mounted around Bethlehem's besieged Church of the Nativity. There, nearly 200 Palestinians, including civilian residents as well as some gunmen, most of them armed police and security officials, had taken refuge when Israel invaded the town in early April. Denied food and medicine and unable to leave, with Israeli sharpshooters picking off several who made last-ditch efforts to pick grass for food in the compound's courtyards, the situation grew desperate.

In response to the siege of Ramallah and the Church of the Nativity (where religious sensitivities regarding the sanctity of the Church compound complicated everything), international negotiations took shape to end the crises. In Ramallah, the focus was on the fate of several Palestinians accused by Israel of masterminding the assassination of far-right Israeli tourism minister, Rehavam Ze'evi. Several of the men had in fact been imprisoned by the Palestinian Authority in Nablus, and they had been transferred to a jail within Arafat's Ramallah compound by US consular officials. But when the compound itself was attacked, the jail was destroyed and the men were moved to the presidential area itself, where they joined the dozens of Palestinian officials and international solidarity activists along with Arafat himself.

In a truncated "trial" held within the compound, the men were convicted. Under pressure from the United States, Arafat agreed that they would serve prison sentences in a jail in Jericho, the only Palestinian city that had not been re-occupied by Israel, but under the custody of a team of American and British guards to ensure they were indeed kept in prison. Palestinian anger grew with the perception that Arafat had traded his own freedom for that of Palestinian prisoners.

Popular unease and anger grew further after the settlement regarding Bethlehem. There, European negotiators as well as representatives of the Vatican were involved, and a resolution was reached under which 26 of the men Israel deemed "wanted" were sent to Gaza, where they were welcomed as heroes. Thirteen more, dubbed "senior terrorists," would be exiled to a variety of European countries. None was arrested, and while EU officials dithered over what the exact status would be of the Palestinians, none faced any charges in any European country (nor, officially, in Israel), and therefore they could not be held as prisoners. But an agreement that sent some Palestinians into exile outside Palestine, however benign some of its conditions, was not one that would win popularity among Palestinians for whom exile from their homeland remained a linchpin of national identity.

The process of internationalization was under way nonetheless. Despite the arrangements in Ramallah and Bethlehem, however, the broad goal of the Bush administration, the real aim of the Zinni, Cheney, and Powell shuttles, as well as those of their underlings who took over when the big men went home, had failed. The objective of stabilizing the region sufficiently so that Arab regimes could safely endorse a US military strike against Iraq without fearing domestic upheaval had not been reached.

OPPOSITION AT HOME

The effort to deal with the Israeli-Palestinian crisis moved further with the Bush administration's announcement of plans for an "international conference" to be held in the summer of 2002. Like the Madrid Conference that followed the Gulf War, early indicators were that Bush officials saw such a conference as both an opportunity to set the parameters for a new US-shaped regional approach to the Israel-Palestine crisis, and simultaneously a chance to bolster support in the region for its anti-Iraq mobilization. Israel was still resistant though, and what was first touted as an "international conference" was soon downgraded in Bush administration parlance to a ministerial-level meeting. Like his father's high-profile meeting in Madrid in 1991, it appeared Bush Junior's so-called "international conference" would serve only as an international launch of separate, uneven, and unequal Israeli-Palestinian, Israeli-Syrian, and Israeli-Lebanese talks, all under an over-arching Israel-protecting American umbrella.

Meanwhile, at home the Palestine crisis brought the Bush administration to its first serious foreign policy challenge from the right wing of its own party. Neo-conservatives, Christian fundamentalists, and other components of the Republican Party's hard right edge moved into an even tighter embrace of Ariel Sharon's Israel, rejecting even Bush's pretense of concern for Palestinian rights. Pro-Israeli sentiment in the United States and support for pro-Israeli lobbies had traditionally been the purview of liberal Jews, and strongest in the Democratic Party. From at least the mid-1990s, however, that had begun to change. Increasingly, right-wing Christian fundamentalists with power in Republican circles emerged as formidable allies of the traditional liberal supporters of Israel. Right-wing leaders like Jerry Falwell and Pat Robertson became regulars on the support-Israel circuit. Part of the reason was theological: many Christian fundamentalists believe that the second coming of Christ requires an "ingathering" of all Jews in the Biblical land of Israel; this belief thus puts these Christians on the side not only of Israel as an existing state, but of Zionism as a political project dedicated to the "ingathering" of the Jewish people. (The inconveniently anti-Semitic fact that the next step in the second coming would be the conversion or death of all those Jews seems lost on the Jewish leaders eager to embrace any influential backers of Israel.) For the Bush administration, the presence of large numbers of pro-Israel, right-wing voters, along with influential leaders of the Republicans' far-right edge, made defense of Israel a significantly higher priority than it would otherwise have been for this oil-industry-oriented administration generally interested in maintaining stability and good ties with Arab oil regimes.

Paul Wolfowitz, ardent pro-Israeli hawk and Bush's deputy chief of the Pentagon, was booed by tens of thousands of pro-Israeli demonstrators at a Washington rally in April when he had the temerity to mention as a brief aside that Palestinian children might be suffering too. Within the Republican Party, the far right uncritically backed Sharon's policy of permanent occupation, settlement expansion, and military attack and destruction of the Palestinian infrastructure. The so-called "moderates," some of them grouped around Bush himself, clung to their traditional concerns about oil and going after Saddam Hussein (something both wings largely agreed on) and maintained the same unequivocal military, economic, and diplomatic support for Israel The only difference was that the moderates talked the language of a Palestinian state. As the 2002 elections came closer, the prospect of a serious division, if not a real split, within the Republican ranks remained a Texas-sized nightmare for the president.

On April 20, more than 100,000 Americans did something that, in the wake of September 11, suddenly seemed very brave: they packed the Washington Mall, marched and rallied from the Washington Monument to the Capitol, and filled the streets of San Francisco. The demonstrations took place as the Bush administration struggled to regroup and recast its Middle East policy following the debacle of the Cheney, Powell, and Zinni failures, and less than a week after a very different large gathering laid claim to the Mall in the name of supporting Israel. The demonstrations brought all the attention back to the foreign policy of the United States, framing the Israeli occupation of Palestine as a crisis of US, as much as Israeli, policy and responsibility.

In Washington they gathered in four separate mobilizations, each focused on a number of separate but related causes—the Bush administration's war in Afghanistan; attacks on Arabs and Muslims and broader civil liberties assaults within the US; the war in Colombia; and corporate-driven globalization and the destruction wrought by its institutional backers, the IMF, and the World Bank. What dominated the entire mobilization, however, was Palestine. And more than just Palestine, the consistent cry was the demand to end the United States support for Israel's occupation of Palestine, its backing of Ariel Sharon, and its funding of Israel's war machine.

The significance of the demonstration lay in the integration, for the first time, of the issue of Palestine and Israeli occupation into the broadest components of the peace and global justice movements. For the first time, the issue was not marginalized for fear of alienating supporters of Israel within those movements. For the first time, the call to end US support for Israeli occupation and its attendant horrors joined the call for a law-based, not war-based, response to the attacks on the World Trade Center. September 11 had changed even the peace movement.

SEVEN

AFTER: THE DANGERS, THE ALTERNATIVES, THE POSSIBILITIES

September 11 had changed the United States domestic politics too. From the first hours after the attacks, partisan division had swiftly dropped off Washington's political agenda. But with the partisan bickering also went virtually any serious critique of the overwhelming shift to the right in civil liberties, in the unchallengeability of the power of the executive branch, in the status and influence of the once-marginalized Pentagon hawks. After an initial period of stunned and acquiescent silence, some critical Congressional voices reemerged, largely centered in the Black and Progressive Caucuses. With only one or two exceptions, however, even those critics kept their focus on the civil liberties issues, the domestic policy side. The war in Afghanistan, the assertion of newly-empowered military unilateralism around the world proceeded largely undisputed.

The ideological side of that assertion continued as well. It was not enough for the Bush administration to reject ratification of the Rome Treaty establishing the International Criminal Court, signed grudgingly by Bill Clinton only hours before the deadline. Clinton himself had made clear that his signature should not be taken as an expression of support (despite the fact that signing a treaty is supposed to indicate exactly that) for the ICC, but rather was a tactical move to ensure an American voice in the debate about how the Court should take shape. Clinton made clear he had no intention of submitting the treaty to the Senate for ratification. But George Bush had to go even further.

On May 6, 2002 the Bush administration formally renounced support for the treaty, and said that the new Court should expect no cooperation from the United States, and that Washington would not provide ICC prosecutors with any information that might help them bring cases against any accused war criminals. US Ambassador-at-large for War Crimes Issues Pierre-Richard Prosper said he could not envision a future situation in which the US would assist the Court. "We've washed our hands. It's over," he said. Secretary of Defense Rumsfeld said that the ICC would "necessarily complicate US military cooperation," and added (in an unintentionally hopeful note) that an international court with jurisdiction over genocide, war crimes, and crimes against humanity "could well create a powerful disincentive for US military engagement in the world."[1] One wonders whether Rumsfeld had suddenly become aware that many people saw too little distinction between unilateral US "military engagement" and war crimes.

It was a move unprecedented in international diplomacy, although for an administration that came into office blithely asserting that the US, its hyper-power unchallenged, would do fine all alone, perhaps it should have been no surprise. The renunciation of a treaty signature had never, according to UN officials, happened before. Under the 1969 Vienna Convention on the Law of Treaties, to which the United States is a signatory, states are prohibited from doing anything to violate or undermine a treaty they have signed, even if they have not ratified it. Signature on a treaty is understood to be a step toward ratification.

The Bush administration's letter to UN Secretary General Kofi Annan stated directly, however, that President Clinton's signature on the treaty was no longer legally binding. "The United States does not intend to become a party to the treaty. Accordingly, the United States has no legal obligations from its signature on December 31, 2000."[2]

Interestingly, the administration's letter was signed by John R. Bolton, the under-secretary of state for arms control. The ICC was not within the purview of his office, but Bolton had a long history of hard-line ideological unilateralism, and he regarded the United Nations as a tactical instrument of US policy since his years as the under-secretary of state for international organizations, the linchpin of the State Department's ties to UN affairs during the Reagan administration. Bolton once said:

> There is no United Nations. There is an international community that occasionally can be led by the only real power left in the world, and that is the United States, when it suits our interest, and when we can get others to go along.... When the United States leads, the United Nations will follow. When it suits our interest to do so, we will do so. When it does not suit our interests we will not."[3]

Some in the Congress saw the decision to reject the ICC as endangering the US fight against terrorism. Senator Russell Feingold noted:

[B]eyond the extremely problematic matter of casting doubt on the US commitment to international justice and accountability, these steps actually call into question our country's credibility in all multilateral endeavors. As we continue to fight terrorism worldwide, we are asking countries around the globe to honor important commitments, to crack down on the financial and communications networks of terrorists and international criminals, and to share sensitive intelligence with the United States. This is not the right time to signal a lack of respect for multilateralism.4

Maybe not for Senator Feingold. But for the Bush administration it seemed exactly the right time.

AN END TO BUSH'S FREE RIDE?

But then came the memos. On May 15, 2002 a trickle—that quickly became a flood—of breathless news reports emerged regarding what President Bush (and/or other high-ranking officials of his administration) knew and when they knew it. The subject was the September 11 attacks, the role of bin Laden, and the threat that might have been known but somehow was not caught. A month earlier, Member of Congress Cynthia McKinney had asked the Bush administration to clarify what they knew about the attacks before they occurred, and she was excoriated by the press and marginalized even by some supporters. No one was quite willing to say that Bush or anyone else in or around the White House actually knew that the September 11 attacks on the World Trade Center and the Pentagon were going to happen and did nothing to stop them. And yet…

One report was of an FBI memo, drafted by an agent in the Phoenix, Arizona field office in July 2001, which had warned of potential danger involving Arab men the agent believed to be suspicious, training at a flight school in the United States. The memo also mentioned al-Qaeda, and when the memo surfaced in May 2002, the CIA matched its names to two of the September 11 hijackers. Another set of reports focused on the top-secret intelligence briefing Bush received on August 6, which was headlined "Bin Laden Determined to Strike in US." That one included background information regarding bin Laden's and al-Qaeda's efforts to "bring the fight to America," at least partly in retaliation for the 1998 US missile strikes on al-Qaeda camps in Afghanistan.5

Taken as a whole, there was certainly legitimate concern about the failure of Washington's vast intelligence apparatus to "connect the dots", as pundits endlessly repeated. The situation was not helped by the claims of Bush administration figures, from Bush and Vice President Cheney on down, that no one could have possibly imagined such an act as those that happened September 11. We only thought regular, old-fashioned hijacking was the danger, they said. If we had ever imagined such a thing as September 11 was possible, of course something would have been done.

"I don't think anybody could have predicted that these people would take an airplane and slam it into the World Trade Center, take another one and slam it into the Pentagon; that they would try to use an airplane as a missile, a hijacked airplane as a missile," National Security Adviser Condoleezza Rice said on May 16.

One problem with that argument, of course, is its implication that old-fashioned, pre-September 11, "regular" hijacking was somehow okay, that using innovative weapons to commandeer an airliner and hold it hostage to demand release of prisoners, as some reports predicted, was not anything requiring any particular concern.

Perhaps more serious was the problem that people not only "could have" but in fact did predict exactly that—people that included not only Tom Clancy (didn't anyone read *Debt of Honor?*) but the former deputy director of the CIA, John Gannon. Gannon chaired the National Intelligence Council, a CIA-linked grouping of a dozen senior intelligence officers assigned to threat-analysis and intelligence priorities. In a September 1999 NIC report, Gannon described how "Suicide bomber(s) belonging to al-Qaeda's Martyrdom Battalion could crash-land an aircraft packed with high explosives (C-4 and semtex) into the Pentagon, the headquarters of the Central Intelligence Agency (CIA), or the White House." The report, entitled the "Sociology and Psychology of Terrorism: Who Becomes a Terrorist and Why?", described suicide hijacking as one of the possible responses al-Qaeda might carry out in retaliation for the United States' air strikes on its Afghanistan camps in August 1998.[6]

Furthermore, equally serious but largely ignored in the media was the clash of civilizations-style racism inherent in the we-could-not-have-ever-predicted argument. Implicit in the claim of unpredictability or unimaginability is the notion that "we"—Americans, westerners, the good guys—are simply incapable of envisioning, let alone carrying out, something so evil. (They must have thought "Tom Clancy" was a

pseudonym for someone named Abu Mohammad.... Only "they"—
Arabs, the bad guys, the others—could envision such a thing.

There was more than a little bit of political opportunism in the
barely-contained glee that characterized some of the Democratic
response to the flood of leaks and debates over who would carry out the
investigation[s]. (After all, the National Intelligence Council memo
had been drafted on Clinton's watch, with equally inadequate
response.) Beyond the partisanship, however, lay the basis for at least
the beginning of the first serious challenge to Bush's unilateralism and
military aggressiveness since September 11 when a tight not-while-
we're-at-war hand was clapped over the mouths of even the most
principled of congressional critics. Many journalists, muzzled by
editorial fiat or self-imposed censorship since September 11, jumped
eagerly into the new fray.

The administration, meanwhile, responded by trying to hold on to
the mantle of "we're all that stands between you and more attacks."
Within days of the reports of the unconnected dots, new warnings
suddenly emerged. Rice and other officials hit the talk show circuit
with dire reports of more "chatter" being overheard among terrorists
in the satellite intercepts. "Something big" was likely under way, but
no information regarding when, where, against whom or what, in the
United States or overseas. According to Vice President Dick Cheney,
another al-Qaeda attack was "almost certain," but it could happen
"tomorrow or next week or next year."[7] Suicide bombings like those
in Israel were "inevitable," according to FBI director Robert S.
Mueller.[8] Secretary of Defense Rumsfeld warned in dire terms that
terrorist organizations "inevitably are going to get their hands on"
weapons of mass destruction and would not hesitate to use them.[9]

Don't worry, White House officials assured Americans. The spate of
alarms and warnings were not part of any White House campaign, nor
were they aimed at deflecting criticism regarding the earlier intelligence
failures. Wow, that was a relief. It would only be luck then, if, as many
anticipated, no terrorist attack occurred in the near future. Officials
could then draw parallels to the pre-September 11 warnings to show
how intelligence material is simply never definitive so the failures are
really no one's fault.

ALTERNATIVES

As the post-September 11 silence began to break eight months later, what remained unspoken was the question of what different kind of response to the horrific attacks might have been considered, what the US reaction might have been. Soon after the September 11 attacks, and as soon as the Bush administration made clear its decision to mobilize for a limitless war in response, it became gospel that the American people were demanding war and that they would not have accepted any other response.

That assessment ignores, however, the fact that in the first hours and first days following September 11, Americans were shocked, grieving, and frightened. For most Americans it was the first experience of being under attack, the first time of suffering through a crime of such magnitude. For many, that led to a kind of paralysis of fear. For them, and for many many more, the desperate search was for answers, for leadership.

Congressman Dennis Kucinich, head of the Progressive Caucus, gave voice to an alternative vision several months later, in February 2002:

> Let us pray that our nation's leaders will not be overcome with fear. Because today there is great fear in our great Capitol.... The trappings of a state of siege trap us in a state of fear, ill-equipped to deal with the Patriot Games, the Mind Games, the War Games of an unelected President and his unelected Vice President. Let us pray that our country will stop this war....
>
> We licensed a response to those who helped bring the terror of September the Eleventh. But we the people and our elected representatives must reserve the right to measure the response, to proportion the response, to challenge the response, and to correct the response....
>
> Because we did not authorize the invasion of Iraq.
> We did not authorize the invasion of Iran.
> We did not authorize the invasion of North Korea.
> We did not authorize the bombing of civilians in Afghanistan.
> We did not authorize permanent detainees in Guantanamo Bay.
> We did not authorize the withdrawal from the Geneva Convention.
> We did not authorize military tribunals suspending due process and
> *habeas corpus.*
> We did not authorize assassination squads.
> We did not authorize the resurrection of COINTELPRO.
> We did not authorize the repeal of the Bill of Rights.
> We did not authorize the revocation of the Constitution.
> We did not authorize national identity cards.
> We did not authorize the eye of Big Brother to peer from cameras

throughout our cities.

We did not authorize an eye for an eye.

Nor did we ask that the blood of innocent people, who perished on September 11, be avenged with the blood of innocent villagers in Afghanistan.

We did not authorize the administration to wage war anytime, anywhere, anyhow it pleases.

We did not authorize war without end.

We did not authorize a permanent war economy.

Yet we are upon the threshold of a permanent war economy. The President has requested a $45.6 billion increase in military spending. All defense-related programs will cost close to $400 billion. Consider that the Department of Defense has never passed an independent audit. Consider that the Inspector General has notified Congress that the Pentagon cannot properly account for $1.2 trillion in transactions. Consider that in recent years the Department of Defense could not match $22 billion worth of expenditures to the items it purchased, wrote off as lost billions of dollars worth of in-transit inventory, and stored nearly $30 billion worth of spare parts it did not need.

Yet the defense budget grows with more money for weapons systems to fight a cold war which ended, weapon systems in search of new enemies to create new wars. This has nothing to do with fighting terror. This has everything to do with fueling a military industrial machine with the treasure of our nation, risking the future of our nation, risking democracy itself with the militarization of thought which follows the militarization of the budget.

Let us pray for our children. Our children deserve a world without end. Not a war without end. Our children deserve a world free of the terror of hunger, free of the terror of poor health care, free of the terror of homelessness, free of the terror of ignorance, free of the terror of hopelessness, free of the terror of policies which are committed to a world view which is not appropriate for the survival of a free people, not appropriate for the survival of democratic values, not appropriate for the survival of our nation, and not appropriate for the survival of the world.

Let us pray that we have the courage and the will as a people and as a nation to shore ourselves up, to reclaim from the ruins of September the Eleventh our democratic traditions. Let us declare our love for democracy. Let us declare our intent for peace. Let us work to make nonviolence an organizing principle in our own society. Let us recommit ourselves to the slow and painstaking work of statecraft, which sees peace, not war as being inevitable. Let us work for a world where someday war becomes archaic....

Let us pray that we have the courage to replace the images of death which haunt us, the layers of images of September the Eleventh, faded into images of patriotism, spliced into images of military mobilization, jump cut into images of our secular celebrations of the World Series, New Year's Eve, the Superbowl, the Olympics, the strobic flashes which touch our deepest fears, let us replace those images with the work of human relations, reaching out to people, helping our own citizens here at home, lifting the plight of the poor everywhere. That is the America which has the ability to rally the support of the world. That is the America which stands not in pursuit of an axis of evil, but which is itself at the axis of hope and faith and peace and freedom.[10]

WHAT MIGHT HAVE BEEN

The seeming unanimity of calls for war (which were not ever as close to unanimous as they were depicted) came not in immediate response to the attacks but later, after hours and days of hearing from the president and high-ranking officials that only war could answer such a crime. No other response was ever posed.

On the day after the attacks, British Prime Minister Tony Blair told Bush that he was confident "American public opinion would give Bush breathing space and adequate time to prepare."[11] Blair was right—but public opinion would also have followed a leadership asserted in an entirely different direction, toward a law-based, rather than war-based, response.

George Bush had a choice on September 11. First, he could have insisted that his pilot land Air Force One in New York City (instead of flying around and landing at obscure refueling stops ostensibly because of claims of threats to the plane) so he could address the country immediately from what was not yet known as Ground Zero. He could have immediately given a very clear and unequivocal speech to his nation and to the world. The president's address might have gone something like this:

"Our people have been the victims of a horrific crime, a crime against humanity.

"We mourn together the victims of this terrible crime, and we pledge to take care of all its victims even as we begin our efforts to understand how and why such a crime could happen and to find and bring to justice the perpetrators of this crime. We recognize today that this attack, like others in so many other countries and places around the world, has international ramifications.

"We recognize even at the beginning of this crisis that we cannot answer this crime alone. This was not an act of war, carried out by a country, and we will not turn to war against any country. That will not find the perpetrators or bring them to justice, nor will it prevent such crimes from occurring in the future. Instead, we need a legal framework that is international in scope and that relies on international law and the United Nations Charter for its legitimacy.

"Even as we continue the task of rescuing the living and burying the dead, we begin with a recognition that we were wrong in the past to reject the International Criminal Court. We understand in a whole new way tonight why such a court must be created, and we now pledge our political and financial support to ensuring that such a court, independent and empowered to act independently, can be built. We know that we cannot rely on the International Criminal Court yet, so we will support the creation of a new international tribunal. This tribunal will be backed by an internationally collaborative and independent police force, drawn in each case largely from countries and regions where suspects may be and who are familiar with the conditions that could give rise to such actions. We know that such a court, such a prosecution effort, must be part of a new kind of international cooperation, one based on democratic equality among and between nations, rather than a coalition of coercion based solely on one country's power. That means that such a court will be used even-handedly—for *we must unite in opposing all terrorists, not just some.* That means all who are responsible for war crimes and terrorism should be brought to justice. Henry Kissinger may be next in the dock with the perpetrators of these latest attacks, and maybe Generals Sharon and Pinochet will be next up. They should not be granted impunity simply because they were backed by the United States.

"We approach this crime internationally because we know that the only sustainable justice is international justice. And justice—not war and not vengeance—is our goal. We will seek the perpetrators and bring them to trial in a legitimate and fair court. And beyond the immediate perpetrators, we will take seriously the challenge of understanding why this happened. Not only the easier question of why a few people would target our people and the symbols of our economic and military power in such a cruel way. But as well the distinct and much harder challenge of understanding why so many more people, in so many parts of the world, thought maybe this attack was not such a bad idea. We will look for root causes in realities of grinding poverty, political disempowerment, and social injustice that together create lives of desperation. And we will search for what role our policies, our economy, our military, our corporations, and our influence have played in creating those conditions. And we will change those realities.

"We will honor the dead not with war but with justice, in their names. We will seek justice, based on international law and the UN Charter, and we will work to encourage internationalism, not our own domination, to do so.

"And I say to you today that I make one more commitment in this time and in this place. There has been too much death today already. Americans and others from more than sixty countries were killed here, and that is already too much. We will prove that we can be different from terrorists who target innocent civilians. I make a commitment now, today, September 11, 2001, that not one more innocent life will be sacrificed in our search for justice."

In the real world, however, on the real September 11, the real President Bush said no such thing. Less than a month later the first bombers would strike Afghanistan. Thousands of civilians would die, and they would continue to die even as the elusive targets of the war remained at large.

Watching George Bush ratchet up the calls for war on that singular night, putting even grief aside to foment anger and vengeance as the only legitimate responses, one might have thought as *The Crucible's* John Proctor did: "I have never knew until tonight that the world is gone daft with this nonsense."

Unilateralism, in all its virulence, was proudly ascendant. US military supremacy was unabashedly the order of the day across the globe. Thirty-six thousand children still die every day as the result of malnutrition and treatable diseases. The possibility of a global challenge to that domination, centered in the United Nations but involving a far broader, more inclusive, and more representative international civil society, remained to be created.

As Kofi Annan noted in his 2002 Nobel Peace Prize acceptance speech, for most people in the world, the world did not change on September 11. "The old problems that existed on 10 September, before the attack, are still with us: poverty, the elimination of poverty, the fight against HIV-AIDS, the question of the environment, and ensuring we stop exploiting resources the way we've been doing," he said. "All these issues.... are still with us and I think we need to focus on them as well."[12]

The promising potential of such an international challenge was taking hesitant shape in the United Nations and elsewhere during the first months of the Bush Junior administration when governments had begun to stand up to the United States bullying. But that challenge was abruptly shut down on September 11. Perhaps that challenge to the new US empire can be rebuilt. "We still believe that another world is possible," wrote Bolivian human rights activist Oscar Olivares to friends in the US on September 12. "We are with you."

NOTES

ONE: THE BUSH ADMINISTRATION STEPS INTO THE WORLD

1 David Gergen, "Bring back the junkets!," *US News & World Report* 27 Oct. 1997.

2 In its effort to ennoble the United States' troops at the heart of the story, the movie ignored the political roots of the 1992–93 US intervention in Somalia, in particular the US refusal to participate in the original United Nations aid protection effort. It was US troops sent into Somalia under a separate Pentagon command, not sanctioned by the Security Council, whose mission in Mogadishu led to the deaths of close to 1,000 Somalis as well as the eighteen US Army Rangers. The movie also ignored the longer history of US involvement in the country, particularly Somalia's role as a Cold War battlefield in which both US and Soviet sponsorship left behind a country awash in poverty and want, with a surplus only of guns, mortars, and landmines.

3 Evan Williams, interviewing Charles Kupchan, "World in Focus," Australian Broadcasting Company, 11 Apr. 2001.

4 Derek Brown, "The US-China spy plane row," *The Guardian* 4 Apr. 2001.

5 "Spy plane breakthrough," BBC, 11 Apr. 2001.

6 Alan Sipress, "New Foreign Policy Ringing In the Old," *Washington Post* 10 June 2001.

7 John Vinocur, "Going It Alone: US Upsets France So Paris Begins a Campaign to Strengthen Multilateral Institutions," *International Herald-Tribune* 3 Feb. 1999.

8 Thomas Friedman, "Noblesse Oblige," *New York Times* 31 July 2001.

9 Walter C. Clemens, Jr., "How to Lose Friends and Inspire Enemies," *Washington Post* 20 May 2001.

10 David E. Sanger, "House Threatens To Hold Back UN Dues for Loss of Seat," *New York Times* 9 May 2001.

11 Harold Hongju Koh, "A Wake-Up Call on Human Rights," *Washington Post* 8 May 2001.

12 Dennis Jett, "The World's Only Super Pouter," *Christian Science Monitor* 14 May 2001.

13 "A More Assertive Europe," editorial, *New York Times* 30 Mar. 2001.

14 John Hughes, "Cheer Up, Ugly Americans," *Christian Science Monitor* 20 June 2001.

15 "Containing America," editorial, *Christian Science Monitor* 15 June 2001.

16 "Powell Fails to Persuade NATO on Antimissile Plan," *Associated Press* 30 May 2001.

17 "A Wary Atlantic Alliance," editorial, *New York Times* 31 May 2001.

18 Marie Isabelle Chevrier, quoted in Vernon Loeb, "Bush Panel Faults Germ Warfare Protocol," *Washington Post* 27 May 2001.

19 "President Bush's Arrogant Negotiating Style Is All Take and No Give," *The Independent* 26 July 2001.

20 Mike Allen and Steven Mufson, "US Scuttles Germ War Conference," *The Independent* 8 Dec. 2001.

21 Keith B. Richburg, "Europeans Object to Bush Approach on Foreign Policy," *Washington Post* 16 Aug. 2001.

22 Michael J. Glennon, "There's a Point to Going It Alone: Unilateralism Has Often Serves Us Well," *Washington Post* 12 Aug. 2001.

23 Thomas E. Ricks, "Empire or not? A Quiet Debate Over US Role," *Washington Post* 21 Aug. 2001.

24 "With regard to the historical aspects, the European Union profoundly deplores the human suffering, both individual and collective, caused by slavery and the slave trade. They are amongst the most dishonourable and abhorrent chapters in the history of humanity. The European Union condemns these practices, in the past and present, and regrets the suffering they have caused.

"Some effects of colonialism have caused immense suffering which still persist today. Any act causing such suffering must be condemned, wherever and whenever it occurred.

"Through these acts of acknowledgement, regret and condemnation, the European Union, aware of the moral obligation incumbent on the entire international community vis-à-vis the victims of these tragedies, shows its firm determination to honour this obligation and to accept its responsibility. It considers that it is the obligation of each individual to remember the suffering caused by events occurring at different points in history, so that they will never be forgotten. The obligation to remember will make it possible to build the future on solid foundations and to prevent the recurrence of the grave errors of the past."

The European Commission, General Affairs Council, "Council Conclusions: On the World Conference Against Racism, Racial Discrimination, Xenophobia and Related Intolerance," 16 July 2001.

25 Hugh Nevill, "US, Israel, pull out of acrimonious racism conference," *Agence France-Presse,* Durban, 3 Sept. 2001.

26 Mahmood Mamdani, "An African Perspective on Contemporary Terrorism," Director, Institute of African Studies, Columbia University, *Pambazuka News* 47.

27 Nevill, 3 Sept. 2001.

28 Nevill, 3 Sept. 2001.

29 BBC World, 4 Aug. 2001.

30 Ofeibea Quist-Arcton, "Delegates Confused by US Stance on Conference," allAfrica.com 4 Sept. 2001.

TWO: THE US IN THE MIDDLE EAST

1 Hisham H. Ahmed, "Roots of Denial: American Stand on Palestinian Self-Determination From the Balfour Declaration to World War II," in Michael W. Suleiman, ed., *US Policy on Palestine From Wilson to Clinton* (Washington, DC: AAUG Press, 1995) 30.

2 David Hunter Miller, *My Diary at the Conference of Paris, With Documents* (New York: Appeal Printing, 1928), cited in Ahmad 35.

3 Miller, cited in Ahmad 36.

4 Sami Hadawi, *Bitter Harvest: A Modern History of Palestine* (Northampton, MA: Olive Branch Press: 1991) 16.

5 Hadawi 16.

6 Hadawi 16.

7 Michael Bar-Zohar, *Ben-Gurion: The Armed Prophet* (Englewood Cliffs, NJ: Prentice-Hall, 1968) 69.

8 Assistant Secretary of War John J. McCloy, quoted in Stephen Rosskamm Shalom, "The US Response to Humanitarian Crises," *Imperial Alibis* (Boston: South End Press, 1993).

9 Cited by Alfred Lilienthal, *What Price Israel?*, (Chicago: Henry Regenery Co., 1953) 194–196.

10 Foreign Office documents on Palestine, 1945, quoted in Salaam.co.uk website.

11 *The Arab Case for Palestine: Evidence Submitted by the Arab Office, Jerusalem, to the Anglo-American Committee of Inquiry, March 1946*, cited in Walter Laqueur, ed., *The Israel-Arab Reader*, (New York: Penguin, 1971).

12 UN General Assembly Plenary Meeting, 2nd Session, 5 (Nov. 1947): 1313–14.

13 Drew Pearson, *Chicago Daily Tribune* 9 Feb. 1948.

14 Benny Morris, "Revisiting the Palestinian Exodus of 1948," in Eugene L. Rogan and Avi Shlaim, eds., *The War for Palestine: Rewriting the History of 1948* (Cambridge: Cambridge UP, 2001) 38.

15 Eugene Rostow, "The Middle Eastern Crisis in the Perspective of World Affairs," *International Affairs* Apr. 1971.

16 Editorial, *US News and World Report* 19 June 1967.

17 Editorial, *Ha'aretz* 30 Sept. 1951.

18 *New York Times* 1 Nov. 1973.

19 Terence Smith, "Mondale Says Begin Agrees to a Parley with Egypt and US," *New York Times*, 3 July 1978, cited in Seth Tillman, *The United States in the Middle East: Interests and Obstacles* (Bloomington: Indiana UP, 1982).

20 Howard Raines, "President Praises Senate's Action as Statesmanlike and Courageous," *New York Times* 29 Oct. 1981, cited in Tillman.

21 Donald Neff, "Israel Bombs Iraq's Osirak Nuclear Research Facility," *Washington Report on Middle East Affairs* June 1995.

22 Cited in Noam Chomsky, *The Fateful Triangle: The US, Israel and the Palestinians* (Boston: South End Press, 1983).

23 Claudia Wright, *New Statesman* 20 Aug. 1982, cited in Chomsky.

24 Yoseph Priel, "Dispatch from Washington," *Davar* 5 Aug. 1982, cited in Chomsky 214.

25 Chomsky 214.

26 Testimony of Israeli Foreign Ministry official Bruce Kashdan before the Commission of Inquiry, in Norman Kempster, *Los Angeles Times* 22 Nov. 1982, cited in Chomsky 368.

27 Cited in Robert Fisk, *Pity the Nation: The Abduction of Lebanon* (New York: Atheneum, 1990)444.

28 Fisk 479.

29 Steven Lee Myers, "US Jets Strike Missile Sites 30 Miles Outside Baghdad," *New York Times* 25 Feb. 1999.

30 Catherine Toups, *Washington Times* 13 Dec. 1995.

31 Butler meeting with UN-accredited disarmament organizations, New York, 12 Feb. 1998.

32 Tim Weiner, "The Case of the Spies Without a Country," *New York Times* 17 Jan. 1999.

33 Laura Silber & David Buchan, "UN-Iraq Accord Faces Early Test," *Financial Times* 4 Mar. 1998.

34 Lee Michael Katz, "UN Waffling on Threat of Force," *USA Today* 3 Mar. 1998.

35 Jonathan Peterson, "Clinton to Iraq: US 'Prepared to Act,'" *Los Angeles Times* 4 Mar. 1998.

36 Iraq Staff Trip Report, 27 Aug.–6 Sept. 1999.

37 Barbara Crossette, "America Moves Apart from the UN on Iraq," *New York Times* 26 Dec. 1999.

38 Amira Hass, "Deceptive Generosity," *Ha'aretz* (English Edition) 13 Dec. 2000.

39 Susan Akram, "Palestinians Refugee Rights: Failure Under International Law," *Information Brief,* Center for Policy Analysis on Palestine, 28 July 2000.

40 "News at Noon," WDBJ-7, Roanoke, VA, 9 July 2000, archived by the Scholarly Communications Project, University Libraries, Virginia Tech University <scholar.lib.vt.edu/VA-news/WDBJ-7/script archives/>.

41 Robert Malley and Hussein Agha, "Camp David: The Tragedy of Errors," *The New York Review of Books* 9 Aug. 2001.

42 Online update, Save the Children, February 2002.

43 Quoted in Fred Hiatt, "Tiptoe Diplomacy," *Washington Post* 28 Jan. 2002.

44 *Lateline*, Australian Broadcasting Company, 8 July 2001.

THREE: THE EMPIRE STRIKES BACK

1 National Public Radio, 1 March 2002.

2 Bob Woodward and Dan Balz, "'We Will Rally the World,'" *Washington Post* 28 Jan. 2002.

3 President George Bush, CNN, 23 Jan. 2002.

4 "Proposed Pentagon Budget Hike More Than Other Countries' Military Spending," *Associated Press* 26 Jan. 2002.

5 "Terror Prompts Huge US Military Revamp," BBC, 1 Feb. 2002.

6 *Lehrer News Hour*, PBS, 11 Mar. 2002.

7 Paul Blustein, "Bush Seeks Foreign Aid Boost," *Washington Post* 15 Mar. 2002.

8 Woodward and Balz, 28 Jan. 2002.

9 Helen Dewar, "In Congress, 'an Unprecedented Reaction,'" *Washington Post* 19 Nov. 2001.

10 William Safire, "That Dog Won't Bark," *New York Times* 24 Feb. 2002.

11 UN DPI Release, Security Council SC/7143, 4370th Meeting, 12 Sept. 2001: "Security Council Condemns, 'In Strongest Terms,' Terrorist Attacks on United States, Unanimously Adopting Resolution 1368 (2001), Council Calls on All States to Bring Perpetrators to Justice."

12 Ambassador John Negroponte, Georgetown University, Washington, DC, 27 Feb. 2002.

13 Negroponte, 27 Feb. 2002.

14 Helen Duffy, "Responding to September 11: The Framework of International Law," Interights, Lancaster House, London, October 2001.

15 Human Rights Watch, "Middle East and North Africa Overview—Human Rights Developments," World Report, (New York: HRW, 1999).

16 Testimony of Secretary of State Colin Powell, House International Relations Committee, 7 Feb. 2001.

17 Tom Nagy, "The Secret Behind the Sanctions: How the US Intentionally Destroyed Iraq's Water Supply," *The Progressive* Sept. 2001.

FOUR: A COALITION OF COERCION

1 Colum Lynch, "Annan Urges Cautious Response," *Washington Post* 25 Sept. 2001.

2 Catherine Toups, *Washington Times* 13 Dec. 1995.

3 Steven Mufson, "US Urged to Target Nations that Aid Terrorism," *Washington Post* 12 Sept. 2001.

4 Thomas E. Ricks and Vernon Loeb, "Rumsfeld and Commanders Exchange Briefings," *Washington Post* 3 Mar. 2002.

5 Patrick Tyler and Jane Perlez, "World Leaders List Conditions on Cooperation," *New York Times* 19 Sept. 2001.

6 Roland Koch, floor-leader of the PDS, DeutschWelle Television, 19 Sept. 2001.

7 Alan Cowell, "Blair Leaves British Awed or Seething Over His Role," *New York Times* 5 Oct. 2001.

8 Jane Perlez, "Blair and Chirac Head to US For Talks and a Show of Unity," *New York Times* 18 Sept. 2001.

9 Perlez, 18 Sept. 2001.

10 Peter Finn, "War Boosts NATO Hopes of Two Nations," *Washington Post* 26 Mar. 2002.

11 Karl Franz Lamers, quoted in Steven Erlanger, "US Officials Try to Assure Europeans on NATO," *New York Times* 3 Feb. 2002.

12 Suzanne Daley, "NATO Quickly Gives the US All the Help That It Asked," *New York Times* 5 Oct. 2001.

13 Daley, 5 Oct. 2001.

14 Hosni Mubarak on "Larry King Live," CNN, 17 Sept. 2001.

15 Perlez, 18 Sept. 2001.

16 Defense Minister Binyamin Ben Eliezer, *Yedioth Aharaonot* (Israel) 14 Sept. 2001, quoted in Jerusalem Media & Communications Center, *News* Sept. 2001.

17 "Sharon warns US not to 'appease' Arabs," CNN, 5 Oct. 2001.

18 Tyler and Perlez, 19 Sept. 2001.

19 Amnesty International: "The backlash—human rights at risk throughout the world," *ACT* 30/027/2001, 4 Oct. 2001.

20 Colin Powell, "United States Position on Terrorists and Peace in the Middle East," McConnell Center for Political Leadership, University of Louisville, Kentucky, 19 Nov. 2001.

21 Tyler and Perlez, 19 Sept. 2001.

22 Serge Schmemann, "UN Delays General Assembly Session of World Leaders

Indefinitely," *New York Times* 19 Sept. 2001.

23 Praful Bidwai, "From Pokharan to Kargil: The Nuclear Danger is No Fantasy," *The Times of India* 2 June 1999.

24 Praful Bidwai, "'Terrorism': India's New 'Strategic' Chance?" *InterPress Service* 13 Sept. 2001.

25 Michelle Ciarrocca, "Arms—Into Whose Hands?," MotherJones.com Feb. 2002.

26 Vernon Loeb, "US Pursues Closer Ties to India," *Washington Post* 6 Nov. 2001.

27 Ciarrocca, Feb. 2002.

28 President George Bush, Washington, DC, 11 March 2002.

29 Interview with Karimov, Uzbek Television First Channel, 9 Oct. 2001, cited in Amnesty International, "Central Asia: No Excuse for Escalating Human Rights Violations," Oct. 2001.

30 United States, Bureau of Democracy, Human Rights, and Labor, "Uzbekistan: Country Reports on Human Rights Practices 2001," (Washington:GPO) 4 Mar. 2002.

31 Ciarrocca, Feb. 2002.

32 Human Rights Watch, "UN Criticizes Uzbekistan for Torture," press release, 13 May 2002.

33 "Kazakh Leader of Opposition Takes Refuge in Embassy," *New York Times* 1 April 2002.

34 Michael R. Gordon and C.J. Chivers, "US May Gain Use of More Air Bases to Strike Taliban," *New York Times* 4 Nov. 2001.

35 James P. Dorian, "Oil, gas in FSU Central Asia, northwestern China," *Oil & Gas Journal* 10 Sept. 2001.

36 Cited in Barry O'Kelly, "Prospect of oil riches speeds the wheels of war," *Business Post* (Ireland) 28 Oct. 2001.

37 O'Kelly, 28 Oct. 2001.

38 "How Oil Interests Play Out in US Bombing of Afghanistan," *Drillbits and Tailings*, Project Underground, 31 Oct. 2001.

39 O'Kelly, 28 Oct. 2001.

40 O'Kelly, 28 Oct. 2001.

41 "Pipeline Politics: Oil, the Taliban and the Political Balance of Central Asia," Special Report, WorldPress.org , Nov. 2001.

42 Cited in Laura Flanders, "Oil Omissions: Bush Sr., Cheney Have Big Stakes in Saudi Status Quo," WorkingforChange.com , 18 Oct. 2001.

43 Joe Stephens and David B. Ottaway, "Afghan Roots Keep Adviser Firmly in the Inner Circle: Consultant's Policy Influence Goes Back to the Reagan Era," *Washington Post* 23 Nov. 2001.

44 Zalmay Khalilzad, "Afghanistan: Time to Reengage," *Washington Post* 7 Oct. 1996.

45 Zalmay Khalilzad and Daniel Byman, "Afghanistan: The Consolidation of a Rogue State," *Washington Quarterly* 23 (2000).

46 Pratap Chaterjee, "Scramble for the Caspian: Big Oil Looks to Divvy Caspian Sea Oil Riches," *Multinational Monitor* Sept. 1998, cited in *Drillbits and Tailings* 31

Oct. 2001.

47 "Pipeline Politics" Nov. 2001.

48 O'Kelly, 28 Oct. 2001.

49 Ahmed Rashid, "Wretched Afghanistan," *Washington Post* 21 Sept. 2001.

50 Mike Shuster, "All Things Considered," National Public Radio, 27 Mar. 2002.

51 Flanders 18 Oct. 2001.

52 Eric Planin, "Peace Groups Are Urging Restraint," *Washington Post* 20 Sept. 2001.

FIVE: AND THE WORLD STANDS SILENT

1 David Ignatius, "Modern Day Rome," *New York Times* 30 Dec. 2001.

2 Margaret Thatcher, "Advice to a Superpower," *New York Times* 11 Feb. 2002.

3 Peter Ford, "Coalition Allies Lament: It's Still 'America First,'" *Christian Science Monitor* 27 Dec. 2001.

4 President George Bush, CNN, 23 Jan. 2002.

5 David Von Drehle, "World War, Cold War Won. Now, the Gray War," *Washington Post* 12 Sept. 2001.

6 Suzanne Daley, "European Leaders Voice Support," *New York Times* 8 Oct. 2001.

7 Steven Mufson and Alan Sipress, "US Gains Allies' Support; Nations Willing to Commit Forces," *Washington Post* 8 Oct. 2001.

8 Daley, 8 Oct. 2001.

9 Steven Erlanger, "Germany Ready to Send Force of 3,900," *New York Times* 7 Nov. 2001.

10 Ford, 27 Dec. 2001.

11 Mufson and Sipress, 8 Oct. 2001.

12 Kathryn Tolbert, "Japan Deploys Ships to Support War," *Washington Post* 9 Nov. 2001.

13 Erik Eckholm, "China Offers Its Wary Support for Attacks," *New York Times* 9 Oct. 2001.

14 Ford, 27 Dec. 2001.

15 Ford, 27 Dec. 2001.

16 Marc W. Herold, "A Dossier on Civilian Victims of United States' Aerial Bombing of Afghanistan: A Comprehensive Accounting," Departments of Economics and Women's Studies, Whittemore School of Business and Economics, University of New Hampshire, December 2001.

17 Luke Harding and Paul Kelso, "Taliban says 20 civilians killed in Kabul," *The Guardian* 9 Oct. 2001.

18 Harding and Kelso, 9 Oct. 2001.

19 "UN Slams Use of Cluster Bombs as 8 Die," *The News International* (Pakistan) 26 Oct. 2001.

20 John Burns, "UN Official Urges Restraint in Bombings to Avoid Casualties," *New York Times* 31 Oct. 2001.

21 Vernon Loeb and Bradley Graham, "Errant Bombs May Have Hit Afghan Civilians, US Says," *Washington Post* 24 Oct. 2001.

22 Rajiv Chandrasekaran, "Villagers Describe Deadly Air Strike," *Washington*

Post 1 Nov. 2001.

23 Susan B. Glasser, "At Hospital, Villagers Tell of US Bombing," *Washington Post* 4 Dec. 2001.

24 Barry Bearak, "In Village Where Civilians Died, Anger Cannot Be Buried," *New York Times* 16 Dec. 2001.

25 C.J. Chivers, "An Afghan Village Where Errant Bombs Fell and Killed, and Still Lurk in Wait," *New York Times* 12 Dec. 2001.

26 Pamela Constable, "Plaintive Afghan's Plea from Community: Stop the Bombing," *Washington Post* 24 Oct. 2001.

27 Loeb and Graham, 24 Oct. 2001.

28 Vernon Loeb, "US Bombs Hit Kabul TV Station," *Washington Post* 15 Nov. 2001.

29 "Michael R. Gordon, "US Tries to Sway Worldwide Opinion in Favor of War," *New York Times* 6 Nov. 2001.

30 Elizabeth Becker and Eric Schmitt, "US Planes Bomb a Red Cross Site," *New York Times* 27 Oct. 2001.

31 Steven Mufson, "Pentagon Changing Color of Airdropped Meals," *Washington Post* 2 Nov. 2001.

32 Neil H. Mermelstein, "Military and Humanitarian Rations Products Technologies," *Food Technology* 55.11 (Nov. 2001).

33 Deborah Zabarenko, "US Offers Lesson on How to Tell Cluster Bombs from Food Packs," *Washington Post* 30 Oct. 2001.

34 Mufson, 2 Nov. 2001.

35 Jim Rutenberg, "Noting 'Shortcomings,' Pentagon Says It Will Remove Some Obstacles to Covering War," *New York Times* 10 Dec. 2001.

36 Mike Allen, "White House Angered at Plan for Pentagon Disinformation," *Washington Post* 25 Feb. 2002.

37 Lucian Kim, "Showdown Looms on German Deployment Decision," *Christian Science Monitor* 15 Nov. 2001.

38 Peter Finn, "Germany Shifts Toward Stronger Military Role," *Washington Post* 11 Oct. 2001.

39 Peter Finn, "Germany Offers 3,900 Troops to Assist US in Afghanistan," *Washington Post* 7 Nov. 2001.

40 Steven Erlanger, "Pressing Greens, German Leader Wins Historic Vote on Sending Troops to Afghanistan," *New York Times* 17 Nov. 2001.

41 Julian Borger, "Powell Loses Power over Pentagon," *The Guardian* 11 Dec. 2001.

42 Colum Lynch, "US Boycotts Nuclear Test Ban Meeting," *Washington Post* 11 Nov. 2001.

43 David Rohde, "Executions of POWs Casts Doubts on Alliance," *New York Times* 13 Nov. 2001.

44 Patrick Tyler, "Powell Says Muslim Nations Should Be Peacekeepers in Kabul," *New York Times* 13 Nov. 2001.

45 Mark Landler, "Bombing Necessary Despite Toll on Civilians, US Envoy Says," *New York Times* 8 Jan. 2002.

46 Thom Shanker and Katherine Seelye, "Behind-the-Scenes Clash Led Bush to

Reverse Himself on Applying Geneva Conventions," *New York Times* 21 Feb. 2002.

47 Michael Ratner, "Follow the Geneva Convention," *Christian Science Monitor* 29 Jan. 2002.

48 T.R. Reid, "US Pressed on Detainees' Treatment," *Washington Post* 17 Jan. 2002.

49 Anthony Lewis, "Captives and the Law," *New York Times* 26 Jan. 2002.

50 Reid, 17 Jan. 2002.

51 Shanker and Seelye, 21 Feb. 2002.

52 Reid , 17 Jan. 2002.

53 Lewis, 26 Jan. 2002.

54 Shanker and Seelye, 21 Feb. 2002.

55 Lewis, 26 Jan. 2002.

56 Fareed Zakaria, "…New Rules for 2002," *Washington Post* 26 Dec. 2001.

SIX: THE AXIS OF EVIL AND BEYOND

1 Chris Matthews, "Who Hijacked Our War?" *San Francisco Chronicle* 17 Feb. 2002.

2 Paul Garwood, "War Commander Gen. Tommy Franks visits troops," *Associated Press* 25 Dec. 2001.

3 David E. Sanger, "A War of Loose Ends," *New York Times* 10 Jan. 2002.

4 Paul Rogers, "No End in Sight," www.opensociety.org, 20 Mar. 2002.

5 David E. Sanger, "The US-Pakistan Relationship Shows the First Sign of Tension," *New York Times* 9 Oct. 2001.

6 Celia Dugger, "US and India Map Path to Military Cooperation; More Arms Sales Are Seen," *New York Times* 6 Nov. 2001.

7 Joanna Slater, "American Focus on Pakistan Grates on India," *Wall Street Journal* 4 Jan. 2002.

8 Pamela Constable and Rama Lakshmi, "India Recalls Pakistani Envoy," *Washington Post* 21 Dec. 2001.

9 Rama Lakshmi, "Missile Test by India Raises Nuclear Ante," *Washington Post* 26 Dec. 2001.

10 Slater, 4 Jan. 2002.

11 Celia Dugger, "Indian General Talks Bluntly of War and a Nuclear Threat," *New York Times* 12 Jan. 2002.

12 Slater, 4 Jan. 2002.

13 Todd Purdum, "Bush Speaks to Leaders and Urges Negotiation," *New York Times* 14 Jan. 2002.

14 Ian Traynor, "Georgia: US Opens New Front in War on Terror," *The Guardian* 20 Mar. 2002.

15 Karen DeYoung, "OAS Nations Activate Mutual Defense Treaty," *Washington Post* 20 Sept. 2001.

16 Alejandro Bendana, unpublished letter, Oct. 2001.

17 David Gonzalez, "Close to US, War Evokes Era of Conflict in Recent Past," *New York Times* 20 Oct. 2001.

18 Gonzalez, 20 Oct. 2001.

19 Sarah Anderson, personal interview, Washington, DC, June 2002.

20 Scott Wilson, "Colombia Seeks More US Aid for a Broader War," *Washington Post* 24 Feb. 2002.

21 Sanho Tree, personal interview, Washington, DC, July 2002.

22 Marc Cooper, "Bush Finds His Vietnam," *LA Weekly* 28 Mar. 2002.

23 George Kourous, "Would Latin America Be Better Off If Washington Just Left It Alone?" *Foreign Policy in Focus* 15 Mar. 2002.

24 Walter Pincus and Thomas E. Ricks, "CIA Fails in Bid to Kill Afghan Rebel with a Missile," *Washington Post* 10 May 2002.

25 "All Things Considered," National Public Radio, 21 May 2002.

26 Douglas Jehl, "Holy War Lured Saudis as Rulers Looked Away," *New York Times* 27 Dec. 2001.

27 Evan Thomas and Roy Gutman, "Iraq in the Balance: The Bush team is looking for some former Iraqi generals to help oust Saddam Hussein," *Newsweek* 25 Mar. 2002.

28 Butler meeting with UN-accredited disarmament organizations, New York, 12 February 1998.

29 CNN.com, 13 Dec. 2001.

30 Andreas Zumach, "No Veto From Moscow if US Goes to War Against Iraq," *die Tageszeitung* 15 May 2002.

31 Peter Slevin, "Bush to Seek Cooperation but Press Issues," *New York Times* 21 May 2002.

32 Colum Lynch, "Firm's Iraq Deals Greater Than Cheney Has Said," *Washington Post* 23 June 2001.

33 United States, State Department, Fact Sheet on the "Goods Review List" for Iraq, 14 May 2002.

34 Security Council SC/7395, "Security Council Approves List of Revised Sanctions on Iraq," United Nations, 14 May 2002.

35 Marlise Simons, "US Forces Out Head of Chemical Arms Agency," *New York Times* 23 Apr. 2002.

36 Simons, 23 Apr. 2002.

37 "Smarter Sanctions on Iraq," editorial, *New York Times* 18 May 2002.

38 Andreas Zumach, "Prag: Truppe nach Kuwait," ("Prague: Troops for Kuwait"), *die Tageszeitung* 11 Jan. 2002.

39 Robert Scheer, "President Bush's Wag-the-Dog Policy on Iraq," *Los Angeles Times* 7 May 2002.

40 William Arkin, " Planning an Iraqi War but Not an Outcome," *Los Angeles Times* 5 May 2002.

41 Henry A. Kissinger, "Phase II and Iraq," *Washington Post* 13 Jan. 2002.

42 Mike Allen, "Bush Resumes Case Against Iraq," *Washington Post* 18 Apr. 2002.

43 Allen, 18 Apr. 2002.

44 Clyde Haberman, "When the Unimaginable Happens, and It's Right Outside Your Window," *New York Times* 12 Sept. 2001.

45 James Bennet, "Spilled Blood Is Seen as Bond That Draws Two Nations Closer," *CounterPunch* 13 Sept. 2001.

46 Alan Sipress, "Cheney Plays Down Arab Criticism Over Iraq," *Washington*

Post 18 Mar. 2002.

47 Mary McGrory, "Speaking From the Sidelines," *Washington Post* 4 Apr. 2002.

48 "UN envoy says Jenin camp 'shocking and horrifying'," CNN.com, 18 Apr. 2002.

49 Physicians for Human Rights Forensic Team, "Preliminary Assessment: Jenin," 21-23 Apr. 2002.

50 Human Rights Watch, "Jenin War Crimes Investigation Needed: Human Rights Watch Report Finds Laws of War Violations," press release, 3 May 2002.

51 "UNSC Avoids Immediate Clash Over Arab Call for Jenin Inquiry," *Agence France Presse* 19 Apr. 2002.

52 Human Rights Watch, "Israel: Allow Access to Jenin Camp," press release, 15 Apr. 2002.

SEVEN: THE DANGERS, THE ALTERNATIVES, THE POSSIBILITIES

1 Peter Slevin, "US Renounced Its Support of New Tribunal for War Crimes," *Washington Post* 7 May 2002.

2 Neil A. Lewis, "US Rejects All Support for New Court on Atrocities," *New York Times* 7 May 2002.

3 John Bolton, Under Secretary of State for International Organizations, speaking at Global Structures Convocation, Washington, DC, 21 Feb. 1994.

4 Lewis, 7 May 2002.

5 Bob Woodward and Dan Eggen, "Aug. Memo Focused on Attacks in US," *Washington Post* 18 May 2002.

6 "'99 Report Warned Of Suicide Hijacking," *Associated Press*/CBS 17 May 2002.

7 Philip Shenon, "Suicide Attacks Certain in US, Mueller Warns," *New York Times* 21 May 2002.

8 Dan Eggen, "FBI Warns of Suicide Bombs," *Washington Post* 21 May 2002.

9 "All Things Considered," National Public Radio, 21 May 2002.

10 Dennis Kucinich Cong (D-Ohio), Americans for Democratic Action convention, Los Angeles, 17 Feb 2002.

11 Bob Woodward and Dan Balz, "We Will Rally the World," *Washington Post* 28 Jan. 2002.

12 "Annan, UN cited for peace work, win Nobel," CNN, 10 December 2002.

INDEX

und

Designed by Graham Round and Brian Robertson
Cover design by Michelle Lawrence

Contents

About this Book

Danger at Demon's Cove is a mystery story with a difference. The difference is that you have to solve the mystery yourself.

Throughout the book, there are puzzles which you must solve for the next part of the story to make sense. Clues and evidence lurk in the words and the pictures.

Keep your wits about you as you read the story and look carefully at the pictures. Don't turn over to the next page until you have found the solution.

Some of the puzzles relate to previous pages so you may have to flick back through the book to find a vital piece of information.

If you get stuck, there are extra clues to help you on page 41. They are printed in a secret way, so you will have to work out how to read them first. If you are completely stuck and have to admit defeat, all the answers are on pages 42 to 48.

Max

Sally

Max and Sally are on holiday. They are camping outside their grandparents' house on the cliff top above Demon's Cove. Between them, they manage to find all the clues and solve the mystery. Can you?

3

A Dark and Stormy Night

It was a dark and stormy night, long ago. A ship called the Indian Queen was on her way home from the East, loaded with spices and silk. There was also a secret cargo belonging to a fabulously rich prince which Captain T. Clipper had pledged to guard with his life – an amazing hoard of treasure, including the Demon's Eye, a huge, priceless, black diamond.

The Indian Queen was lashed by fierce waves. The Captain struggled to steer the ship and desperately looked out for the lighthouse beam.

Meanwhile, the three evil Grabbitt brothers waited on the cliffs above Demon's Cove, sending a false signal to lure the ship onto the rocks.

The Captain spotted the signal. The doomed Indian Queen unwittingly sailed onto the treacherous rocks and began sinking fast.

Denzil, Jago and Joshua Grabbitt eagerly hauled the cargo onto the shore, without a thought for the crew of the wrecked ship.

The Indian Queen sank without trace, while the brothers inspected their booty. Denzil, the most evil of them, prised open the chests.

The greedy Grabbitts stared incredulously at the glittering jewels and amazing treasure, hardly able to believe their luck at such a haul.

Tom paused and gazed out to sea. Sally shivered. She could picture it all clearly.

"But what happened to the treasure?" asked Max. "What did the Grabbitts do with it?"

"It's said that they hid the two treasure chests in the maze of smugglers' tunnels at Demon's Cove," Tom continued. "But within months the brothers had mysteriously perished and the secret of the treasure was lost with them.

Some say the Demon's Eye diamond held a curse. No one knows for sure. But even now, ghostly cries are heard echoing through the caves and on stormy nights the phantom Indian Queen can be seen sailing in the bay at Demon's Cove."

5

Flashing Lights

L ater that night, Max and Sally were asleep in their tent on the cliffs above Demon's Cove. A sudden loud roar of thunder woke Sally with a start.

She peered out through the tent flap as lightning lit up the bay. Sally rubbed her eyes in disbelief. Was this the ghostly Indian Queen . . . ?

Then the flashing lights began and she realized it was a modern boat. By now Max was awake and they watched as a series of long and short flashes beamed across the bay.

"Perhaps it's a signal," said Max, as a lorry drew up on the cliff top opposite.

Sally quickly grabbed a notebook and started to scribble down the sequence, using dots for short flashes and dashes for long flashes. Max rummaged through a bag stuffed with useful equipment and pulled out his pocket codebook. He flicked through it until he found the page he was looking for and handed it to Sally.

"This will help us work out what it means," he said.

DON'T TURN THE PAGE YET

Can you decode the signal?

Watching Demon's Cove

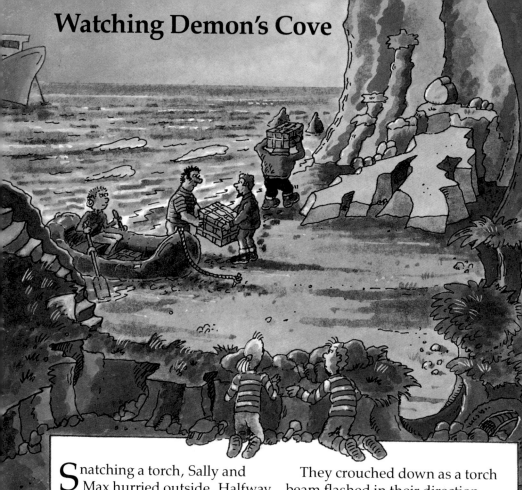

Snatching a torch, Sally and Max hurried outside. Halfway down the steps to the cove, there was a wide ledge where they could hide and watch the beach.

A small dinghy pulled ashore. Two men clambered out and glared around, suspiciously. They began unloading some large, wooden crates. What was going on? Were they smugglers? Max leant out to get a better look and dislodged an avalanche of stones and pebbles.

They crouched down as a torch beam flashed in their direction, scanning the rock face again and again. They waited, hearts pounding, until at last a gruff voice gave the all clear.

Sally and Max stayed well hidden behind the rocks. They couldn't risk being discovered now. They heard muffled voices fading into the distance, but could see nothing. Soon there was silence and, in spite of the cold, they both felt very sleepy…

Max woke suddenly, sunlight dazzling him. He jumped to his feet, but the people and dinghy had vanished. He shook Sally and dashed down to the beach.

Max thought he caught a glimpse of the boat, but Sally was puzzled by the footprints. She could see three sets of tracks heading in one direction towards the cliff where they stopped. Someone must have rowed the dinghy away, but where had the other three people gone?

Sally stared at the cliff face, looking for a clue. She thought back to last night. Something had changed.

DON'T TURN THE PAGE YET

What has Sally noticed?

9

Message in a Bottle

Sally stared up towards the large boulder, sure it was hiding something. She took a deep breath and jumped onto the rocks. She scrambled up to the wide, grassy ledge with Max struggling behind.

Sally leant against the boulder and pushed. It was surprisingly light and rolled away to reveal a narrow opening. Max peered into the gloomy darkness. Sally flicked on the torch and they stepped cautiously through the gap to investigate.

They found themselves in a small cave. The torch beam disturbed some bats, but otherwise the cave was empty. Footprints in the sand matched the ones on the beach and showed that three people had walked into, but not out of, the cave. So where had they gone?

"Perhaps there's a secret tunnel," said Max.

Sally began tapping the walls, but they felt disappointingly solid. Max looked for hidden levers or buttons. But they found nothing.

Suddenly, Sally spotted a block of stone that had been firmly wedged into the wall. After a lot of tugging and a final wrench that sent Max tumbling backwards, they pulled it free and stared into the hole at an old, cobwebby bottle. Sally lifted it from its hiding place and Max pulled out a crumbly roll of paper. It was torn at the edges and faded by damp and age, but they could still see the clear outlines of a map and peculiar, sloping writing that was almost impossible to read.

DON'T TURN THE PAGE YET

Can you work out what the writing says?

Enter throughe thee trapp dorr in thee cauve above thee cove

Bewayre atte Highe Tyde when tunnells floode ~ these be drawne inn blue ~

Snake passage

DEMON'S COVE

This belongs to Jago Crafott

Tricky Trapdoor

Sally studied the paper, thinking hard about what it meant. This was only part of a map and she wondered what had happened to the rest of it. She was sure the map was important, why else would Jago Grabbitt have hidden it so carefully? Could it have something to do with the treasure from the Indian Queen?

Max scuffed his way across the floor, searching for signs of a trapdoor. Suddenly he caught his foot in a ring half buried in the ground and tripped, knocking over a heavy, metal pole. He lay sprawled on the floor, but at least he knew where the trapdoor was.

Just then, Sally noticed an unusual, carved stick lying on a rock. She tucked it into her bag, then began to help Max brush away the sand from a heavy, old, oak door.

The rusty, metal ring was embedded in one side of the trapdoor. Max lifted up the ring and tugged.

Together, Sally and Max heaved, pulled and yanked, but still they couldn't lift it. The door wouldn't budge.

They gave up, this was getting them nowhere. There HAD to be another way of opening the trapdoor. Max gazed around the cave searching for inspiration, but there didn't seem to be anything that would help. Then he had a brainwave.

"This should be easy," Max exclaimed, confidently. "I know how to open it."

DON'T TURN THE PAGE YET

How can they open the trapdoor?

13

Into the Smugglers' Tunnels

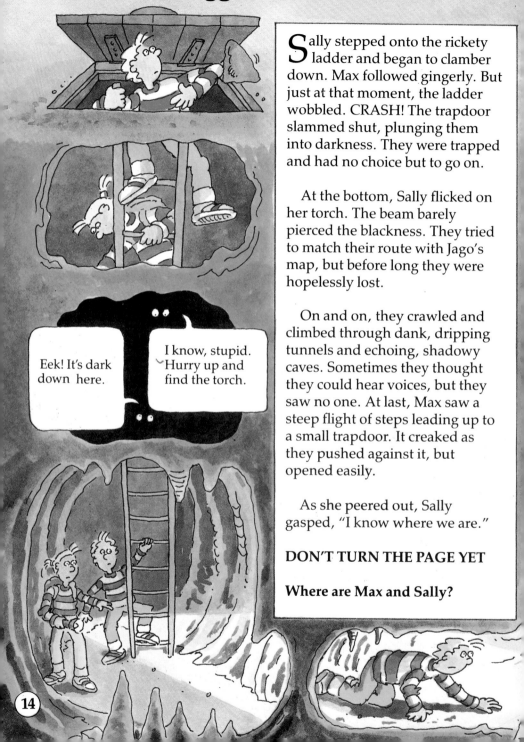

Eek! It's dark down here.

I know, stupid. Hurry up and find the torch.

Sally stepped onto the rickety ladder and began to clamber down. Max followed gingerly. But just at that moment, the ladder wobbled. CRASH! The trapdoor slammed shut, plunging them into darkness. They were trapped and had no choice but to go on.

At the bottom, Sally flicked on her torch. The beam barely pierced the blackness. They tried to match their route with Jago's map, but before long they were hopelessly lost.

On and on, they crawled and climbed through dank, dripping tunnels and echoing, shadowy caves. Sometimes they thought they could hear voices, but they saw no one. At last, Max saw a steep flight of steps leading up to a small trapdoor. It creaked as they pushed against it, but opened easily.

As she peered out, Sally gasped, "I know where we are."

DON'T TURN THE PAGE YET

Where are Max and Sally?

The Mystery Thickens

Silence. The cottage was deserted. Max and Sally pushed open the trapdoor and scrambled out.

They gazed at the cluttered room. Every corner and shelf was crammed with an odd assortment of curios collected from around the world. But there were also several puzzling things that seemed very unlikely possessions for a fisherman like Tom.

Suddenly, something made Sally stop and stare, a name she remembered from Tom's story of the Indian Queen.

DON'T TURN THE PAGE YET

What has Sally spotted?

17

The Old Sea Chest

Max tried the chest. It was unlocked. Sally looked doubtful; she didn't like the idea of snooping through someone else's things.

"There's something going on, and I want to find out what," said Max.

The chest was packed with mementoes from the Indian Queen – the Captain's logbook, ancient charts and old doubloons and pieces of eight . . . Max tried out the telescope, but it didn't work. He just stared into luminous, inky, blackness.

Then a recent newspaper cutting caught his eye. Max was certain he had seen the man in the photo before. He racked his brains trying to remember where.

As he read and reread the stories, a worrying suspicion began to grow in his mind. Everything that had happened started to make sense.

DON'T TURN THE PAGE YET

Where has Max seen the man before? What does he suspect?

18

Nov. 10th. Took on freshe water and supplyes. Our scurvey sufferers seeme grently cheered. A fayre wind is behinde us and full sails are set. Offered two guineas reward for first sight of lande.

Nov. 11th. Made goode speed during the night, but now the barometer is falling and the wind has changed to a Sou'Westerly direction. We are in for a blow. The crewe seeme cheerfull and long to be home.

Nov. 12th. Barometer still falling. Have battened downe the hatches and furled the mainsail. Never have I felte

suche a gale, nor seene suche waves. Doubled the men's grog rationes to keep them in goode spirits.

Nov. 13th. Weather still worseninge. Bosun Smollett sighted lande firste but 'tis an evill night. I feare he will never collect his two guineas, nore will we see our homes againe.

All is lost, we are wrecked. The shippe is being torn apart. I must secure my speciall charge.... Place one's eye to the eye-piece, where the eye shall see nowt but the Eye.

FREE AGAIN

From our man in Cairo

Two members of the notorious Doppel Gang were released yesterday without charge, following the reappearance of the famous six-toed Lost Idol.

They are Gloria Goldfinger, jet-setter and collector of expensive jewellery, and John Smith, alias Luigi Macaroni, Hans Sauerkraut and other names – a ruthless master of disguise.

Both wore dark glasses and John sported a new beard, as they boarded a private plane last night with top lawyer, Eustace Whimpe, bound for an unknown destination.

DARING HELICOPTER JAILBREAK

At dawn this morning, another member of the Doppel Gang, Silas 'Spikey' Scarface, was airlifted from Turnquay prison where he

was serving a sentence for tax evasion. Other prisoners looked on spellbound as the helicopter hovered overhead and Spikey was hoisted by rope from the roof. As yet, there is no clue to his whereabouts.

DAILY SCOOP COMMENT

Could these two events be connected? The Doppel Gang, led by the infamous Baron Grabbitt, is suspected of masterminding numerous robberies, involving ancient gold, jewels and art treasures. So far, Gang members have avoided arrest for any of these crimes.

The Doppel Gang is rumoured to have a new mission and to be on the trail of an amazing lost treasure. Baron Grabbitt, questioned at his country residence, Grabbitt Hall, refused to comment but described himself as being on "family business".

Tom Acts Suspiciously

Sally and Max slowly repacked the chest, their heads buzzing with unanswered questions.

Had they been watching the infamous Doppel Gang at Demon's Cove last night? Was the Gang searching for the lost treasure from the Indian Queen? And what was Tom's part in all this? It was very suspicious.

Heavy footsteps came closer and closer until they stopped outside the front door. Sally and Max watched in horror as the handle slowly turned. What should they do now? Max scooted into the open trapdoor. Sally shut the chest and dived behind the sofa, hardly daring to breathe as Tom sat down in it. She was trapped.

The silence was broken by a strange, crackling sound, followed by a high-pitched whine. Sally cautiously peeped out over the sofa as Tom leapt to his feet and rushed across to the radio.

He sat down at his desk, adjusted the radio and listened intently through the headphones. He was writing something down and seemed to be checking a notebook.

Max opened the trapdoor and saw a carved stick drop to the floor. It was the same size and just like the one Sally had picked up.

Minutes, later the door banged shut and Tom's brisk footsteps faded into the distance. Sally and Max emerged from hiding.

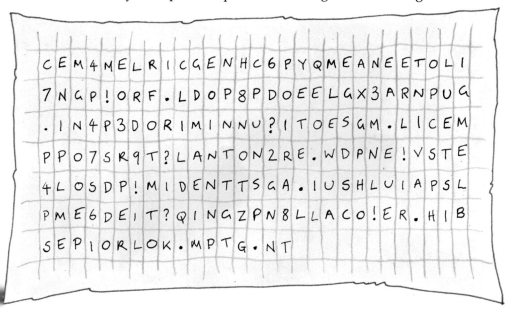

C E M 4 M E L R I C G E N H C 6 P Y Q M E A N E E T O L I
7 N G P ! O R F . L D O P 8 P D O E E L G X 3 A R N P U G
. I N 4 P 3 D O R I M I N N U ? I T O E S G M . L I C E M
P P O 7 S R 9 T ? L A N T O N 2 R E . W D P N E ! V S T E
4 L O S D P ! M I D E N T T S G A . I U S H L U I A P S L
P M E 6 D E I T ? Q I N G Z P N 8 L L A C O ! E R . H I B
S E P I O R L O K . M P T G . N T

The paper Tom had been writing on was lying on his desk next to the radio. He had neatly written seven rows of letters on the squared paper, but they didn't appear to mean anything. Sally was totally puzzled.

"It's a code," said Max. "And I know how to read it."

DON'T TURN THE PAGE YET

What does the message say?

Looking for X

The message confirmed their worst suspicions, but where WAS the usual meeting place? Max slumped down into a chair. All their detective work seemed to have come to nothing.

Then Sally spotted Tom's notebook lying on top of the radio. It was open at a map marked with a red cross. Could this be the meeting place? It was a long shot, but it had to be worth trying. It was their only lead.

There were no labels, but Sally was sure it was a map of Nether Muckle. She and Max ran outside to the back of the cottage and stared at the village. If only they could match the map to the roads and buildings.

DON'T TURN THE PAGE YET

Can you work out which building is the one marked X on the map?

23

The House on the Cliff Top

Max and Sally sprinted through the village and ran on along the cliff road, past the Smuggler's Head Hotel and ruined abbey. Finally, they turned into the lane leading to the strange house on the cliff's edge.

The steep hill in front of the house made a good viewpoint. Max and Sally scrambled to the top using the thick gorse bushes as cover. Gasping for breath, they crawled to the edge and stared down at Grabbitt Hall, home of Baron Grabbitt. If this was the meeting place, they had to get inside, but finding a way in would be tricky.

DON'T TURN THE PAGE YET

Can you find a safe route into Grabbitt Hall?

GRABBITT HALL

Inside Grabbitt Hall

The meeting is in the round room at the end of the passage leading off the drawing room. You know the entry procedure.

Grabbitt Hall was ominously quiet. Max and Sally sneaked downstairs and along a deserted corridor. Now they had to find out where the meeting was being held, without being discovered.

Max and Sally heard the buzz of voices ahead. They ducked behind a large suit of armour and peered out. A man was standing in the hallway giving directions to two familiar-looking people.

They waited impatiently for the man to walk slowly away down a flight of stairs and then silently tiptoed after the two visitors. Sally and Max turned into a wide, blue-carpeted corridor in time to see them disappearing through a doorway.

A minute later, Max turned the doorhandle and peeped into the room. It was empty. He looked for a door or passage, but the only door was this one. It was very strange, there HAD to be another way out. The two visitors couldn't have vanished into thin air.

The labels in the portraits read:

DENZIL GRABBITT · JOSHUA GRABBITT · JAGO GRABBITT · WORZEL GRABBITT · ROBIN GRABBITT · JEAN-PAUL GRABBE À LOTTE · EBENEZER GRABBITT · ABIGAIL GRABBITT · GORDON III BARON · SHEILA GRABBITT · JASPER I BARON · HORATIO II BARON AND ESMERALDA IN THE DRAWING ROOM · GRIZELDA GRABBITT · BRIAN IV BARON

Sally looked around. The walls were covered with portraits of the Baron's Grabbitt ancestors. But something was puzzling Max. Looking at one of the paintings, he could see the room had hardly changed over the years, but one thing was different. What was it?

"I've got it," Max exclaimed. "There's a secret passage, and I know where it is."

DON'T TURN THE PAGE YET

What has Max spotted? Where is the door to the secret passage?

27

The Round Room

Max stood face to face with the portrait of Baron Grabbitt.

"He's not very friendly," he muttered, wondering how to open the door.

Then he saw that one of the Baron's rings had a button where the jewel should have been.

There was a loud whirring as Max touched the button. The Baron slid slowly aside to reveal an eerie, wood-panelled passage, lit only by candlelight. There was no one around, so Max and Sally tiptoed in, not knowing what, or who, to expect. It was a bit spooky, but they reached the open door at the end, unchallenged.

They peeped into a deserted room. Sally glanced around nervously. Where had the two visitors gone? She spotted some scattered papers and part of an ancient-looking map on the table.

"Property of Den . . . it must be Denzil Grabbitt," Sally exclaimed, reading the bottom line of writing.

She delved into her rucksack and pulled out Jago's map. She knew it would match Denzil's. Max whipped out his new, mini camera. CLICK and the picture was taken.

"Now we've got a copy of the map and no one will know we've been here," he said, stuffing the camera into his pocket. "Let's go."

Sally was looking at the map. There was still one piece missing, but she was sure the writing would give them a clue to where the treasure was hidden.

The writing on Denzil's map was very strange, but as she stared it began to make sense.

DON'T TURN THE PAGE YET

What is written on the map?

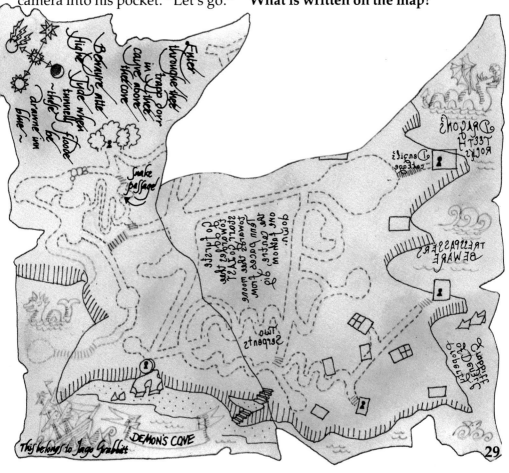

29

Trapped

There was an ominous scraping sound. A panel opened revealing another room and gloomy passage. Framed in the doorway stood Baron Grabbitt and the Doppel Gang.

"I'll take that," the Baron snarled, snatching the map from Max. "We've been watching you sneaking through the Hall on the TV screen."

Max groaned. Closed circuit television; they should have guessed. He looked around, but they were surrounded with no hope of escape. Sally watched miserably as the lady with orange hair studied their map. At least they still had the camera and film. Spikey grabbed Max and a man called Harry pushed Sally towards the dark passage.

They were marched down a flight of wide, stone stairs and through a huge cave to a long passageway. Harry hurried them straight on, ignoring the tunnels on either side, until they came to seven steep steps.

At the bottom they turned left and carried on into a small, round cave. Even Sally had to duck as she stepped into the low tunnel that twisted down and down. There were more steps, but these were so wet and slippery that Sally, who was trying to memorize their route, lost count.

Finally they came to a small, damp cave where the two men left them tied up. Max wriggled across to some jagged rocks and began to saw at the rope around his wrists. Luckily, it was easy to cut. Meanwhile, Sally had worked out where they were and was trying to find the best route out of the caves, avoiding Grabbitt Hall. Her brilliant memory meant she could picture the map clearly.

DON'T TURN THE PAGE YET

Where are they? Which is the shortest route out, avoiding Grabbitt Hall?

31

Escape through the Tunnels

S ally and Max ran so quickly, they were gasping for breath by the time they reached the Snake Passage. But at least there was no danger of being followed here. The tunnel was so narrow, it was a tight squeeze even for Max and Sally.

At last they came to a wider passage which sloped steeply upwards towards a small wooden door. But as Max fumbled with the catch, they heard footsteps, running. A tall figure loomed suddenly from the dark shadows behind them.

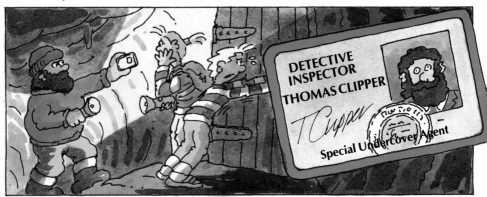

DETECTIVE INSPECTOR
THOMAS CLIPPER
T Clipper
Special Undercover Agent

"I thought I'd never catch you," a gruff voice wheezed.

Tom! They were trapped. Max shoved against the door, trying desperately to open it. Then Tom whisked out a plastic identity card.

"We thought..." Sally began.

". . . I was one of the Doppel Gang," Tom finished. "I realized that. I came to rescue you and guessed you would make for here, but I had to go the long way round."

They set off at once for Tom's cottage where he could develop their film. As they scrambled out and made their way through the wood and across the fields, Tom told them the rest of the story.

The Grabbitts made an ingenious plan to hide the treasure, until the hunt for it had been called off.

They hid it in the confusing maze of tunnels at Demon's Cove and drew a map to show the hiding place.

But the brothers didn't trust each other so they divided the map into three parts. Each wrote a vital clue on his portion. When they died, the map was forgotten.

I'm very interested in the case of the Indian Queen treasure, as Captain Clipper is my great great great grandfather.

Baron Grabbitt is Denzil's great great grandson. Gloria Goldfinger discovered Denzil's map while going through some of his old books.

I have been trailing the Gang for months, investigating their activities.

This is how the Doppel Gang's hunt for the treasure and for the missing parts of the map began.

Photo Identification

Tom led Sally and Max into a tumbledown barn behind his cottage. They gazed around in amazement. Inside, the barn was transformed into a high-tech office. Tom opened an important-looking box marked "Police File". It was packed with photographs.

"I want you to help with evidence," Tom explained, making Max and Sally feel very important. "Pick out every photo showing members of the Doppel Gang."

Tom disappeared into the darkroom with their film while Max and Sally spread out the photos. He particularly wanted them to identify the two new gang members. At first it seemed impossible, but they soon spotted familiar faces and some which were cleverly disguised. They could also name most of them.

DON'T TURN THE PAGE YET

Find all the photos of the Doppel Gang and name as many as you can.

THE DOPPEL GANG:

BARON GRABBITT Millionaire, Gang leader. Power-crazy, highly dangerous.

GLORIA GOLDFINGER The brains of the Gang. Tall, slim and vain. Can't resist expensive jewellery. Often changes hair colour.

JOHN SMITH Now known as Harry Loimeswolde. (Other aliases: Luigi Macaroni, Angus McHaggis.) Ruthless master of disguise. Small scar on left jaw.

SILAS 'SPIKEY' SCARFACE Expert thief. Left leg shorter than right leg. Scar on right cheek.

EUSTACE WHIMPE The Gang's lawyer. Short, skinny and weedy.

+ TWO RECENT RECRUITS

SWINDELLS
BANK
Lutzdor, Switzerland

NAME : GRABBITT (Baron)
FORENAMES : Brian Archibald
ADDRESS : GRABBITT HALL
Nether Mackie.

ACCOUNT NO : AX 12345

35

The Missing Link

Tom studied the photos of the two new Gang members and frowned.

"Fingers Golightly and Dinah Might. Notorious villains," he said.

Tom held out the newly-developed print showing the two portions of the treasure map. He locked the barn and led Sally and Max across the garden towards his cottage.

As he opened the back door, all three heard a suspicious, scuffling noise.

They were just in time to see a man disappear through the front door.

Tom glanced across at his safe. It was open and he knew it was empty.

Sally dashed to the window and saw Spikey running towards a van. He was brandishing a small piece of paper. The engine revved, Spikey jumped inside and the van roared away.

Tom lifted down a dusty tin.

"The Doppel Gang must know who I am," he said. "They've taken my copy. But . . . I've still got the original."

Copy? Original? What was Tom talking about? He took a small scrap of yellowing paper from the tin. It was the third piece of the Grabbitt brothers' map.

"But how did you find it?" asked Sally, not quite believing her eyes.

This portion of the map had belonged to Joshua Grabbitt, the youngest of the brothers. For Tom was not only descended from Captain Clipper, but also from Joshua Grabbitt. The Captain's grandson had married Joshua's grandaughter. Just last week, Tom had found the map rolled up and forgotten in the attic along with Captain Clipper's chest. Now they could work out where the treasure was hidden. But they would have to move fast to get there before the Doppel Gang.

DON'T TURN THE PAGE YET

Can you work out where the treasure is hidden?

Treasure from the Indian Queen

They raced out to Tom's jeep and set off. Tom radioed for reinforcements and the jeep lurched down the gravel track. With Max in the lead, they scrambled through the trapdoor and down into the maze of dark tunnels, to the Demon's Lair. The Doppel Gang had yet to arrive.

Large boulders made a screen around one side of the cave. It was impossible to hear anyone approaching because it was high tide and the sound of the sea roaring in the tunnels echoed through the cave. Tom found a good hiding place where they could keep watch. They switched off their torch and waited.

It was not long before Max spotted a torch beam. The Doppel Gang marched into the cave. Harry counted ten paces from the centre and the Gang set to work with spades, while Gloria and the Baron watched.

At last there was a shout, the Gang had found the treasure. It was time to put Tom's plan into action. The special microwave radio crackled to life. As Tom struggled to hear what was being said, he turned very pale and began to look very worried.

"There's been a delay," he whispered. "The plan won't work. We only have enough men to guard one tunnel and there are four exits from the cave."

Sally's mind whizzed into action. She thought back to the plan of the caves and realized there WAS only one way out. Sally, Max and Tom edged their way out of the cave, while the Gang were busy with the chests. Tom radioed his instructions.

DON'T TURN THE PAGE YET

Is Sally right? Which exit should they guard?

39

The Demon's Eye Diamond

The plan was a success. Almost before Max and Sally knew it, the six members of the Doppel Gang were safely in police custody. Tom, Max and Sally followed as the Gang were led through the tunnels to Demon's Cove, where a police launch was waiting. Outside on the beach, Tom opened the chests. Max and Sally gazed in amazement at the treasure. But they quickly realized something was wrong. The red leather box that should have held the Demon's Eye diamond was empty.

Had one of the Doppel Gang secretly taken it? Sally didn't think so. She was convinced the Grabbitt brothers had never found the famous jewel all those years ago. But if she was right, where was it now? Sally remembered Captain Clipper's logbook, she knew that it held the answer.

DON'T TURN THE PAGE YET

Where is the Demon's Eye diamond?

40

Clues

Answers

Pages 6-7

The message is in morse code. This is what it says:

Diving party landing with equipment and wreckage from Indian Queen. Standby to receive at Demon's Cove. End of message.

Pages 8-9

One thing has changed. The large boulder on top of the ledge has been turned round. It is ringed in both pictures.

Large boulder

Pages 10-11

The letters are written in an old-fashioned way and where the letter s comes in the middle of a word, it is written like an f. Some words are also spelt differently.
This is what it says:

Enter through the trapdoor in the cave above the Cove.

Beware at high tide when tunnels flood – they be drawn in blue.

This keyhole symbol shows there is a door.

Demon's Cove

This belongs to Jago Grabbitt

Snake Passage

Pages 12-13

They open the trapdoor using the metal pole Max knocked over as a lever. They balance the pole on top of the rock which then acts as a pivot.

This means they need less effort and strength to open the door.
These diagrams show how Max and Sally open the trapdoor.

The pole is pushed through the ring

Metal pole lever

Pivot rock

They push here to lift open the trapdoor

Pages 14-15

Stained glass window

The trapdoor opens into Tom's cottage. Sally knows this because she spots the stained glass window which she saw from the outside on page 5.

Pages 16-17

Sally has spotted the name Captain T. Clipper on the sea chest. He was captain of the Indian Queen. You can see the name ringed here.

The other puzzling things Max and Sally have noticed are labelled.

Gun in holster

Powerful binoculars

Radio transceiver

Camera and lenses

Pistol

Pages 18-19

Max saw the man in the photo last night. He was one of the people on the beach at Demon's Cove.

Here is the man from the photo.

Max suspects the Doppel Gang are looking for the lost treasure from the Indian Queen. His main reasons are: the Doppel Gang's interest in ancient treasure; the message Max and Sally decoded on page 7; the fact that

Baron Grabbitt, the Gang leader, has the same surname as the Grabbitt brothers who wrecked the Indian Queen.

Pages 20-21

Max decodes the message using the carved stick that Sally found on page 12. Place the stick below each line of writing. Lines on the stick match the letters on the paper. To break the code, read the letters which are above notches on the stick.

Here is the message:

Emergency meeting of Doppel Gang in 30 minutes. Important new developments. Usual meeting place. Be prompt.

Pages 22-23

The building marked X on the map is ringed in black.

Tom's cottage is here.

Pages 24-25

The safe route into Grabbitt Hall is marked in black.

Pages 26-27

In the painting above the fireplace, Max spotted a door where the life-size portrait of Baron Grabbitt now hangs. The entrance to the hidden passage must be behind this picture.

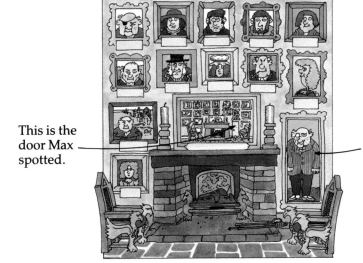

This is the door Max spotted.

The door is behind this portrait.

Pages 28-29

The words on Denzil's portion of the map are written backwards. This is what it says:

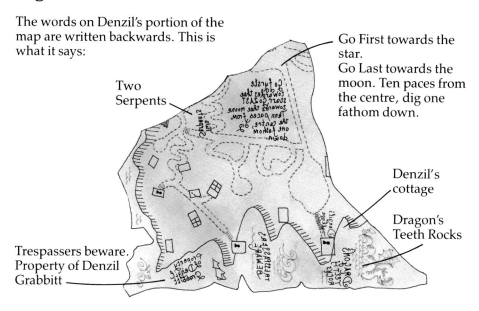

Go First towards the star.
Go Last towards the moon. Ten paces from the centre, dig one fathom down.

Two Serpents

Denzil's cottage

Dragon's Teeth Rocks

Trespassers beware. Property of Denzil Grabbitt

Pages 30-31

The shortest way out is marked in black.

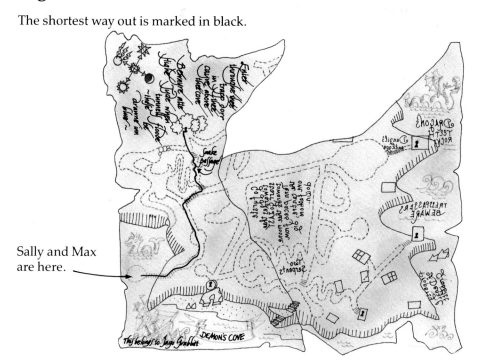

Sally and Max are here.

Pages 34-35

Here you can see the members of the Doppel Gang.

Silas 'Spikey' Scarface

Dinah Might

Eustace Whimpe

Gloria Goldfinger

Harry Loimeswolde

Fingers Golightly

Silas 'Spikey' Scarface

Eustace Whimpe

Dinah Might

Fingers Golightly

Fingers Golightly

Harry Loimeswolde

Gloria Goldfinger

Harry Loimeswolde

Baron Grabbit

Pages 36-37

Written in order, the clues say:
Enter through the trapdoor in the cave above the Cove. (Map page 11.)
Go First towards the star. (Map page 29.)
Second, look left from the Brigand's Boot and then descend the stair; steer by the comet into the Demon's Lair. (Map page 37.)

Go Last towards the moon. Ten paces from the centre, dig one fathom down. (Map page 29.)

(One fathom is equal to six feet.)

You can see where the treasure is buried on the completed map, shown on the next page.

47

The treasure is buried here.

The Grabbitt brothers' route to the treasure is marked here in black.

Pages 38-39

Sally is right.
This is the only tunnel that must be guarded.

This tunnel is blocked.

It is high tide and so this tunnel is flooded.

This tunnel leads to the Snake Passage. It is too narrow for anyone larger than Sally and Max to squeeze through (see page 32).

Page 40

Read the last entry in Captain Clipper's logbook on page 19. This tells you the Demon's Eye diamond is hidden in the telescope which Max tries to look through on page 18.

You can see the diamond gleaming here.

This edition first published in 2007 by Usborne Publishing Ltd.,
Usborne House, 83-85 Saffron Hill, London EC1N 8RT, England.
www.usborne.com Copyright © 2007, 2002, 1998 Usborne Publishing Ltd.

Sons of the Church
The Witnessing of Gay Catholic Men

Acclaim for
Sons of the Church:
The Witnessing of Gay Catholic Men

"I didn't so much read this book with my head as felt it with my heart. The witnesses whom Stevenson has assembled divulge not only the wounds of being gay in the heterosexist culture, but also the joys of appreciating their sexual orientation. This book is a must-read for pastoral educators and counselors."

—Sister Jeannine Gramick, PhD
Executive Codirector,
National Coalition
of American Nuns

"The stone that was rejected has become the cornerstone. Many gay Catholics have discovered they cannot live out the teaching of the Roman Catholic Church on homosexuality without destroying themselves psychologically and spiritually. They have gone through a maturing process, which led them to find the voice of God from within themselves and their own experience. This book recounts that spiritual maturing process in the lives of many gay men. These people are the foundation for a mature church whose authority is no longer based on the parent-child relationship, but on an individual discernment of spirits."

—Father John McNeill, PhD
Author of the groundbreaking book
The Church and the Homosexual
and numerous other books on gay spirituality;
ousted from the Jesuits by the Vatican
for his ministry to gay and lesbian Catholics

Sons of the Church
The Witnessing of Gay Catholic Men

Thomas Stevenson

HPP

Harrington Park Press®
An Imprint of The Haworth Press, Inc.
New York • London • Oxford

For more information on this book or to order, visit
http://www.haworthpress.com/store/product.asp?sku=5599

or call 1-800-HAWORTH (800-429-6784) in the United States and Canada
or (607) 722-5857 outside the United States and Canada

or contact orders@HaworthPress.com

Published by

Harrington Park Press®, an imprint of The Haworth Press, Inc., 10 Alice Street, Binghamton, NY 13904-1580.

PUBLISHER'S NOTE
The development, preparation, and publication of this work has been undertaken with great care. However, the Publisher, employees, editors, and agents of The Haworth Press are not responsible for any errors contained herein or for consequences that may ensue from use of materials or information contained in this work. The Haworth Press is committed to the dissemination of ideas and information according to the highest standards of intellectual freedom and the free exchange of ideas. Statements made and opinions expressed in this publication do not necessarily reflect the views of the Publisher, Directors, management, or staff of The Haworth Press, Inc., or an endorsement by them.

PUBLISHER'S NOTE
Identities and circumstances of some individuals discussed in this book have been changed to protect confidentiality.

Cover design by Jennifer M. Gaska.

Library of Congress Cataloging-in-Publication Data

Stevenson, Thomas B.
    Sons of the church : the witnessing of gay Catholic men / Thomas
B. Stevenson.
        p. cm.
    Includes bibliographical references (p.   ) and index.
    ISBN-13: 978-1-56023-580-4 (hard : alk. paper)
    ISBN-10: 1-56023-580-2 (hard : alk. paper)
    ISBN-13: 978-1-56023-581-1 (soft : alk. paper)
    ISBN-10: 1-56023-581-0 (soft : alk. paper)
    1. Catholic gay men—Religious life. 2. Homosexuality—Religious
aspects—Catholic church. I. Title.
BX1795.H66S74 2006
248.4'82—dc22
                                                                                    2005019193

For Eddie

And for Katherine,
who once said to me,
"Love is love is love."

ABOUT THE AUTHOR

Thomas Stevenson, PhD, received his BA in the Program of Liberal Studies (the Great Books Program) from the University of Notre Dame, his MA in philosophy from Boston College, and his PhD in Systematic and Philosophical Theology from the Graduate Theological Union in Berkeley, California. He has taught philosophy and religion for a number of years.

CONTENTS

Foreword

One of the ironies of the current teaching of the Vatican congregations concerning homosexuality is that it effectively makes it impossible for Catholic authorities to teach the Catholic faith to gay and lesbian people. This is because current teaching talks only about a "they" who are described as objectively disordered. By definition, an objectively disordered "they" cannot be engaged in meaningful conversation as a "you" and therefore cannot become an "I" or a "we" as part of the fruit of that conversation.

The nearest parallel I can think of is attempting to have a rational conversation with someone in a pub who has had several drinks too many. You would not attempt to engage such a person rationally about his car keys, and why you have removed them from his pockets. You would not treat him while he is drunk as a real "I" who could be meaningfully addressed as "You." You would simply take the car keys and trust that when he is sober, tomorrow, he will be glad of what you have done unilaterally, and his real "I" will be able to say so.

The problem with the parallel is, of course, that no evidence suggests that gay people will be ungay tomorrow. In their case, no ungay "I" will surface with the dawn to thank you for your refusal to be drawn into the self-deception of their altered state of the night before. As a result of its defective characterization of what being gay consists of, Church authority is currently locked into the position of constantly removing the keys, yet never reaching the moment when the conversation concerning the act of love or concern which that removal of keys was supposed to show can take place.

doi:10.1300/5599_a

Luckily, God is not trapped by our foolishness, whether ecclesi-astical or gay, and has already started to have the conversation with us which calls us forth as "I" or "We." God has started to show that Catholics as gay people can be, and frequently are, treated as "You" by God and are able to develop a "we" and an "I" that is recogniz-able as being both Catholic and gay. Some of the quiet, unsen-sational evidence that this conversation is well advanced is to be found in the pages which you are about to embark on. God seems to be filling the gap left by Church authority, making available Christian teaching for beloved sons and daughters through witness such as this.

Tom Stevenson has done us all a great service in providing us with the fruits of his tender listening and very highly skillful order-ing. His book is not a demand that "Church authority listen" to some victim voice. Instead it shows what happens when a gay Catholic listens and starts to find out for himself what the life of the Church really is and can be for gay Catholics. What the official pas-tors have ruled themselves out from doing, the Good Shepherd is starting to do through and for his sheep.

What is most surprising, and wonderful, about Tom's book is how quiet, unprotesting, and normal it is. He was surprised by how much joy he found in those he interviewed. And this is a surprise, and a joy, which he shares beautifully. A much more wholesome picture of what many gay Catholic kids picked up in their child-hood emerges than might have been expected. It is fascinating to see how early on some were able to make the saving distinction be-tween the voice of God and the voice of society, sometimes canon-ized by Church authority.

There is no attempt to run away from uncomfortable truths, and Tom's chapter on promiscuity, rather than being a piece of moral-ism or a flight from moral discourse, is instead a beautifully gentle piece about real phases of people's lives. The perspective of mercy, of awareness of what can be lost, yet what people can become is, it seems to me, distinctively Catholic and a sign that truth can be told, and heard, when people are addressed as "You" by one who is like us. Even the rhetoric of sternness can have its place when the overarching message is one which says, "I'm not going to take away the keys, but I'm going to stay with you until you are sober, and be with you when you drive, and, if necessary, do some of the driving for you."

This morning I received an e-mail from a friend in Mexico telling me of a gay Catholic friend of his who rang him up at 4 a.m. to tell him that he wanted to kill himself. This is the book I would love to have been able to give him to put into his friend's hand, praying that that friend would have the patience to allow himself to hear the depth of such quiet words. He would be able to receive an unexpectedly loving and gentle regard from One who loves him and would be able to relax into the knowledge that that love is already long at work speaking people like himself into lives of joyful faith.

Please make sure that Tom's book gets into hands like his!

James Alison
London, January 2005

Acknowledgments

When I first began to work on this book I was amazed by the ways guys came forward to be interviewed. I often had the feeling that these guys were not so much interested in appearing in a book as much as they were interested in being helpful to others. Somehow they knew their stories would be of service to others. They were and are a remarkable bunch of good guys. I owe a special thanks to Mark Matson for the way he coordinated several of the interviews for me.

As I neared the end of the work on the book another great gift came to me in the presence of Mary Allen. Mary is the author of *The Rooms of Heaven* and a graduate of the Iowa Writer's Workshop and a sometimes visiting professor in the Creative Nonfiction Writing Program. Mary's editing help was invaluable. She can be reached at MAllen1215@aol.com.

I am very grateful to James Alison, the noted theologian, for writing the foreword for this book.

Scott Perry and Ricky Ricardo (mentor of all mentors!) have supported and encouraged me as both good and trusted friends and as discerning dialogue partners about the book. Marion Edward Bothe, Terry Schubert, and Cheryl and Chris were also valuable readers.

In the background was the support of other friends: Chandran A., Marcia B., Mary B., Matt B., Ligia C., Paul K., JP L., Sarah M., Roger M., Maureen N., Tom S., and Justine T.

I want to thank the support group for gay Catholic people in Tempe who read and commented on the book.

Thanks to Bill Palmer and everyone at The Haworth Press.

doi:10.1300/5599_b

Thanks to Dawoods.com for designing the Web page sonsofthe church.com.

My family has been a constant source of support. My parents, Grant and Loretta, have provided steady and constant love, and Dad provided the financial backing without which this book would not have been possible. My siblings Cheryl (my champion), Renee, Bob, and Gina have also been a constant source of love and support, as have their families.

I'll conclude by thanking four women who have been lights in my life: Loretta, Cheryl, Katherine, and Marcia.

Introduction

Near the end of his book *The Unhealed Wound: The Church and Human Sexuality,* the highly regarded Catholic author Eugene Kennedy makes a suggestion for the Catholic Church: "What would the Institution lose if, instead of issuing statements, such as those about the 'objective disorder' of homosexuality, it sat, as a good pastor might, and willingly listened to the world and its sexual woes?"

When I began to interview a number of gay Catholic men for this book, I expected to hear stories of woe. Perhaps my own experience was coloring my expectations; I am gay and Catholic, and as I entered midlife I was increasingly saddened by it all. Shame and guilt regarding my sexuality had weighed me down for years. My participation and indulgence in the glitz and glamour of gay life had left me merely sad. And I was increasingly saddened by the Catholic community, where for too long I was uncomfortable or afraid to bring myself as a homosexual person to the table.

Perhaps behind the inspiration to interview a bunch of gay Catholic guys was my need for some wisdom and advice—and who better to turn to but those who have struggled with the same experiences? But my inspiration to work on this project went beyond the desire for advice. I thought the men I planned to interview would have something to say to others. I hoped they would have something to say to gay people, particularly to those still suffering in their experience of being homosexual. And I hoped they would have something to say to Catholic people about how their faith has informed their experiences with their homosexuality.

I expected to hear stories of suffering, but as I began to interview the remarkable men who make up this book, I was also surprised by the joy I was hearing. Between 2000 and 2004 I interviewed forty-four men for this book. All of these men identify themselves as homosexual and Catholic. Their ages, at the times of the interviews, ranged from twenty-six to sixty-eight. The majority of the men come from Chicago, Illinois, and Columbus, Ohio, with others coming from various locales in Iowa, Ohio, Louisiana, Connecticut, Arizona, and England. Forty-one of the forty-four people interviewed are laypeople and three others are priests. As one could surmise by the makeup of the respondents, the focus of this book is to look generally at homosexuality in relation to being Catholic; it is not a book about homosexuality and the priesthood, although there are implications. Furthermore, and unfortunately, the discussion of homosexuality in this work is limited to the experiences of men; the voices of lesbian women in the Church need to be heard too, but that was beyond the scope of this work. It should also be noted that some of the respondents opted for anonymity; therefore, some of the names are pseudonyms.

This book does not intend to be a scientific, statistical study of what it is like to be gay and Catholic, but rather to get at some common truths of what it is like to be gay and Catholic. Although the men I interviewed are largely located in Chicago and other parts of the American Midwest, it is my hope that the truth of their stories will find echoes in Dublin, Sao Paulo, Sydney, and everywhere else.

In referring to the interviewees I also need to introduce my use of the words *witness* or *witnesses* throughout the book. I choose to call the interviewees "witnesses" because again and again they try to come to terms with their homosexuality by returning to the source of their faith. And insofar as I understand a witness, theologically speaking, to be a person who reveals the source of his or her faith, or who inspires faith, hope, or love in another, I can attest to the fact that these interviewees did inspire me.

In this book, one story—the story of what it is like to be gay and Catholic—is told through a variety of stories, and a narrative arc arises organically out of the material. The first two chapters of the book deal with experiences of childhood and youth, focusing more on homosexuality in Chapter 1 and more on experiences of Catholicism in Chapter 2. In Chapter 3 we move to how our "witnesses" accept and integrate their homosexuality. Chapters 4 and 5 deal with how these men come to terms with their sexuality in relation to others, in terms of promiscuous behavior in Chapter 4, and in terms of intimate relationships in Chapter 5. We then move beyond sexual relationships to view various ways our witnesses come to terms with larger communities, with aspects of the gay community in Chapter 6, and finally with the Catholic Church in Chapter 7. In other words, the arc of the book starts with childhood and develops through ever-broadening experiences of relationality: relationships with one's self, with one's sexual and intimate partners, with the culture of gayness, and finally with the Catholic Church. Throughout, there is an attempt to discern how our witnesses' faith in God guides them through various experiences and issues they face.

The words of Sister Jeannine Gramick, written in 1983, still resonate today: "Above all, meet with and learn from lesbian and gay people themselves." With the spirit of Sr. Jeannine's words in mind, I invite the reader to listen, as Eugene Kennedy suggests that "a good pastor might," to these gay Catholic men.

"How can you be gay and Catholic?" This is a question I and others have faced for years. The tone of the questioner, whether he or she is a gay conversation partner at a bar, an academic, a student, or, indeed, at times a fellow Catholic, is often one of incredulity. Underlying the question seems to be an impression that being gay and being Catholic are irreconcilable. The viewpoint of this book is that being gay and being Catholic are reconcilable. The words and stories of numerous gay Catholic men, woven throughout the text, illustrate this truth in a variety of ways.

This book, then, is a journey into some issues and concerns of homosexual Catholic men. It is divided into seven chapters. The first two chapters deal for the most part with issues concerning our witnesses in their youths. The rest of the book covers a variety of issues that relate to their adult lives. We'll begin our journey by addressing the theme of discovery of sexual attraction during our witnesses' youths.

Scott C., who was forty-four when I interviewed him and lives in a suburb of Chicago, went to an all-boy's high school. He states simply, "I found myself being attracted to many of my classmates and also some of the upperclassmen." Mark M., forty-five, from a suburb of Columbus, Ohio, shares, "I remember we had a doctor come in seventh grade to talk to us about the facts of life. I knew that I was supposed to be attracted to girls because the other guys were talking about it. And I was of course attracted to them [the other boys]." John F., thirty-nine, from Chicago, speaks of his developing attractions, "When I was eighteen and that time frame. You don't have to be explicit, but in the locker room at gym change I can't figure out how I'm not going to look even though I

doi:10.1300/5599_02

really want to." Finally, Greg P., forty, also from Columbus, adds his own somewhat humorous story. "I'm Finnish by heritage, so it was what we would do in the ethnic area when they'd have the Finnish steam bath. You have the women on one side, the men on the other. All the men are there nude. And I was always fascinated by men. And I guess it was like, huh, I always wondered why Dad stopped taking us. He knew my eyes were traveling too much."

Notice the language of Scott C.: "I found myself being attracted to." In the testimonies of the more than forty Catholic men interviewed for this book, not one person spoke, with particular regard to his youth, of choosing to be attracted to other boys or to men. Instead, the language, better yet the experience, speaks, in one way or another, of *finding one's self* being attracted to boys or men. Such descriptions give the lie to an argument which implies, if not advocates, that homosexuality is a choice. More often than not the predisposition within this argument is to view homosexuality as immoral. For something to be immoral there has to be culpability or responsibility, and culpability or responsibility by their nature entail choice. So goes, it seems to me, the basic reasoning of some people, in particular some Christians, with regard to homosexuality.

As an initial response to this argument, it is worth pointing out that, in their youth, if given the choice, many of our witnesses might very well have chosen *not* to be homosexual. (Although you should keep in mind that this would have been a stance in their youth. In later years they will speak differently, indeed much more affirmatively, of their homosexuality.) For example, Jeff M., forty-five, from Columbus, referring to his youth, states matter of factly, "I didn't want to be gay." Mitch S., thirty, from Des Moines, Iowa, says, "I always thought, I can't be gay. Everything is too good for me. I'm smart. I'm athletic. I'm popular. I'm going to be successful. There's just no way. I don't have a problem with people who are gay, but I can't be gay." A prayer that Mark M. says he would have imagined for his youth certainly does not indicate that he would have chosen to be homosexual: "Remove this from me. Take this away." Indeed, perhaps this prayer does voice a choice—a choice *not* to be homosexual.

Furthermore, as I hope this entire book will bear out, our witnesses do face or have faced moral choices in terms of their sexuality. Contrary to the argument that views homosexuality itself as a choice, these witnesses experience homosexuality as a condition of their existence, a given in their life, in relation to which choices will be made. Homosexuality itself is not chosen. This given condition is what Andrew Sullivan, in *Virtually Normal,* calls the "involuntariness of homosexuality." Moreover, it is acknowledged by the American Catholic Bishops when they say in their 1997 message "Always Our Children," "Generally, homosexual orientation is experienced as a given, not as something freely chosen."

It is in relation to this given condition that many of our witnesses had to navigate in their youths through some very painful and alienating waters. One such initial experience was commonly understood in terms of being *different.* John M., fifty-eight, who grew up in Poland, shares his experience of this phenomenon: "I sort of always knew I was different. I didn't know why. But I knew I was left-handed and that was something that was accepted. So I was different in that way, but there was also something else and I wasn't sure what it was. I never associated any of this as bad. But I did feel the loneliness. Being different sort of set me apart and that made me sad. . . . By the time I was a teenager, I realized there was something wrong, because some people were beginning to point fingers at me. And, in fact, I really tried to turn away from it. I still didn't feel like it was sinful, but I felt like I was a weirdo."

For now we'll shy away from the damaging repercussions of believing one's homosexuality is sinful or believing that one is a weirdo. The point I wish to take note of here is the confusion or lack of understanding John experienced in relation to feeling different. He didn't even have words for it. The experience of Jerry G., sixty-eight, from Chicago, parallels this: "I didn't fit into the social picture at school. I didn't know why or what was the matter, but from early on I knew there was something different about the whole thing. So much so that after my first year in high school the Brothers called my father in and said. 'Maybe it would be best for him to change schools and areas *where he's not known'* [emphasis added]. That was the best advice that ever came up because I went to a neighborhood where the kids were from all over the place. *They didn't know me. I didn't know them.* We didn't have to communicate."

Notice again, in the story of Jerry, the lack of understanding about being different. And, notice also, that although the good Brothers may have been saving Jerry from persecution, nonetheless there is a logic that says he needs to go somewhere *where he's not known.* The implication is that he could not be known as the person he was, with his difference, where he was. For many, such an experience might make them feel like less than a person. Fortunately, for Jerry it did not turn out so.

The confusing and alienating experience of being different is also related by Mark M.: "The only negative experience I had in grade school was the increasing awareness that I was different from the other guys, and I didn't know what to do with that at all. And of course that became worse by seventh or eighth grade. Now what is interesting to me is that I thought I was the only person in the world like me, because I was so isolated." Mark's experience of being different continued through high school: "I was president of my class, on student council. I think that's kind of the way I dealt with being different. I was very sociable. I was a person who bridged groups. I'd go to dances and I had to of course find somebody to go with. Other than that I didn't date. My parents never raised questions about that. It seems odd in retrospect. So, I didn't have any trauma to reflect on in terms of being in school. It was just the increasing sense of being really different and that my difference was something that, as long as I didn't have to discuss it with anybody, was kind of not real. Maybe that's because I'm extroverted, so once I say it, it becomes real, so I just didn't talk about it."

But what is it that Mark could have said? What word could he have put to his difference? John M. and Jerry G. did not put a word—homosexuality, gay, or whatever—to their differences either. Whereas any young person's growing awareness of his or her sexual feelings and attractions might be somewhat confusing, the difference and added difficulty for many people experiencing homosexuality, especially those of older generations, is that they commonly encountered silence about it.

For some of our witnesses it was a common experience not to even hear the word *homosexuality,* as if the word was somehow anathema itself. Leo R., forty-nine, from Columbus, succinctly describes such an experience: "It was understood that *that* [homosexuality] was not to even be discussed, thought about, talked about. No way possible. It doesn't happen here." Bob S., forty-three, also from Columbus, is equally succinct in voicing an external attitude regarding homosexuality in his youth: "We're certainly not going to talk about this [homosexuality]."

Michael S., thirty-nine, from Chicago, who grew up in a very faithful and loving Catholic family, nevertheless echoes the sentiments of Leo and Bob in a story describing how he tried to understand homosexuality and how, in a way, that attempt was silenced by the response of his father (in what could have been a well-intentioned response on his father's part): "A big thing that happened to me when I was about twelve was, I did ask my father, because I had seen, I'll never forget it, in the TV guide, there was a summary of that movie, *That Certain Summer,* which was a made-for-TV movie, the first made-for-TV movie that dealt with homosexuality. And so I asked my dad, I didn't even know what that word was, I said, 'Dad, what is this word, homosexuality, there's going to be a movie on this week?' And my dad was very, and he hardly was ever this way, but he seemed to get a little angry, and he was like, 'Don't concern yourself with that, that's not anything you would want to really know . . . but that's basically when two men do what a man and woman would do. And that's wrong.'"

Michael interprets his father's response: "It was like, get that out of your mind, was basically what my father was saying. Don't think about it. So I know that sounds like a contradiction [from the way he generally describes an open and loving atmosphere to his family]. . . . But that was one time he was very stern, would be the word. So you know, when I think back about that, if I did have any feelings I was pushing them out of my head."

Chris T., twenty-nine, from Cedar Rapids, Iowa, in describing confusion about his sexuality and abuse by other young people when he was young, indirectly describes an environment in which he could not talk about his difference, his homosexuality: "At some points there was some gender confusion there about should I really be a girl if I'm attracted to a boy. But it wasn't that this is wrong or that I necessarily wanted to change, but I didn't see that as an option of two boys or two girls getting together. I thought that it had to be a boy and a girl. So that presented some confusion.

"So I just kind of kept that inside and didn't really talk about that a lot. But there were all sorts of things going on around that same time when I was discovering this. I started getting teased a lot by classmates and members of the community and that was happening in fourth grade on until I graduated from high school. It started small but then it peaked around eighth or ninth grade and then it started going back down. There were the verbal taunts that escalated to physical intimidation and violence and some sexual intimidation and all of that. So that was pretty tough to deal with and there wasn't really an outlet that I could talk to anybody about that with. You know, no friends or family or counselors that I felt comfortable talking with."

Whereas Chris could not share his story because he felt there was no human ear to hear him, Mitch S. was alienated by the stories of others in which his experience was not reflected. The alienation occurred when "Craig, Dan, everybody was having these sexual [heterosexual] experiences and of course telling stories and I never had the stories to tell. I think that was the most difficult because it was very clear in my mind that I was not having the same experience that everyone else was."

Leo, Bob, Michael, Chris, and Mitch all describe experiences in which words or stories about homosexuality were not heard. An alienating silence reigned. We need to stop and examine this phenomenon. Imagine, if you will, a conversation with a friend wherein your friend, after listening to your experience, shares a story of his or her own that relates to it and thus confirms your experience. Or imagine a therapeutic context in which you have been grappling with a painful experience and are finally able to put a word or a name to the experience. In either case, it seems to me that the spoken word or story that comprehends your experience can be a liberating event. Perhaps such experiences can leave you with a sense of being liberated from feeling abnormal, from feeling you are less than a person, and from feeling you are outside the community of your fellow human beings. Indeed, perhaps you feel like you are returned to yourself, returned to life. Conversely, the lack of a word or story that fits your experience can be a depersonalizing event, leaving you alienated or isolated from normality, from the human world. Although times are changing, and stories, movies, and television shows increasingly bring homosexuality into the larger context of human life, most of our witnesses encountered a lack of words and stories integrative of homosexuality while growing up. So, if I might rephrase an old adage, whereas a silence that is full of listening, or wonder, or appreciation, or adoration, or even sorrow, may indeed be golden, not all silence is golden. In order to become a person, to integrate one's experiences, there is a need for words and stories that comprehend those experiences, even if, I might add, the silence of prayer is the horizon for those words.

Silence, then, is one way our witnesses received in their youths a nonaffirming message regarding their homosexuality. But outright condemnation was encountered as well. As we have already seen, Chris T. spoke of being taunted and intimidated in his youth because of his difference, his homosexuality. Brian H., forty-nine, from Chicago, echoes Chris in describing why he had to keep his homosexuality a secret during high school: "Oh, because I was always afraid. This was an all-boys' school. And you know, I was sort of earmarked as being gay. You know, just in the way boys do other boys. I think probably it was just teasing me and stuff. But, because of that, I just played it carefully. I didn't know what to do. What do you do when you are sixteen or seventeen years old, you know, in 1972?"

There are more extreme stories of victimization. Tim D., in his thirties and from Ohio, shares an experience from his youth: "I have to say growing up gay I've been through lots of ugliness. It's good because to me it's something that I want to make sure I never do to anyone else. So if I have a huge group of friends and I share . . . things that I've been through or other people've been through it opens doors to people by thinking, 'I never knew people could do that.' One incident, it's so sickening today. I look back and have issues with it.

"I worked at Houlihan's. I was a cook. I got along fine for the first year. The second, this girl made a mistake, she said, 'Tim, you can tell me anything. I love you, you're my friend. Are you gay? I'm just curious. You don't have to tell me but I love you anyway. My brother's gay.' Finally, one day I said, 'Yes.' Damn, did that fly like wildfire. In five, ten minutes that whole place knew I was a 'faggot.' The cooks found out. It's hard to forgive what they did. I ordered a buffalo chicken sandwich hamburger and what the cooks did is they went back into the restroom, they dipped it into the toilet, and they peed all over it. There's witnesses to it so I know it took place. Oh, and they ran it on the floor, too, in all the grease and everything on the bare floor. I had not a clue that this took place, but I knew something was wrong because everyone was watching me eating it. I thought they put hot sauce on it. I just started eating it and the girl that let me know, she was watching me, her friends were watching me, the prep cooks were watching me. I probably had ten people watching me and the only thing I thought was they put hot sauce on it. I never thought they'd go that low. That's why I was naive. I ate it and ate it and they were laughing and cutting up and I thought I'm going to bite into a pepper anytime. Well, I didn't. Later, about three-quarters of the way, I just threw it away because I thought something's not right. Later, they told me, another girl, bless her heart, she was a waitress and I liked her and she came back and told me. And she started screaming and hollering and she told me what they did."

Tim bears witness in a powerful way to the victimization by others for being homosexual. He is the "faggot." The person, Tim, is denied. He is forced to eat like an animal. The person, Tim, is treated with disdain and degradation. Beyond denial, beyond degradation, would be, it seems to me, destruction. If a person or group of people are not worthy of being treated as people, then it is not a far stretch to view them as worthy of destruction.

Sean F., who is sixty-seven and lives in Columbus, shares a story that bears witness to the possibility of destruction at the hands of others. (And, although this story does not refer to his youth, it does refer to the potential violence that has so often been a condition of a young gay person's life.) Approximately thirty years ago, Sean was "cruising" for other men in a park in Cleveland. The park was in a wooded area on a bluff overlooking Lake Erie. While wandering in the park he spotted and overheard a few guys talking about faggots. They in turn saw him, came after him, and then, "They pushed me off of the cliff. It's sixty feet into the water. But there were some trees at about forty feet and I hung onto those. They didn't see me and I stayed there as long as I could and then gradually made my way up and over to get my car. I got in my car and started out and, bingo, they came right behind me. There was a carload of them. I got to get to the police station. Yes, they're following me. We're well over the speed limit. I make it through a traffic light; they don't. They come around anyhow. They swerved around cars. They were intent. One fellow had a baseball bat and they tried to pull up next to me and bang on the window and knock me and that sort of thing. I got pretty well bashed over the eye. They pulled right into the parking lot behind me as I pulled right up to the door of the police station. About three policemen came out and so that car disappeared real fast out the driveway."

Consciously or unconsciously, to some degree homosexual people have lived in fear. Perhaps we can understand our next topics, the ways our witnesses fought with themselves about being homosexual, or pretended not to be homosexual, or, perhaps most commonly, engaged in some form of secrecy, hiding, or isolation, as responses to this threatening atmosphere, to living in a fearful world.

Jeff M. speaks of not wanting to accept his homosexuality for a number of years in his youth: "As far as being gay, I first realized it when I was probably about fifteen and pretty much fought it up until my early twenties. Basically during my late high school years and my early college years I kind of avoided any type of sexual situation by either drinking too much or smoking too much pot, or doing some other type of drug, so that I wouldn't have to deal with it."

Pete L., fifty-five, from Louisiana, speaks to this theme of fighting his homosexuality: "Until I was out of college, I really refused to come to terms with the homosexuality and fought it for many years, quite a long time. I knew very early on, as I think most gay people do, in my opinion, that they were attracted to guys and not the girls. I tried to cover it over by dating . . . lots of experiences with dating, trying to be a regular person by dating. And enjoying girls. I enjoyed dates and had fun, but there was very seldom a sexual element involved and when there was I was very uncomfortable. I remember one particular one when I was in high school was in a play, *Annie Get Your Gun,* and I played the lead, Frank. I was very young to be playing that but this very buxom, fabulously sexy girl who was a year older than me took me aside at the cast party and tried to teach me what sex was like. I remember being absolutely rigid as she attempted to excite me and I didn't know what to do. It was strange."

Another predominant way our witnesses responded to their homosexuality, and the social rejection associated with it, was through some form of hiding from life, or isolating. Mark R., from London and in his twenties, speaks to this theme of growing up homosexual in Scotland: "I became very isolated, and I think mentally I was very aware that I was gay and I think I repressed it for I would say seven to eight years. I think that happened because of my awareness of being gay and I didn't really have much awareness of the gay community or homosexuality in general, but I knew that my gayness and my difference was unique to me. At that point that's all I knew and that there were other people like that but they weren't necessarily people the Catholic Church, or indeed my peer group, would approve of."

Leo R. likewise speaks of isolating, particularly during his high school years: "I think I did isolate because it [his homosexuality] prevented me from establishing friendships that could have developed. I purposely didn't pursue friendships, especially with other male friends for fear they would find out. You can get close but not too close. I could be the life of the party at a dance or school or a function but don't call me at home, don't visit me. That kind of distancing you do. So I felt very isolated in one sense. It was kind of a difficult period."

In a remarkable and strong book, *Know My Name: A Gay Liberation Theology,* Richard Cleaver speaks more generally to the experience described by Mark and Leo. According to Cleaver, "profound isolation . . . is still, most of the time, the most typical experience of lesbians and gay men in the United States."

In conclusion, the themes we have covered in this chapter give testimony to a fairly substantial degree of suffering and oppression in the lives of young homosexual people. Whether it be through the silence surrounding homosexuality or the possibility of violence often associated with homosexuality, the culture or society around such young people generally conspired to make them feel abnormal, or less than a person, because of their homosexuality. In turn, because of such an atmosphere, our witnesses in their youths often fought with themselves, denied their sexuality, or isolated.

It is my guess that the experiences our witnesses describe were common to many homosexual people in their youth whether they were Catholic or not. But what happens when Catholicism is intertwined with the experience of homosexuality? Whereas in this chapter the Catholicism of the witnesses' youths has been in the background, in the next chapter the Catholicism of these witnesses in their youths is brought to the foreground.

It might be surprising to some, in particular to those who think gay people should just discard the "baggage" of being Catholic, that many of our witnesses have cherished memories of the Catholic heritage of their youths. Romeo C., thirty-eight, from Chicago, is grateful for the ways he learned about prayer and love: "Growing up I had a strong faith based on a lot of prayer. My mother's family was Italian; my father's family is Puerto Rican. My father's mother was very devout, in a very Latin American sense. She did go to Mass every Sunday, but to her the most important thing was prayer, so we prayed lots. And she was a very positive influence on my perception of Catholicism because it was everything to her and she was a very loving and giving person."

Romeo continues, "Another thing would be my parents who in a certain way were very religious, had a strong faith even though they didn't go to church nearly as much as my grandmother. Sometimes they wouldn't go at all. But they did have a type of morality that stemmed from their Catholic faith that has impressed me since I was young. In some ways I was envious of it because their morality was based on loving and giving and sharing and the big sin out of all sins is being selfish and egotistical. I tend to be pretty self-involved, so it's very difficult. I always felt I was doing wrong and it had nothing to do with sexual practices or anything like that. The guilt came from, 'Am I being too selfish? Am I not giving?' I thought that was kind of healthy for me. I mean, I think it's healthy not to be too selfish."

Romeo talks more about prayer and love than he does about his sexuality. But prayer and love will become, as we shall see in upcoming chapters, guiding lights for dealing with many of the concerns surrounding homosexuality. We will see, for example, ways in which prayer facilitates a process of acceptance and integration of homosexuality. And we will see, as further examples, the loving ways our witnesses respond to the promiscuity in their midst, and the ways love is experienced in their intimate relationships.

Michael S., whom we met in Chapter 1, was likewise deeply influenced by a faithful, loving family: "Let's see. I was born and raised on the southwest side of Chicago. Grew up Catholic and I would characterize my family as devoutly Catholic, but not sternly Catholic. As a family we did not pray a lot together but we were devout and it was very serious. My parents were pretty low-key about everything in their life and they were kind of low-key about their Catholicism in that they led by example. They went to Mass every Sunday and took it seriously and the one thing that I treasure about my parents is that they lived their faith without being real . . . stern." Michael continues, "Catholicism is a big part of our family. My uncle is a priest, and I had a great-aunt who was a nun, another cousin who was a priest, and they fit in really well and were treated just like everybody else. They were very loving people. I consider myself very blessed having grown up in a home that was loving and faith based and, as I said, not stern or legalistic." When asked to encapsulate in a nutshell the message he received from and about Catholicism in his youth, Michael concludes, "It was about family and being close-knit but not overly demonstrative in a way. So there was a little bit of formality, but it was about service to the community, and it was about being loyal and obedient to the Church, and to previous generations, and being faithful and being loving. Good education was intertwined since we all went to Catholic grade schools. Being respectful of authority too, an authority would be the nuns and priests who were prominent in our lives and our education. . . . My parents taught me to live by the principles of Christ, but they didn't evoke his name a lot. But here I was going to school and hearing his name a lot and hearing what I was supposed to hear."

Like Romeo, Michael is grateful—indeed feels blessed—in having been part of a prayerful and loving family. Both men also have a clear appreciation for the communal dimension of their experience of growing up Catholic. A third example of the latter is offered by Matteo P., thirty-eight, from Chicago: "I am Catholic and I was raised Catholic. My family has always been very involved in the Church. My background, being Italian, the Italians occasionally get emotional with their beliefs in their church and they get close. Growing up we weren't just people who attended church but we also knew the priests, and the priests and the people that represented the Church would even come to our homes for parties or for house blessings or after christenings or things. . . . Also, with my family, they helped to build a church in a small community. They were instrumental in being the pioneers in helping to establish a church that has now, today, in this year, become a very huge parish. It has an elementary school and a nursery school and it carries a very good name and it's a very well-established parish. So my feeling about the Church in general has always been not to fear it because it was something that has been my friend." Matteo's sense of belonging to the Church even carries him through a humorous first confession. "I remember the first time I went to confession, I was unaware of how the light situation worked above the door and I walked in on somebody while they were in the middle of theirs. Finally when it did get to be my turn I was so frustrated by the fact that that had happened that I didn't know what to mention for sins because these priests had known me all my life. So I just made up a few things and I felt good about that because it was a sense of wanting to belong, if that makes any sense. Even at a young age. And of course I was forgiven for the things I hadn't even done."

Just as prayer and love can be formative, so too can the experiences of belonging and community. We will see, for example, the ways in which our witnesses' understanding of community embraces as well as conflicts with the gay community. And we will see how their experience of community plays a part in why they stay Catholic now.

But first, we need to include the stories of a few witnesses who had, to use Michael's word, a more "stern" familial experience of Catholicism. John F., who grew up in a military family, encapsulates the experience of Catholicism in his youth in the following way: "Do your duty, so to speak. I have a hard time separating the Catholicism part of it from the military part of it because it is all blended together for me. But it is very this-is-the-rules and there is no deviation from the rules. Those rules came both from the family and the priests at church. It was a very strict environment. . . . There are certain expectations in your life and what you're going to do. You're going to go to college, get married, have kids. That's the path you're going to take." And, being a self-described "good boy," that is the path that John took. Despite his homosexuality he married and had children, as we will hear later.

Don P., thirty-three, from Chicago, speaks of growing up with mixed messages. On the one hand, he very much experienced the stern form of Catholicism, yet he also received a less stern message: "Well, I think there were some messages that were taught by older people, some of the nuns in school, and, perhaps my father in particular, who believed in more of an absolute or militant Catholic experience. Militant and absolute equal going to hell; well, first of all the idea and expression of going to hell because of dot, dot, dot. . . . On the other hand, the younger nuns or priests or lay teachers didn't have such a militancy to Catholicism . . . the emphasis being on being a good person, following the ideas and ideals of the gospel and religious teaching in general."

Later in this chapter we will return to the stories of John and Don and how the generally stern experience of Catholicism was linked specifically with an attitude that homosexuality is evil. But here I'd like to take what some might consider an unexpected turn with regard to this perspective. My guess is that it might be unexpected because, since I am trying to present a more positive or appreciative understanding of homosexuality, it might seem likely that I would be dismissive of the stern or legalistic approach to life within Catholicism. But instead of being dismissive, and notwithstanding that the entire thrust of this work counters a perspective that sees homosexuality as evil and homosexual acts as necessarily immoral, I'd rather search for some common ground with this stern perspective. And a common ground might be found in, of all places, the awareness of evil in life. If the stern perspective might be wrong as to what it categorizes as sinful, it might be right in reminding us that we are sinners, in danger of losing our participation in the personal life God offers us. In other words, if evil can enter into all aspects of the human condition, then the question for this work will become one of how evil is experienced in relation to being homosexual, according to our witnesses. Maybe here we could talk about evil in terms of the depersonalization of homosexual people at the hands of others in society and religion, or the exclusion from communities of faith, or the lack of sexual integration in a person, or the turning of others into objects for sexual pleasure, or in terms of the absolutization of gayness, or, as may be common to all people, the ways we betray or reject ourselves, others, and God. Depending on the situation, perhaps a stern response to evil can be appropriate. But again, just as with the other themes we've mentioned, a clearer appraisal of this will come in subsequent chapters.

So far we have focused on familial experiences in examining the Catholic Christianity of our witnesses' youths. Now we'll turn our focus to Catholic educational experiences, considering whether influences in this realm foreshadow how our witnesses will deal with their homosexuality.

We might start with the experience of James B., forty-eight, of Chicago. At a young age James learned about following Christ, and these formative educational experiences continue to serve him as he responds to various issues regarding his homosexuality.

"I suppose most importantly for me it's like going back to grade school but it's something I've always carried with me, the corporal and spiritual works of mercy. In that sense of being a follower of Jesus because I can feed the hungry or clothe the naked or visit prisoners or whatever. I really do find that my life is guided by that, not by these moral principles but because in my being Catholic I feel my relationship to God is understood. Like who I am, God's love for me, His redemption in Christ, my being joined to Him in Christ, consciously a deep sense of His love for me."

Like James, several other of our witnesses spoke of their Catholic educational experiences in glowing, positive terms. Dave H., fifty-five, from Chicago, for example, does not relate a specific message impressed upon him by the nuns who taught him as much as he received an overall impression of the goodness or grace the nuns embodied: "I just have such fond memories of the nuns that taught me in grade school. I can name every one of them from first grade through eighth grade. I had one that was bad, but fortunately the others were all good. In high school I remember thinking to myself, these women, half of them really seem to have this glow about what they're here for and all about." We will see how a discernment of goodness is present in our witnesses' acceptance and integration of their homosexuality. And we will see how a discernment of goodness or grace can be found even in highly promiscuous settings.

Romeo C. speaks with gratitude for the influence of a particular nun who taught him the value of social justice: "One nun who particularly laid a positive impression on me was a missionary. She was in the same order as Sr. Jeannine Grammick. She was in the School Sisters of Notre Dame. She was a missionary in Paraguay and I was in first grade and she was the first person to inform me of any sort of social cause or social justice issues. I took to that. People don't understand how formative those years can be and that has stayed with me."

Another witness, Brian H., remembers a core message he received from his Catholic education. He says, "These Jesuit priests were very progressive and taught you to do good works, and listen to your heart, it's in your soul." *Listening to your heart* may be nearly the same as discerning and following your conscience. A memorable part of the education of Ron G., forty-three, from Columbus, was indeed the formation of conscience. He describes how he understood this: "One of the things I can remember—and my friends crack up because they say, 'I can't believe you remember this,' but I swear on a Bible I do—I remember very, very early on in grade school being taught the whole idea that you have to form your conscience based on all the things you know and that you have to make decisions based on what you believe is right. I very distinctly remember that." The experiences of Brian and Ron will help illustrate, further on, how the discernment process that takes place in following one's conscience relates to integrating one's homosexuality, dealing with promiscuity, being in a homosexual relationship, or participating in gay culture.

It is in fact through following Christ, or subsidiarily, following their consciences, praying, loving, discerning goodness, or acting justly, or confessing sinfulness, or needing and participating in community, that our witnesses as adults try to reconcile their homosexuality and their Catholicism. However, a more comprehensive understanding of such integration lies ahead, since it was generally only with difficulty, if at all, that our witnesses were able to reconcile the two in their youth.

As we turn to the question of how our witnesses, as young people, struggled to integrate their homosexuality with their religious beliefs, distinctions need to be made. A few of our witnesses distinguished between society, as the chief purveyor of negative messages about homosexuality, and their religion. David D., thirty-five, from Chicago, speaks of having to suppress his homosexuality because of social rather than religious factors: "As far as experiencing the attraction to another man, . . . in high school it was definitely existing but I suppressed that tremendously." He suppressed it because "it was socially unacceptable then. Probably still is in some areas of the metropolitan Chicago area." And, in response to my question about whether this meant he experienced his homosexuality as something bad, David adds, "It was a social factor. It wasn't moralistic. It wasn't religious by any means."

Robert P., thirty-six, also from Chicago, makes a similar distinction when asked, regarding his teenage years, whether he had any thoughts or feelings along the line of his homosexuality being something bad: "Yeah, but it was not from the religion, it was from the society. Because I was in the South, I was in Florida at the time. There was pretty much a lot of prejudice against gay people and there still is. And so, it just was . . . definitely not the thing to be. So I got the guilt from society. That was the biggest thing, to come to grips with that from peer groups and society. It's still like that down there. It really hasn't changed."

Finally, with regard to this theme, let's return to the story of John M., who appears in Chapter 1. John, who grew up in Poland, felt there was something wrong because of his homosexuality: "By the time I was a teenager, I realized there was something wrong, because some of the people were beginning to point fingers at me. And in fact I really tried to run away from it. I still didn't feel like it was sinful, but I felt like I was a weirdo." Describing the negativity surrounding his homosexuality, John says, "It was a social message, not a Church message. I'd never heard the Church stance on the issue. . . . It was a social taboo and the Church never said anything about it. And when the Church was pressured to make a statement, they had to go along with the rest of the world."

Setting aside for now John's statement as to how the Church came to a position on homosexuality, I would like to point out once again the distinction he makes between social oppression of homosexuality and homosexuality as something sinful. In fact, according to John, social oppression played a part in his leaving Poland. In a voice that could have been echoed by countless young people who left, for example, Iowa or Alabama for San Francisco, or places in Latin America for Miami, John says, "There were many reasons for coming to America, but one of them was to get away from there and start a new life."

The capacity for distinguishing between social and religious messages about homosexuality raises some interesting questions. Were our witnesses who speak of this theme able, even at young ages, to sort things out in their consciences? Does conscience, at its best, tap into a dimension that transcends, and thus allows for critique of, what might be called a social dimension of life? Did the fact that some of our witnesses failed to hear a negative message from the Church on homosexuality have something to do with the Church being silent on it? If so, were they able in that silence to find something valuable, whereas other of our witnesses experienced something oppressive?

Before we turn to the issue of silence within the Church concerning homosexuality, we also need to listen to those who said they did hear an explicitly condemnatory message regarding homosexuality from the Church. It is interesting to note that two of our witnesses who will attest to this are John F. and Don P., who described a more stern or militaristic experience of Catholicism in general. John F. says, "One of the things that you always heard as a child was that homosexuality is evil. You heard it explicitly, not only from my parents because they talked about some . . . students getting kicked out . . . because maybe they were deviants. You also heard it from the priests." In Don's case, a question his mother posed to him when he came out to her as homosexual is most likely linked to a more legalistic, stern, or militaristic experience of Catholicism. As described by Don, his mother said, "What do you say to people when you tell them you're gay and then they say you're going to go to hell because you're gay?"

More common than explicit condemnation, however, was the experience of silence from the Church concerning homosexuality. Chris T. may touch on a common experience of growing up Catholic and homosexual when he says he doesn't remember hearing *anything* about homosexuality from the Church. He speaks of this in terms of his typical experience of going to Mass: "My mom would have us there and she'd have little things for us to do or tell us to be quiet and I'd play games with her or whatever in the church pew. So I think that also explains why I don't have a lot of hang-ups about being Catholic or raised Catholic because maybe I missed something. But what I don't remember, though, is anything about our priest talking about homosexuality. I don't remember any of that."

Although homosexuality is increasingly addressed by the Church, one gets the impression that in the past, even recently, and still, I would presume, in some present situations, homosexuality was and has been experienced as such a taboo in the Church it couldn't even be talked about. Leo R., in speaking of his youth, refers to the way silence about homosexuality existed within the context of a cherished communal Catholicism. Describing this context, he says, "We lived in a very blue collar, Catholic, working-class family. We had eight kids in the family, the Izzis next to us had ten kids. The Cheeseboroughs had six kids, and the Martins had seven kids. The parish church was three blocks away. The founding pastor of the parish who had been there since 1930 or 1935 or whatever was good friends with my parents. I served the early Masses. We had novenas every Monday. I would serve the novenas and benedictions. My father was a letter carrier, so he got me up at five o'clock in the morning to go serve six a.m. Mass. Catholic grade school; Catholic high school . . . it was a very tight-knit community." Within this tight-knit community, which he remembers with fondness, Leo refers to no explicit messages about homosexuality but, repeating a message we heard from him in the first chapter, he did internalize a rather harsh implicit message: "It was understood that that [homosexuality] was not even to be discussed, thought about, talked about. No way possible. It doesn't happen here."

Again, perhaps like countless others, Leo did not receive a message that was outrightly condemning of homosexuality as much as he encountered silence on the issue. But it was a silence that was often condemning, if not disastrous, in its own way. In a dramatic story that doesn't refer to his own youth, but to the young life of a person he met while working as a counselor in a Catholic high school, Mark M. shares what he believes can be the repercussions of such silence: "When I was a counselor in the high school, . . . one of the significant events there was when there was a student whose name was 'Joshua.' I knew he was gay. I could just tell. I could see my own story in him. That's all. He was a very handsome guy so he was popular with the girls but he wasn't athletic so he wasn't with the guys and I knew he was getting ribbed for being queer. I had just heard it at different times with kids. Anyway, one day he had enough of it and attempted to take his life. His mom left him in the house, ran out to buy groceries, on her way realized she had left the list behind, debated whether she should go back or not. She had a long list; she thought, 'I better go back, sure as anything I'll forget it and have to come back anyway.' So she turned around and went back home. And when the door went up on the garage, her son was hanging from the rafters. Leaving her list behind is what saved his life. That's when she found out her son was gay and what torment he was going through."

Mark continues, "Of course, it's when I also found out what torment he was going through. It had a profound impact on me because I should have been able to be a mentor to him. I was a gay, adult man in the Church and I could have helped him, talked him through. But he couldn't access me because I was living in my own cage of fear as well. And the Church had put us there. I felt I had really let him down."

Just as children absorb the silent messages of family life, homosexual people in the Church almost certainly have absorbed, and in matters of degree still do absorb, the silent message that homosexuality is something so bad it can't even be spoken about. The repercussions of such silence were and often are terribly damaging.

Whether condemnation was communicated through silence or through explicit messages that being gay was somehow abnormal, bad, evil, or sinful, guilt and shame about one's sexuality could easily result. Joe G., fifty-two, from Columbus, shares this story of confiding his homosexuality to a priest: "In eighth grade I told this priest that I was homosexual. He denied that could be the case. So he gave me a book on Royal Canadian Air Force exercises and I was to learn to build up my body and I was to learn on the threat of him 'kicking me in the butt' how to play baseball."

This priest was undoubtedly well-intentioned in his advice to this young adolescent, but it was advice that nevertheless denied Joe's homosexuality and advocated that he be other than he was. It would be difficult not to experience guilt for acting, or shame for being, homosexual, in the face of such an attitude.

Mark M., referring now to his own youth, did not go to a priest, but he looked up "homosexuality" in a catechism book: "Oh yes, I remember discovering a book down in the basement of the house. It was an old Catechism book but it was clean. I ran across this book and started looking at the table of contents and there was a chapter on homosexuality. And I read it and of course it said terrible things, that it was terribly sinful and a perversion and so forth. I remember that it was really traumatic to me." It isn't surprising that, in light of this memory, when asked how he might have prayed about his homosexuality in his youth, Mark answered, "A prayer would have been, 'Remove this from me. Take this away.'"

Doug D., thirty-nine, from a suburb of Columbus, speaks of the shame he experienced for being homosexual within a Catholic familial and social context: "I think it was all that internal shame, but I don't know if I can pinpoint a message or a time when I felt shameful for my sexuality. I grew up in a family where even heterosexuality wasn't talked about, so homosexuality was nowhere near the conversation. But there was just this innate sense that to find someone of the same gender attractive was not right. . . . I think the origin of this attitude was at least in part from my religious background. I do remember the scripture texts and the ones that referred to homosexual practices being immoral. I remember those being quoted. I don't remember if they were preached on, but I remember them being used." In response to my question as to whether he prayed about his homosexuality at that time, Doug adds, "I did. I said, 'God, take it away. This is a phase. When is this phase going to be over?'"

In response to my question of whether he ever hoped that his homosexuality was just a phase, Mitch S. embarks on a profound and sorrowful story. He says, "Oh, yes, because what I saw is that I'd had a very close relationship with a lot of students, my classmates I grew up with, and there were some experiments and different things like that. I just assumed I would grow out of it just like obviously they all had. I was kind of physically behind, just a little kid. I was kind of small, so I assumed I'd just grow out of it. When I was nineteen, on this retreat, I realized I'm not growing out of this. I'd realized it all along but this was like throwing in the towel. This is who I am."

The story of Mitch's "throwing in the towel" continues: "I'll dive in when I came out to myself. I was on a TEC retreat—Teens Encounter Christ. Lots of stuff was stirring up and I went on this retreat and I realized this is who I am and it's not going away. As a ritual, when you pick up your TEC cross you can pick it up and say something if you want or you can just take it or whatever. When it got to be my time . . . I was going to come out to a priest, my former pastor from when I was growing up, and I was going to go to reconciliation and tell him I was gay in reconciliation, but it didn't happen or work out that way. . . . I also knew there was a lot of brokenness in my life around this issue. So I saw reconciliation as a healing. . . . So what I did is, I picked up the cross and I turned to everyone and I said, 'I never wanted this cross but I'm taking it.' So I put it on and I went back. I immediately began to sob. My friend Michelle was there so she embraced me. . . . So that is when I came out to myself."

For Mitch it appears there were at least three dimensions to his bearing of a cross. First, there was some acceptance of who he was. With regard to his homosexuality, this is when, as he puts it, he came out to himself. Second, there was healing. The healing absorbed "the frustration, the brokenness around feeling different, feeling alienated all those things." Perhaps Mitch's sobbing was a way of grieving about all the brokenness and alienation that encompassed his being homosexual. Perhaps he was also experiencing the love of Christ who gave him the freedom to grieve in his suffering.

Third, Mitch speaks of bearing a cross in terms of "the acceptance of a burden. It was the acceptance of, 'I guess there's a reason why I am gay and I'll deal with it and that's going to be hard and burdensome.'" There's an openness in this statement. It leaves open, for example, a question of whether the difficulty of bearing homosexuality is something inherent to homosexuality, as if one has to bear a disorder and learn to live with it, or, whether, perhaps, the difficult burden stems more from communal alienation and rejection. (Indeed, what was Jesus bearing on the cross if not in part a rejection by humanity.)

What is clear is the difficulty, pain, and sorrow of being homosexual in this young Catholic person's life. What is not so clear is whether the "burden" of homosexuality is just something he will have to learn to live with, something which is not deemed good or valuable as much as it is something that has to be put up with, or whether this burden, which includes an acceptance of himself, will become a way in which he can grow in a life of love that finds, despite the difficulty and sorrow, his homosexuality valuable and, indeed, good. The language of burden might lead one to believe that in his youth Mitch felt the former, but the subsequent journey of Mitch will reveal the latter—an attempt to integrate what he will come to see as the goodness of his homosexuality into a life of love.

Finally, it will prove worthwhile to listen to two of our witnesses who, when they prayed or turned inward, did not pray some variation of "take this away." We will return first to the story of Brian H. As cited earlier, Brian paraphrases the messages he received in a Jesuit high school as follows: "These Jesuit priests were very progressive and taught 'do good works, listen to your heart, it's in your soul.'" In part due to the influence of one particular teacher of theology, Brian was able to come to terms with his homosexuality in a more positive way. He says, "We had a head of the boys' religion department whose name was Father Mark. And he had written these books on how to talk to God, how to pray, that—my understanding was—were pretty well respected. He'd teach theology to high school students, and I had him as a teacher. And somehow I got the message [referring to homosexuality] that God still loved you. Yet . . . I still played the double-edged thing, you know, I'm keeping this [homosexuality] a secret, but if God knows, then I'm okay." Describing how he prayed about his homosexuality, Brian adds, "I never had 'Please take this away.' I had, 'Please, make this easier for me to get through.'"

There is ambiguity in Brian's comments. Some might interpret his statement that God *still* loves him as implying that God loves us even with all of our shortcomings, failures, and sins, and homosexuality falls into one of these categories. But it might also mean that his relationship with God, in contrast to his relationship with a rejecting society around him, nonetheless confirms him in the goodness and lovability of his homosexuality. Indeed, this does become the trajectory for how he will deal with his homosexuality as an adult.

Despite negative external messages concerning homosexuality, Leo R. likewise came to an understanding of the goodness of his homosexuality in his youth. Speaking about this, he says, "It was like, I love this. This is great. But none of the other boys that I'm aware of identify as gay." He continues, "This is where the tension lies. Inwardly I knew it was good and part of my salvation, becoming more aware of who I am. I knew who I was in a sense. . . . I just knew it was somehow good in a way, even though all the messages I was getting, either verbally or nonverbally, said it's not good. I knew instinctively inside that it was somehow good."

The experience of viewing homosexuality as good, as part of one's salvation, was not acknowledged by many of our witnesses when speaking of their youth. Nevertheless, it might prove worthwhile to look at such an experience as a kernel, which although acknowledged by only a very few in their youths will be something all our witnesses discover and grow in. The next chapter will show the development of this kernel, of the salvific significance of "becoming more aware of who I am."

3 ∞ The Acceptance and Integration of Homosexuality

People often tell us to be ourselves. But just as common sense, according to the adage, is not all that common, perhaps "being yourself" is not all that common either. In response to such a prescription, one might feel like the character Archbishop Romero in the movie *Romero,* who responds to another character's advice just to do God's will by saying, "What is that?" Being yourself often seems like more of a journey than a fact. Many particularities, or, if we were to speak more religiously, gifts, make up who we are. And although such particularities may be natural to us, discovering, accepting, and integrating them, opening up about them with others, and seeing and sharing them as gifts are not automatic. This chapter will show the ways our witnesses came to accept and integrate their homosexuality.

One particular witness, Mark M., serves as an excellent initial guide in the matter of accepting oneself as homosexual. He begins, "In the beginning of my journey . . . I was outside of myself. I was afraid of what was instinctive to me and what was constitutive to me. I kept constantly distancing myself. I said, 'Nope, can't go there. Nope, can't do it.' When I acted on those [homosexual] inclinations—I felt like that's terrible, that's shameful, must confess to God, can't discuss it with anybody, conceal it. All that."

Mark cites the reason for being outside of himself as having given himself over to those voices who were not affirmative of homosexuality. In particular, in having given himself over to what the Church had to say; the consequence of this was shame: "I had allowed the Church to shame me." Within a circle of shame he hid: "I had been hiding all this time."

doi:10.1300/5599_04

Deeply underlying the shame, incorporating his "hiding," was a profound sense that Mark was losing himself, being alienated from himself: "I had been honoring someone else's truth all along. By trying to live my life, by trying to live up to other people's expectations of me, I was becoming . . . increasingly alienated from myself. I became depressed. I went into therapy for depression. And the alienation was really at the root of my depression."

Mark's evolution from alienation to integration was sparked by two key experiences: "The first time I felt that my life started to get integrated was when I found my college roommate in bed with his girlfriend, because it was the first time I really experienced the pain [of loneliness and alienation in his own life]. Isn't it funny? I still feel it. I allowed myself to grieve what loss I had suffered because of trying to be something other than who I was to please my mother, to please the Church, to please whomever. So that was the first time there was integration because I got in touch with that feeling. Before then I was just kind of trying to be happy-go-lucky, just pretending it didn't matter. The second time was when I found love and had sex and admitted to God this is who I am and God accepted me."

Whereas the first experience described by Mark highlights mourning over what has been lost, the second experience highlights what, we might say, he will find. After Mark finished college he went into a seminary, and while there met someone who became a partner. He explains, "It started out, of course, as a friendship, so I could still rationalize that. But one night we were out in the woods walking and he turned around and knelt down and engaged me in oral sex. I, of course, was dumbfounded. I didn't stop him. That was the moment I could no longer play intellectual games with myself. I had now had gay sex. And I knew what the Church said about that. And that was a real moment. You would think that the shame would have come rushing down afterwards. It was so wonderful that I concluded that this cannot be evil. I went into the chapel that night, in the darkened chapel, and I had a conversation with God and I said, 'Well, God, I guess I'm homosexual.' Now, I don't get answers to prayers very often, but I got a response that time. Inside my gut was, 'I'm glad you finally know and maybe now you can stop running from me.'"

Mark continues: "I had this feeling of acceptance, like God was just waiting for me to get to this point. No condemnation. And so my relationship flourished.

"I think these moments—I call them grace-filled moments, because in spite of all the evidence to the contrary I could spend a moment in the chapel with God and experience acceptance and unconditional love—was pure grace. It was a gift, because I know people like myself who experience condemnation. I don't know why I was lucky, but thank God that I had that experience."

Mark further interprets these experiences in terms of discernment of conscience. "You could say those were the moments when I really got in touch with my conscience in the sense that there was always the voice inside me that said to me, 'You're okay.' But all the clamor and noise on the outside said, 'You're not okay.' And I listened to those outside voices."

Mark's story describes a journey from alienation to integration. His alienation from himself, others, and God occurs in giving himself over to a cacophony of condemning voices, not the least of which were Church voices, regarding his sexuality. Indeed, Mark more or less says that in running from himself, he was also running from God and from personal relationships with others. Again, he is claiming that God is calling him to be the person who he is. In so doing he can also be more genuinely in relationship with others.

The process of moving from alienation to right relation with oneself, others, and God is echoed in the experience of David D. who speaks of this in terms of moving from hiding to honesty. He describes this in the context of the low point and high point of coming to terms with his homosexuality: "I think the low point in dealing with my homosexuality was that I was living life in a lie and that I really couldn't live with myself that way. The high point was when everybody knew because at that point I no longer had to worry about it."

David adds, "When I came out to everybody, yes, I saw it as being good in that I found myself and I no longer had to hide this part of me." David's movement from hiding to honesty is a movement from not being known to being known. "The low point was when no one knew me and that's exactly right. . . . After coming out . . . when I spoke at a family gathering or at a dinner table people knew where I was coming from. That's what is fun about coming out is that when you come out you're no longer just the son that's different, that no one knows why, but now they know where you're coming from. People know you when you talk to them. If they want to know they'll know you and they'll enjoy everything you have to say."

Like David, Michael S. emphasizes the importance of becoming honest with himself. In his case this is partly inspired by the honesty of a friend. "A good friend of mine, who had been fighting with his homosexuality, came out to me. He had been away at college, I was at home, going to a college here in Chicago, and so when he came back and was living back here in Chicago he did come out to me. Now, about four years earlier, in our senior year, he did make a sexual advance towards me. But that was stopped by me and I put it out of my head. Because, I just thought, 'No, this is wrong. And I don't think I'm going to enjoy this.' Now, it's funny that for four years our friendship went on intermittently because he was away at college, but it went on and we never talked about that. And finally he came out to me and it was only a matter of months before I said, 'He's honest, maybe I should be honest with myself and with him and come out too, because those are feelings that I have as well.' Let's see, that's when I was about, so it was 1984, I was about twenty-one."

Michael then describes the effects of being honest with himself. "I felt liberated in . . . a very personal, private way. But I knew that I was going to have to keep this in, too. I would make gay friends, and certainly my friend introduced me to other people, but my immediate thought was, 'Well, I don't think I'll be dealing with this with the family for a while.' So it took a couple years before I started coming out to members of my family."

Whereas the effects of being honest with his family will come in time, there were immediate benefits from being honest with himself: "I felt like I didn't have to chase those thoughts from my head anymore. I could simply acknowledge them and be gay and enjoy that or live that way. And I was ready to explore that and there was no more bottling up of that.

"I felt that I should be true to myself. My parents had always taught me to be honest. Their example was to be honest, so this was consistent with that. Why shouldn't I be honest with myself, first and foremost? So that felt good, that really did. Now I will say, that shortly thereafter I did decide to go to confession and talk to a priest about this. Just to see where this fits in my life anymore. I think I had a good experience because when I went to confession, I said, 'Father, I do want to tell you this, that, how does the church feel about homosexuality?' And I felt that I had to ask about that, because it was 1984, before the '86 pronouncements. So, in the confessional, the priest said, 'Well, the important thing is that you are chaste or monogamous. It's okay to be that way.' And I remember him using the words be chaste or monogamous. You do this in a responsible manner. That was another kind of liberation for me."

As Michael's story highlights, the process of becoming honest with oneself can take time. In some cases it can take a long time. Bob S. refers to the long-term process of his coming out. "It took me forever to get to a point of being totally comfortable with myself and being out to my parents and things like that. I and my partner were in our late thirties before we were totally out. We were just together all the time; we lived together. We never made mention to friends about being gay or anything like that. It was funny, people we knew for years, like, once we finally said, 'We've been living together for the last fifteen years and we're gay.' It took some people by such surprise, like, what the heck are you doing? But, yes, it took us a very long time to come out. But that's part of the story, that it took us a long time, and I'd have to say once we came out we really came out."

Bob continues, "My late thirties was the change, where it's not something I'm going to hide from everybody. That was probably the point when I said, 'This is my life. I love my life, and that is the way it is.' At work I'm out. I'm not afraid to say that Ron is my partner. His boss has Christmas parties and so he always takes me to his Christmas parties. So we're just very out and happy to be out, trying to stake our little claim to happiness."

Some of our witnesses were married when they began the journey of accepting themselves as homosexual. There are some common threads in the stories of these men, including homosexual experiences prior to or during their marriages; familial, social and or religious pressure to be married; the realization that they were not being themselves in the marriage; hurt spouses; depression; and, ultimately, self-acceptance.

Let's look first at the experience of John F. Earlier we heard John speak of how his homosexuality didn't fit into the Catholic and military background in which he was raised. John speaks explicitly of the expectations that existed during his background: "You're going to go to college, get married, have kids . . . this is very ingrained in myself, where I was supposed to go in life. The dutiful son."

John talks about meeting his future wife in college. "I never got in trouble, did everything they wanted me to do, went to college, didn't even dare explore any other side of me. Now some people take that as an opportunity away from home finally to explore. No, no, no. That's just the message I had for my whole life. So I made friends with this woman who was a really nice person. She was a Spanish exchange student here and we just really hit it off. We had a great friendship and I thought maybe this is what I'm supposed to do. I ended up saying I'm going to force myself, I'm going to get married. I'm going to do what I am supposed to do, what my family says I'm supposed to do, what my religious beliefs say I'm supposed to do. Even after college I'm the dutiful son attending religious services on a regular basis and didn't deviate from any of that.

"Looking back on it twenty years later, in my parents' eyes and probably God's eyes, anybody who was looking at me thought, 'Oh, that good boy.' So I ended up getting married to 'Jennifer.' Looking back on things, if I had the strength I have today, no way would that have happened. But we got married. We had a great time with each other; she was a very nice person. We ended up having two daughters too.

"Over the years I became increasingly depressed. I put on weight. I couldn't get motivated about things. Probably about a year before I took any action, I started thinking about what's going on here. Do I need to see a psychiatrist? At that time I didn't want to because to me that would admit defeat. But I saw the war in myself and I got a hold of some information. This was in 1989, 1990. I was just starting to get connected online. I was connected to AOL at the time, so you were able to get a little more information available to you. I was able to start thinking about this whole sexuality thing and exploring that and then found some communities on AOL that were geared toward people who were possibly homosexual but in a situation like I was, married. So that was kind of a relief. I thought, 'Oh my gosh, I'm not the only one in this situation.' And two or three people across the nation, there was a guy in California, there was one in Utah and another guy. Through the e-mail we could chat and stuff, you got to really explore yourself. Probably being anonymous helps in a way, that you could really lay down your feeling for someone and start thinking about the part you've repressed for so many years.

"From the time I started to the time I said, 'I've got to end this,' this helped in my depression."

What John needed to end was "the phony marriage and the phony life that I've been living all these years (trying to live for others). . . . So it was about a year later in 1991 . . . my wife found out. This is the one area I'm not very proud of. I'm a very trusting person and I expected to be trusted. Right near the end I met somebody. Bob and I had a little affair for awhile. That was it, but she found about it. You look back upon it and think maybe I wanted her to, maybe it was the easiest way for her to find out. I left the house. I started seeing a psychiatrist and I haven't looked back."

When asked about his religious sensibility and or prayer life during this time, John adds, "I would still go to church every Sunday and I can remember praying, 'God, give me something, give me some help here. I've got to make some decisions and I don't want to hurt anybody.' You end up with this woman—I end up marrying and divorcing. She ended up being hurt. I do feel some sense of guilt in that arena. But yes, I was looking for direction, but direction doesn't come like a lightening bolt. More you find some inner strength in you and that's one of the things I think has been . . . a blessing. One of the things I do think is a blessing for myself is the strength to be able to address this, my homosexuality, and become completely comfortable with myself."

John expounds on the "blessing" of being himself: "I think that's a blessing because I have a lot of strength and I've endured a lot. . . . I think that's a blessing. I have a friend who's three years older than me and lives nearby. He just struggles. He didn't get married and have a kid or anything but he just can't accept himself. So I think that's one thing I've been blessed with and that is an inner strength."

There are parallels to John's experiences in the stories of Leo R. and Michael D. First, as with John, there were familial, social, and/ or religious pressures to get married. Leo, for example, speaks about some of his motivations for getting married: "Right out of high school I went to work and that's where I met my wife. We were working together at the post office and she was at OSU and I was going to Franklin University. So we'd meet and study. Things developed and she became pregnant and that's why we got married. As a matter of fact, that was my first sexual experience. I had very limited sexual experiences other than jack-off sessions with friends. . . . So we ended up getting married and I thought, 'If we get married and I work hard and keep my nose to the grindstone, these feelings will soon dissipate. We'll have the house in the suburbs.'"

During this discussion, I asked Leo a few questions regarding earlier statements he had made that in his youth he believed his homosexuality to be something good:

Q: You've got this tension because you had been saying that on the inside your homosexuality was good.

LEO: Inside I knew it was good. I knew I was gay.

Q: But you wanted it to go away because it wasn't accepted by other people?

LEO: Yes, because culturally it wasn't acceptable. I thought if I get married then [my homosexual feelings] will go away and then everything will be okay and then things will all fall into place.

Michael, in his forties and from Columbus, describes similar hopes that by getting married he would change his homosexual orientation: "Well, I was married for twenty years and I have three children and two grandchildren, and I think growing up Catholic made it harder for me to accept myself than maybe some. For me, I think it's one of the reasons I got married, I told my wife about a week and a half before the wedding that I had tendencies, not knowing really what that meant. I just knew there was and I had a guy, I wouldn't call him a lover because in those days I wasn't sure, but I played around with him from age fourteen until the night before my wedding. When I told my wife I had tendencies, I thought, 'Well, I'll give her an out.' I think it was sort of maybe hoping that she would say no and do the job for me instead of saying I can't do this. But I seriously felt that first of all I had to change."

Q: You had to change this orientation, because it was bad?

MICHAEL: Yes, because it was bad. . . . I was raised in a family that I think I heard enough about and people make fun of and all growing up I was never the really most masculine of my brothers and I was teased a lot, so I just kind of kept to myself and was kind of quiet. But obviously what they saw was true. But instead of a society where it's okay to be who you are, instead we feel we have to change to fit the world that everyone else has for us.

So when I went into the marriage, I really thought I could do it. My wife, I guess I relieved my guilt from telling her what I told her and I felt and she felt that if we loved each other enough we could change it together. She would help me. And while I was having children and going through the routines and everything, I really stayed on the straight and narrow pretty much.

So with Michael, just as with John, background pressures and even a desire not to be homosexual played a part in the decision to be married. And, just as John speaks of living a "phony life" in his marriage, Leo and Michael echo this in their own ways. First, to continue Michael's story: "For fifteen years . . . I was a good little Catholic boy and I was on the parish council and I was on other city things . . . but in my heart I never felt right about how I was living. It was okay, I think, the first five years, and then as reality set in, I just felt dishonest. And yet I didn't know how I was going to . . . come to terms with this, but I also knew that life was going to make me deal with it."

Leo, likewise, addresses this theme of living a phony life: "So then Chris was born the first year we were married. We had another child two years later and then another child three years later. So we had three kids within a five-year span. After the birth of the last child in 1975, I really knew that being married was not going to work and the homosexual feelings came back stronger.

"I thought I was living a lie. I wasn't being true to myself. Here I am, I'm teaching fifth grade religion class, the CCD class, which is on the sacraments. One of the exercises we have to get through is the examination of your conscience. I'm reading the teacher's edition, the questions you should ask the students, and I'm doing it for myself and the answers I'm getting—I don't want the answers to these questions. Finally I'm thinking, 'It's not fair to me, it's not fair to my kids, it's not fair to everybody else to be doing this. It's not right. She's not with someone who can love her totally. I'm not with someone I can love totally—sexually, physically, emotionally, spiritually. It's not what marriage should be, so somehow we got to stop this.'"

Just like John, Leo and Michael speak of an increasing sense of depression while in their marriages. Leo continues his story: "I internalize and process internally. I guess I learned that from being gay and having to work it out in my head always. It took a few years; it took probably another three years. Then my mother died. My mother had heart disease and she died early. She was forty-nine when she died. That's really what started it. I thought, 'I could die at age forty-nine.' Here I am, I was twenty-nine or something. I said, 'I could die in twenty years. What would I have?' I think you do that in your thirties; you become more reflective. You start looking back because pretty much you're either in the career you're going to have or you're soon to be in the career you're going to have, so that's done and most of your education's done and most of your lifestyle is set. So now you start to ponder what does all this mean? Have I chosen the right path, and if I haven't what path should I choose? That's pretty much what I did; I worked through that process. It was very difficult. I remember the more I pondered on it the more depressed I got. The more depressed I got the more I withdrew. I remember my wife saying, 'I don't know what the hell is wrong with you. You're not talking with me.' We weren't interacting physically, sexually. I just couldn't, so I was dysfunctional, and she said, 'I don't know what's wrong with you but you need to go talk to someone.' I kept saying, 'No, no, it's work and I'm working too hard.' I was working all the overtime I could get to stay out of the house and kept thinking I'm actually working overtime for the good of the family. In retrospect I was really working overtime to get out of the house so I would have the excuse to be too tired to do anything else.

"We did have, on the outside, the perfect family. Three kids, two dogs, two station wagons. We had the house on the cul-de-sac. We had it all going. She did music in the church, music groups; she was the leader of that. I taught CCD and she taught CCD also. We were on the parish council. We were *the* Catholic family or poster child, so it was very difficult. But it came to a head, I remember it was the summer of 1980, because it was right after Dad died in 1979, she said, 'I can't take it anymore. I'm going to take the kids. I'm going to go on vacation for a week. You see who you have to see, you talk to who you have to talk to, but when I come home I want answers.' I couldn't avoid it anymore. So I thought, 'Oh shit. Now what do I do?'"

It was at this point of crisis that Leo reached out for help and came to an acceptance of himself as homosexual: "So I called the mental health center and said, 'I need to get in to see somebody,' and they said I couldn't see anybody for over a month. I said, 'You don't understand.' So I knew the Shrine Center, which is a local Catholic center here, has a priest on there and he has an open office and you can go in and talk. I thought, 'I'll go in.' I went in and saw him and told him my whole story and what I suspected, that I thought I may be gay but I didn't know any other gay people because I lived way out in the suburbs. There are no other gay people, I hadn't been in the gay world, hadn't been out, hadn't acted on it or anything since I was married. Nothing. I wasn't sure, but I thought I might be." At some point in the conversation the priest apparently referred in a somewhat derogatory tone to the local Newman Center, which was known for being supportive of gay people. According to Leo, the priest said, "'Those people down at the Newman Center.' *Those people*. So I knew that conversation was over.

"Fortunately, I did call the Newman Center, so that was very good and I got in right away and I saw a priest, Paul. I talked to Paul for two or three hours and he said, 'You're coming out. That's what's going on. You probably need to see a psychologist.' So he recommended a few names and so I went to see some guy."

Through the help of this conversation with Father Paul, Leo's acceptance and integration of his homosexuality finally took root. "It was what I needed to hear. I needed some affirmation of what I knew was true all along but didn't want to deal with."

In Michael we see a similar painful progression from and through depression to acceptance of his homosexuality. "I dealt with depression, never had to deal with depression, and I was amazed at how I could put on a happy face at work. No one had a clue because I talked deeply about it with a guy that I met there. Even my wife couldn't tell all of what I was feeling. I had not told my kids that I was gay, and I just had come to where I couldn't deal with it anymore. I was totally worn out. We were going to church at the time but I couldn't get into that church. God was in my heart but I couldn't feel anything at church. I remember that through this whole depression I was still spiritual.

"Later when I analyzed that I thought that was so weird. I never lost God in the whole thing. But I had one day that was really, really bad and I just wanted out and I am ashamed today that I went that far because this day I had planned. I knew when she was coming home. I knew when the kids would be home. I planned that she would be the one that would find me. I thought I just wanted to write a few things down. I did mat cutting so I had razor blades. I had figured out how I was going to do it. I was going to go up my arm instead of across because they say that's a surer way, it would be harder for them to save you. I thought I'll go into the bathtub so I wouldn't make a big mess in the apartment."

Prior to this day, however, Michael had befriended a person, "Doris," and had told her something about his depression and had promised her that if things ever got dire he would call her. So on this day, in which he was planning his suicide, he was haunted by this promise. "I called her and she said, 'Mike, are you scheduled to work today?' I said, 'No.' I don't remember why I wasn't working that day, unless I hadn't got a job yet. I can't remember. Anyhow, she said, 'Get out of there and come down!' because she lived on the other end of town.

"So I'm driving down and feeling smaller and smaller as I'm going through this and feeling like crap and ashamed and embarrassed and all of this. When I got to her house she had her Baptist minister there. He had come over. Then I thought, 'Brother, now I'm going to hear all this,' and it was funny because he didn't do that at all. As a matter of fact he made me feel so comfortable. He told me that it was time to give up the marriage. I thought, 'He believes I'm wrong anyway and I've already done this sinful thing so she's free so let her off the hook.' I kept thinking, 'This is why he's

being nice to me, he's just convincing me this and that.' But he basically said, 'You are who you are and that's what you are, so you
just need to get away from your wife and live your life.'" Perhaps
it's the "You are who you are" message that marks the spot where
the acceptance of himself as homosexual took root for Michael.

Again, it's interesting to note several common themes in the stories of the three witnesses who had been married, not the least of
which is that in not being themselves with regard to their sexuality
they were not able to participate in fully personal relationships with
their wives. Listen again to Leo's words as he describes how his
marriage was unfair: "She's not with someone who can love her totally. I'm not with someone I can love totally—sexually, physically,
emotionally, spiritually. It's not what marriage should be." Having
said that, however, I'm not sure how fair it would be to generalize
from these marriages to the marriages of all people in which one
partner is gay. First, there may be legitimate questions about bisexu-
ality. Second, I'm not sure there couldn't be reasons for staying in
a marriage even if one of the partners is homosexual. (I remember a
conversation with an elderly gentleman, not one of the interviewees for this book, who spoke of himself as gay but also married, of
having been married for years. He told me about how, in coming to
terms with his homosexuality at a late age, during his sixties, he
came out to his wife. He told her he was gay, and she responded, "I
know. Can we go get something to eat?") Third, and perhaps most
important, the stories of the spouses married to homosexual people
and the stories of the children of such unions don't seem to get
much of a hearing. Whereas there is an increasingly public voice regarding the concerns of homosexual people, where are the voices,
or the concern, for those who were married to such people, or for
their children? Their hurt, their anguish, their shame, their confusion, their anger, and—it is to be hoped—their coming to terms
with things need to be listened to and addressed.

The witnesses have shown us the struggles they went through in
the process of accepting themselves as homosexual. Other witnesses put this struggle for acceptance into a broader perspective.

Jerry G. speaks of the importance of integrating one's homosexuality in terms of wholeness: "It's part of the whole person. If you haven't discovered that, if that is indeed who you are, you haven't got the whole pie, you haven't got the whole picture. That person would be pretty miserable who doesn't know where they fit into this."

Robert P. gives his perspective on the importance of accepting oneself as homosexual by saying, "If you're living a lie you're not going to have peace." And, according to Robert, joy comes from being yourself. "It is the greatest gift to yourself to be who you are. I used this in my coming out group. It's the greatest gift to be giving yourself, to be gay and allow yourself to be gay. It's the greatest gift you can give yourself and it's a gift from God. And it is a joy to be yourself."

Wholeness, peace, and joy as the gifts of being oneself are accompanied, in the perspective of Ryan O., in his forties, from Dayton, Ohio, by life-giving energy. "Whatever your sexual orientation is about, to me there ought to be a sense of integration. You ought to have a sense that it informs how you think about things and it gives you a certain energy with which you can change the world or make life better for yourself or your family or whatever it gives. And that's what sexuality is for; it's supposed to be life giving."

To conclude this chapter, I'll turn to one final story. Here, in Jim L., fifty-six, from Chicago, we'll see a person who struggled with his homosexuality, tried to discern in his conscience what to do with it, and then reached an acceptance and integration of it that is marked by peace, joy, and, as he describes it, liberation.

Jim describes how, for much of his early adult life, he struggled with his homosexuality. There was "guilt, anguish, and everything that was associated with that, and of course not being able to talk to anybody about it, having to deal with it on my own. I was living at home most of the time. I was thirty-two years old before I moved out and got my own apartment. Prior to that there was no reason for me to do so, so I didn't. Then all of a sudden I needed to get a life of my own. But the life I had lived was a life in a protected area that had walls around it so high and so thick that no one could break through and it hurt me."

The walls Jim refers to were walls around himself, walls which inhibited him from sharing himself with others, and from letting others share themselves with him. He continues, "It was very late in life when I came out. I was thirty-eight before I even met another gay man. There was no sexual activity or anything before age thirty-eight. But I had known I was gay and I had dealt with it alone as no one knew."

Yet in his years of struggle and dealing alone with his homosexuality, Jim also turned to prayer or, as he puts it, to conversations with God. "I had conversations with God about it. And for a long time, because I didn't know if it was right or wrong, I stopped going to communion because I thought if I'm doing wrong then I can't go to communion, although I continued to go to church every Sunday. For six years I didn't go to communion—and then it almost bordered on revelation—that all of a sudden I knew that it was alright to be who I was and the very next Sunday I went to communion."

While in one respect Jim's revelation may be seen as the culmination of a process of struggle and prayer, it also refers to a particular experience that took place during a weekend retreat at a Jesuit retreat house near Cincinnati. There he met with a spiritual director, and "the program he put together for me was to do a lot of spiritual reflection on the grounds while walking around and praying. I brought one of the hymn books from the church with me and would sing out in the woods all my favorite songs."

Jim describes what happened on one of his walks. "I was walking along the pebble beach alongside the river and it was a cloudy kind of day. It was warm for October and I was looking up at the sky and even though it wasn't a vision, He appeared, Jesus appeared in the clouds, smiling down at me. I knew He wasn't there and it was just my mind, this is where we are and this is the answer I was looking for. To actually see Him, He just smiled on me and I knew what He was smiling about. . . . It was me, and, 'Jim it's alright to be who you are and what you have is a special gift.' And I believe at some point in my life I'm going to find out why. I don't know yet why but sometime in the future I'm going to find out why God decided that I was going to be gay. There's a reason for it. It's a gift He's given to me and a gift that very few other people have and I don't know yet what my purpose is, but it's there and I'll find out. That was the crowning moment of that three-day weekend."

The effects of this experience on Jim included peace and the transformation of uncertainty and doubt into a faithful, liberating confidence. "I was completely at peace all of a sudden, where for all those years before there was always the uncertainty, the doubt. I didn't need anybody to tell me it [being homosexual] was all right. If He told me then I didn't care what anybody else said. I know they couldn't do anything about it. They couldn't prevent me from going to Heaven, or sentencing me to Hell. They couldn't do that so all of a sudden their power over me was gone. And that was a liberating experience."

The witnesses in this chapter describe, for the most part, a process of accepting themselves as homosexual. And "process" is probably the correct word for what they went and continue to go through, for what person can speak as if they have totally experienced self-acceptance or integration? Indeed, in a way that can be confusing, a gay man may actually be "out" to family and friends (and in that sense has accepted his homosexuality), but continue to struggle with sexual behavior that on some level he finds shameful. Perhaps nowhere in the lives of gay men is the accepting and affirming love of Christ needed more than in unbinding the layers of shame that can often, like cloth surrounding a mummy, encircle gay men and their promiscuous behavior.

A child who grows up unloved may find it very difficult to love. Likewise, homosexual people who have grown up with their homosexuality unloved may in turn find it very difficult to love through their sexuality. This difficulty, intertwined with a natural sexual desire, may get near the bottom of the common experience of promiscuity among gay men.

Promiscuity is one of the most complex and challenging areas of experience for gay men, and, surprisingly, it is not often thoroughly addressed. In this chapter we'll first listen to what some or our witnesses have to say about their experiences with promiscuous sexual behavior and how they regard it. After that we'll return to the question of an underlying lack of love.

Jerry G., who is sixty-eight and is one of our older witnesses, describes, not without humor, what it was like to be homosexual when he was younger. "That's some era to come from. The only good thing about it was you didn't have to be afraid of things you have to watch out for today. . . . There was a lot of promiscuity then; that was the norm. I rather enjoyed that. It got ridiculous. I'd be out with somebody in the early part of the day, then toward evening I'd be with somebody else, then late at night somebody else again. Not all the time. But it did happen like that on occasion. Every other week or so was party time. That was anything goes, too. You go to these parties and you all ended up on the floor in no time. I'm sure they don't do stuff like that now. I don't know; I don't go to parties anymore. At my age, I'm lucky to do what I do."

Notwithstanding the good-humored and even slightly nostalgic attitude with which Jerry recalls his experiences, a tinge of sadness enters his words as he contrasts promiscuity to lasting relation-

doi:10.1300/5599_05

ships. "I believe in relationships, I really do, instead of promiscuity. . . . I believe in loyalties. But being in a relationship wasn't as easy to do then as it is now. People today are looking for a relationship. I see it with the young people. They pair off more and that's a good thing."

Brian H. is in his late forties and thus comes from a younger generation than Jerry, but he too describes a scene that illustrates the pervasiveness of promiscuous behavior. In Brian's case the experience involved a bathhouse in Chicago in the 1970s. "When I came out in the '70s there was a lot of sex, you know. I went to Man's Country, I want to say in '76, '77, and I remember walking around and there were hundreds and hundreds of men having sex."

Brian goes on to share his struggles with sexual behavior in the context of a bathhouse. "Not that I wasn't there to have sex," Brian says, "and I did have sex—but . . . it was never a part of me to go into the orgy room and let whatever happens happen. And I think that's partly based on religious dealings. I think it's respect for self. I've been accused of being hypocritical about it, because I've been to the baths and will do one thing and not another. But it just seems different to me. It seems different to be in a room and invite someone in or let them come in and be treated with a modicum of respect, versus other stuff you can do."

Matteo P., who's in his thirties, talks about promiscuity in his life. "I had a wild time of drinking and carousing during my early college years and I would even have to say I lived kind of dangerously. . . . I was experimenting with sexual promiscuity to a point that, whether I was gay or whether I was heterosexual, would not have been acceptable to my person, to my way of life."

Matteo continues, "It was becoming an obsession to have just the sex and I wasn't experiencing the joy that I had felt in my earlier experiences with gay sex and even [when I had] heterosexual sex. It just wasn't good for my spirit. My spirit was saying, this isn't good and something's not right there . . . meeting someone in a bar and getting drunk and going home and then waking in the morning and not feeling good led to some self-loathing."

Mark R., who's in his twenties, describes his experiences, growing up in Scotland, looking for sexual encounters in parks and public restrooms. "At first going to parks and stuff was really exciting and I thought it was really cool, but in my mind I was just really confused. At the end of the day I realized I was confusing sex and emotions. . . . Sometimes if I would see the same guy a few times I would . . . get a bit stuck on him."

Mark continues, "At the end of the day I knew that I wanted something different. This wasn't the way I wanted to go. Now I can look back and see that I wanted something all along. . . . I wanted one person. I didn't want all this [promiscuity]. As exciting and decadent as it was, I wanted one person . . . partly because I've seen [being with one person] work. I was brought up that way."

Mark acknowledges that he still struggles with promiscuous behavior, and perhaps his words have some compassion for himself and others in them: "It is still a bit of a struggle. I haven't really resolved that, in the sense that I realize what I need is someone to love."

Jerry, Matteo, Brian, and Mark in sharing their experiences with promiscuous behavior are making descriptive and evaluative statements. With Jerry and Mark their engagement with promiscuous behavior is intertwined with a value placed upon personal relationships. With Matteo and Brian their engagement with promiscuous behavior is intertwined with a concern for self-respect.

Turning to further evaluation of promiscuity, we'll listen first to those of our witnesses who voice their concerns or warnings about promiscuous behavior. In the context of an outreach Mass for gay and lesbian people, James B. paraphrases the counsel of a priest during the homily: "'For gay men here, I want to say that in your relationships, if you just go after the sex, you're never really going to touch the person you're with.' Gay men need to hear that," James continues. "In a community of gay men a priest can say, 'In your relationships you cannot use one another. Sex is part of who you are but it can destroy you or give you empty lives. It can draw you down just as anything else can draw you down.'"

Mitch S. relates the story of his father warning him about how people can sometimes lose themselves with sex. "My father said, 'When people start to experience their sexuality it is very powerful and it can change them.' To me, what could be more affirming than my dad saying, 'Be who you are. The person I love in you is this and this and this. Caring, compassionate, sensitive, honest, all those things. And what he was saying was, 'Don't lose that.'"

Bill H., twenty-six, from Chicago, voices his sentiment that promiscuity is not soul nourishing in the way long-term relationships are. "I would even say most gay men would prefer to have a long-term relationship. There's the emptiness of one-night flings. Some people feel bad about them because sex is such a personal event and. . . in a way one-night stands . . . depersonalize it and I think that does have an effect on a person's psyche." Bill's concern about *depersonalized* experiences of sexuality is echoed in the comments of some other witnesses. Bob S. says, "I try not to be judgmental; I've got my Midwestern values, blah, blah, blah. . . . But at times the promiscuity—I'm not comfortable with it, let's put it that way. Because I've had very limited times, but I've had sexual encounters that I didn't feel good about. . . . It was impersonal and it was not in a loving situation."

Brian H. doesn't use the terms *depersonalize* or *impersonal,* but he gets at the essence of what Bill and Bob are concerned with. "Have you ever gone home with somebody and . . . you're having sex and all of a sudden you realize, you know, you're just a dick and there's no real connection there?"

Whereas many of these witnesses express their concerns about the loss associated with promiscuous behavior, a few other of our witnesses speak of good things that can happen during, or arise out of, promiscuous sexual behavior. For example, while Brian H. was concerned about the lack of connection that can happen in promiscuous behavior, Leo R. understands that for some gay people it may be through promiscuous behavior, even anonymous sex, that they are trying to connect with others. "I don't necessarily dismiss anonymous sex. It's not totally bad at all times for all people. It can be good in some sense because if we are to connect with one another and if you're working out who you are, sometimes that's the only way you can work it out. Even in its raw bathhouse sex mode—I don't know you, you don't know me—there's still this connection that happens between two individuals. Even there you can find goodness. So in that sense it can't always be bad."

Greg P. doesn't deny that something good might happen in a one-night stand. "Even one-night stands can be kind of fun. It's not just fun, it's like there can be a bonding experience that is transcendent."

And young Mark R. says simply, "I'm reluctant to be in any way negative about sex outside a relationship for the simple fact that . . . I enjoy sex. I don't know whether it is fair to say sex can be a recreation or whatever, but I think at the end of the day we all need sex."

Some of our witnesses point to situations in which anonymous sex, bathhouse sexual encounters, or one-night stands can be positive. Other of our witnesses emphasize the dangers of losing oneself or disrespecting others in promiscuous sex. Underlying this apparent conflict on the surface, however, is perhaps a common ground, and that is the concern for sexuality taking place within a personalized context. Perhaps the concern for a personal, rather than impersonal, attitude toward sexuality is voiced more strongly in our witnesses who lean toward being critical of promiscuous behavior. Nevertheless, can we categorically say that all so-called promiscuous behavior is lacking in personal relating? Can goodness be found in some occasions of casual sex as Leo R. points out? Can there be one-night stands where bonding and transcendence occur as Greg P. points out? Is there room for choices, which may be more or less personal, within the context of sexual relating in a bathhouse as Brian H. suggests? No doubt, as we shall see, a greater degree of personal relating can take place more commonly within the context of a growing committed relationship. But that is not to say, categorically, that personal relating can never take place within so-called promiscuous behavior, notwithstanding the very prevalent dangers of depersonalization that so often surround and happen with promiscuous behavior.

Perhaps another way to speak of the distinctions being made about promiscuity is to say, in a manner that will appear tautological, that there is a difference between losing oneself and *losing* oneself. On the one hand, our witnesses are concerned with the ways in which promiscuous behavior can leave one with a sense of emptiness, or destroy one's self-respect or even one's life. These are very real possibilities of losing oneself. On the other hand, there is the losing of oneself in an ecstasy of giving and receiving persons. Whereas the first way of losing oneself tends to lead, in matters of degree, to nothingness, the second tends to lead, in matters of degree, to fullness and bliss. (But then, approaching things from yet another angle, it can happen that in taking the path of pursuing empty relating, one realizes one's need for redemptive love. Alas, all roads can lead to God).

Furthermore, speaking of ecstasy, perhaps there can be an ecstasy of pleasure in promiscuous sex, but what might be missing is the ecstasy of joyful communion. Remember Matteo P. comments as to how the obsession with sex resulted in a loss of joy. To partake in joy is to partake in something personal.

Yet this distinction between personal and impersonal forms of sexual behavior alone does not adequately address the ways gay men have so often been bound to or frozen in more impersonal forms of sexual behavior. To understand this phenomenon of being bound to impersonal forms of sexual behavior returns us to the sentence at the beginning of this chapter, that "a child who grows up unloved may find it very difficult to love."

As a direct consequence of the profound lack of love for their homosexuality—lack of love from families, from society, from religions, from other gay people—the spirits and sexualities of gay people are often broken. As a result of this brokenness, I believe there are often two predominant, related, and calcified responses to sexuality in the lives of gay people. These are self-hatred and despair.

As a response to the hatred of homosexuality by society, a homosexual person may, at some deep level, hate himself for being homosexual. Mitch S. says, "I think there's some pathological stuff that plenty of my straight friends are engaged in too, so it's not just about being gay. But I think it gets manifested in gays because there's so much brokenness. . . . There's this piece—at least for myself, and I think a lot of gay men would concur—there's a piece of self-hatred that never goes away. So you always have that shadow of potential demons that get expressed and emerge. I just think about all the things that you can associate with gay sex, whether it's fisting or water sports. I think that's violent."

Self-hatred turns to hatred in sexual behavior. Greg P. gives an example of a hateful attitude within sexual behavior: "What I'm talking about is where you no longer have love coming out of your soul, but something else. And when I say something else, it's when you're callously wicked and wantonly cruel. Where, [for instance], it's some old man and . . . you're putting him down and you're acting superior."

Whereas one possible turn as a response to growing up unloved as homosexual is hatred, another complementary turn is that of despair. The despair might be put into words in the following way: *I'm not loved in my sexuality and I'm not going to be loved in my sexuality.* Hope for the possibility of love is killed. The connection between despair and promiscuity could then be phrased as follows: *Since I'm not loved in my sexuality, and I feel no real expectations that I will be loved, then I'll just settle for less personal forms of sexual relating.*

One of our witnesses, Max B., forty-seven, from Illinois, explains how despair about his homosexuality affected his life. "Well, let's see, I was raised Catholic and went to a Catholic college. And I really believe I learned about love from the Catholic people in my life. But homosexuality was never even talked about in my upbringing. By the time I graduated from college I was increasingly aware of my homosexual feelings. I started grad school out in the Bay Area after college and used to go into San Francisco, and I would go to a few bars, and more than anything I think the wildness of it all scared the hell out of me. I actually left the Bay Area and moved back to the Midwest. I was about twenty-three then and I think that was an easier and less threatening place for me to come to terms with things. There I met someone, John, who I fell in love with—heavy duty. I really cared for this person, and in my heart still do so. But he more or less rejected my love. It took me years to realize that that experience of falling in love with John, of loving John, and of not being loved in return, along with all the lack of love for being homosexual in general, led to my shutting down the possibility of loving someone and being loved by someone."

In part it seems that Max's heart was broken by John. Now perhaps hearts are broken every day with regard to romantic and sexual relations. But the heartbreak of Max, and perhaps other gay people like him, came against the backdrop of "all the lack of love for being homosexual in general." Max then "shut down." Perhaps his shutting down is another way to speak of despair, of giving up on, as he puts it, "the possibility of loving someone and being loved by someone." Indeed, perhaps the painful experience of heartbreak further reinforced a sense that his homosexuality was not natural, good, or lovable, for, despite the love he did receive in his upbringing, there were apparently no messages of love for or regarding his homosexuality.

Max then explains his involvement in promiscuity. "I just settled for casual sex: going to bathhouses, bookstores, one-night stands, pornography, lots of porno movies, even male escorts, that kind of stuff for years. I remember seeing one therapist for two years. I kept talking about my sexual behavior and my guilt, but we never got to the bottom of it. Because here I am, the people in my life have known I'm gay for years, I've lived in all kinds of gay meccas, but I don't know I still struggled with sex, or my ways of having sex. And this therapist kept trying to address the behavior but we never got at the underlying causes. Then I went to another therapist, and this was in California, and he was gay, so maybe that explains part of the attitude, but anyhow I still had guilt about my behavior. His basic message was, 'Hey, you are young, you are single, what's the big deal.' Well I kind of liked that message because it was so accepting, but it also never really got at the bottom of things. Plus, even though I had all these sexual encounters there was also lots of loneliness and depression, culminating in almost a two-year depression in my late thirties, early forties, when in ways I dropped out of life. And now, after all these years, I know what was at the bottom of it all. I didn't feel I was worthy of love and deep down I didn't *really* believe my homosexuality was good. And all my friends never got why I wasn't partnered up with someone, but I really couldn't be available to another person because of that deep-seated block. I had sex but not love."

Whether it be Max B. talking about despair or Mitch S. talking about self-hatred, underlying the despair or self-hatred is a wound, a wound of feeling unlovable which is the logical result of growing up gay in a society that finds homosexuality unlovable. This wound may very well be unconscious. It can be covered up by many things. Addictions are a prime example. Hedonistic fun is another example of something which masks, at times garishly, an "I'm not lovable" attitude. It can be masked by a loquaciousness which betokens an inability to silently address the self-hatred or despair. And it can be masked by an obsessive need for attention.

Perhaps Bob S. sums up this wound of feeling unlovable when he paraphrases a darker attitude toward sexuality: "It's like, if I'm a piece of shit, what difference does it make if I go out and suck somebody's cock three times tonight. I'm going to hell anyway so I might as well have fun in the process."

It seems to me that, and as the words of many of our witnesses attest, the antidote to this wound is a compassionate affirmation of people in their homosexuality. In considering this compassionate affirmation that is needed for healing the wound of unlovability, it might be best to begin by contrasting it to other understandings of compassion for homosexual people. It is not a compassion that is cloaked in pity or sorrow for the homosexual person because he or she is homosexual. Nor is it a compassion that Christians sometimes describe as "loving the sinner, but hating the sin," as if you can help the homosexual person by not affirming their homosexuality. The danger of such perspectives is that they still deny the naturalness, goodness, and lovability of being homosexual. And until one can affirm such naturalness, goodness, and lovability, there will be no ultimate healing or wholeness.

Our witnesses affirm the naturalness, goodness, and lovability of their own and others' homosexuality in at least three different ways that foster healing. First, many of them express compassion for the hardships gay men face, for the suffering gay men endure. Second, they are concerned with affirming and integrating their sexuality into themselves and with moving in the direction of personal relationships. Third, in what may be the most profound expression of healing, they experience their sexuality as a gift. (Perhaps I should add that I don't necessarily think healing is a strictly linear process, as if one first understands the hardships gay men face, then moves toward bringing an integrated self to more personal relationships, and then finally rejoices in the gift of one's sexuality. Although there may be a progression, there may also be more cyclical movement; one might, for example, appreciate the gift of one's sexuality but still sometimes struggle with the hardships of being gay.)

Our witnesses understand the difficulties gay men face; they have compassion around promiscuity, considering it in light of the underlying conditions that lead to more impersonal forms of sexual behavior. Return, for example, to the voice of Jerry G., our oldest witness. A remarkable spirit of joyfulness and peacefulness permeated Jerry's countenance as he discussed the widespread promiscuity of an earlier era. His compassion regarding this behavior is captured by the very simple statement, "Being in a relationship wasn't as easy to do then as it is now."

Leo R. has an understanding of and compassion for gay people and their promiscuous behavior because of the "homonegative" culture they grow up in. Indeed, perhaps his words also have a reverberatory power for helping us to further understand the self-hatred and despair that afflict gay people. "I think the culture we define ourselves in is a very homonegative culture. So it's difficult to find a lot of gay people who are very positive about being gay. I've met quite a few people who are kind of conflicted." Echoing Leo R.'s sentiments, Matteo P. has compassion for gay people and their sexual behavior in light of the lack of positive models for homosexual relating. "I feel sometimes that a lot of our community is uneducated and they're not given the opportunity to be . . . shown a different path."

In this and the previous chapter, many of our witnesses speak of the need for integration of one's sexuality into one's whole person, and of the power of such integration to heal and transform. Mark M. talks about being outside of himself until he accepted his homosexuality. Jerry G. speaks about how people will be pretty miserable if they don't have the "whole pie" of who they are. And Ryan O. describes the "life-giving energy" that comes from integrating one's sexuality. Finally, referring to the healing power of integrating one's sexuality, let us return to the story of Max B.: "As I was going through this long period of depression I got help, important help and counsel from this nun who is a pastoral counselor. She was amazing, so full of compassion and joy. It's funny—even her joy was so helpful! From our conversations, and I guess through my own prayer and reflection, I came to realize a few things. First, I realized that my homosexuality was natural to me. This may sound kind of strange because obviously over the years I had all these sexual encounters, but accepting it as natural made a difference in that it brought more ease and relaxation. Second, and most important, I came to realize God loves me as gay. That is so important I don't even have words for it. . . . Where this leaves me now, well, it's still a struggle. I'm very grateful for the ways I feel more at ease and relaxed about accepting what's natural for me. But God knows, I now have a lifetime of habits! But it's funny; I'm more at peace with all of it."

I want to underline the importance of Max B.'s acceptance of his nature. Part of the richness of the Catholic tradition, as I understand it, is that what is natural is not to be ignored, escaped from, or considered evil. The natural realm, however, has been weighed down by sin, and thus salvation is a restoration *of,* a salvation *of,* not a salvation *from,* our nature and the world. It is just such a loving restoration of people in and to their homosexuality that I am trying to show in the pages of this book. And, indeed, working backward, if we witness this loving restoration then we also have to acknowledge the naturalness.

These messages underscore the healing power of compassionately affirming gay people as they are, in their homosexuality. Compassion itself is a personal event. Thus, compassion for the whole person, *if received,* will organically lead to a need and desire for more personal, rather than impersonal, relations. James B.'s description of a priest's counsel regarding the dangers of impersonal sex provides an example of how messages delivered with compassion and in the spirit of acceptance of the whole person can be most effective. The priest's perspective is also powerful because it sees personal homosexual relationships as good and as the goal toward which sexuality can be directed. The power and goodness of long-term, committed, loving relationships between gay men will be explored in more detail in the next chapter.

Perhaps the healing power of the compassionate affirmation of homosexuality is most wondrously and joyously conveyed by those of our witnesses who speak of the "gift" of their homosexuality. As described in Chapter 3, Jim L. experienced this after many years of struggling and being alone with his sexuality; during a meditative walk near a retreat house, Jim discerned the voice of Jesus saying to him, "Jim, it's all right to be who you are and what you have is a special gift." Robert P. echoes Jim when he says, "It's the greatest gift to be giving yourself, to be gay and allow yourself to be gay. It's the greatest gift you can give yourself and it's a gift from God." And Max B., after all his years of loneliness and despair seems to imply an understanding of the giftedness of his homosexuality when he is finally and peacefully able to accept his nature and that God loves him as gay. Our witnesses speak of experiencing God as affirming, loving, and indeed *giving* them their homosexuality. Indeed, perhaps an awakening of awareness to the "gift" of homosexuality is the ultimate healing for all of the brokenness that surrounds homosexual behavior.

In having described the compassionate affirmation that is needed for healing the wound of unlovability in gay people, it needs to be underlined that a crucial choice, perhaps even a choice of life and death, for the gay person who suffers from such a wound, and who is stuck in more impersonal forms of sexual behavior, is whether he will open himself to receive such compassion and affirmation which may be imperfectly given by oneself and one's friends, partners, family members, therapists, pastoral counselors, and churches; or perfectly and unconditionally given by the ultimate source of love, the creator of nature and the healer of our brokenness. What is the alternative? Further despair, self-hatred, or hard-heartedness? Compassion will inevitably lead to more personal forms of relating, including sexual relating, even amid continuing promiscuous behavior.

The important choice of the homosexual person who suffers from a wound of unlovabilty to get help is one side of things. Another side is that of how social justice relates to promiscuity among gay men. Perhaps it might sound a little surprising to relate social justice to promiscuity for there has been a tendency in ethical thinking to consign sexual matters to the private rather than the public realm. But if Matteo P. is correct that a lot of homosexual people are uneducated or confused with regard to ways of relating sexually aside from promiscuous behavior, and if Leo R. is correct about the effects on gay people of existing within a homonegative culture, and if Mitch S. is correct in his understanding of how self-hatred affects many homosexual people, and if Max B.'s experience is indicative of the despair that affects many gay people, and if I am correct in saying that gay people have been inflicted with a wound of feeling unlovable around their homosexuality, then it seems to me that the impersonal forms of sexual relating that result from all these conditions are a social justice issue. The culture that surrounds any given group of people and the education and models they receive are public matters. Just imagine how different things might be if, for example, Catholic parishes and schools affirmed the goodness and lovability of people *in* their homosexuality. Not just religion and parochial education, but laws, public schools, and popular culture could all evolve—or perhaps continue to evolve, since in some respects they already have—in ways that would heal the wound of feeling unlovable and open the lives of homosexual people to more personal forms of relating. And given the naturalness, goodness, and lovability of homosexuality, it is the right of gay people to expect such justice.

To conclude, some religious thinking on the issue of homosexuality says something to the effect that homosexuality can be accepted, even affirmed, as long as it is in the context of committed, loving relationships. Whereas in the next chapter we will look at the light and love which can in fact be found in such relationships, and whereas such relationships can indeed model, witness to, and inspire the lovability of homosexual people, nevertheless, it seems to me that one should not say that homosexuality should be expressed only in the context of a committed relationship. For if, as I have been trying to show, many gay people feel unlovable with regard to being homosexual, then it may be unrealistic to expect them to move directly into loving relationships unless they have gone through some kind of healing process. Indeed, such expectations might perpetuate a cycle of feelings of worthlessness, and add more guilt, shame, and anger for gay people, because their sexuality is not living up to these expectations.

The great Cardinal Newman once wrote, referring to a different context, that "in a particular instance, it might easily happen, that what is only second best is best practically, because what is actually best is out of the question." These words bring to mind Jerry G.'s comments earlier in the chapter about how many gay people of his generation, including himself, settled for more casual sexual encounters because being in a relationship wasn't as easy to do then. The conditions for relationships for gay people, although improving in some parts of the world, are still often weighed down by immense difficulties. If what is best for personal sexual relating is found in a committed relationship, and if such relationships are difficult for gay people to find, are neither encouraged nor supported, are in fact discouraged by the Church and others, and are even cause for severe and extreme punishment in some parts of the world, then who are we to cast blame when gay people settle for sexual relating that might be considered second best? Perhaps, as Cardinal Newman suggests, when the best is out of the question, the second best is best practically. And what is the next best thing to a committed sexual relationship? I believe it is personal sexual relating that lies somewhere between a committed relationship and not hurting others or oneself.

Healing and justice can help alleviate the sense of unlovability that often lies at the heart of the experience of homosexuality. Healing and justice, at their best, are deeply personal experiences. Healing, at its best, takes place in the face of a compassionate person who cares for us as a person, and justice takes place when right relations between persons are restored. Sadly, however, as day-to-day life often poignantly bears out, healing and justice, in this life anyhow, are limited. Facing these limits, we fall upon our need for God, the same God who is the source of healing and justice, the source from whom we understand the ways to act and love personally. For it is God who calls us by name, who loves us *personally*.

5 ဆ Commitment

"There are some loves whose very power in us moves us to commitment." So says Margaret Farley, the well-respected Catholic ethicist, in her article "The Meaning of Commitment." The purpose of this chapter is to look at our witnesses' experiences of commitment in their relationships. Just as married heterosexual Catholics might speak of God bringing them together, of God drawing each toward a deeper intimacy with the other, and as commitment being the glue which sustains and deepens their intimacy, so, likewise, will we see such themes in the relationships of our witnesses.

We'll start with the story of Leo R. and Joe G. from Columbus. As we shall see, Leo and Joe believed their meeting to be providential—even though, at first glance, so to speak, they did not like each other. In describing their meeting, Leo shares, "When I first moved out [from the house and the marriage], I was going to a gay support group at the Newman Center and . . . Joe just happened to be there. The meeting I went to . . . had this panel on couples. After the panel discussion, there were forty of us in the room so you could go around and say your name and share what you wanted to about yourself. I remember I was on the side of the room that went first. I said I was presently married, in the process of coming out, had three small kids. Joe was on the other side of the room and when we came around to him I remember him saying, 'I don't know what these clowns are talking about up here. They're full of shit. These relationships don't work. It's all about the sex, guys, it's all about the sex.' I'm thinking, 'This guy is the biggest loser I have met in my life. Who in the hell would even talk to this guy more than two minutes?' He dismisses me too because of the kids—he hates kids.

doi:10.1300/5599_06

"So we go to the next meeting, and I happened to be the first one at the meeting and he was second. He remembered my name so we just said hi, but I didn't want to talk with him because I didn't like him. I thought he was a jerk. . . . Two more weeks went by. At one of the meetings he asked me what I was doing for Thanksgiving, because the holidays were coming up. He knew I was really depressed about not being able to see the kids and being just separated. Very, very strange. He asked me what I was doing and I said, 'Not much.' He said, 'Would you like to go to a party?' I said, 'I guess.' My psychologist said, 'You need to experience and see more people. Broaden your horizons a bit. Go out and test the waters.'

"So we went to this small party . . . it was a pot luck. I got there last for some reason. . . . Joe was in the kitchen cooking meatloaf. I couldn't believe he was making meatloaf. It was a real huggy, kissy, touchy-feely type of group, so I know I came in and I hugged everybody. And Joe said, 'You hugged everybody but you didn't hug me.' Well, I didn't want to. But we hugged and it was just something. It was like kismet. Something happened; something was very weird. . . . It was like, 'Wow.' After the meal was ready we sat on the couch and happened to be seated side-by-side and we started talking about our—the same grade school, had pretty much the same teachers. My sister, who was killed in an automobile accident, was in his class. That's the only girl he remembers. . . . We had many of the same experiences so we ended up talking for like four hours that night. . . . It was like no one else was there, like we were alone. Then we started seeing each other after that and here it is nineteen years later."

In concluding his story, Leo speaks of the mystery of providential meetings. "We knew in retrospect we were brought together for some reason. I honestly do think we were brought together . . . and meant for each other, because I tend to complement and strengthen his weaknesses and he does the same for me. . . . Joe's experience is totally different from mine. He got shit on from the get go, by his family, his church, by people he got in touch with. He got the totally opposite messages that I ever got. That's why I think it was so important that we came together, because I was able to bring him out of where he was and he was able to inform me when I had on rose-colored glasses."

Joe picks up the story of their burgeoning relationship. "After Christmas, the whole group was going to get together for a New Year's Eve Party. Leo said, 'Are you going to be there?' I said, 'No, I'm going to be in New York.' 'Well, call me,' Leo said. Now, I really had my sexuality kind of out there, so I intended to be at the Mineshaft [a notorious bar in New York at the time], midnight, New Year's Eve. I said, 'Leo, my dear, there's no phone. . . . I'll think about you but I won't be able to call.' I was meeting a friend in New York, and I had already told this guy I intended to go the Mineshaft.

"So I flew to New York. I met this guy—and our friendship was strictly friendship—and we were going to go out that night. Well, we got talking—and with this particular individual, he could put me so much at ease—it was cold, and we decided, you know, I don't even want to do this, I'll just stay right here. We'll watch the balloon come down, we'll be fine. And to this day I truly believe that if I had gone to the Mineshaft that night I would have gotten AIDS. I just believe I would have."

Joe pauses to paint a foreboding picture of the other way he could have gone with his sexuality in general, in contrast to the intimacy he now shares with Leo; he gropes for words to describe a feeling of being under the influence of larger forces—what one might describe as divine intervention—gently pushing him in the latter direction. "Once before I'd been to the Mineshaft—I was able to go to the Mineshaft anytime I wanted when I was in New York—and I'd felt, there is evil here. On the surface it could have been like, Look at this kind of sexuality; there's something obviously disturbed about it. But it had never bothered me before, so why would it bother me then? No, I can't. . . . All I know is that I felt there is something evil here. In retrospect, I have written in my journals that I truly believe that spiritually and physically I could easily have died if I had stayed [in New York]. So I left."

Joe returns to the story of New Year's Eve, 1981-1982. "I did call Leo up at midnight. He picked up the phone and he said, 'Oh, I knew it was you. . . .' And he said, 'Oh, if you were here I'd tell you so much.' We got off the phone, and I said, 'Oh dear God, the guy's in love with me. What in the hell am I going to do now?' My friend said, 'You're going to go back and tell him to slow up a bit.'

"This friend had an ability to get me to really get deep. At one point we talked about Leo, we talked about my maybe going home earlier. He also said at one point during that discussion—because I had such an image problem, like why would someone be interested in me? I grew up with that, I didn't get it—and he tried to tell me people like me because they like me, because of something good in me. Anyhow he said, 'What would God say about you? What does God see in you?' And it was like the answer was right there. I said, 'When God looks at me, God sees himself.' I just couldn't believe that came out of my mouth, and yet it was so profoundly true.

"I paid more to get my ticket changed. I couldn't get hold of Leo. Got to the Columbus airport, called Leo. No answer. Finally, after an hour, Leo answers the phone. He says, 'Where are you?' I said, 'I'm in the Columbus airport.' He said, 'What in the hell?' I said, 'It's a long story, Leo. Can you pick me up?' 'Sure.'

"So he picked me up and I didn't know how to do this. I didn't know how to ask him, can I stay the weekend. I'm trying to figure out how to say it. I said, 'You want to go for a cup of coffee?' And he says, 'Well, yes.' I stopped to think about it. I said, 'Oh, Leo, I'm not good at this. What I'd really like to know is can I spend the weekend with you?' 'Oh, sure.' We went to the store; we got food; I spent the weekend with him."

In contrast to a more loveless direction he could have gone with his sexuality, Joe describes his process of being drawn toward intimacy, of being drawn toward a goodness he recognized in and with Leo. "We started to date. . . . I was scared to death. I had so separated sex from emotions that in the past every time I put the emotion into it I got left at the altar. I had said screw it. But I knew there was something about this man. He wasn't my ideal physically—I found out later that I wasn't his either—but he was a good person. I saw this man as so good that I didn't want to lose him, and yet I was scared to death. So I went into therapy again to deal with how to be intimate.

"I finally got enough courage to tell Leo I was in therapy and I was hoping he wouldn't think I was a mental case. Not a problem. So I asked him to come to therapy with me. I was saying, 'I can't feel, I can't feel anything toward Leo. . . . The one time I get somebody who's really good and I'm turning off my feelings. There's something wrong with this picture.'

"And I didn't know what in the hell to do with somebody who said they were in love with me. The therapist told Leo, 'Leo, you have to know something about Joe. Joe was raised on conditional love and when somebody says they love him he wants to know what the bottom line is. What's he going to have to do? What's he going to have to give? What's the cost of this? And you need to know that.'

"Anyhow, we made a contract which we renewed every three months. Yes, a contract that we would stay together even if I went out or said I couldn't feel and it was horrible. . . . The last contract was up November 12, 1982. I just knew in my heart of hearts, we never talked about it, but I knew in my heart of hearts Leo wasn't going to renew. He was in therapy with this guy, too, for a while, and I guess they were talking about, 'What are you going to do if Joe says he can't do it?' And I wasn't privy to that, but on November 11, 1982, I came to . . . some prayer; I said, 'I'm scared to death to commit to that man, but there is no way in hell that I will ever walk out on him.'"

We'll return to the story of Leo and Joe at the end of this chapter, but suffice it to say for now that, notwithstanding Joe's fears, their relationship did continue after November 12, 1982.

Another story concerns the coming together of Norman P. and Doug D., which, although not exactly a parallel of *When Harry Met Sally,* is similar in that it involves two people who meet when they are younger but must wait many years before becoming a couple.

Norman and Doug met initially while both were seminarians, and a major theme in their story is of how they learn that intimate love between two people can be a way of responding to God's love just as being a priest can be. Norman describes how he and Doug first met: "Doug and I actually met at the seminary fifteen years ago. . . . It's funny, because we were an item there our first year and then split up for about thirteen years and then got back together and are now getting married, or we're having a union ceremony next September."

Doug picks up his side of their story. "The reason for the split was that I still felt called to the ordained ministry. Norman left during the year and I went on and finished theology and professed vows. But I didn't profess final vows. I really loved Norman, but I didn't feel like I could spend my life with a person at that time. I felt like this was fun, this was experimenting, this was helping me make an informed decision about my vocation, but I did not feel like being in a relationship was the stuff of life vocation. When I finally decided to leave the seminary was when I realized I could fall in love with someone I wanted to spend my life with."

After Norman left the seminary, Doug was still there and he met another person and fell in love, and this accelerated Doug's struggle with discerning what he was called to in life. "I remember agonizing in prayer when I was still under vows and having this relationship and not knowing where my life was going to go. I really experienced this moment of grace where I felt the spirit say to me, '*Doug, all I call you to is a life of love. How you live that life is up to you.*' . . . That helped me to realize that celibacy was a way of living and a relationship was a way of living. . . . For years I had to compromise my needs for intimacy, and I always felt I had these deeper needs that the community was not able to satisfy. Whenever I went to the community with these needs it always came back to me that you need to meet those needs on your own. I was just getting continually frustrated with that."

Despite his frustration, however, Doug doesn't deny the many values and gifts of seminary life. Indeed, his process of discernment seems to be one of integrating these realities into his intimate relationships. What he valued in seminary life included "Communal prayer, making a difference for other people, living life in a spiritual framework, and everything comes out of that. I had not experienced those things with any male in order to be able to say that this was my life vocation. Then when I experienced that in a relationship in my last year of seminary, . . . my life just turned upside down and I realized this is possible. So . . . I decided to leave the seminary to pursue what was my passion. Unfortunately, that person did not go on board with me. But what that did for me was, it made it so that I didn't leave for a person. I left for a life I knew was possible. That freed me to look at relationships in a more, I think, healthy way and to look at myself in a healthier way, that I was really worth it and I didn't have to compromise on those needs anymore."

Norman, too, after he and Doug went their separate ways, went through a process of discernment regarding his vocation, his homosexuality, and his need for intimacy. "My coming out was a very positive experience. It's very interesting because it's my recollection that Doug and I were involved before I came to terms with the fact that I was homosexual. I guess that probably made the process easier. Doug mentioned that we split up because we were going to different seminaries for further studies. So he went to one in the East and I went to one in Colorado. . . . Being in the Colorado seminary was a very good experience for me. . . . I had a . . . very good spiritual director out there who was very affirming of my gayness."

While at the seminary in Colorado, Norman sums up briefly how he became clear regarding his vocation. "I kind of had a moment of catharsis on the side of the mountain on a swing set in Colorado. I realized I was better with other people when I was with one significant other and it kind of hit home to me—I should be in a relationship because I'm better for everyone."

Norman and Doug were reunited in the late 1990s. They have created a home together and, as was said, were planning a commitment ceremony at the time of their being interviewed.

Robert B., forty-two, from Dayton, Ohio, furthers our discussion of the themes of falling in love and intimacy by emphasizing the importance of choosing someone who would make a good long-term partner. "I have often said to people, I've done some matchmaking work in my time, and I say, 'Date those people that would make good friends. You don't date the person with the biggest arms, or the hugest chest, or the biggest . . . heck. It's not going to do you any good when they have no personality. And here [speaking of his partner] is someone whose heart I love deeply. It's like, this is what we love. The package isn't always pretty, you know, but here is someone really loving and caring and who has such a strong sense of justice that it's like the person can draw more out of you than you may realize and that to me is what love is. Did you ever read *The Road Less Traveled?* M. Scott Peck talked about love being encouraging spiritual growth in another person."

Robert contrasts the kind of love he has with his partner to the more party-like atmosphere of gay culture. For one year while his partner, Ryan, was working in California, Robert did go to gay bars and other places. He contrasts the value he sees in his relationship to what else he experienced in gay culture during that year. "I had some things happen and I thought, you know, this is not what I want. I met some really interesting people. I had a lot of fun, but, what did I say?—'I've been to Oz and I'd much rather be in Kansas. Because Oz was fun, but good God Almighty!'"

Continuing our discussion of intimacy, Robert P. defines intimacy in terms of loyalty and trust. "I believe in loyalty and commitment. I don't think we can have friendship without loyalty. And the same with an intimate relationship—you know, without loyalty or commitment you really can't be intimate with someone because you don't have that trust level. Intimacy is like a lot of trust. You can't be intimate with people if there's no trust."

Indeed, it was the lack of trust that played a major part in the breakup of an early relationship in the life of Tom A. Tom speaks of a time in his life when he was going back and forth from Chicago to his childhood home in western Illinois to visit his ailing parents. At the same time he was involved with 'George.'

"During the time I was [at my parents'] home, my partner, George, met somebody, and when I got back here . . . two weeks later, all of a sudden there was this lame excuse about why he wasn't going to be home one night and basically he was seeing another person. The next morning he told me the truth and he told me what had happened. Of course I was completely devastated and he couldn't understand why I was devastated but I was."

After both of his parents died and Tom started graduate school, Tom turned to his Catholicism, along with therapy, for solace and also for help in discerning what was right for him to do in his relationship. "I was in therapy for about two years and it was just a real, real trying time. I think I looked to the Church for some strength and some support, and fortunately I did find some there. It took me a long, long time but . . . in the course of the therapy and in the course of doing my own soul-searching and my own reflection on myself and my religion, . . . I finally had the strength to say, 'George, if this ever happens again I can't go through this and our relationship will be over.' That was after two years of trying to re-build the trust that I had prior to this incident. It was complete lack of trust. Every time he was gone longer than I thought he was going to be gone or wasn't home from work when he said he was going to be home from work, my inside thought was, he probably met somebody. I struggled and struggled to regain that trust and was never really able to do that.

"What happened then was, he met somebody else and at that point it was very clear for me—okay, this is a sign that this is over. . . . I think, as kind of sick as it may sound, that was the point where my healing began and everything was clear in my mind that I've tried for the last two years to reconcile this and make this thing work and it's not going to happen."

Tom concludes his story by contrasting the predominant values of gay culture, as he experienced them, with those of his religion. "I think there's a huge difference between the values of gay culture and the values of normal organized religion. When . . . George . . . . met this other person and had a little fling, he said: 'Well, look at our friends. All of our friends have experiences outside their relationship.' I just looked at him and said, 'That's fine for them but that's not necessarily fine for me.' I think what I was espousing was what I saw as the values that organized religion, especially Catholicism, kind of ingrain in a person as they're brought up in that faith. I know that the value that I adopted at a young age by my family influence, as well as my religious influence, was that at some point in your life you make a commitment to another person."

What is commitment? Margaret Farley defines it this way:

> [A] commitment to love is not a prediction, not just a resolution. It is the yielding of a claim, the giving of my word to the one I love—promising what? It can only be promising that I will do all that is possible to keep alive my love and to act faithfully in accordance with it . . . it's purpose is to assure the one I love of my ongoing love and to strengthen me in actually loving.

Echoing Farley's comment that a commitment "can only be promising that I will do all that is possible to keep alive my love and act faithfully in accordance with it," Doug D. speaks of commitment in the following way: "I think commitment is so much more than just a physical, sexual act. It's saying, 'I'll be there for you; I'll be there with you. In good times and in bad, in sickness and in health. I will be there to talk about my day with you and I'll be there to hear what your day was like. I'll be there to hold you. I'll be there to rejoice with you.' It's about intimacy through life. It's saying 'I'm going to commit to this relationship even when it doesn't feel comfortable, I'm going to work at this because you're worth it. And I will hear what you say to me because I care what you say to me because I care about you.' That is what commitment is to me. And it's to say that we're in this forever."

Other of our Catholic witnesses describe ways in which their religious faith helps them do "all that is possible to keep alive their love." Two categories of action in particular stand out in their stories. These are sacrifice and prayer.

James B. describes how "the discipline" of loving another person reflects his Catholic values and adds goodness and grace to his life. "I suppose you have to get into a relationship where you really start loving someone, and you realize the goodness of that love, that it does no harm, it does good and it builds up and it deepens one's life. . . . It teaches you the discipline of loving someone, of being considerate, going through difficult times without thinking of yourself, of thinking of someone else. This is what people do in relationships and this is how my relationship is. My relationship is a relationship that includes who I am, that is who I am, but I do it out of Catholic values."

Jim speaks of the roles of sacrifice and personal responsibility in his relationship with his partner. "So like with 'Dave,' very often it's like I have to say—and I'm sure he does this with me too—it can't just be the way I want things. I have to make a sacrifice. . . . I have to realize that there's someone here and it's not just about me. I have to have the strength to address myself. Have I wronged him? Have I hurt him? On the other hand, have I shown him in other ways that I respect him, that I love him? It's a conscious thing. It's the same thing you would do in a straight relationship or a marriage." And, not coincidentally, Jim's relationship with God reinforces his responsibility to and commitment with his partner. He adds, "When I go to Mass, I really find that I'm saying—not all the time—'I feel guilty before You, because of something I've said to Dave or something I failed to do.'"

Kevin N., forty-eight, from Chicago, talks about the conscious effort needed to build and maintain a successful relationship. "When I started the relationship a lot of friends said, 'It's not going to work. He's not going to be there sometimes.' I said, 'Nothing's . . . going to work out if you don't . . . put any work into it. It's like any relationship, if you don't put work into it and you don't try to work things out if they're not working, no relationship is going to last.'"

Ron G. and Bob S. have to make sacrifices in their relationship in order to take care of Bob's mother. Both men describe these difficult sacrifices as acts of love that keep them grounded in themselves and in their partnership, and see these sacrifices, as well as the relationship itself, as God's way of helping them live the lives they were meant to live. Ron says, "It's kind of funny because I think both of us are better people because of our relationship. I'll give you an example of what we're going through. Bob's mother lives with us and that's very difficult for me, but he's said to me before, 'I couldn't do this without you.' If I put that into a perspective of spirituality and the things God asks us to do, I believe there are relationships that help us with living lives that God intended them to be."

Bob gives his perspective on the same situation. "We're in a difficult situation now because my mom's been staying with us for the last couple of years. At times she can be in a confused state which I can deal with more easily than Ron can. . . . I think having faith has helped us get back to the reality, or to the real point of the situation, which is to help my mom."

Bob follows up the story regarding his mother by speaking more generally of his relationship with Ron. "Granted, having your mother live with you kind of puts a damper on your sexual activities, but I truly feel that our relationship is spiritual and God-blessed." Perhaps inspired by the awareness of how his relationship is "spiritual and God-blessed," Ron adds a caveat where he stands up to a sometimes Church assumption that gay people should be celibate. "It would be a sin for me to follow the Church's rules to be celibate. It would truly be a sin. That's why it just burns my ass when they come out with stuff like that."

Whereas sacrifice is one way our witnesses do "all that is possible to keep alive their love," prayer is another. Just as many Catholics pray for the people in their lives, many of our witnesses speak of praying for and with their partners.

Norman P. speaks generally about the role prayer plays in his relationship with Doug. "I've had a lot more experience with relationships than Doug has had, but this is the first one that has been spiritually centered. It works on so many different levels. The fact that we do mass together and we pray, not daily—we'd like to do it daily but we're still working on getting there—but we pray often together."

Other of our witnesses talk about addressing more specific concerns with their prayers. Jim L. speaks of how he prayed that "Terry" would become more understanding of others, especially those who are more homophobic. "I've prayed for Terry all the time, that he would be a little more compassionate for other people. He was always angry. But I think that's what I prayed for the most, for him to be more understanding of other people, about what their reactions were to him, to try to see their side of it also. It took me a long time to accept who we are. It may take them just as long to accept who we are, so we have to understand that also."

John F., who because of his work is often away from home, prays for his partner to have the strength to deal with that reality. "I pray for both of us. I pray for him to give him strength . . . because I travel a lot for work. The last year especially was very tough for me because for nine months straight I was on the road almost every week, Monday through Friday. I'm just starting up a cycle again right now. I traveled last week and this week. I pray for him that he can deal with it because it bothers him a little bit. So I pray for the strength in our relationship to continue."

Michael S. speaks generally about praying for and with his partner, and then even offers an example of praying before sex. "It's every week or whenever I do pray [for my partner]. I like it when we pray together, but we don't do that very much. It still feels a little odd to us. But when we've done that it's been really good. And I even heard a story about a couple that would occasionally pray before they had sex. And we did that and it really turns out nice. It's sex that's very giving. All of a sudden you're doing it with a blessing over you or with a higher purpose in life."

Finally, with regard to the specific theme of prayer, let's listen to Tim D. as he speaks of communicating with his departed lover. "There's times in bed that I . . . feel his presence and immediately I'll start talking to Chuck because he's there. I don't see Chuck and he's only there for a few minutes and then he's gone. . . . But . . . he never left my side after he died. . . . Now he comes back every once in a while to check on me, but before he left—it was almost a year or so ago—we were talking . . . I knew what he was saying and it's almost like I was saying, 'You have to go, don't you? I know I'm strong now.' It was almost like he said, 'Are you sure?' . . . It was like saying good-bye but it wasn't a good-bye where that person actually leaves your sight. He's on a banister. I see all my friends on a banister and they're all looking down. The more of my friends that die . . . they're all getting together up there and they're not lonely anymore. They have one another. Then I have that many more people looking after me. And you know what? I know if I call on Chuck he'll be there."

To conclude this chapter, let's return to the story of Joe G. and Leo R., as narrated by Joe. Here, in particular, we will see Joe address the committed dimension of their relationship. He shares how this commitment affects other people, deepens the intimacy between him and Leo, and helps each to experience the presence of God in their relationship. Joe says, "On our fifteenth anniversary we were going to have a big celebration and renew our vows publicly. I would have a small affair; of course, Leo, he wants to invite the whole world and who cares what it costs. So we were going to have it on November 9, 1996. That whole nine or ten months before, . . . I went through all my intimacy fears over again. And I had to work it out again about this relationship and what was I supposed to do. And what was I committing to, and where was God.

"We went through the ceremony. There were one hundred seventy people. We had a Mass; it was done in the Protestant church, but we had a Catholic Mass. We had a Catholic priest who went unidentified from another diocese. We had our work people there, straight and gay, our brothers and sisters, our siblings. (All of our parents are dead.) And we said our vows. When we said our vows, our voices were all choked up. . . .

"I'm going to tell you what I said to Leo because it is still really meaningful. I said, 'Leo, when I first met you fifteen years ago, I never believed that I would find someone who would love me and care for me and share my life. Because of your gentleness, kindness, loyalty, and unconditional love for me, I have learned to live without guilt, and my spirituality and sexuality are far more integrated into my personality. Because of you, Leo, I am alive today. For all eternity I will thank God for the gift of you, pure grace in our life. Today, Leo, I renew my commitment to you and to our relationship. I will continue to take care of you, to love and to care for you to the best of my ability. I'll be with you in the good years and the difficult ones and I will continue to care for and love you to the best of my ability in this life and I look forward to spending eternity with you and with God. I love you."

Joe and Leo's commitment to each other, publicly and religiously celebrated, was an inspiration to other people in the community, even to some people who weren't always sympathetic to the idea of gay relationships. "Later, after the whole ceremony . . . we got phone calls from people thanking us for inviting them. I invited one aunt who was very close to my mother; my mother used to cry to this aunt over me. So I invited her and her daughter, and in the receiving line [at the reception] she said, 'Joe, I'm eighty years old, over eighty, and I have never been to a wedding this beautiful.' And a psychologist called and said, 'Joe, I have three people in therapy as a result of your ceremony. I have never been to something so affirming in my life.' Another guy, who was one of our ushers—this guy never shows emotion, he's always Mr. Macho—but a year later, we went out to dinner [with him] and he said, 'I watched during your ceremony, I was watching you. The place was so full of love. People are absolutely in awe of what was taking place. It was truly a sacramental moment in my life.'"

The commitment between Leo and Joe reinforces and deepens the intimacy between them. It also reinforces the experience of

God in their relationship. As Joe says, "The intimacy with Leo just, it changed. It got deeper. I can remember . . . dancing at a bar with him and at one point . . . I held him and I was aware that God was here; God was in my relationship.

"My relationship with Leo is a spiritual communion. Sometimes when I make love with him—I can be really selfish during sex sometimes—but sometimes I can be very aware that God is here in this very midst. We have a kind of habit, after we have sex, we lay in each other's arms and turn on really nice music and just hold each other. . . . This is the man I love. Me, who never believed I would be committed to one person, not with my past. . . . (I must have slept through New York.) I'm with a man who's Catholic, who accepts, who understands my values. . . . And, God's irony, me, who had told my sister I never wanted to have children, marries someone who has three. And they are good kids—they're all adults now, but they were fine children. And I feel whole with Leo."

Joe concludes his story about his relationship with Leo by backtracking a bit to describe his fears and concerns prior to their commitment ceremony. He shares how he went to a monastery, and Joe had had an attraction to monastic life, and prayed about his relationship with Leo. "I told you how in 1996 when we had the ceremony I was scared shitless. I was down at the monastery, Memorial Day weekend, and I was praying, What should I do? What do you really want me to do?" He continues, "I started to write and I wrote the answer but I didn't realize it till later, till the next day when I read what I wrote, [which was], 'Lord, you know me through and through, who I am and why I am. You know I worry about my relationship with Leo, about my lack of or lessening of passion, about my attraction to others at times. What am I to do? You know I often doubt whether you love me as gay."

Joe then shares how he discerned the Lord's answer to his prayers. "And then I wrote, 'Joseph, I love you with every fiber of my being. I love you whether you're gay or straight, like a light, good or bad. You are precious to me and I will never let you down, no matter what. Life is life and in the midst of problems and questions, I exist in you. Through it all, I am here with you. Joseph, you asked me what you were to do with Leo and the idea of being a monk. In both cases I gave you an answer. Remember and relive it. I told you to find me in Leo. . . . And I also told you I will make you holy in the world. Both answers, my son, are still valid. You have what many others desire, a relationship that is based on love and affection. Leo loves you and is faithful to you. You also love Leo in spite of your fears and ambiguities. You are not a celibate, Joseph, and I didn't ordain you to be. Stop worrying about a lifestyle that isn't yours. Again, I ask you, how many have what you have? Not many. Grow together with Leo. Develop each other's strengths and forgive each other's weaknesses. I live in him, Joseph, and I live in you, too. I bless your relationship and I have ordained it to be a vehicle for your salvation, wholeness, and growth.'"

6 ☙　The Absolutization of Gayness

I recently heard a commentator on a television news show mention "the gays." This relatively common use of language is symptomatic of a larger issue. This is the problem of absolutization so brilliantly written about by the Jesuit priest William Lynch in the 1970s. Lynch wrote about an absolutizing instinct in human beings. Quite simply, this means the tendency to take part of life and turn it into the whole. Since the part is not the whole, absolutizing involves reductionism. Wholeness is lost in the fixation on something particular, and human beings are reduced to a single aspect of who they are.

This chapter addresses our witnesses' concerns about the ways gayness is absolutized. Although it is undoubtedly true that homosexuality and homosexuals have been absolutized by society as a whole, in this chapter our witnesses mainly speak about their concerns about absolutization within and by the gay community and the ways in which they try to broaden the scope of their own lives.

We'll begin by looking at some of our witnesses' concerns— often related to the point in their lives when they were coming out—that they could be consumed by a culture transfixed by gayness. John F. says, "I didn't want to have to go to bars all the time. I didn't want to have to go to a gay doctor if I didn't want to. I didn't want to have to live in the gay ghetto. I didn't want to have to wear boas. . . . I don't care so much how people live their lives. I just wasn't comfortable with everybody in the gay community having to be under this gay lifestyle umbrella, because everybody's life is different and there is no gay or straight lifestyle; it's just the way you live your life. That's probably what bothered me. I was afraid I'd get sucked into that [homogeneity]."

Doug D. also refers to aspects of gay culture that could have "sucked him in." "I remember at some point in my own development—this was before I left the seminary—I had a couple gay friends and everything about them seemed to center around being gay. I remember looking at that and thinking, 'I don't want that.' It seems so reductionistic, like everything boils down to the fact that I like someone else's penis. At that point I thought I needed to be a priest because I wasn't attracted to the gay community, at least to that expression of it."

Mitch S. also speaks of his concerns about being consumed by being gay. "What's hard about being in the gay community is that I become consumed with being gay and want to tell everybody my story. Some of that's healthy and some of it's important, but I'm looking for that gay situation where it's just not an issue because of course you're gay, but you're a human being."

Mitch continues, "My friend Doug . . . helped me to see, as we both talked about being frustrated, as he talked about being straight and not meeting people, that a lot of what I'm experiencing is not because I'm gay, it's because I'm a human being. I think sometimes in the gay community that gets lost. It's all about we're gay instead of all about we're humans. We're human beings."

Mitch explains how his concern for maintaining a sense of humanity relates to where he lives. "One of the reasons I'm much more comfortable in Des Moines than I was in Las Vegas is that if you live in a big enough city [like Las Vegas] you can put yourself under the umbrella of being gay. You go to the gay doctor, you may work with some straight people, but all of your other social interactions are with gay men. I think it's important to have relationships with a wide variety of people."

Scott C. also relates his fear of being "consumed by being gay" at the time when he was coming out. "I first came out really publicly when I was thirty, and at the time being gay wasn't a new experience for me, but being publicly known as gay obviously was. I was counseled by many gay friends who said, 'Your life is really going to change and you're going to find that all of your close friends are gay and you're probably going to be cutting yourself off from other friendships and relationships you have in your life. Maybe not consciously,' they said, 'but the reality is that in time that will happen.' I said, 'No, I don't buy that. Being gay is just one piece of who I am.' And while I expected that perhaps my closest friends would probably be gay, that really hasn't been my experience. In the sense of close intimate relationships, yes, but I also have some very, very close straight friends."

Scott continues, "There is this preconceived notion that once you are publicly gay you're going to shut off all these other pieces, components of your life. I know people who do that and I think that's kind of sad because it's that diversity that stretches us, and we can find all kinds of things in relationships with straight people. It's not a we-they type of thing, or at least it doesn't have to be and it isn't with me."

Many of our witnesses address the issue of labeling. John M. says, "I hate labels. I hate labels. Because once I put a label on you, I have to look at you as that. And very often everything else goes by the wayside. . . . You've missed the person. . . . And I think many people who are gay pay attention to gayness and nothing else. . . . I have to look at you as a whole person and not just the fact that you're gay. Big deal."

Tim D. is likewise concerned with the problem of labeling. "I am me. I am Tim, and God looks down on me and says, 'I love you for whoever you are.' He takes out the labels—gay, lesbian, whatever—that society puts on you. So when God looks down on us He looks straight down and sees our soul and our love. Society is the one that puts the labels on."

Tim continues, voicing his way of understanding the divisiveness of labeling. "I have to go back to Dr. Seuss. I relate Dr. Seuss so much to the world today. If you remember, Dr. Seuss writes about the Xs and the Os, and the Xs play together and the Os play together. Then somehow an O got an X so he had to create a machine to take all the Os off all the Os and give them Xs. Then things got complicated and the machine broke down and everybody was getting triangles. I think that's the way society labels, you're an X, you're an O. If we have that then we put them in our own categories and we know who they are. If we put them in that machine and it takes everything off, then you know what, how are we going to react? The only thing to do is what you would normally do if they all had Xs, all had Os, all were triangles, you'd accept it. But once you start giving people labels, then you divide. I don't think we need to divide."

Perhaps with labeling one does not have to deal with the ambiguity of human life. One can neatly pigeonhole, categorize, or stereotype people and not have to relate to them as whole, complex people. Steve B., thirty-nine, from Chicago, bemoans the stereotyping he has experienced from other gay people. "One of the first individuals I dated—and at the time I was gay, Catholic, and Republican—oh, my God! They just completely shut down. They wanted nothing to do with me."

Steve continues, more generally addressing the issues of labeling and the absolutization of gayness. "I think that sometimes within the gay community we're our own worst enemies in terms of discriminating. We complain about being discriminated against but then we return it in spades. . . . There is this model that if you're gay you'd better be a Democrat, you've got to do this, you've got to do that, you've got to be an activist. There's this whole checklist of things and if you don't fall into that, well, you're not a 'good' gay or lesbian."

In his book *Images of Hope,* William Lynch says that a way out of the trap of fixation upon, or absolutization of, the particular, is through a "human imagination that can circle around the mountain of the human until it sees all that is there." For gay people, circling around the mountain of the human might mean two things: First, viewing oneself as more than gay, and second, striving for connection with the personhood of others, with humanity as a whole.

We'll conclude this chapter by listening to some of our witnesses as they express their experience of being more than gay and their experience of needing and wanting to connect with humanity as a whole.

Matteo P. "circles around the mountain" of his own personhood when he says, "I'm more than gay. I am my job. I am a brother. I am a son. I am a good friend. I am a leader in certain things. I'm many more things than just being gay. I am a Catholic. I am a person. I'm trying to grow spiritually and I hope I'm making some progress that way."

Doug D. echoes Matteo's concerns about limiting the focus of one's personhood to being gay. "I'm gay and I'm Catholic and I'm a lawyer. It was interesting, when we were approached with this project and somebody said, 'This guy wants to interview you about being a gay Catholic.' I thought, 'That works for a lot of people because it's important to them that they're gay Catholics, that's their center.' I was kind of hesitant to take this interview largely because I'm like, I'm going to give him a view that isn't like the other views, and if it's not the view he's looking for maybe he's not going to want to have this interview with me. Because being Catholic is very important to me and being gay is very important to me and being a lawyer is very important to me and being an actor is very important to me."

Circling around the mountain of the human should also be experienced with and between people. As Kevin N. says, "I guess what I've learned through time is that I don't like groups that are exclusively gay because I think, unfortunately, we slant things at times and much to our demise. I'd rather have a larger scope." Kevin continues, "If you choose to live your life exclusively as a gay person, then I would say you're not living your life as a Christian, because you're segregating yourself from the community that is supposed to be all together, all believing, all caring. . . . Christ did not come out and put a lifestyle on Himself or a label as such. I think—and I'm sure people would disagree with me on this—but I don't think you need to carry a label. I think, when it comes down to it, if you're a good caring person, if somebody finds out you're gay, it's not going to be an issue with them if they're good people."

Kevin may fail to address certain important failures to integrate particularities into the whole on the part of society: the ways in which gay people have been excluded from Christian churches or have sometimes been considered bad people because of their homosexuality. Nevertheless, his call for a larger scope still stands.

Mark M. speaks of opting to move beyond exclusively gay situations in terms of the Eucharist: "I call that living in the ghetto. Gay ghettos, black ghettos, Hispanic ghettos, feminist ghettos—for whatever reasons—you pull into yourself and disconnect from the larger community and that's not a Eucharistic event. The Eucharist keeps calling us into connection with others and God."

Mark continues. "Now my challenge is trying to help other people understand what it's like to be gay. My friends kid me about living out in the suburbs, that I have a diplomatic outpost because most of my neighbors are married with kids and so forth. I would say my living here has helped many of my neighbors to understand that a gay man isn't a pedophile, doesn't throw wild sex parties all the time. People are envious of my lawn and garden. On the other hand, I've also become more sensitized to the challenge of parenting, the love of these people in trying to raise their children. In many ways I'm much more selfish than they are. They give tremendously of their time. I watch them, I watch daddies come home from their day at work and then go out . . . just taking the little kid out and playing ball or taking him for a walk. I know if that were me I'd think, 'I've got all these things I've got to do.' Our priorities are different, so I've come to respect people unlike myself as well."

Finally, Tom A. describes his desire for a larger scope, both within himself and in his relationships with others. "It all gets back to the question of what is the most important element. Is the important element who I am as a person or is it that fact that I'm a gay person. . . . I'm one of those living testimonials to, 'I'm a person first and I'm gay second.' Although I have no problem telling anyone I'm gay, I don't have an issue with that at all. But when George and I broke up we had a significant number of friends . . . and when we told them we were breaking up ninety-nine percent of them automatically assumed that I was going to move to Boystown [a predominantly gay neighborhood in Chicago]. I said, 'There is no way. It's just way too homogeneous of a community. To me, that's not a healthy environment. I think there's a whole distortion of life in general, because all of a sudden you're in an environment where it's nothing but gay values, gay community, and everything like that. So I chose to live in my current neighborhood because I knew that there was ethnic diversity there as well as diversity within the people themselves. . . . There are young professionals, there are older professionals, there are blue-collar workers, there are Asians, there are Hispanics, there are African Americans. I don't surround myself with gayness because I don't feel like I need to. And I personally feel gay people could make more inroads into the general community if they didn't isolate themselves and didn't create this almost isolated structure of who they are and what they are."

William Lynch believed that fixation on a particular aspect of life is a cause for hopelessness because one is trapped and isolated by the particular. Hope comes from moving from this isolation and entrapment to embracing the mountain of humanity. The movement from isolation to community is also a question of church. At the heart of Catholic Christianity has always been an openness to and concern for humanity as a whole.

7 ∞ How Can You Be Gay and Catholic?

I began this book with the question "How can you be gay and Catholic?" To conclude this book I want to return to and then try to give an answer to this question.

I think we should acknowledge that one way a person might hear this question is as less of a question and more of a statement: "How can you be gay and Catholic!" This statement often expresses exasperation, anger, resentment, or even hatred on the part of people, often other gay people, toward the Catholic Church.

Our witnesses give voice to how this anger or hatred toward the Church surrounds them. Mitch S. describes his experience of the exasperation of others: "People say, how can you be Catholic, how can you be Christian in a Church that persecutes you, hates you!" Greg P. has experienced something similar. "I got that a lot when I was going through RCIA [Rite of Christian Initiation for Adults]. From Catholics, from past Catholics, from gay people in general. They'd all be like, 'Why do you subject yourself to that? Run away. Run away!'"

Brian H. and Michael S. relate how people just cannot understand why they participate in AGLO, the Archdiocesan Gay and Lesbian Outreach of Chicago. Says Brian, "A lot of people have a problem with me being a member of AGLO because they can't understand how I reconcile who I am with what the Church teaches, and they don't understand why I bother trying to do that." Michael says, "I don't think that going to AGLO is hip for a lot of gay people. I've had arguments with people who think I'm being an apologist for the Church or an accomodationist in my own person because I go back to the Church."

doi:10.1300/5599_08

93

Steve B. shares the experience of a near argument over such concerns at a dinner party. "My partner, Mark, is a realtor. One of his associates. . .had a dinner party. We were the only gay couple there. . . . Somehow the group got on a religious topic that kind of evolved to Catholicism, and Mark, my partner, who's a Methodist, said, 'If you want to talk about Catholicism and being gay, here's the man you need to talk to.' This woman was very agitated. 'How can you be gay and actively practice? I don't understand why you people don't just start your own church!'"

Perhaps those who would advocate that gay people leave behind their Catholicism fail to see that while our witnesses affirm their homosexuality there is still something in their Catholicism that they do not want to let go of.

In order to summarize what I believe our witnesses find in their Catholic Christianity—in order to understand why they remain Catholic—I would like to adopt as a framework a traditional Catholic perspective on the human condition that speaks of ways of death and ways of life. The testimony of our witnesses with regard to the experience of being homosexual speaks, in a similar fashion, of ways of death and ways of life.

We often deny or ignore ways of death and destruction. For example, such ways can be ignored in a particular contemporary perspective on homosexuality which equates the experience of homosexual people with the experience of heterosexual people. This perspective might be paraphrased as "We're just like you. We fall in love; we have our families; we pay our taxes. We have the right to get married." Although such a perspective may get at the truth of a shared humanity, it may also, for the sake of promoting equality, shove under the rug the ongoing destructive behavior on the part of many homosexual people—behavior arising in part out of the social, historical, and religious history of homosexual people, history which still has too much impact to this day.

The ways of death include—often during but not limited to the growing awareness of one's homosexuality in their youth—denial, hiding, lying, fighting one's sexuality in some Sisyphean manner, isolation, loneliness, silence, confusion, and shame and guilt simply for being homosexual. Too many times these ways of death have literally led to suicide.

If one does not feel loved in one's homosexuality it is not surprising that one might live out this homosexuality in unloving ways. Underlying sexual behavior in which one gives one's body but not one's heart, often because one's heart is steeped in despair or hatred, is an impersonal form of sexual behavior. Sex becomes not about persons but about types, techniques, power, and oblivion. The ways of death enter directly into sexual behavior.

The ways of death also infiltrate into experiences of community. If the homosexual person despairs of community, then lonely isolation may be his or her lot. As Richard Cleaver said earlier in this work, "profound isolation . . . is still, most of the time, the most typical experience of lesbians and gay men." Gay communities may offer alternatives to isolation. However, insofar as these communities are based on resentment or hatred of another community— gays versus straights, gays versus the Catholic Church—then they become bracketed and isolated. Bracketed, isolated communities that are not striving for connection with humanity as a whole diminish the humanity of their members. This diminishment of humanity is in itself a way of death.

Insofar as the Catholic Church and other churches continue to categorically ascribe sinfulness to homosexual actions, and insofar as people continue to degrade, exclude, and victimize gay people, and insofar as gay people continue to internalize such destruction, we will be caught in a vicious circle. The homosexual person is not loved in his or her homosexuality and may return that lack of love with destruction toward himself or herself, toward his or her sexual partners, and toward churches and larger communities.

Our gay Catholic witnesses speak of a love that frees them from the vicious circles of death and destruction for more life-affirming ways of being homosexual. Love is the animating principle for the ways of life. Love is at the center of Catholic Christianity—the love of God for us and our love for others. When asked to encapsulate what is essential about their Catholicism, several of our witnesses speak of this love.

Greg P., in explaining why he is Catholic, says, "I believe in the love and trust, and that's tantamount. And from Mass, and through praying, I can feel the loving presence of God in Christ and the working of the Holy Spirit. . . . The love of God in Christ and through the Holy Spirit for us is transformed into our love for others. . . . That's why I'm Catholic. Now I am also gay. I'm a gay Catholic."

Steve B., in describing what he believes is essential to his Catholicism, speaks of Jesus' love for us and of the Golden Rule. "What it comes down to is that Jesus came on to earth to save humankind and died for that. . . . Furthermore, I guess the precepts really come down to the Golden Rule: Do unto others as you would have them do unto you, and love one another as you love yourself. That's the core."

Tom A., in describing the value he places upon homosexual relationships, likewise goes back to what he believes is essential to Christianity, namely—again—love. "I know that people go out there and pull precepts from the Bible to back up whatever they want to back up. My fundamental belief in religion and what religion has taught with Jesus being our savior is that it all comes down to the ability to love people."

Our witnesses speak of how the loving, compassionate affirmation of their homosexuality, often with regard to youth but not limited to it, frees them from the destructive denial, hiding, or fighting of their homosexuality. This freeing of themselves as homosexual opens up to new life that is marked by honesty, peacefulness, wholeness, and the experience of the naturalness, goodness, and giftedness of their homosexuality. As Robert P. shared in Chapter 3, "It is the greatest gift to yourself to be who you are. . . . It's the greatest gift to be giving yourself, to be gay and allow yourself to be gay. It's the greatest gift you can give yourself and it's a gift from God. And it is a joy to be yourself."

Our witnesses speak of how love enters into their sexual relationships. They speak of the tendencies toward destruction in impersonal
sexual relationships and of being freed from such destructiveness for
a new life of personal relationships marked by joy, sacrifice, commitment, loyalty, prayer, forgiveness, and a sense of giftedness. Joe
G. had this to say about homosexual relationships, including his
own, before he met Leo R: "These relationships don't work. It's all
about sex, guys, it's all about sex." Joe admits that he could very
well have continued on a destructive path with his sexuality. But at
his commitment ceremony with Leo, Joe publicly affirmed the following: "Leo, . . . because of your gentleness, kindness, loyalty, and
unconditional love for me, I have learned to live without guilt, and
my spirituality and sexuality are far more integrated into my personality. Because of you, Leo, I am alive today. For all eternity I will
thank God for the gift of you, pure grace in our life. Today, Leo, I
renew my commitment to you and to our relationship. . . . I'll be
with you in the good years and the difficult ones and I will continue
to care for and love you to the best of my ability in this life and I
look forward to spending eternity with you and with God."

Our witnesses speak of being freed from bracketed, isolated gay
communities. Our witnesses are freed for an experience of community, Christian community, where there are no divisions of gay versus straight or gay versus Catholic, or at least where they can meet
the challenge of struggling for the healing of such divisions and for
a justice that breaks down such divisions. Mark M. speaks of how
the sacrament of the Eucharist gives us an experience of community that counters communities based on particular identities:
"Gay ghettos, black ghettos, Hispanic ghettos, feminist ghettos, or
whatever, for whatever reasons you pull into yourself and you disconnect from the larger community and that's not a Eucharistic
event. The Eucharist keeps calling us into connection with others
and with God."

Many of our witnesses comment on the ways a gay person can remain Catholic while being critical of Church teaching. Our witnesses make distinctions about what is essential or central to their

Catholicism and what is not. What is essential is summed up by the words of Greg P., quoted earlier: "The love of God in Christ and through the Holy Spirit for us is transformed into our love for others." From this core, from this center, one can be critical of Church teaching that homosexual actions are necessarily sinful. Tom A. comments, "It's like, how can the Lord all of a sudden flip the coin and say, 'Because you love another man that's not the right kind of love that I'm expecting.' To the best of my knowledge there's never been any clear definition that that's a good love or a bad love. . . . It's love. . . . I have a hard time believing that that love is any less significant than a love between a man and a woman."

This distinction between what is essential and what is not is brought home by a few of our witnesses. James B., for example, is grateful for the way the Church nurtures what is essential, but he also understands how the Church brings in other teachings, such as those about homosexuality, which in his view fall outside of the essential. "I understand my relationship with God through the Catholic tradition. . . . I think it has to do with the simple fact that our life with God is mediated through the Church; there's just no way around it. And that the Church in its role as mediator is a sacramental role, so we receive the life of Christ through the Church and its sacramental activity. . . . That's wonderful. . . . The doctrines of the Church tell us how it is." He continues, "But along with those doctrines come other beliefs and ideas, including one about homosexuality. In a sense it falls outside the essential. I hate to say it that way. The essentials, of course, are the sacraments and the life of Christ they bring us and then how that transforms us into action in the world. . . . We only know and believe that because the Church teaches that, but then the Church teaches these other things and these other things sink into the mind too."

Mitch S. also has had to struggle and come to an understanding of what is essential to his Catholicism. In his words, "One of the things I wrestled with at the beginning of seminary was that I started to move the Church into the position of God. I started to think canon law and all this stuff really was the entry point to God.

And I started to get really pissed because I didn't like some of the things I was being taught. I didn't like some of the attitudes. . . . Then I realized what I was doing. I said to my spiritual director one day, 'It's like God is the hook that the Church hangs on. . . . What I've been doing is I've been making the Church the hook that the rest of reality hangs on. No, God's the hook.'"

Mitch is not saying that the Church does not attend to God. "On the important stuff—go with it. The Church has got it right. It's not that the Church has it right; it's that the Church is paying attention to who God is."

John McNeill, who has been on the forefront of the Catholic Church in responding to the needs of gay and lesbian people, calls gay and lesbian people to pay similar attention to who God is. In his book *Freedom, Glorious Freedom: The Spiritual Journey to the Fullness of Life for Gays, Lesbians and Everybody Else,* McNeill also makes what I believe is the most succinct and powerful criticism that can be made of Church teaching on homosexuality:

> When we gay and lesbians discover that we cannot follow the fallible teachings of our religious authorities without destroying ourselves, then we are forced to search out what God is saying to us through our experience and take personal responsibility for the choices we make.

The experience of our gay Catholic witnesses speaks of returning to the center of their Catholicism, to the experience of the God who loves us and transforms us for loving others. Through their experiences, through the voices of their consciences which have been witnessed to in this book, we see how this life-affirming love embraces the goodness of homosexuality, finds a home in personal relationships, and strives for a community where all are included. If one truly experiences and witnesses this love, then one must also see that the Church teaching that believes homosexual actions are inherently and always sinful is in fact an unloving teaching. To go along with such a teaching, which is counter to love, would entail, as McNeil wisely points out, the destruction of oneself.

In other words, the Catholic Church teaching that ascribes inherent sinfulness to homosexual actions is itself complicit in the destructive behavior of homosexual people. What's bred in the bone comes out in the flesh. If what is bred in the bone of a homosexual person is that homosexual actions are inherently sinful, incapable of being expressed lovingly, then it should be no surprise that gay people who are molded by such teaching will tragically act out their sexuality in destructive, unloving ways. (And there may be implications here for understanding part of the story, while granted not the whole story, of why some homosexual priests have acted out their sexuality destructively.)

In yet other words, the Church's teaching that imputes inherent sinfulness to homosexual actions is itself a way of death.

Challenging Church teaching, however, does not mean giving up on the center. At the center of Catholicism is this love of God for us, this love of God in Christ and through the Holy Spirit for us that in turn transforms us for loving others and returning love to God. A hymn I heard in the Catholic Church in my childhood goes, "We will know they are Christians by their love." The experience of the remarkable witnesses who speak in this book points to how this love saves. This love saves by encouraging us to affirm and integrate our homosexuality rather than fall into disintegration; by helping us cultivate personal relationships instead of giving in to the deadening impact of impersonal relationships; by allowing us to have an experience of community that is open to all people, not one that is trapped by particularities. Indeed, I would add, this love so towers over bracketed, isolated communities that it opens up a path toward and a vision of eternity. Perhaps, above all, the experience of our witnesses points to how this love saves through forgiveness. Too often we fail at loving ourselves as homosexual, or we fall into despair or hatred, or we treat one another impersonally, or we fail in our loyalties, or we resent if not hate other communities. This love at the center of Catholic Christianity, this essence of what it means to be personal—given to us by He who became human—forgives and frees us from ways of death for ways of life.

Our witnesses return again and again to this Center and in their consciences make distinctions about what is not essential in Church teaching, what, according to their lights, is not loving. They do not give up on this Center; rather they challenge from it. To give up on this Center, this Love which is salvific, would itself be destruction.

How can you be gay and Catholic? By returning again and again to this Love.

Bibliography

Cleaver, Richard. *Know My Name: A Gay Liberation Theology.* Louisville, KY: Westminster John Knox Press, 1995.

Farley, Margaret. "The Meaning of Commitment" in *Perspectives on Marriage,* eds. Kieran Scott and Michael Warren. New York and Oxford: Oxford University Press, 1993.

Gramick, Sr. Jeannine. "Prejudice, Religion and Homosexual People," in *A Challenge to Love, Gay and Lesbian Catholics in the Church,* ed. Robert Nugent. New York: Crossroads, 1983.

Kennedy, Eugene. *The Unhealed Wound: The Church and Human Sexuality* New York: St. Martin's Press, 2001.

Lynch, William. *Images of Hope.* Notre Dame, IN: University of Notre Dame Press, 1974.

McNeill, John J. *Freedom, Glorious Freedom: The Spiritual Journey to the Fullness of Life for Gays, Lesbians and Everybody Else.* Boston: Beacon Press, 1995.

Newman, John Henry. *The Idea of a University.* Notre Dame, IN: University of Notre Dame Press, 1982.

Sullivan, Andrew. *Virtually Normal.* New York: Vintage Books, 1996.

United States Catholic Conference of Bishops. "Always Our Children: A Pastoral Message to Parents of Homosexual Children and Suggestions for Pastoral Ministries." Washington DC: United States Catholic Conference, Inc., 1997.

Order a copy of this book with this form or online at:
http://www.haworthpress.com/store/product.asp?sku=5599

SONS OF THE CHURCH
The Witnessing of Gay Catholic Men

_____ in hardbound at $24.95 (ISBN-13: 978-1-56023-580-4; ISBN-10: 1-56023-580-2)

_____ in softbound at $14.95 (ISBN-13: 978-1-56023-581-1; ISBN-10: 1-56023-581-0)

Or order online and use special offer code HEC25 in the shopping cart.

COST OF BOOKS_____

☐ **BILL ME LATER:** (Bill-me option is good on US/Canada/Mexico orders only; not good to jobbers, wholesalers, or subscription agencies.)

☐ Check here if billing address is different from shipping address and attach purchase order and billing address information.

POSTAGE & HANDLING_____
(US: $4.00 for first book & $1.50 for each additional book)
(Outside US: $5.00 for first book & $2.00 for each additional book)

Signature_____

SUBTOTAL_____

☐ **PAYMENT ENCLOSED:** $_____

IN CANADA: ADD 7% GST_____

☐ **PLEASE CHARGE TO MY CREDIT CARD.**

STATE TAX_____
(NJ, NY, OH, MN, CA, IL, IN, PA, & SD residents, add appropriate local sales tax)

☐ Visa ☐ MasterCard ☐ AmEx ☐ Discover
☐ Diner's Club ☐ Eurocard ☐ JCB

Account # _____

FINAL TOTAL_____
(If paying in Canadian funds, convert using the current exchange rate, UNESCO coupons welcome)

Exp. Date_____

Signature_____

Prices in US dollars and subject to change without notice.

NAME_____

INSTITUTION_____

ADDRESS_____

CITY_____

STATE/ZIP_____

COUNTRY_____ COUNTY (NY residents only)_____

TEL_____ FAX_____

E-MAIL_____

May we use your e-mail address for confirmations and other types of information? ☐ Yes ☐ No
We appreciate receiving your e-mail address and fax number. Haworth would like to e-mail or fax special discount offers to you, as a preferred customer. **We will never share, rent, or exchange your e-mail address or fax number.** We regard such actions as an invasion of your privacy.

Order From Your Local Bookstore or Directly From
The Haworth Press, Inc.
10 Alice Street, Binghamton, New York 13904-1580 • USA
TELEPHONE: 1-800-HAWORTH (1-800-429-6784) / Outside US/Canada: (607) 722-5857
FAX: 1-800-895-0582 / Outside US/Canada: (607) 771-0012
E-mail to: orders@haworthpress.com

For orders outside US and Canada, you may wish to order through your local
sales representative, distributor, or bookseller.
For information, see http://haworthpress.com/distributors

(Discounts are available for individual orders in US and Canada only, not booksellers/distributors.)

PLEASE PHOTOCOPY THIS FORM FOR YOUR PERSONAL USE.
http://www.HaworthPress.com

BOF06